THE PARAMETERS OF WAR

THE PARAMETERS OF WAR

Military History from the Journal of the U.S. Army War College

Edited by

Lloyd J. Matthews

and

Dale E. Brown

Introduction by

Edward N. Luttwak

Published under the auspices
of the U.S. Army War College Foundation, Inc.

PERGAMON-BRASSEY'S
INTERNATIONAL DEFENSE PUBLISHERS
(a member of the Pergamon Group)
WASHINGTON · NEW YORK · LONDON · OXFORD
BEIJING · FRANKFURT · SÃO PAULO · SYDNEY · TOKYO · TORONTO

U.S.A. (Editorial)	Pergamon-Brassey's International Defense Publishers, 8000 Westpark Drive, Fourth Floor, McLean, Virginia 22102, U.S.A.
(Orders)	Pergamon Press, Maxwell House, Fairview Park, Elmsford, New York 10523, U.S.A.
U.K. (Editorial)	Brassey's Defence Publishers, 24 Gray's Inn Road, London WC1X 8HR
(Orders)	Brassey's Defence Publishers, Headington Hill Hall, Oxford OX3 0BW, England
PEOPLE'S REPUBLIC OF CHINA	Pergamon Press, Room 4037, Qianmen Hotel, Beijing, People's Republic of China
FEDERAL REPUBLIC OF GERMANY	Pergamon Press, Hammerweg 6, D-6242 Kronberg, Federal Republic of Germany
BRAZIL	Pergamon Editora, Rua Eca de Queiros, 346, CEP 04011, Paraiso, São Paulo, Brazil
AUSTRALIA	Pergamon-Brassey's Defence Publishers, P.O. Box 544, Potts Point, N.S.W. 2011, Australia
JAPAN	Pergamon Press, 8th Floor, Matsuoak Central Building, 1-7-1 Nishishinjuku, Shinjuku-ku, Tokyo 160, Japan
CANADA	Pergamon Press Canada, Suite No. 271, 253 College Street, Toronto, Ontario, Canada M5T 1R5

First edition 1987

Library of Congress Cataloging in Publication Data

The Parameters of war: military history
from the journal of the U.S. Army War
College.
1. Military art and science – History
I. Matthews, Lloyd, J.   II. Brown, Dale E.
III. Parameters
355'.02'09   U27

British Library Cataloguing in Publication Data

The Parameters of war: military history
from the journal of the U.S. Army War
College.
1. Military art and science – History
I. Matthews, Lloyd, J.   II. Brown, Dale E.
III. Parameters
355'.02'09   U27

ISBN 0-08-035547-1 Hard cover
ISBN 0-08-035546-3 Flexi cover

*Printed and bound in Great Britain by
Hazell Watson & Viney Limited,
Member of the BPCC Group,
Aylesbury, Bucks*

Contents

IV. Civil-Military Relations

V. History as a Prelude to Doctrine

Maps

Acknowledgements

Our first duty, our most pleasant duty, is to thank the several authors whose articles make up this volume. Alone among the contributors, it was their time, their labor, and their sense of history that called forth the ideas herein preserved.

The path had been well prepared. Major General Franklin M. Davis, Jr., the U.S. Army War College Commandant from 1971 to 1974, set out to move the College to its rightful place at the center of the contemporary defense dialogue. This impulse was continued by his successor as Commandant, Lieutenant General DeWitt C. Smith, Jr., who advanced *Parameters* as a prime forum for the propagation of seminal military thought. The current Commandant, Major General James E. Thompson, has continued in the same tradition, providing needed impetus to *Parameters* as a practical extension of the College's educational arm. We are indebted as well to the Army War College Foundation, Inc., whose sponsorship of this publishing effort was indispensable, and to the Foundation's Executive Director, Colonel LeRoy Strong (U.S. Army, Ret.), whose support has been faithful and unstinting.

We also delight in mentioning past *Parameters* editors: Colonels Paul Goodman, Alfred J. Mock, Paul R. Hilty, Jr., Roland R. Sullivan, and William R. Calhoun, Jr. Their salutary influence, though rarely acknowledged, is always felt. And last, for special emphasis, we mention Mrs. Lisa A. Ney, who as the *Parameters* Editorial Assistant transcended the untranscendable in producing immaculate text; and the Assistant Editor, Mr. Gregory N. Todd, he of wise head, fine hand, and steadying presence.

The Editors

Introduction

This collection of essays reflects twin advances – in the attention that military history receives in the country's premier military journal, itself both a symptom and one of the causes of the intellectual renaissance of the U.S. Army since Vietnam; and in the practice of military historiography, whose rising scholarly quality and enhanced academic standing have been widely noticed of late.

Such a revival implies a prior decline, and it is certainly true that the study and writing of military history have been recovering in recent decades from a secular decadence, which coincided perversely with the advance of historical studies in general, and which was a most unexpected sequel to their splendid classical antecedents. After all, for the Greeks as for ourselves, the greatest of all historians was Thucydides, teacher of every enlightened generation since his own, and most definitely a military historian; then in the next era, to explain the Roman ascent to imperial primacy as Thucydides had unforgettably illuminated the decline of Athens, it was once again a military historian who stood above all others, Polybius of Megalopolis. Indeed, among the Roman historians of the first rank, from Sallust of the late Republic to Ammianus Marcellinus of the late empire, only one was not a military historian, though the exception, P. Cornelius Tacitus, was admittedly the most profound thinker of them all.

It was not merely that they wrote of wars that made Thucydides, Polybius, Sallust, and Ammianus Marcellinus military historians, along with many others from Arrian to Xenophon – for virtually all historians of the ancient world did likewise – but rather that they explained the detailed military content of fights won or lost, and how the armed strength of nations that derived from demographic, economic, and political sources rose or fell with the passage of time. To do so persuasively, they had to address military operations as well as tactical questions, the branch composition of the armed forces, and the nexus between ultimate sources of strength and the military power obtained from them. That in turn required a definite expertise, which they all acquired on the scene of war in one way or another, although only Ammianus Marcellinus and other later writers could be professional officers. It was only in the late empire that soldiering had become a life-time career for educated men, and no longer just a social obligation and a stage in the course of political advancement.

The achievement of these men stands as high as any in the universe of human culture, and it is only their enduring influence on our minds that paradoxically prevents us from recognizing just how much we have learned from them. Thucydides' *History of the Peloponnesian War* is of course on sale in every respectable bookshop throughout the lands of Western culture from Vladivostok to Hawaii, but it is not generally recognized to what extent prevailing notions about war and peace usually attributed to native common sense actually derive from that one text. Our debt to Thucydides is hardly forgotten, but of the many who have some knowledge of the struggle between Rome and Carthage, and of the style and ethos of the Roman legions, only a few know that much of it comes originally from Polybius. Again, the caustic brevity of Sallust has always attracted many readers, who have directly learned from him the prototypical ideas of both guerrilla and counterinsurgency warfare (*History of the Jugurthine War*) and of the political coup d'état (*Conspiracy of Catiline*); but of the great many people who recall the formidable strength of the Huns, as well as the outlines of the catastrophic Roman defeat of Adrianople at the hands of the Goths, very few know that their knowledge derives almost entirely from Ammianus Marcellinus – who is so little read even though very much worth reading, being himself a prominent victim of the prejudice against all late-Roman writers.

Given these magnificent beginnings, how can one explain the decline of military historiography in the modern era? For while its products have been widely read and commercially successful from the dawn of printing till our own days, there is no doubt of the shoddy quality of the mass of would-be scholarly writings that fill our libraries and bookshops, whose defects range from a shallow antiquarianism that describes everything and explains nothing, to a provincial reliance on national sources alone that is peculiarly inappropriate to the subject, and which is usually motivated by no better reason than ignorance of the required foreign languages.

For the historian who must confront the truly difficult task of explaining human actions, sufficient linguistic knowledge to consult the appropriate documents should be a trivial accomplishment, and indeed it is demanded as a matter of course in general historiography. The conclusion is inescapable that the still lower quality of popular works, often undocumented even when their counterparts in general history would be, reflects the poor example set by the literature with scholarly pretensions.

As for the paucity of scholars of the first rank who have emulated the ancients in devoting themselves to the study of war, it is both symptom and cause of the marginal status of the study of military history in academic institutions. Virtually absent in the past, the subject is only now becoming established in relatively few universities of the Western world, and in still fewer is there a separate department of military history, with only a single one in the United States.

There have always been exceptions, of course, and historians such as Michael Howard as well as D. Clayton James (well represented in the present volume with ''MacArthur's Lapses from an Envelopment Strategy in 1945''), Jay Luvaas (author of two studies in this volume, including the symptomatic ''Military History: Is It Still Practicable?''), and Russell F. Weigley (author of ''Shaping the American Army of World War II: Mobility versus Power'') among others, deservedly acquired wide reputations that transcended the boundaries of military historiography as such.

Perhaps the easiest explanation of the decadence of the subject would be one that casts the blame upon an unfortunate coincidence. On one hand, the general progress of learning and the particular outlook of the statistical age induced historians to adopt a much more *systematic* approach, exemplified by the comprehensive historical surveys that did so much to elevate the study of ancient history, the great documentary collections, and the collective national histories that saw their origins in the middle decades of the last century. On the other hand, war was becoming much more complicated than ever before, much more resistant to comprehensive analysis.

The transformation of war that coincided more or less with the emergence of modern historiography was certainly much more than a mere expansion in scale, though of course armies and navies did expand, and to a spectacular degree. Wars in which the troops on all sides number in the millions, and battles are fought by hundreds of thousands, need not for that reason alone be more refractory to systematic study than their earlier counterparts that engaged mere fractions of such numbers. A given maneuver by ten or a hundred thousand men is as easily encompassed by analysis as the same maneuver by five hundred men, while conversely the historian who engaged himself in the study of each and every episode could find a lifetime of employment in any battle sufficiently documented, even if fought on a modest scale.

The real difference made by the transformation of war, which began long before but was most clearly evident in the Napoleonic campaigns, was the increasingly distinct *stratification* of its levels.

There has always been a *technical* level in warfare, but the interaction of a handful of diverse small arms, longer-range munitions, and warships gave way to a steadily broader interplay of weapons more and more diversified, in a process that continues till this day with the successive emergence of novel categories of weapons. The military historian has thus been confronted with technical questions less and less transparent to the non-expert observer, while at the same time more and more weighty in the totality of military affairs.

Again, there has always been a *tactical* level of warfare that encompasses the conduct of forces of any given type in specific forms of combat, and the historian has always been faced with the necessity of understanding both the role of the human intangibles of morale, cohesion, and leadership, and also the specific tactics they sustained. But the insight needed especially for the human factors was much more accessible when there were only a few forms of combat, which moreover many military historians experienced directly in the course of the normal vicissitudes of pre-modern life.

The *operational* level of war, comprehending the interaction of diverse forces, has long been neglected in Anglo-Saxon military thought. (If I may inject a personal note, the rediscovery of the operational level was seemingly prompted by my article, "The Operational Level of War," in *International Security,* Vol.5, 1980–81, pp. 61–79; the Army drafters of the new version of Field Manual 100–5, *Operations,* informed me immediately after the appearance of my article of their intention to include its central theme in the new manual.) Of course, the operational level was not equally important during every era of warfare. While usually associated with a higher level of command in action, and a broader perspective on the part of the historian, the actual content of the operational level depends on the incidence of maneuver within it, or rather the locus of the action in the attrition-maneuver spectrum. If an entire army is engaged in the execution of the same invariant tactics of attrition, then the operational level of war has no real content of its own, and what can be observed in that broader perspective is not more nor less than the same tactical actions repeated many times.

Thus the operational level of the idealized melee of feudal warfare was equally devoid of significance for those in command at the time, and for the future historian engaged in explaining what happened. The same has been true of some notable cases of modern warfare as well, as in much of the trench fighting of the First World War for example, but modern-era military forces with their increasingly organized structures have allowed increasing scope for maneuver and when that potential has been exploited, the significance of the operational level has increased pro rata. Hence even in the analysis of the campaigns of Gustavus Adolphus, and certainly in dealing with Napoleonic warfare, the historian has to differentiate between the tactical and the operational levels, because the latter is no longer an aggregate of the former.

If one considers a form of warfare at the extreme maneuver end of the spectrum, the classic German *blitzkrieg* of 1939-1942, then the observation of tactical events at each remove can be positively misleading: it is only at the operational level that the making of battle-winning encirclements can be recognized in the totality of separate tactical moves, each of which seems desperately fragile on its own, as the long, thin columns of penetration present highly vulnerable flanks throughout their advance.

For the historian there are twin problems: first, the difficulty of coping with contradictory or merely divergent observations in the two levels of war, the tactical and the operational; second, the need for procedural as well as substantive military expertise to study the operational – that being the expertise of staff officers and generals, and as such much less likely to have been casually acquired by historians during their own experiences of war.

Finally, the level of *theater strategy* also became much more important in modern-era warfare, because of the exclusive delimitation of national territories, the formation of fronts (i.e., lines of contact) that extend the full length of the affected borders, the counterpart staging of offensives of equivalent magnitude, and the growth in the size of the armed forces that made it possible to carry out defensive and offensive warfare on such a large scale. Historians faced no novel difficulty in their analysis of the political factors that play such a large role in theater strategy, but again the military aspect calls for expertise more likely to be found among professional soldiers than professional historians, unless they specialize their studies accordingly.

That indeed has been the response of successful military historiography to the phenomenon of stratification across the board: specialization by levels has been added to specialization by periods and regions. Instead of the thin gruel of "multi level" studies, bound to descend into superficiality when encountering the levels least congenial to the historian, we now have a growing corpus of meaty technical level military historiography, mostly found in journal articles of course but which has also yielded very satisfactory monographs (e.g., Alfred Price's 1978 work *Instruments of Darkness* on electronic warfare) that illuminate the subject they touch upon in toto even while concentrating on the technical issues as such.

Tactical level historiography has naturally attracted the interest of professional military writers more than professional historians (see, for example, in the present volume, James W. Rainey's "Ambivalent Warfare: The Tactical Doctrine of the AEF in World War I," but note John M. Gates' "Indians and Insurrectos: The US Army's Experience with Insurgency." But the same has not been true of operational-level historiography; John Erickson's two volumes on Soviet warfare on the Eastern Front in World War II, for example, are very largely focused on that level, as is the very interesting article "Jackson's Valley Campaign and the Operational Level of War" in the present volume. Also in an operational vein, albeit with an institutional focus, are the two present articles on the rise of mechanized warfare, a very interesting matched pair (William J. Woolley's "Patton and the Concept of Mechanized Warfare" and Robert A. Doughty's "De Gaulle's Concept of a Mobile, Professional Army: Genesis of French Defeat?").

Because of the salience of political goals and constraints within it, much historical work has concentrated on the theater-strategic level, which provides a middle ground between general historiography and the more specialized forms of its military counterpart. Aside from D. Clayton James's work already noted, two articles of the volume are pitched at the theater-strategic level (Richard F. Timmons' "Lessons from the Past for NATO" and James A. Blackwell's "In the Laps of the Gods: The Origins of NATO Forward Defense").

Research in military history has also been favorably influenced by the new emphasis on institutional questions in the discipline of government (or "political science"). While the study of bureaucracies and bureaucratic interactions has yielded much less than was promised for the analysis of state conduct, it has been more fruitfully applied to interpret military decisions and events, as illustrated in two articles of this volume (Keith D. McFarland's "The 1949 Revolt of the Admirals" and Douglas Kinnard's "McNamara at the Pentagon"). Because of the more intense loyalties they command, or rather because of their nature as approximations of "total institutions" in sociological terms, and because of the more explicit and more rigidly bounded nature of their repertoires, military bureaucracies tend to act much more predictably *as* bureaucracies than their civilian counterparts, thus increasing the plausibility of explanatory models based on their institutional characteristics.

The study of history should be its own reward, but from its beginnings claims of practical worth have been made for military historiography. The Greeks were generally cautious in that regard, knowing that all the variables vary too much for deeds to be successfully repeated in unvaried form ("one may not step in the same river twice"), but in Roman times the likes of Frontinus and Polyaenus among others did not hesitate to offer fortunate stratagems and effective tactics as ready-made examples for direct emulation.

Since those days, the accelerating evolution of weapons has further eroded the authority of "lessons" drawn from the past; indeed the entire notion that such instruction can be obtained at all has come into question. As the aphorism goes, "the only valid lesson of history is that mankind learns nothing from history"; but that, surely, is a moralist's exaggeration. What is certainly true – and too obvious to be belabored – is that attempts to repeat stratagems, tactics, methods of operation, and strategies extracted from their original context, without an extreme sensitivity to that context, are apt to have very unfortunate results.

No better words of caution in that regard can be found than the article by Jay Luvaas already cited, while Benjamin F. Cooling III ("Military History for the Military Professional") is persuasive in showing how historical knowledge can inspire as well as educate the practitioner. That the Great Captains of the past learned any of their arts from their reading of history cannot be proved; but what *can* be proved is that almost all of them did read as much military history as they could. Certainly there is no excuse for willfully ignoring the record of human experience at war when preparing to assume responsibility for its conduct – at any level.

Edward N. Luttwak

I. MILITARY HISTORY:

The Nature and Practice of the Historian's Craft

1

Military History:
Is It Still Practicable?

by JAY LUVAAS

There was a day, before the advent of the A-bomb and its more destructive off-spring, before smart bombs and nerve gas, before computer technology and war games, when professional soldiers regarded reading history as a useful pastime. Many who have scaled the peaks of the military profession have testified to the utility of studying military history.

Most of these, however, seem to be commanding voices out of the past. MacArthur, steeped in family tradition and familiar with many of the 4000 volumes inherited from his father, was never at a loss for a historical example to underscore his point of view; Krueger, as a young officer, translated books and articles from the German military literature; Eisenhower spent countless hours listening to the erudite Fox Conner on what could be learned from military history; Marshall and his contemporaries at the Army Staff College at Leavenworth reconstructed Civil War campaigns from the after-action reports; Patton took the time in 1943 to read a book on the Norman conquest of Sicily nearly nine centuries earlier and to ponder "the many points in common with our operations";[1] and Eichelberger summoned from memory a passage he had read ten years before in Grant's *Memoirs* (which ought to be required reading for all officers) and thereby stiffened his resolve to press home the attack at Buna. These Army commanders were all remarkably well versed in history.

So were many of their civilian superiors. President Franklin D. Roosevelt was an avid reader of naval history, and Harry Truman frequently acknowledged the pertinent lessons that he had gleaned from a lifetime of exposure to history:

Reading history, to me, was far more than a romantic adventure. It was solid instruction and wise teaching which I somehow felt that I...needed...It seemed to me that if I could understand the true facts about the... development of the United States Government and could know the details of the lives of... its political leaders, I would be getting for myself a valuable...education... I know of no surer way to get a solid foundation in political science and public administration than to study the histories of past administrations of the world's most successful system of government.[2]

Because the military is a "practical" profession geared much of the time to

3

problem-solving, soldiers – like engineers and scientists – tend to be pragmatic about what is meant by the word "practicable." History is "practicable" if it yields lessons, especially exemplary lessons in tactics and strategy that can be directly applied to some current situation. History is "useful" in illustrating points of doctrine, in instilling in the young officer the proper military values or an appreciation for our military heritage. The "practical" man often scans the past for some magical formula that may ensure success in war, like Field Marshal von Schlieffen's theory of envelopment, or Captain B. H. Liddell Hart's strategy of indirect approach.

Such assumptions inevitably determine the way military history is taught. Because an important duty of the officer in peacetime is to teach, and because in the Army *teaching* usually involves *explaining*, it is often assumed that history, to be taught, must be explained. The emphasis therefore is on organizing and presenting information in a lucid, often lavishly illustrated lecture, in which tidy answers outrank nagging questions in the minds of everyone involved. The inference on the part of most students, if not the instructor, is that a person who remembers the lecture will somehow have learned history. It's a mistaken assumption we all make.

It is also true that no other field of history is under as much pressure as military history to provide "practical" answers to some current problem. If military history cannot provide such answers, why study it? The specialist in Renaissance diplomacy is rarely solicited for his views on foreign policy but, rather, is left alone to concentrate his thoughts on the cold war with the Turks in the 15th century. Nor is the scholar who has spent a lifetime studying the ramifications of the French Revolution apt to be consulted when news breaks of still another palace coup in some Latin American banana republic. But let a historian or journalist prowl around in some remote corner in the field of military history and often he will be expected, even tempted, to function as a current-affairs military analyst.

Perhaps we think this way because, as a society, we are largely ignorant about both the facts and the nature of history. In high school, European history no longer is required, having been replaced by something called "Western Civilization." We know astonishingly little about the history of other societies, and most of us, unfortunately, care even less. Students voting with their feet in colleges and universities across the nation have caused enrollments in history courses to plummet as they turn to "more practical" subjects such as economics, psychology, biology, engineering, and business administration. In the Army's schools, history has become a casualty of the Vietnam War; clearly the emphasis now is upon training. Even at the Military Academy, the required course in the military art was severely curtailed several years ago and only recently has been restored to its logical place in the curriculum. For that matter, how many officers who have invested off-duty hours to work toward an advanced degree have taken it in history? In the officer corps of today, the subject is rarely considered "practicable."

More to the point, is the Army as an institution as historical-minded as it was in the past? For without even a rudimentary understanding of history and its processes, there is no way that the past can be made to offer object lessons for the future. Professor Pieter Geyl, a distinguished Dutch historian, reminds us that it is useless to talk about "the lessons of history" when the historian "is after all only a man sitting at his desk."[3] The lessons that we would learn are his – the fruits of *his* labors, the creation of *his* imagination, perhaps the idea that *he* is to sell to the reader. For, as a German general asserted a hundred years ago, "it is well known that military history, when superficially studied, will furnish arguments in support of any theory or opinion."[4]

Common Fallacies

Perhaps the most frequent error in the abuse of history is to take historical examples out of context. Once removed from its historical context, which is always unique, a battle or a campaign ceases to offer meaningful lessons from history. According to Napoleon, "old Frederick laughed in his sleeve at the parades of Potsdam when he perceived young officers, French, English, and Austrian, so infatuated with the manoeuvre of the oblique order, which (in itself) was fit for nothing but to gain a few adjutant-majors a reputation." Napoleon appreciated that the secret of Frederick's successes was not the oblique order, but Frederick. "Genius acts through inspiration," Napoleon concluded. "What is good in one case is bad in another."[5]

One of Frederick's own soldiers demonstrated that in another environment even Frederick's maneuver's might fail. When Baron von Steuben, who had served in the Prussian Army throughout the Seven Years' War, was trying to make soldiers out of Washington's shivering, half-starved volunteers at Valley Forge, he knew better than to waste precious time teaching those complex maneuvers he had mastered under Frederick. Instead he selected only those that were essential to meet the unique conditions that prevailed in America, where volunteers had only a few months instead of years to master the intricacies of Frederick's drill, and where officers had to learn to lead by example instead of relying upon the severity of the Prussian system. Soldiers, Frederick repeatedly had warned, "can be held in check only through fear" and should therefore be made to "fear their officers more than all the dangers to which they are exposed.... Good will can never induce the common soldier to stand up to such dangers; he will only do so through fear."[6] Whatever may have motivated Washington's amateur soldiers at Valley Forge, most certainly it was not fear.

If there is a lesson here for us, it is simply that solutions to problems are not to be viewed as interchangeable parts. Even the Germans in World War II apparently failed to heed this lesson in drawing conclusions from their own war experiences. In addition to displaying a tendency to generalize from personal or limited experience, they often indiscriminately applied the experiences of one situation to entirely different circumstances. Thus the German Supreme Command "applied the experiences acquired on the Western Front in 1940, unchanged, to the war against Russia" despite the "greater tenacity" of the Russian soldier, his "insensibility against threatening the flanks," the scarcity of roads, and the vast space involved "giving ... the opponent the possibility of avoiding decision." In the words of one German general, not only did this misapplication of experience influence the operational plan against Russia, it also "contributed to the final disappointment."[7]

It is also a distortion to compress the past into distinctive patterns, for it is as true of history as it is of nature that "each man reads his own peculiar lesson according to his own peculiar mind and mood."[8] History responds generously to the adage "seek and ye shall find." At the turn of the century the Chief of the German General Staff, Count Alfred von Schlieffen, was faced with the need to plan for a war on two fronts. His solution was to point toward a quick victory on one front in order to avoid ultimate defeat on both, and his inspiration for the battle of annihilation essential to a quick victory came, at least in part, from reading the first volume of Hans Delbrück's *Geschichte der Kriegskunst*, which was published in 1900. Delbrück's treatment of the battle of Cannae in 216 B.C. convinced Schlieffen that Hannibal had won his lopsided victory by deliberately weakening his center and attacking with full force from both flanks. The much publicized Schlieffen Plan was an adaptation of this idea. Having thus discovered the "key," Schlieffen turned in his writings to the idea of envelopment to unlock the secrets of Frederick the Great and Napoleon, both of whom, he claimed, had always attempted to envelop the enemy. Similarly, Captain B. H. Liddell Hart was to discover from his research for a biography of Sherman that the key to Sherman's success lay in a strategy of indirect approach. When he turned to history at large for confirmation, of course he "discovered" that nearly all successful generals, whether they had been aware of it or not, had employed something akin to the strategy of indirect approach. The future British field marshal Sir Archibald Wavell, who always found Liddell Hart's ideas stimulating whether he agreed with them or not, once slyly suggested to the captain: "With your knowledge and brains and command of the pen, you could have written just as convincing a book called the 'Strategy of the Direct Approach.' "[9] Wavell appreciated that it was Liddell Hart and not the muse of history who preached this attractive doctrine.

Moreover, nothing is necessarily proven by citing examples from history. There are many works on military theory that provide examples of bad argument from analogy or authority; such faulty use of historical examples, according to Karl von Clausewitz, "not only leaves the reader dissatisfied but even irritates his intelligence." The mere citation of historical examples provides only the *semblance* of proof, although the reader who understands little about the nature of history may set aside his book convinced of the essential truth of some new theory, and the audience exposed to a well-organized and seemingly cogent lecture sprinkled with examples from history is equally vulnerable. "There are occasions," Clausewitz noted,

> where nothing will be proven by a dozen examples . . . . If anyone lists a dozen defeats in which the losing side attacked with divided columns, I can list a dozen victories in which that very tactic was employed. Obviously this is no way to reach a conclusion.

And if the author or lecturer has never mastered the events he describes, "such superficial, irresponsible handling of history leads to hundreds of wrong ideas and bogus theorizing."[10]

Perhaps the greatest disservice to history and its lessons comes from its frequent association with a given set of military principles or doctrine, and here the celebrated Swiss theorist Baron de Jomini may have had an unfortunate influence. Drawing upon an exhaustive examination of 30 campaigns of Frederick and Napoleon, Jomini deduced certain fixed maxims and principles which he claimed were both eternal and universal in their application. If such maxims would not produce great generals they would "at least make generals sufficiently skillful to hold the second rank among the great captains" and would thus serve as "the true school for generals."[11]

To future generations of young officers, Jomini said, in effect: "Gentlemen, I have not found a single instance where my principles, correctly applied, did not lead to success. They are based upon my unrivaled knowledge of the campaigns of Napoleon, much of it acquired at first hand, and of the basic works of Thiers, Napier, Lloyd, Tempelhof, Foy, and the Archduke Charles. Thanks to my labors you need not invest years of your own time in scrutinizing these voluminous histories. Did not Napoleon himself confess: 'I have studied history a great deal, and often, for want of a guide, have been forced to lose considerable time in useless reading'? You have only to study my principles and apply them faithfully, for 'there exists a fundamental principle of all the operations of war' which you neglect at your peril."[12]

Jomini had many prominent disciples, and their books were nearly all written on the assumption that battles and campaigns, ancient as well as modern, have succeeded or failed to the degree that they adhered to the principles of war as explained by Jomini and could be confirmed by the "constant teachings of history." But where Jomini read history, many of his followers read primarily Jomini and thus were one step removed from history and its processes.

The emergence of doctrine (as late as the American Civil War there were only drill manuals) and the introduction of historical sections on most European general staffs after the Prussian victories in 1866 and 1870 meant that increasingly, in the eyes of professional soldiers at least, military history was linked to doctrine and more specifically, to the principles of war as these principles were rediscovered and refined. Since World War I it has become fashionable to use history to illustrate the official principles of war as they are variously defined.

There are three dangers inherent in this approach. In the first place, pressed into service in this way history can only *illustrate* something already perceived as being true; it cannot prove its validity or lead to new discoveries. This is probably the terrain on which most soldiers first encounter the subject, and they would do well to heed the warning of Clausewitz that if "some historical event is being presented in order to demonstrate a general truth, care must be taken that every aspect bearing on the truth at issue is fully and circumstantially developed – carefully assembled . . . before the reader's eyes." In other words, the theorist ought to be a pretty good historian. Clausewitz goes so far as to suggest that, even though historical examples have the advantage of "being more realistic and of bringing the idea they are illustrating to life," if the purpose of history is really to explain doctrine, "an imaginary case would do as well."[13] Moreover, to use history primarily to illustrate accepted principles is really to put the cart before the horse. If one starts with what is perceived as truth and searches history for confirmation or illustrations, there can be no "lessons learned." How can there be?

A second weakness in linking history to doctrine is the natural tendency to let doctrine sit in judgment of historical events. Sir William Napier, who had a healthy respect for Jomini's theories, used his maxims as a basis for rendering historical judgment on the generalship of French and British leaders in his classic *History of the War in the Peninsula*. Similarly, Major General Sir Patrick MacDougall "discovered" that these maxims could also serve as criteria for judging the generalship of Hannibal, and Matthew F. Steele's *American Campaigns*, which was published in 1909 and endured as a text at the Military Academy and other Army schools even beyond World War II, used the maxims of Jomini, von der Goltz, and other late-19th-century theorists to form the basis for historical commentary on the generalship of individual American commanders.

Most serious of all is the ease and frequency with which faith in doctrine has actually distorted history. This was happening frequently by the end of the 19th century as each army in Europe developed and became committed to its own doctrine. It is the primary reason why the tactical and strategical lessons of the Civil War, which in many respects was the first modern war, went unheeded.[14] Even the elaborate German General Staff histories on the wars of Frederick the Great and the wars of liberation against Napoleon never failed to drive home the soundness of current German doctrine,[15] and the German official histories of the Boer War and the Russo-Japanese War similarly serve to demonstrate above all else the continuing validity of German doctrine. The Boers had applied that doctrine and *therefore* usually won, at least in the earlier battles before the weight of numbers alone could determine the outcome. British doctrine was faulty, if indeed the British yet had a doctrine, and *therefore* the British suffered repeated defeats. The Germans had trained the Japanese Army and the Japanese had won in 1904-05, "proving" again the superiority of German doctrine. Had a trained historian instead of an officer serving a tour with the Military History Section analyzed the same campaigns, surely he would have asked some searching questions about the differences in the discipline, morale, and leadership of the two armies. Did the Japanese cavalry win, for example, because of superior doctrine based on shock tactics or because it was better disciplined and led? To the officer corps of the day, the results demonstrated the weakness of the Russian Army's mounted infantry concepts in the face of shock tactics, whereas 10 years later, in a war that, at the outset, was strikingly similar in the conditions prevailing on the battlefield, shock tactics did not prevail anywhere for long.

Thus military history distilled by Jomini and his disciples ultimately found itself shaped by a commitment to doctrine, and the instinct of most professional soldiers before World War I was to explain away exceptions to the official rules rather than to use history as a means of testing and refining them.

Facts in History

Although it is not always evident in a lecture or a textbook, we can never be completely certain – and therefore in agreement – about what actually happened in history. Frederick and Napoleon knew this well. Skeptical both of the historian's motives and of the reliability of his facts, they evinced a healthy skepticism about the ability of the human mind ever to recreate an event as it actually had happened.

"The *true truths* are very difficult to ascertain," Napoleon complained. "There are so many truths!"[16]

Historical fact . . . is often a mere word; it cannot be ascertained when events actually occur, in the heat of contrary passions; and if, later on, there is a consensus, this is only because there is no one left to contradict . . . . What is . . . historical truth? . . . An agreed upon fiction . . . . There are facts that remain in eternal litigation.[17]

A Union staff officer whose corps bore the brunt of Pickett's charge at Gettysburg put it a different way:

A full account *of the battle as it was* will never, can never, be made. Who could sketch the charges, the constant fighting of the bloody panorama! It is not possible. The official reports may give results as to losses, with statements of attacks and repulses; they may also note the means by which results were attained . . . but the connection between means and results, the mode, the battle proper, these reports touch lightly. Two prominent reasons . . . account for the general inadequacy of these official reports . . . the literary infirmity of the reporters, and their not seeing themselves and their commands as others would have seen them. And factions, and parties, and politics . . . are already putting in their unreasonable demands . . . . Of this battle greater than Waterloo, a history, just, comprehensive, complete, will never be written. By-and-by, out of the chaos of trash and falsehood that newspapers hold, out of the disjointed mass of reports, out of the traditions and tales that come down from the field, some eye that never saw the battle will select, and some pen will write what will be named *the* history. With that the world will be, and if we are alive we must be, content.[18]

This writer intuitively understood that as soon as the historian begins to impose order on something as chaotic as a battle, he distorts. If his narrative is to mean anything at all to the reader he must simplify and organize the "disjointed mass of reports." He must, for lack of space, omit incidents that did not contribute to the final result. He must resolve controversies, not merely report them, and he must recognize that not every general is candid, every report complete, every description accurate. Orders are not always executed; not every order is even relevant to the situation. At Gettysburg, the watches in the two armies were set 20 minutes apart, and after the battle Lee had some of his subordinates rewrite their after-action reports to avoid unnecessary dissension. Well may it be said that "on the actual day of battle naked truths may be picked up for the asking; by the following morning they have already begun to get into their uniforms."[19]

During World War I, German General Max Hoffman confided to his diary: "For the first time in my life I have . . . seen 'History' at close quarters, and I know that its actual process is very different from what is presented to posterity."[20] *Plutarch Lied* is the descriptive title of an impassioned indictment of the French military leadership on the other side of no-man's land:

Men who yesterday seemed destined to oblivion have, today, acquired immortality. Has some new virtue been instilled in them, has some magician touched them with his wand? . . . Civilian historians have studied historical events from a point of view which is exclusively military. Far from trusting to their own judgment, they have not considered it respectful to exercise their critical faculties on the facts as guaranteed by a body of specialists. An idolatrous admiration for everything which concerns the army has conferred upon them the favour of having eyes which do not see and memories which are oblivious of their own experiences . . . . An incredible conspiracy exists in France at this very moment. No one dares to write the truth.[21]

Even with the best of intentions and an impartial mind, it is difficult to reconstruct what actually happened in history. This truth was given eloquent expression by a French pilot on a reconnaissance flight to Arras in May 1940 as he reflected on the chaos engulfing a dying society 30,000 feet below.

Ah, the blueprint that historians will draft of all this! The angles they will plot to lend shape to this mess! They will take the word of a cabinet minister, the decision of a general, the discussion of a committee, and out of that parade of ghosts they will build historic conversations in which they will discern farsighted views and weighty responsibilities. They will invent agreements, resistances, attitudinous pleas, cowardices . . . . Historians will forget reality. They will invent thinking men, joined by mysterious fibers to an intelligible universe, possessed of sound far-sighted views and pondering grave decisions according to the purest laws of Cartesian logic.[22]

Even where there can be agreement on facts, there will be disagreements among historians. "To expect from history those final conclusions which may perhaps be obtained in other disciplines is . . . to misunderstand its nature." Something akin to the scientific method helps to establish facts, but the function of the historian is also to explain, to interpret, and to discriminate, and here "the personal element can no longer be ruled out . . . . Truth, though for God it may be One, assumes many shapes to men."[23]

This explains the oft-quoted statement of Henry Adams, the famous American historian: "I have written too much history to believe in it. So if anyone wants to differ from me, I am prepared to agree with him."[24] No one who does not understand something about history could possibly know what Adams meant by this apparently cynical statement. Certainly he did not intend to imply that history, because it lacked unerring objectivity and precision, is of no practicable use to us. Quite the contrary. To recognize the frail structure of history is the first essential step toward *understanding*, which is far more important in putting history to work than blind faith in the validity of isolated facts. History tends to inspire more questions than answers, and the questions one asks of it determine the extent to which the subject may be considered practicable.

Making History Instructive

What, then, can the professional soldier expect to learn from history? If it can offer no abstract lessons to be applied indiscriminately or universally, if it cannot substantiate some cherished principles or official doctrine, if the subject itself is liable to endless bickering and interpretation, what is the point of looking at history at all?

Here Napoleon, whose writings and campaigns formed the basis of study for every principal military theorist for a hundred years after his death,[25] provides a useful answer in his first major campaign. When he assumed command of the French army in Italy in 1796, he took with him a history of a campaign conducted in the same theater by Marshal Maillebois half a century before, and more than one authority has noted the similarity in the two campaigns. "In both cases the object was to separate the allies and beat them in detail; in both cases the same passes through the maritime Alps were utilized, and in both cases the first objectives were the same."[26] In 1806, when he sent his cavalry commander, Murat, to reconnoiter the Bohemian frontier, he recommended that Murat take with him a history of the campaign that the French had waged there in 1741, and three years later Napoleon approved the location of pontoon bridges at Linz because Marshal Saxe had successfully constructed two bridges there in 1740. In 1813 he sent one of his marshals "an account of the battle fought by Gustavus Adolphus in positions similar to those which you occupy."[27]

Obviously history served Napoleon not so much because it provided a model to be slavishly followed, but because it offered ways to capitalize on what others before him had experienced. History, Liddell Hart reminds us,

is universal experience – infinitely longer, wider, and more varied than any individual's experience. How often do we hear people claim knowledge of the world and of life because they are sixty or seventy years old? . . . There is no excuse for any literate person if he is less than three thousand years old in mind.[28]

By this standard Patton was at least 900 years old after studying the Norman conquest of Sicily.

Napoleon also proposed, in 1807, the establishment of a special school of history at the College of France that would have practical application for officers. Trained historians would teach the military student how to make sound historical judgments, for Napoleon understood that "the correct way to read history is a real science in itself." He regarded the wars of the French Revolution as "fertile in useful lessons," yet apparently there had been no systematic effort to retrieve them. This too "would be an important function of the professors in the special school of history." For similar reasons Napoleon ordered his War Minister in 1811 to have the Depot of War prepare comprehensive records of the sieges and attacks of the fortified towns captured by the French armies in Germany, not for publication but for ready reference. And he did not discourage the printing of a similar volume on the sieges in Spain.[29]

Napoleon thus conceived of history as serving a purpose similar to that of the publications of the Old Historical Division and its ultimate successor, the Center of Military History. He would have applauded the appearance of the *Guide to the Study and Use of Military History*,[30] for some way had to be found to steer the military student through the "veritable labyrinth" of campaign studies, technical treatises, and memoirs. Like Frederick, who viewed history as "a magazine of military ideas,"[31] Napoleon would have been delighted with the official histories of the campaigns of World War II, Korea, and Vietnam, and with the extensive monographs on specialized subjects such as mobilization, logistics, and medical services.

On St. Helena Napoleon spoke of the need to publish manuscripts in the Imperial Library as a way of establishing a solid foundation for historical studies. Probably one of the first proposals of its kind, it anticipated by half a century the decision of the US War Department to publish in 128 meaty volumes *The Official Records of the Union and Confederate Armies*, a unique compilation of the after-action reports and official correspondence of Union and Confederate leaders. Napoleon also gave the first impetus to official military history when he created a historical section of the General Staff and named Baron Jomini to head it.[32]

His most enduring suggestion, however, was the deathbed advice he offered to his son: "Let him read and meditate upon the wars of the great captains: it is the only way to learn the art of war."[33]

Because Napoleon occasionally mentioned certain "principles of the art of war," he is often thought to have meant that the study of the Great Captains is valuable because it leads to the discovery of enduring principles or illustrates their successful application in the hands of genius. While acknowledging that these Great Captains had "succeeded only by conforming to the principles" and thus had made war "a true science," Napoleon offered more compelling reasons for studying the campaigns of Alexander, Hannibal, Caesar, Gustavus Adolphus, Turenne, and Frederick:

Tactics, the evolutions, the science of the engineer and the artillerist can be learned in treatises much like geometry, but the knowledge of the higher spheres of war is only acquired through the study of the wars and battles of the Great Captains and by experience. It has no precise, fixed rules. Everything depends on the character that nature has given to the general, on his qualities, on his faults, on the nature of the troops, on the range of weapons, on the season and on a thousand circumstances which are never the same.

The Great Captains must therefore serve as ''our great models.'' Only by imitating them, by understanding the bases for their decisions, and by studying the reasons for their success could modern officers ''hope to approach them.''[34]

Napoleon agreed with Frederick, who considered history ''the school of princes'' – princes, that is, who are destined to command armies – and who wrote his own candid memoirs in order that his successors might know ''the true situation of affairs . . . the reasons that impelled me to act; what were my means, what the snares of our enemies'' so that they might benefit from his own mistakes ''in order to shun them.'' And both would have endorsed Liddell Hart's observation that ''history is a catalogue of mistakes. It is our duty to profit by them.''[35]

Whereas Jomini concentrated upon *maxims*, Frederick and Napoleon focused their attention on *men*. They stressed the need for a commander to view a military situation from the vantage point of his opponent, and for the military student to become privy to the thinking process of successful commanders. This was the advice Prince Eugene, Marlborough's sidekick and the greatest commander who ever served the Hapsburgs, gave to young Frederick when, as the heir to the Prussian throne, Frederick accompanied the Prussian contingent serving with the Imperial Army along the Rhine in 1734. After he had become the foremost general of his day, Frederick urged his own officers, when studying the campaigns of Prince Eugene, not to be content merely to memorize the details of his exploits but ''to examine thoroughly his overall views and particularly *to learn how to think in the same way.*''[36]

This is still the best way to make military history practicable. ''The purpose of history,'' Patton wrote shortly before his death,

is to learn how human beings react when exposed to the danger of wounds or death, and how high ranking individuals react when submitted to the onerous responsibility of conducting war or the preparations for war. The acquisition of knowledge concerning the dates or places on which certain events transpired is immaterial . . . .[37]

The future field marshal Earl Wavell gave similar advice to a class at the British Staff College shortly before World War II:

The real way to get value out of the study of military history is to take particular situations, and as far as possible get inside the skin of the man who made a decision and then see in what way you could have improved upon it.

''For heaven's sake,'' Wavell warned,

don't treat the so-called principles of war as holy writ, like the Ten Commandments, to be learned by heart, and as having by their repetition some magic, like the incantations of savage priests. They are merely a set of common sense maxims, like 'cut your coat according to your cloth,' 'a rolling stone gathers no moss,' 'honesty is the best policy,' and so forth.

Merely to memorize the maxim "cut your coat according to your cloth" does not instruct one how to be a tailor, and Wavell reminded his listeners that no two theorists espoused exactly the same set of principles, which, he contended, "are all simply common sense and . . . instinctive to the properly trained soldier."

To learn that Napoleon in 1796 with 20,000 men beat combined forces of 30,000 by something called 'economy of force' or 'operating on interior lines' is a mere waste of time. If you can understand *how* a young, unknown man inspired a half-starved, ragged, rather Bolshie crowd; how he filled their bellies, how he out-marched, out-witted, out-bluffed, and defeated men who had studied war all their lives and waged it according to the text books of the time, you will have learnt something worth knowing.

But the soldier will not learn it from military texts.[38]

Sometimes military history is treated, in books and lectures alike, as though it exists primarily for the future field commander. Frederick might have assumed something of the sort in his own writings, but he wrote more about such practical subjects as feeding and drilling an army, the gathering and evaluation of intelligence, and how to treat friendly and hostile populations than he did about strategy. Likewise, Napoleon was concerned about military education at every level, and his advice to his son on studying the decisions of the Great Captains should not obscure the fact that he believed strongly in military history in his officers' schools and also as a practical subject for research.

History can be made practicable at any level. The future field marshal Erwin Rommel did not have future corps commanders necessarily in mind when he wrote *Infantry Attacks* in 1937. His lessons, deduced from the experiences of his battalion in World War I, could indeed have been of value to any company or field grade officer. For example, describing the events he witnessed in September 1914, Rommel concluded:

War makes extremely heavy demands on the soldier's strength and nerves. For this reason make heavy demands on your men in peacetime exercises.

It is difficult to maintain contact in fog . . . . Advances through fog by means of a compass must be practiced, since smoke will frequently be employed. In a meeting engagement in the fog, the side capable of developing a maximum fire power on contact will get the upper hand; therefore, keep the machine guns ready for action at all times during the advance.

All units of the group must provide for their own security. This is especially true in close terrain and when faced with a highly mobile enemy.

Too much spade work is better than too little. Sweat saves blood.

Command posts must be dispersed . . . . Do not choose a conspicuous hill for their location.

In forest fighting, the personal example of the commander is effective only on those troops in his immediate vicinity.

The rain favored the attack.[39]

Rommel drew his own conclusions from his experiences, but a discriminating reader could probably have extracted them for himself.

These observations were not lost on Patton, who probably shared similar experiences and had been involved in training troops. During the Saar campaign in early 1945, Patton confided to his diary:

Woke up at 0300 and it was raining like hell. I actually got nervous and got up and read Rommel's book, *Infantry Attacks*. It was most helpful, as he described all the rains he had in September 1914 and *also the fact that, in spite of the heavy rains, the Germans got along.*[40]

And so, shortly, did the Third Army.

Another book of this genre is *Infantry in Battle*, which was prepared at the Infantry School in 1934 under the direction of then Colonel George C. Marshall and revised four years later. Written on the assumption that "combat situations cannot be solved by rule," contributors to this book fell back upon numerous examples from World War I to introduce the reader to "the realities of war and the extremely difficult and highly disconcerting conditions under which tactical problems must be solved in the face of the enemy."[41]

Military history has also been used to test the ability of military students. In 1891 a British colonel published a tactical study of the battle of Spicheren, fought 20 years earlier. In the introduction he explained:

To gain from a relation of events the same abiding impressions as were stamped on the minds of those who played a part in them – and it is such impressions that create instinct – it is necessary to examine the situations developed during the operations so closely as to have a clear picture of the whole scene in our mind's eye; to assume, in imagination, the responsibilities of the leaders who were called upon to meet those situations; to come to a definite decision and to test the soundness of that decision by the actual event.[42]

Learning from History

What Frederick, Napoleon, Rommel, Patton, Wavell, and many others referred to here have shared in common can be summed in one word: *reading*. An English general in the 18th century urged young officers to devote every spare minute to reading military history, "the most instructive of all reading."[43]

"*Books!*" an anonymous old soldier during the Napoleonic wars pretended to snort. "And what are they but the dreams of pedants? They may make a Mack, but have they ever made a Xenophon, a Caesar, a Saxe, a Frederick, or a Bonaparte? Who would not laugh to hear the cobbler of Athens lecturing Hannibal on the art of war?"

"True," is his own rejoinder, "but as you are not Hannibal, listen to the cobbler."[44]

Since the great majority of today's officers are college graduates, with a healthy percentage of them having studied for advanced degrees, they have probably long since passed the stage at which they can actually benefit from a conventional lecture on history, with the emphasis on factual content and the expectation of a clear conclusion. The leading question therefore becomes: How do we teach them to learn from history? J. F. C. Fuller, coauthor of the concept that later became known as *blitzkrieg*, had this problem in mind when he addressed a class at the British Staff College a few years after World War I. "Until you learn how to teach yourselves," he told the students, "you will never be taught by others."[45]

Fuller did not specify how this was to be accomplished, but he probably would insist that to teach the officer how to teach himself should be the avowed objective of every course in military history. Certainly he would agree that no course in military history can really do much good if the officer is exposed every half dozen years throughout his career to no more than a structured course of only a few months' duration, especially if in the process he has gained little understanding of history as a discipline or a scant appreciation for how it can be used and abused. Assuredly such a voracious reader as Fuller – who at age 83 confessed to having recently sold off all of the books in his library that he could not read within the next 10 years – would argue that there would be no point to any history course whatever if the student is not stimulated to spend some time afterwards poking around the field a bit on his own. "Books," Fuller once wrote, "have always been my truest companions."[46]

Any student of history must learn to identify with the men and events he reads about, seeking above all to understand their problems and to accept the past on its own terms. The student must also learn to ask questions, not of the instructor necessarily, but of his material and especially of himself. Historians usually worry more about asking the right questions than finding definitive answers, for they know from experience that no document or book can answer a question that is never asked. Had Patton read Rommel's book when the sun was shining, for example, and all was going well, chances are he would never have paid any attention to the casual observation that rain seemed to favor the attack. Cannae was an important battle to Schlieffen because the double envelopment achieved by Hannibal suggested a method by which a battle of annihilation might be fought in a war against France and Russia. But to Colonel Ardant du Picq, the foremost French military theorist of the 1860s, Hannibal was a great general for a quite different reason – "his admirable comprehension of the morale of combat, of the morale of the soldier."[47] The two men were searching for solutions to different kinds of problems, and in reading about Cannae each responded to his individual interests.

In the old Army, when there was enough leisure time for reading, riding, or a regular game of golf, it was probably understood that the burden of learning from military history must rest primarily upon the individual officer. The annual historical ride to the Civil War battlefields – which had been preserved by Act of Congress "for historical and professional military study"[48] – directly involved students from the Army War College in the unending dialogue between past and present. Students were frequently asked on location how they would have handled some problem in tactics or command and control that had confronted a commander during battle. "It is not desirable to have the question answered," the instructions specified. "Some will know the answer, but all who do not will ask themselves the question."[49]

This is the only way to learn from history. The textbook or the instructor can organize information, but only the student can put it to work. "Mere swallowing of either food or opinions," Fuller reminds us, "does not of necessity carry with it digestion, and without digestion swallowing is but labour lost and food wasted."[50]

Today there is a shortage of both "labour and food," as other budgetary priorities and manpower shortages have forced severe cutbacks in history courses throughout the Army.

But in a sense this blinds us to the real problem, for it does not necessarily follow that more money and instructors must be the solution. A formal course in military history, however desirable, is not the only way and may, in fact, not be the best way to teach students how to teach themselves history, which is the goal. George C. Marshall, as future Chief of Staff, regarded his two years at the Army Staff College in 1906-08 as having been "immensely instructive," but not because of the quality of the courses there. "The association with the officers, the reading we did and the discussion . . . had a tremendous effect . . . . I learned little I could use," Marshall wrote, but "I learned how to learn . . . . My habits of thought were being trained."[51]

Marshall's words touch upon the essence of practicability. Military history may be of indeterminate value for the immediate future (if World War III were to be fought next week, for example), but among the captains in the career courses today are the Army's top administrators and leaders of tomorrow, and not all graduates of the war colleges in June will retire in the next six or eight years. Those that remain are bound to benefit from anything that can heighten their understanding of society, of other armies, of the political process, of leadership, of the nature of war, of the evolution of doctrine, and of a dozen similar areas of human activity in which history, pursued by an intelligent and inquisitive reader, can still be strikingly practicable to the modern soldier.

To any set of military maxims, whatever their origin, perhaps the following literary maxims should be added:[52]

The history that lies inert in unread books does no work in the world.

If you want a new idea, read an old book.

'Tis the good reader that makes the good book.

A book is like a mirror. If an ass looks in, no prophet can peer out.

Jay Luvaas

NOTES

1. As quoted in Martin Blumenson, *The Patton Papers*, Vol. II: *1940-1945* (Boston: Houghton Mifflin, 1974), p. 283.
2. Harry S. Truman, *Memoirs*, Vol. I: *Years of Decision* (Garden City, N.Y.: Doubleday, 1955), p. 119.
3. Pieter Geyl, *Napoleon For and Against* (New Haven: Yale Univ. Press, 1963), p. 15.
4. As quoted in Prince Kraft zu Hohenlohe-Ingelfingen, *Letters on Artillery*, 2d ed. (London: Edward Stanford, 1890), p. 108.
5. *Memoirs of the History of France during the reign of Napoleon,* dictated by the Emperor at Saint Helena . . . (7 vols.; London: Henry Colburn and Company, 1828), VI, 18-27; Ernest Picard, *Preceptes et jugements de Napoleon* (Paris: Berger-Leurault, 1913), pp. 405-06.
6. *Frederick the Great on the Art of War,* ed. and trans. by Jay Luvaas (New York: The Free Press, 1966), pp. 77-78.
7. Lothar Rendulic, "Mistakes in Deducing War Experiences," Historical Division, European Command, 10 October 1951. Italics added.
8. Herman Melville, as quoted in John Bartlett, *Familiar Quotations,* 14th ed. (Boston: Little, Brown, 1968), p. 698.
9. Wavell to Liddell Hart, 15 March 1934, Liddell Hart Papers, States House, Medmenham, England.
10. Karl von Clausewitz, *On War*, ed. and trans. by Michael Howard and Peter Paret (Princeton: Princeton Univ. Press, 1976), pp. 170, 172-73.
11. Baron de Jomini, *Summary of the Art of War* . . . (New York: Greenwood Press, 1954), p. 329.
12. The quote from Napoleon is found in his "Observations on a plan to establish a special school of literature and history at the College of France," 19 April 1807, *Correspondance de Napoleon Ier* (32 vols.; Paris: Imprimerie Imperiale, 1858-70), XV, 107-10.
13. Clausewitz, *On War*, pp. 171-72.
14. See Jay Luvaas, *Military Legacy of the Civil War* (Chicago: Univ. of Chicago Press, 1959), pp. 119-69 *passim.*
15. See Alfred Vagts, *A History of Militarism*, rev. ed. (New York: Meridian Books, 1959), p. 26; A. L. Conger's remarks in "Proceedings of the Conference on Military History," *Annual Report of the American Historical Association for the year 1912* (Washington: GPO, 1914), pp. 162-74.
16. As quoted in J. Christopher Herold, *The Mind of Napoleon* (New York: Columbia Univ. Press, 1955), p. 50.
17. Ibid.
18. Frank L. Byrne and Andrew T. Weaver, eds., *Haskell of Gettysburg* (Madison: State Historical Society of Wisconsin, 1970), pp. 200-01.
19. Ian Hamilton, *A Staff Officer's Scrap-Book during the Russo-Japanese War* (2 vols; London: E. Arnold, 1906), I, v.
20. B. H. Liddell Hart, *Through the Fog of War* (London: Faber and Faber, 1938), p. 227.
21. Jean de Peirrefeu, *Plutarch Lied* (New York: Alfred A. Knopf, 1924), pp. 10, 23.
22. Antoine de Saint-Exupery, *Flight to Arras* (New York: Reynal & Hitchcock, 1942), pp. 133-35.
23. Geyl, pp. 15-16.
24. As quoted in B. H. Liddell Hart, *Why Don't We Learn From History* (London: George Allen & Unwin, 1946), p. 10.
25. Our basic principles of war first appeared in their modern form in the early writings of J. F. C. Fuller, who in turn had deduced them from his reading of the printed *Correspondance* of Napoleon. J. F. C. Fuller, *The Foundations of the Science of War* (London: Hutchinson & Co., n.d.), pp. 13-14.
26. J. Holland Rose, *The Personality of Napoleon* (New York: G. P. Putnam's Sons, 1912), pp. 95-97.
27. Camon, *Pour Apprendre l'art de la Guerre* (Paris: Berger-Leurault, n.d.), p. 4.
28. Liddell Hart, *Why Don't We Learn from History,* pp. 7-8.
29. Napoleon, *Correspondance*, XV, 107-10; XXI, 378-79.
30. John E. Jessup, Jr., and Robert W. Coakley, eds., *A Guide to the Study and Use of Military History* (Washington: US Army, Center of Military History, 1979).
31. Frederick, *The History of the Seven Years War* (2 vols.; London: G. G. J. and J. Robinson, 1789), I, xii.
32. Rose, p. 244; S. J. Watson, *By Command of the Emperor: A Life of Marshal Berthier* (London: The

Bodley Head, 1957), p. 185. Napoleon may in fact have been the first to distort the official history of a campaign by applying pressure on the historian to twist his narrative to suit his own ends. See General Camon, *Genie et Metier chez Napoleon* (Paris: Berger-Leurault, 1930), pp. 33-44 *passim*.

33. Herold, pp. 255-56.
34. Napoleon, *Correspondance,* XXXI, 365.
35. Frederick, *The History of My Own Times* (London: G. G. J. and J. Robinson, 1789), ix; Liddell Hart, *Thoughts on War* (London: Faber and Faber, 1944), p. 138.
36. *Frederick the Great on the Art of War*, p. 50. Italics added.
37. Blumenson, II, 750.
38. As quoted in John Connell, *Wavell: Scholar and Soldier* (2 vols.; London: Collins, 1964), I, 161.
39. Field Marshal Erwin Rommel, *Attacks* (Vienna, Va.: Athena Press, 1979), pp. 16-60 *passim.*
40. Blumenson, II, 571. Italics added.
41. US Army, *Infantry in Battle* (Washington: US Army, 1939), introduction.
42. G. F. R. Henderson, *The Battle of Spicheren . . .* , 2d ed. (London: Gale & Polden, 1909), pp. vi-vii.
43. *A Series of Letters recently written by a General Officer to his Son, on his entering the Army . . . ,* 1st American ed. (Salem: Cushing and Appleton, n.d.), I, v.
44. *Hints to Young Generals,* by an old soldier (John Armstrong) (Kingston: J. Buel, 1812), pp. 7-8.
45. J. F. C. Fuller, *Memoirs of an Unconventional Soldier* (London: Ivor Nicholson and Watson, 1936), pp. 417-18.
46. J. F. C. Fuller, *The Last of the Gentlemen's Wars . . . .* (London: Faber and Faber, 1937), p. 112. In 1961 Fuller told the writer that he was unloading the books he could not hope to read during the next 10 years.
47. Ardant du Picq, *Battle Studies: Ancient and Modern Battle* (Harrisburg: Military Service Publishing Co., 1947), p. 68.
48. Ronald F. Lee, *The Origin and Evolution of the National Military Park Idea* (Washington: Office of Park Historic Preservation, 1973), pp. 33-35.
49. US Army War College, ''Memorandum: Instructions for students designated to be present on Historical Ride,'' Fort Humphreys, D.C., 4 May 1937.
50. Fuller, *Memoirs of an Unconventional Soldier,* p. 417.
51. Quoted in Forrest C. Pogue, *George C. Marshall: Ordeal and Hope 1939-1942* (New York: Viking Press, 1966), p. 101.
52. The ''maxims'' quoted come from Clark Becker, Lord Lytton, Ralph Waldo Emerson, and Georg Lichtenberg.

This article appeared in the March 1982 issue of *Parameters.*

2

Military History for the Military Professional

by BENJAMIN F. COOLING III

Two decades ago, at the height of the Korean conflict, a renowned military historian claimed that military history as a specialty had largely lost its function. ''If military history is to have more than antiquarian interest, it must, it would seem, turn away from the study of past wars to the study of war itself in its broadest, possible terms,'' declared Walter Millis.[1] Since that time professional historians who devote their careers to analysis of military affairs have worked to refute Millis' contention. At the same time they have tried to overcome the aversion of their colleagues to military history. Lately, antagonism toward war in general, and to the war in Viet Nam in particular, have further blurred any signs of progress.

Some blame for the rejection of military history rests with military historians themselves. Often they have reflected Millis' impression that his compatriots were adrift, unsure of their destination and uncertain as to whether they were even carrying the correct cargo. Millis thought that military history should become less military and more civilian. It would have to make better use of the resources of political philosophy, economics, and sociology as well as the applied sciences. He felt that its success as a useful discipline would depend upon its return to the general study of man and his society. Twenty years after Millis' stricture it seems that the guild of military historians continues to suffer from the old malaise. The eminent scholar Peter Paret recently concluded:

Far too much military history is being written in America. In this respect, at least, its condition does not differ from that of other fields of history. But with few exceptions, the character of the work produced is extremely conventional–descriptive history, centering on leading figures, campaigns, and climactic battles, often with a strong antiquarian bent. Few enterprising minds are interested in war and in military institutions for their own sake.[2]

If civilian professionals have moved slowly to reshape one of the more ''relevant'' subdisciplines of history in the post-Korea period, many military professionals have been equally reluctant to study past experience in order to apply the knowledge gained to the practice of their own craft. In a way, they have reflected the reluctance of so many Americans to think about the past. Facing backward, it would seem, would impede progress in our future-oriented nation. But this does not mean that military men have failed to show great interest in certain facets of military history. They are among the most ardent devotees of Civil War and Second World War battles and campaigns. They rally to societies like the American Military Institute, the Company of Military Historians, and the Council of Abandoned Military Posts. The very abundance of military museums (fifty-nine for the Army alone at last count) attests to the interest in the heritage of the military profession.[3]

This so-called "drum and trumpet" history is frequently scoffed at by civilian academicians. But experience has shown that maintaining a link with the past yields rich dividends in the present by helping young and old soldiers alike to identify with unit lineages and to learn many technical lessons that are useful for the future.[4] Disciples of Clio, the muse of history, can muster many reasons why senior armed services professionals need to take another look at the experiences of their forefathers. Indeed, the extensive locations and variety of US military commitments around the world, and the increasing scope of Army educational programs in recent years support the need for emphasis on historical perspective. Concern with command and management, strategy, national security policies, economics and politics, international and domestic conflicts and tensions, the composition of the Army, and the impact of technology only reinforces the need for a new and innovative approach to military history by the military leader – "Military History for the Military Professional" let us call it.

Such military history may be studied either in the classroom or independently. This paper will suggest ten areas that might be included in such a program. There are others, but a program that incorporates the elements of these ten areas can do much to prepare the military professional to face the challenges of the future.

First, a military leader must comprehend *The Nature and Scope of Military History*. If past remains prologue, then there must be an understanding of the endless, complex, and perplexing contrasts and inconsistencies of the past and their applicability to the future. The relationship of military history to other disciplines, i.e., economics, sociology, political science, the physical sciences, and even other areas of history must be highlighted. Such an introduction can come from the reading of sound military historiographical work.[5] Specific questions might be posed on the role of the military in the study of war and conflict, the use and abuse of military history by the military profession, historical methodology, and the facilities and agencies for the study of the craft. At this stage the professional soldier should concern himself with understanding history as a means for clarifying man's proclivity for conflict.

Next, the military professional might proceed to a historical analysis of the relationship between *Armed Forces and Society*. A premise may be made here that a successful military institution must be a viable part of and reflect the culture of which it forms the sword and shield. In view of this premise it seems important that there be an examination of the fabric of societies and their military establishments throughout history. A wide variety of societies suggest themselves for study. For instance, the Ancient World, which should include not only Greece and Rome (that have interested Western scholars for so long due to their influence on the spawning of modern institutions), but also China, a society that has contributed so much to civilization. Similarly, attention should be given to a study of the cultural-military ancestry of those nations which operate under the socio-political system of Islam. Finally, the impact of the tribal societies of the great Zulu and Botswana should be compared with the influence exerted by European colonialism. Such study can illuminate shadowy areas of civil-military relations and the interaction of military affairs and society in those polyglot African political entities emerging in the wake of disimperialism.

American military professionals may feel that they understand fully the subtle relationships between military and civilian sectors of Western European nations and the United States. But they might benefit additionally from a periodic review of how the American military profession reflects Anglo-American civilization and its development.[6] Such inquiry can help to reinforce a sense of pride on the one hand, while serving as a timely reminder that the Anglo-American tradition places the soldier's roots in an essentially civilian society. Failure to keep this basic fact in mind at all times could lead to the disasters that have occurred in various European, Asian, and other nations which have made the military a caste apart from civilian society.[7]

A third area for possible scrutiny encompasses *Command and Control Through the Centuries*. There are recognizable aspects of high command and management as we examine the past thirty centuries. The biographical approach to military history is hardly new. "Great Captains" have been studied many times in the past. Today, this concept can include more than an analysis of leadership styles and the way in which the so-called principles of war were practiced. Such a study can clarify varying nationalistic terminologies and interpretations of command, staff concepts, and participatory leadership. Special attention must be paid to the evolution of Napoleonic, Suvarovian, German, and Anglo-American leadership modes and styles.[8] However, today's military professional can utilize both ancient and modern examples of leadership, and Eastern as well as Western. If Mao and Giap are currently in vogue, their forebears are legion, and there appears to be no dearth of material for more conventional "Great Captains," from Scipio Africanus and Saladin to Zhukov and Montgomery.

The conglomerate, multi-social makeup of contemporary American society as reflected in our military forces points to a fourth area, *The Historical Human Composition of Military Forces*. The wide ethnic and nationalistic variations in armies might explain the success and failure of employing non-white or alien military units and individuals in American and Western European forces. The

Roman use of Gauls, Iberians, and Franks as *Auxilia*; the Turkish employment of Janissaries, a foreign military elite; the French utilization of Senegalese and Tonkinese Tirailleurs; the British experience with Indian sepoys; the American practice of all black units, Indian "scouts," and Philippine Constabulary; the Russian integration of a Cossack minority group; and the International Brigade's participation in the Spanish Civil War, are subject areas which could offer some lessons in this regard.[9] VOLAR planners may discover some very useful information if they investigate why and how these alien units found employment – their advantages and disadvantages in terms of discipline, morale, efficiency – as well as the question of their social position within the military institution itself and the chance of their being assimilated and being advanced in society.

The continued high priority of national security policy formulation by senior planners dictates a fifth need: an understanding of the common and unique elements of *National Security Policies Through the Ages*. An analysis of the issues of vital national interest over the centuries can be richly rewarding for the continued evolution of American programs. There are numerous strands of continuity between the concerns of the modern world and the historic interests of Republican and Imperial Roman expansion and defense, Byzantine concern with survival, the counter-thrust of Russia against invasions and "enemies on all sides," German *Reich*-building, French mesmerization with nationalism and prestige, British home island defense and protection of the trade routes for survival, and interaction between insular Japan and China, the continental giant. In addition, military planners of the present and future should be aware of the passage of the United States through three distinct stages of security concern. These include America's transition from emerging nation, through her continental expansion, to participation as a major nation-state in the world power struggle with relationships to the national security concerns of other nations.[10] Nowhere have such developments taken place in isolation. Indeed, to appreciate modern security requirements throughout the world it would seem fundamental for American military officials to appreciate certain traditional elements and causative factors in these requirements.

The *Interaction of Military, Political, and Diplomatic Affairs* provides still another area for serious investigation by military professionals. Throughout history the military man has been more than simply the servant to diplomats and civil authority. Rather, armed forces personnel have also been diplomatic representatives in their own right, involved in activities ranging from daily relations with foreign citizenry to higher roles as makers of policy and alliances. The phenomenon is not new and it continues to comprise a major phase of military activity. The soldier-as-diplomat can be studied in the experiences of counselors like Max Bauer, Chiang Kai-Shek's first German military adviser; missions such as Perry's naval expedition to Japan in 1854; participants in postwar peace negotiations such as Panmunjom; or disarmament negotiations in London and Washington after World War I. Expeditionary operations like the Allied maneuvers in northern Russia; occupation activities which pinned down Federal troops in the Reconstructed South; pacification programs of European powers in Africa; and formulation of military alliances such as the Imperial Defence Agreement of 1887 between Great Britain, Australia, and New Zealand, all displayed the military man in a quasi-diplomatic role.[11] Simply put, the modern senior officer should be aware of the role of the military as it interacted with political and diplomatic affairs from *Pax Romana* to *Pax Americana*. Might not the study of such experiences as American pacification of the Philippines after the Spanish War have enabled our policy makers to avoid the frustration accompanying recent efforts of this nature in Southeast Asia?

Likewise, the modern officer should find useful the historical perspective of *Internal Crisis and Military Force*. Domestic disturbances are far from unique to the present generation or even to the American scene. Military organizations throughout history have been charged with the promotion and protection of domestic tranquility as well as defense against external threat. Rebellion took place in Republican Rome, and domestic unrest has long been endemic to the Far East in China and India. The French Revolution, English experiences in North America as well as their home islands during the Industrial Revolution, and twentieth century manifestations of internal disturbances in Mexico, Ireland, and Russia can all contribute to any discussion of the role of the military in domestic crises from ancient to modern times. Certainly the role of American airborne units patrolling the streets of Washington in 1968 fits the pattern of our experience from the Whiskey Rebellion to modern labor and racial unrest.[12] It should prove enlightening to examine the actions of the French line army during the early stages of the French Revolution, or the Petrograd garrison in the outbreak of the February 1917 revolution in Russia. Perhaps the conduct of the Roman legions, thwarted for years by Palestinian revolt, will not seem so strange when in 70 A.D. they levelled Jerusalem, sparing neither buildings nor inhabitants.

Balancing this portrayal of the military as guardians of internal order, sometimes at the expense of personal freedom, would be the eighth area of concentration, *Nationbuilding Activities of the Military*. Indeed, the man in uniform has often contributed to society in ways other than with a rifle at the ready. Military institutions have been called upon frequently to participate in nonwar-related endeavors and national projects because of critically needed skills. High levels of organization, discipline, concentration of available aptitudes, and administrative abilities have led the military into historic roles in engineering, technology, medicine, education, and social involvement. From Roman road building to American flood control projects; from the introduction of the stirrup by the Mongols to US Army supervision of the Manhattan Project; from Napoleonic medicine to American cure of yellow fever; from West Point and St. Cyr as the early collegiate institutions oriented toward scientific training to the democratizing element of military service for immigrants to American shores, the uniformed services have built as well as destroyed in the name of civilization.[13] The man on horseback has not always been a threat to the state; witness the contributions of Kemal Ataturk, George Washington, or Oliver Cromwell. Senior officers might very well find knowledge of such phenomena very useful when countering the derogatory image of their profession held by so many civilians today.

We should be particularly curious about a ninth area in our new approach to military history: *Unpopular Wars and Military Operations.* Certain military episodes in history have produced sharp divisions between governmental policy and public support. Citizen approval in periods of conflict remains directly related to achievement of military goals and performance. It is important for the modern officer to examine historically the viewpoints of man as he went about fulfilling his obligations vis-à-vis the nation, especially in wartime. The nature of governmental involvement in a specific unpopular war or operation can shed light upon public relations, the goals of popular opposition, and the impact on state policy. Analysis of specific wars may include the War of 1812, which nearly tore apart the youthful, struggling American republic, and produced cases of militia refusal to invade foreign soil during major operations. Similarly, the Mexican War, the Philippine Insurrection, and British participation in the Boer War and Suez operation of 1956 produced deep cleavages in the body politic.[14] French involvement in Indochina toppled one government at home in the late nineteenth century, and we are all aware of the impact of that same area, together with Algeria, upon the stability of modern France. One may suspect that this topic will continue to interest present and future generations of American military planners, especially as increasing numbers of informed citizenry wonder why we remembered nothing and forgot nothing from the experiences of Frenchmen on the Asian mainland.

Just as military affairs have been affected by social and technical change, military affairs have had a continuous effect upon the shaping of technology and society. Thus, *Technology, Culture, and Warfare* provides an appropriate capstone to this one approach to military history for the military professional. The interaction has been continuous and accelerating, with long historical roots and antecedents. The modern officer need not be held captive by specifics of the screw propeller, the machine gun, or the atomic bomb. Instead, he should be more concerned with the full scope of technology and society since the Industrial Revolution. He might consider the constructive versus non-constructive aspects of the interaction of war and technology without subverting his professional integrity. In fact, all segments of society need to become more aware of the "case for war" school of thought whose disciples like Warner Sombart, Lewis Mumford, F. W. Nietzsche, and Stanislav Andreski have stressed the positive force of war in societal and technological progress. Their antagonists, including Arnold Toynbee, John U. Nef, and others have countered that war and its concomitant military burdens have always been the "proximate cause" of the breakdown of every civilization in the past.[15]

If this exercise appears too ephemeral or esoteric to the average professional soldier he need only remember that the place of conflict in society remains central to the continuing issues of our times. Questions of modern economics, organization and administration, labor, product standardization, conflict limitation, civil government, democracy, nationalism, and culture and the arts – as they relate to military affairs – must be considered and understood by all military professionals.

The United States Army stands at another critical juncture in its history. Officers should be encouraged to look at the past in order to make the present and future more meaningful. This does not imply that they should be preoccupied solely with the Army's past and with lineage rosters or with glorious deeds of valor and sacrifice, however praiseworthy this approach. Instead they should examine the way in which the American military profession fits into the broader stream of the history of military affairs. Military professionals need not be tied uncritically to the past with its mistakes or successes. They should not accept facts on face value. They should be acutely aware that the study of military history can offer guidelines that can prevent their "reinventing the wheel." General George Patton said, "To be a successful soldier you must know history." We think he was right.

NOTES

1. Walter Millis, *Military History* (American Historical Association Teachers Service Pamphlet 39), Washington, 1961, pp. 17-18.
2. Peter Paret, "The History of War," *Daedalus,* Spring 1971, p. 381.
3. U.S. Department of the Army, Office of the Chief of Military History, *Directory U.S. Army Museums*, Washington, 1968, lists fifty-nine Army museums, ten National Guard and at least seventeen non-Army military, Naval, and Air museums.
4. Recent encouraging signs along this vein include increased instruction in military history at the U.S. Military Academy, at various ROTC institutions, and the Command and General Staff College as well as the deliberations of the Department of the Army Ad Hoc Committee for the Study of Military History in the Army. The author wishes to acknowledge that many of the ideas expressed in this paper evolved while developing a military history elective for the US Army War College with Dr. Don Rickey, Jr., Assistant Director for Research, US Army Military History Research Collection.
5. In addition to the works of Millis and Paret, cited above, the following are also useful in this regard: Michael Howard, "The Demand for Military History," *The Times Literary Supplement* (London), 13 November 1969; John K. Mahon, "Teaching and Research on Military History in the United States," *The Historian*, February 1965, pp. 170-184; and Allan R. Millett, "American Military History: Over the Top," in Herbert J. Bass, ed., *The State of American History*, Cleveland, Quadrangle, 1970, pp. 157-182.
6. See for example Russell F. Weigley, ed., *The American Military: Readings in the History of the Military in American Society*, Addison-Wesley, Reading, Mass., 1969.
7. Credit for stimulating the author's memory on this point belongs to Ambassador Hermann Fr. Eilts, Diplomatic Adviser to the Commandant, US Army War College.
8. Few boundaries exist for the biographical approach to military history, and a useful example of reinterpretation is James Marshall-Cornwall, *Grant as Military Commander,* New York, Van Nostrand, 1970. LTC James B. Agnew's "Coalition Warfare: A Successful Experiment in Combined Command, 1914-1918," *Parameters*, Spring 1971, pp. 50-64, illustrates a useful approach to historical evaluation of command and staff work.
9. This relatively new field of investigation includes such works as William H. Leckie, *The Buffalo Soldiers: A Narrative History of the Negro Cavalry in the West,* Norman, University of Oklahoma Press, 1967; and George H. Dodenhoff, "A Historical Perspective of Mercenaries," *Naval War College Review*, March 1969, pp. 91-110.

10. National Security policies may be viewed from historical perspective in Vern L. Bullough, "The Roman Empire vs. Persia, 363-502: A Study of Successful Deterrence," *Journal of Conflict Resolution*, March 1963, pp. 54-75, or Fred Greene, "The Military View of American National Policy; 1904-1940," *The American Historical Review*, January 1961, pp. 354-377.

11. See for instance, Alfred Vagts, *The Military Attache*, Princeton, Princeton University Press, 1967; John Gimbel, *The American Occupation of Germany: Politics and the Military, 1945-1949*, Stanford, Stanford University Press, 1968; or Henry F. Graff, ed., *American Imperialism and the Philippine Insurrection*, Boston, Little, Brown & Co., 1969.

12. Historical appreciation of this continuing problem may be gleaned from Carlton Younger, *Ireland's Civil War*, New York, Taplinger, 1968; and Robin Higham, ed., *Bayonets in the Streets: The Use of Troops in Civil Disturbances*, Lawrence, Kan., University Press of Kansas, 1969.

13. Studies of non-combat activities of the military include: William H. Goetzmann, *Army Exploration in the American West*, New Haven, Yale University Press, 1959; Edgar Hume, *Victories of Army Medicine . . .*, Philadelphia, J. B. Lippincott, 1943; or Dankart A. Rustow, "The Army and the Founding of the Turkish Republic," *World Politics*, July 1959, pp. 513-552.

14. See for instance Samuel Eliot Morison, Frederick Merk, and Frank Freidel, *Dissent in Three Wars*, Cambridge, Harvard University Press, 1970, or E. B. Tompkins, *Anti-Imperialism in the United States: The Great Debate, 1890-1920*, Philadelphia, University of Pennsylvania Press, 1970.

15. This broad topical area can be approached through I. B. Holley, *Ideas and Weapons*, New Haven, Yale University Press, 1953; Stanislaw Andrezejewski, *Military Organization and Society*, London, Routledge and Kegan Paul Ltd, 1954; and John U. Nef, *War and Human Progress, An Essay on the Rise of Industrial Civilization*, New York, W. W. Norton and Co., 1968 edition.

This article appeared in the winter 1972 issue of *Parameters*.

3

S.L.A. Marshall (1900-1977): In Memoriam

by HUGH M. COLE

The death of Brigadier General S.L.A. Marshall last December ended a lifetime of personal devotion to the United States Army and a career dedicated to chronicling the deeds of the American fighting man. Samuel Lyman Atwood Marshall himself wore the Army uniform in four wars. Although this paper will not attempt to list all of his original 24 published books, it is significant to note that all but four deal with the US Army and its history. These books – and scores of newspaper and magazine articles – appealed to and were read by serving soldiers and civilians alike, gaining Marshall a reputation as the leading American historian, critic, and analyst of ground warfare.

The long association between Marshall and the Army began in World War I with combat service in the American Expeditionary Force. In France, he received what would be his only formal military education, this in the various basic schools established for noncommissioned officers. He also won a battlefield commission to become the youngest second lieutenant in the Army. In the preface to his first book, *Blitzkrieg* (1940), Marshall later wrote:

The only schools from which I have ever graduated have been army schools. The United States Army in wartime is a great University. To the service, I owe a great deal and the debt may some day be paid.

Back home in El Paso after having resigned his commission, Marshall experienced the rootlessness of many young veterans, finally joining the 1st Cavalry Division. Adna Chaffee encouraged the young man to write articles about the divisional polo team, and the results led Marshall to believe that he could make a living with his typewriter. In 1922, he got a job on the *El Paso Herald* and, by 1927, had made a national mark as a newspaperman and had been hired by the *Detroit News*.

The years with the *El Paso Herald* were crucial to Marshall's career. Fort Bliss was a way station for a host of Army officers who would rise to high rank. Here Marshall made Army friendships that lasted for the rest of his life. In these years, too, he commenced to read military history as a conscious process of self-education in the military art. But most important, in these years, were the rough-and-tumble associations formed by a tough editor in the frontier environment of West Texas. Marshall became involved with the ''outlaw'' baseball teams formed in defiance of Judge Kenesaw Landis, then the Commissioner of Baseball; he helped manage the football teams sponsored by the mining companies; and he wrote the wire stories on once-great pugilists making their last fights in the Juarez Bull Ring. It would be said of Marshall in later years that he had mastered the art of communicating with the common soldier, of whatever race or social status, on a footing of mutual respect, and with compassion and understanding. No Army career course in the psychology of leadership could have given Marshall the finely-honed ability to perceive the verities of human response to life and death, challenge and despair, danger and fatigue, which he developed in those West Texas years.

In Detroit, as military critic and editorial writer for the *News*, Marshall also began to write his first articles for the *Infantry Journal*, establishing a professional connection which would last for many years – and serve the Army well. His personal tie with Joe Greene, who, as editor, had proclaimed that the *Infantry Journal* was ''the Infantry's unofficial 'magazine for fighting men,''' was particularly fruitful. Both men had a keen appreciation of the human factor in war; both loved fine literature and savored the masters of the written word; and both could repeat without pause the longest patter songs from Gilbert and Sullivan.

With the onset of World War II, Marshall published two books, *Blitzkrieg* (1940) and *Armies on Wheels* (1941), which firmly established him in the company of the leading military writers of the day. Indeed, General J. F. C. Fuller wrote a laudatory preface to the second volume. Strangely enough, these two early books represent Marshall's only full-scale examination of armored warfare.

In 1942, Marshall was recalled to duty as a major in Washington and was named Chief of Orientation in the Special Services Division of the War Department. After a few frustrating but productive months, during which he established the Army News Service, a stroke of good fortune brought Marshall to the new Historical Section of the War Department General Staff. Sent to the Pacific in 1943 as a lieutenant colonel to develop methods of battlefield research, he took part in the Gilberts Campaign and the battle for Kwajalein.

In battle, Marshall discovered, in his words, ''a new method of covering combat.'' The method was simple in theory, albeit complex in execution. The survivors of an action were gathered as a unit, immediately after combat, and interviewed collectively in an attempt to recreate the events of the battle and the role played by each participant. At Kwajalein, Marshall was able to work with six rifle companies and cover a complete segment of the operation. The product of this effort, *Island Victory* (1944), deserved the unique judgment delivered by the editors of the *Infantry Journal:* ''No book like it has ever appeared before.''

In an appendix to *Island Victory*, Marshall described his original method and told that what he had learned of applying the rules of evidence was "how the truth of battle is found." Not surprisingly, the rules he discovered were those which had been taught for years in graduate courses on "Historical Method." Marshall, however, had added new dimensions: first, the oral interrogation of an entire unit as a corrective to the personal bias of the individual witness (this with a resulting richness of detail); and, second, the possibility of prompt corrective action through the lessons learned by participants as the story of combat unfolded in the interview process.

Transferred to the European Theater of Operations in 1944, Marshall, now a colonel, worked with the D-Day forces, most importantly helping the airborne divisions to recreate the story of the initial drops into Normandy. Indeed, without Marshall's efforts, much of this story would have been lost. The close ties Marshall forged with the younger airborne officers later bore fruit in his book, *Bastogne: The Story of the First Eight Days* (1946).

As the great German counteroffensive unfolded in the Ardennes, Marshall found himself in operational control of the numerous combat historical teams attached to the American forces. Under his direction commenced what may be the most intensive historical coverage of a major military campaign ever attempted, comprising hundreds of combat interviews and the collection of actual journals, situation maps, and other working records before they were lost or destroyed. In the last months of the war, Colonel Marshall – by now the Theater Historian – used his considerable prestige and long-time Army associations to make certain that the history of the US Army in the European campaigns would be written and the lessons recorded for the future Army. General Frank Ross, a friend from his El Paso days, helped Marshall and his staff save the tons of European Theater combat records from routine disposal and probable oblivion in a Liege depot.

Then came peace, and in 1946, Colonel Marshall again left the Army. He spent his terminal leave writing a slim volume in which he attempted the distillation of his wartime experiences and observations. This book, *Men Against Fire* (1947), came from the presses of the *Infantry Journal* at a time when military thinkers were groping around the apparition of the atom bomb. Although Marshall here was concerned with the physical and psychological aspects of tactics, he delivered a strong cautionary message about the new strategic weapon, exhorting the nation and the Army not to "risk the national future" by misreading this new form of military power and dismissing the *man* on the battlefield of the future. *Men Against Fire* developed the simple thesis that success in future combat will depend on new training techniques and standards of battle discipline which are designed to provide "more and better fire" in battle. Unfortunately, Marshall's message was obscured at the time by a single quotable statisic: Only 25 percent of the men in battle ever fire their weapons (a statistic which, it should be said, was open to grave question).

Back in an editorial chair at the *Detroit News*, Marshall continued to reflect on the experiences of the recent war. But what he said and wrote was a direct reflection of the problems facing the Army in the post-war period and a call to reaffirm the nation's dependence on the attributes of courage and steadfastness shown by the soldier who has "a will to fight."

Two books argued for a better understanding of the whole nature of the soldier and what it is that either assists him in battle and hardens his will or "stops him and strangles his best intention." The first, *The Soldier's Load and the Mobility of a Nation,* initially appeared as a series of articles in the *Infantry Journal* and was a strong indictment of the folly, as Marshall saw it, perpetrated by those in the Army who would rely on machines and discount the role of the fighting man. The message was simple: "Mobility is only present when there is a will to fight." In this day of cruise missiles and laser beams, *The Soldier's Load* still merits a careful reading. It is, however, normally shelved by Army libraries in the dust-covered section labeled "Uniforms and Equipment."

The second 1950 book, *The Armed Forces Officer*, appeared under the aegis of the Secretary of Defense without Marshall's name. This volume – styled as a "manual on leadership" – is the source of oft-repeated quotations and pertinent anecdotes. It is also a very wise book whose lessons and guidance are valid today despite the intervening years and the experiences of two unfortunate wars. It is still a widely-used official Department of Defense publication.

The Korean War brought Marshall again to the field in varied roles as a war correspondent, a combat analyst, and a serving staff officer. In 1951, he was promoted to the rank of Brigadier General. Korea gave Marshall raw material for some of the finest stories of man in combat ever penned by an American author. But his first mission was utilitarian:

> To analyze our infantry line and its methods under pressure, to estimate whether troops are good or bad, to see what is wrong or right in our tactics and to recommend such corrections as are indicated.

His analysis of Chinese infantry tactics stripped away the mystique which had surrounded the Chinese night attacks, clever use of terrain, and camouflage of movement. When the two sides dug in for the long war of position, Marshall did his best to rectify the most alarming inadequacies in the American field works but was defeated by the rotation policy which, as he saw it, shuttled officers and noncoms so briskly through the theater that they seldom had either the time or the inclination to learn the tedious business of trench warfare.

It is sometimes forgotten that Korea was an unpopular war and that the American press attacked the green American troops and castigated their leadership. When American troops broke and ran, Marshall became – as the *New Yorker* had it – "spokesman for the rabbits."

In *The River and the Gauntlet* (1953), he sought to rectify the injustice done the men of the Eighth Army by popular reports following the defeat inflicted by the Chinese Communist forces in November 1950. He gave the drama of the longest retreat in American history the full treatment, from the initial intelligence failure to the moment on Christmas Day when the 2d Division could once again be considered a going concern. Marshall tackled this story of military disaster because it was of epic proportions; but his eye was on the men in the rifle companies. Thus, the chapter called "The Stonewall Company" is designed to record the bravery of an infantry company which, after a magnificent fight, found itself with no typewriters and, therefore, no decorations!

A second book, *Pork Chop Hill* (1956), lacked the sweep of the first and was, after all, only the account of a small fight by some men of the much-maligned 7th Division on "a contemptible hill." Nonetheless, many consider *Pork Chop Hill* to be Marshall's finest book. As he had done in *Island Victory,* Marshall appended a description of his after-action technique and the way in which the 50,000 words of testimony on the battle entered his notebooks.

The Korean War may be reckoned as ending in the truce tent at Panmunjom, but bitter controversies over the American conduct of the war continued apace; in these, Marshall was deeply involved. When an all-service commission was convened to draft a new Code of Conduct for future American prisoners of war, Marshall was instrumental in wording this code. He recognized then – and would argue later in connection with the *Pueblo* incident – that the retention in Article V of the old "name, rank, serial number, and date of birth" injunction would negate the practical wartime application of the code. Indeed, much of the testimony in 1977 before the Defense Review Committee for the Code of Conduct confirmed that American experience in Vietnam with the "big four, nothing more" rule tracked with what Marshall had originally predicted.

In the years between Korea and Vietnam, Marshall used his typewriter in vigorous battle against the prevailing "bigger bang for a buck" syndrome. In a series written for *Army* in 1957, he pleaded for "men, not gimmicks," reminding his military readers that American forces in Korea had possessed vastly superior firepower and mechanized means but had been forced to accept a wasteful stalemate "because we had no reserve of trained, willing people." And again: "A nation will get what it trains for – not more or less. When it overrates the products of science and undervalues the human heart, it bids for oblivion."

One small nation had retained a sense of the human value in combat, and Marshall was drawn emotionally, as well as professionally, to write the story of the Israeli Army in the Sinai campaign of 1956. The Israeli civilian-soldiers eagerly welcomed the interest expressed by such a famous military student, and in following years Marshall was given free access to the Israeli troops and to many of their councils.

When American involvement in Southeast Asia heated up to the boiling point, it was inevitable that General Marshall would again don the uniform. He had written a newspaper article about the war which his old friend Harry

Kinnard felt was not entirely correct, so Kinnard suggested that Marshall come over and see how it really was. Even though he was 66 years old, Marshall hastened to get himself dispatched to Vietnam, where he joined the 1st Cavalry Division in the Central Highlands.

Marshall would have no doubts about the morality of American involvement in Vietnam. He regarded the treaty obligations assumed therein as binding on the nation, even at the cost of American blood and treasure. He was equally certain that most of the reportage of the war was biased, amateurish in all military matters, and calculated to confuse the American public. His views of the Saigon press corps were caustic in the extreme: ''Never before have men and women in such numbers contributed so little to so many.'' He despised ''the young man who calls himself a war correspondent when he spends his time chasing after riots in Saigon,'' but he had genuine admiration for the camera crews and TV reporters who took their chances in battle alongside the infantry.

General Marshall had none of the euphoria introduced in high circles of the Kennedy Administration by extravagant reliance on the Army's Special Forces; nor could he accept any one of the several and particular doctrines of limited war then passing for strategic wisdom in the Pentagon and the State Department. Although he was an honored guest in the US Army field headquarters off and on from 1966 to 1968, and a sometime representative of the Army Chief of Staff, Marshall never swerved from the task of recording the story of the fighting man and seeking lessons which could be applied to increase his chances of survival and success in battle.

In retrospect, it may be said that the peculiar conjuncture of political, military, and social factors which marked American operations in this unpopular war, plus the national search for a nostrum of easy application, negated Marshall's attempts to find and teach tactical lessons – even when supported by the Chief of Staff and the major field commanders. His almost single-handed crusade to communicate the basic facts of this confusing war and to remove some of the moral onus heaped on the American soldier likewise had little impact. In the Korean conflict, Marshall had been a kind of emotional link between the American combatant and the American people. Apparently, in the era of Vietnam, the forces at work to divorce the soldier from the nation simply could not be overcome.

The My Lai atrocity left Marshall deeply disturbed and puzzled. He would recall that he had personally covered some 48 actions in Vietnam, from patrols to division-size operations, and had found nothing like My Lai. Indeed, in the book *Fields of Bamboo* (1971), he would record numerous incidents in which American troops had taken unusual personal risks so that civilians might be protected. To the end of his days, Marshall could not understand how My Lai happened. He was certain, however, that this episode should not be charged to the account of the thousands of American fighting men in Vietnam who risked and sustained death and mutilation in the service of their country.

The five books written from Marshall's Vietnam combat interviews deserve mention, for they have been submerged by the spate of moralistic tomes and juicy recitals of Saigon high life and misdeeds. *Battles In The Monsoon* (1967), *Bird* (1968), *Ambush* (1969), *West to Cambodia* (1968), and *Fields of Bamboo* (1971) are works which speak eloquently for the fighting man. They also, to repeat Marshall's final judgment, show the American forces universally "violating the principles of war in matters large and small."

When he finished his last Vietnam book, Marshall wrote to a friend about the Army failures there:

Some of the fault is at field level and above. The mistakes became apparent. But most of it is at junior leadership rank. The kids are too careless. Haven't they always been that way? The trouble is that in this kind of war the cost is higher and the mistakes look more glaring.

Marshall was competent to judge these mistakes, for he had behind him a record of 40 years in which he warned of the errors in battle which persist from war to war and of the cost of disregarding the lessons displayed in past combat.

Will the writings of General S. L. A. Marshall be read by the next generation of soldiers? The most recent official Army *Contemporary Military Reading List* no longer contains reference to any of his works. Yet the basics which Marshall held up to view will hardly escape notice by new generations of Americans – soldiers and civilians – because of the lasting quality and popularity of these masterfully written books. In 1976, when then-Major General DeWitt C. Smith, Jr., Commandant of the US Army War College, presented individual copies of Marshall's *The Armed Forces Officer* to the incoming War College class, he may have given ultimate definition to Marshall's abiding worth: "He makes you look into a mirror at your real self, and he makes you remember the nation we serve and the men and women we lead. These are important things to do."

This article appeared in the March 1978 issue of *Parameters*.

II. GREAT BATTLES FROM THE PAGES OF *PARAMETERS*

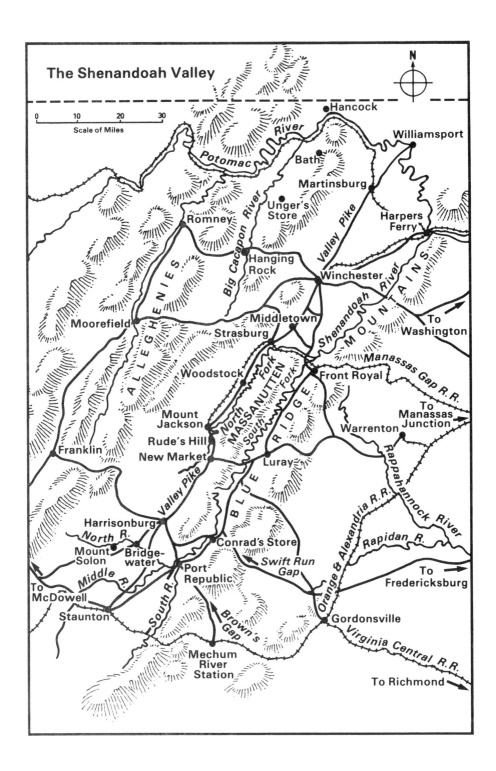

The Shenandoah Valley

Scale of Miles
0   10   20   30

N

Hancock

Williamsport

Potomac River

Bath

Martinsburg

Unger's Store

Romney

Big Cacapon River

Harpers Ferry

Valley Pike

Hanging Rock

Winchester

Shenandoah River

ALLEGHENIES

Moorefield

Middletown

Strasburg

To Washington

MOUNTAINS

Manassas Gap R.R.

Woodstock

North Fork

MASSANUTTEN

South Fork

Front Royal

BLUE RIDGE

Mount Jackson

Warrenton

To Manassas Junction

Rude's Hill

Franklin

New Market

Luray

Valley Pike

Rappahannock River

Harrisonburg

Orange & Alexandria R.R.

North R.

Conrad's Store

Rapidan R.

Mount Solon

Bridge-water

Swift Run Gap

Port Republic

To Fredericksburg

To McDowell

Middle R.

South R.

Staunton

Brown's Gap

Gordonsville

Mechum River Station

Virginia Central R.R.

To Richmond

4

Jackson's Valley Campaign and the Operational Level of War

by WALTER P. LANG, JR., J. FRANK HENNESSEE, and
WILLIAM E. BUSH, JR.

The US Army has recently acknowledged the existence of a previous gap in its framework of theoretical reference by including the concept of the operational level as a category of military activity distinct from the tactical and strategic levels in its family of manuals. This expansion of the basis on which we view warfare is likely to have a profound effect on American soldiers for a long time and should be studied thoroughly by those responsible for the direction of the nation's armed forces.

Our recognition of the operational level owes much to European military experience and thought. However, the operational art in warfare should not be considered an alien concept. Rather, it should be viewed equally as an American development, which sprang from the same basic source (the study of the wars of Napoleon Bonaparte) as continental military theory and developed here in parallel with European ideas on the subject.[1]

Although latent in recent years, the flowering of operational art in America is vividly portrayed in our military history. The Shenandoah Valley Campaign of 1862 must certainly be among the most remarkable campaigns in this respect. It is certainly not the only good example which can be found in the American Civil War. Grant at Vicksburg and Sherman in Georgia are names which come readily to mind. The Valley Campaign is a superior example, however, because its ratio of forces gives greater clarity to the issues of operational art.[2]

Background

At the beginning of November 1861, Thomas Jonathan Jackson was promoted to Major General, Confederate States Army, and made commander of a geographical command encompassing the Shenandoah Valley and much of what is now northern West Virginia: the Valley District. The command had been called into being because Joseph Johnston's move over the Blue Ridge for the first Manassas operation had denuded the valley of trained troops, and the citizens were complaining of the threat of occupation by Northern forces located in the Hagerstown, Maryland, area as well as in trans-Allegheny Virginia.

Upon his arrival Jackson assumed command of what was really a subdivision of the eastern theater of war. The Confederate government at that time faced a number of severe threats in the east. The most serious of these was the huge Federal army being trained and equipped in the vicinity of Washington by a soldier of high reputation, Major General George B. McClellan. The future movements of this imposing force could not be predicted, but it clearly posed the largest threat. Additional Union forces were located in western Maryland and might at any time descend upon the northern Shenandoah Valley, a region of great economic and political importance to Virginia. There were also substantial Federal forces disposed in the western portion of Virginia, a region that showed increasing signs of political disloyalty to the Southern cause. Those Federal forces located in what is now West Virginia might with little warning descend upon the valley in the area of Staunton/Harrisonburg or farther north (Strasburg/ Winchester), approaching from the direction of the south fork of the Potomac River.

Jackson apparently felt that his duty lay at this point in: (1) protecting his district, its people and economic resources; (2) taking action to forestall a permanent separation of Western Virginia from the rest of the Commonwealth; and (3) causing as much confusion and disarray in the Union high command as he could with the limited forces available to him.

The Romney Expedition

As Jackson gathered the elements of his Valley Army near Winchester in late December 1861, it was clear to his men that action was imminent. Jackson's major concern was that Federal forces to his north (Major General Banks) along the Potomac River and to his west (Major General Rosecrans) in the Alleghenies would unite in the vicinity of Martinsburg. This union would have amassed such superior strength that Confederate retention of the Shenandoah Valley would have been in jeopardy. To preempt such a potentiality, Stonewall had argued for and gained reinforcement by Brigadier General W. W. Loring's division to permit an attack to seize Romney.

On 1 January 1862, the Valley Army, now approximately 9000 men, departed its camps around Winchester without knowledge of its destination. Speculation ran high that Jackson was launching an offensive to seize Romney, where Union forces roughly equal to Jackson's were encamped. Romney was, in fact, Jackson's objective, but his movements in the succeeding week would breed confusion concerning his real objective, not only among soldiers and politicians of 1862, but also among military historians to this day. General Jackson's Confederate forces forsook the road to Romney and moved north toward Bath (now Berkeley Springs, West Virginia), an obscure Union outpost along the Potomac, where contact was made on 4 January with a Union force of three regiments.

Jackson attempted and failed to outflank the Federals and block their retreat northward, and thereafter he likewise failed to pin them against the Potomac and destroy or capture them. These tactical actions were unsuccessful because of lethargy and tactical ineptitude among Jackson's subordinate leaders. The Union forces fought an effective rear guard action and crossed the Potomac by boat and fording with minimum casualties.

Jackson was far too prudent to try to force a crossing; he settled for destruction of the important Baltimore and Ohio Railroad bridge over the Big Cacapon River several miles to the west, severing many miles of railroad track and telegraph lines. He also shelled the town of Hancock, Maryland. These actions were not without their rewards, as they effectively cut communications between Banks and Rosecrans and apparently did substantial damage to the supply lines to Union forces in the Alleghenies.

To the surprise of everyone except Jackson, this relatively ill-fated excursion to Bath opened the door to Romney without a fight. As his men marched southward from Bath to occupy an assembly area near Unger's Store, Jackson received word from Major Turner Ashby, his cavalry commander, that the Federals, after a raid against the Confederate outpost at Hanging Rock, had withdrawn from Romney. Jackson moved westward to fill this void as quickly as the difficult terrain and the bitter winter weather permitted, and by 10 January the Valley Army occupied an outpost line (Bath, Romney, Moorefield) which effectively negated the threat to the Shenandoah Valley from the west.

The Romney expedition was Jackson's first as a major independent commander and it reveals some factors that contributed to his later success. The paramount characteristic of Jackson's success was his inclination toward the indirect approach. Given Jackson's mission, most commanders would have focused on Romney as the objective and would have moved with all due urgency to attack the Union forces there. A particularly astute commander might even have pursued his goal by conducting a tactical envelopment of the Northern forces in the vicinity of Romney.

Jackson's budding genius at the operational level devised a plan which effectively maneuvered his foe out of the objective area by striking at another point. The purpose of the strike to Bath remains cloaked in obscurity even today. Most historians seek to explain this strike as either a shakedown operation for his green troops or as a raid on the line of communication of the Union Army in the Alleghenies with little real relationship to his expressed objective of seizing Romney. Few have appreciated his skill in choosing an initial objective which would cause such concern to the Union chain of command that the garrison at Romney would be weakened or abandoned. Thus General Jackson demonstrated at the earliest stage of the Valley Campaign his mastery of the subtleties of operational maneuver, developing plans that would accomplish his aims without risking his precious few troops in a direct attack against superior combat power; he sought a point of enemy weakness which, if attacked, would create such a disruptive effect on the psyche of the enemy command that important gains could be achieved without confronting the enemy head-on.

Among Stonewall's laudable attributes were his inclination toward operations security, his skill in intelligence operations, and his proficiency in using the reconnaissance and security forces which produced much of his intelligence. Throughout the planning and execution of the Romney expedition, Jackson's intelligence preparation of the battlefield gave him an unqualified advantage which he retained throughout the Valley Campaign.

Another Jacksonian characteristic in evidence here was his willingness to take great, yet prudent, risks to achieve success. His move to Bath opened enemy approaches to Winchester, Jackson's headquarters and support base, from both north and west. If he had taken counsel of his fears based on enemy capabilities, this success would not have been possible.

On the opposite side of the ledger, Jackson displayed characteristics which tended to constrain his successes. First was his uneven tactical ability. His failure to coordinate and control the operation effectively at the tactical level cost him even greater rewards at Bath. It is perhaps more important for the military professional who aspires to senior command to note that tactical success in every battle is neither a necessary nor sufficient condition for success at the operational level. Although the Valley Army suffered through a tactical fiasco during this phase of the campaign, success at the operational level was gained.

Second, Jackson's obsession with secrecy, which was carried to such an extreme that his subordinate commanders often did not know the tactical objective or his concept of the operation, was evinced in this expedition. Although he did not pay a high price for this proclivity in January 1862, he was later to have his potential successes limited considerably by lack of flexibility and initiative among subordinates. This can be attributed directly to Jackson's overly taciturn behavior concerning his campaign and battle plans.

Winchester to Rude's Hill to Kernstown

The spring of 1862 found Jackson's Valley Army at a strength of less than 5000 men. His mission was to hold as many Union forces as possible in the valley. When Union forces under Banks moved into the northern valley in strength in March, Jackson was forced to withdraw from Winchester to a more defensible position in the vicinity of Rude's Hill (about 45 miles south of Winchester), where an S-turn in the Shenandoah River is overlooked by a relatively low height which nevertheless dominates the river valley to the north. Banks failed to press the Valley Army, and based upon a perception of Jackson's weakness and the need for additional Union forces in eastern Virginia, Banks moved the majority of his force east of the Blue Ridge. Jackson reacted immediately. Stonewall pushed his men northward in a forced march, attempting to gain contact with the Union forces remaining in the valley under Brigadier General James Shields. Although Shields' forces still outnumbered Jackson's two to one, Jackson attacked without delay. On 23 March a bloody battle ensued at Kernstown, just south of Winchester, in which the Valley Army was soundly defeated.

Again, confused, piecemeal commitment of forces to a battle and a general lack of good command and control cost Jackson dearly. Nevertheless his boldness, daring, and timing brought great success without tactical victory, for the battle at Kernstown caused McClellan to direct the return of significant Union forces (approximately 25,000) under Banks to the Shenandoah. Major General Irvin McDowell's Union corps was held near Washington rather than proceeding south toward Richmond. Additionally, Major General Blanker's division was dispatched west to the Alleghenies to reinforce Major General John C. Fremont, who had replaced Rosecrans there. Coming at a time when the North had just embarked on a grand maneuver to seize Richmond through an amphibious envelopment on the Peninsula coupled with a supporting attack due south from Washington, the distraction in the valley was extremely costly in that it caused a diversion of forces which the Union could ill-afford.

Kernstown to Swift Run Gap

After the tactical defeat at Kernstown, Jackson withdrew south to preserve his force. Initially, he moved to occupy again the position along Rude's Hill. He was pushed out of his position by mid-April. At this point, although his Valley Army had grown to about 6000, he was badly outnumbered and could not afford a major battle. He withdrew again; however, in so doing he discarded two obvious alternatives. With the absolute necessity of protecting his support base – the important city of Staunton with its strategic rail and road junctions – the temptation must have been powerful to establish a strong defensive position on the most defensible terrain north of Staunton in the Shenandoah Valley. Alternatively, he could have recalled Brigadier General Edward Johnson who was deployed with a brigade-sized force west of Staunton protecting that city from Fremont's forces in the Alleghenies. With the scarcity of forces under his command and the growing Union strength, concentrating his forces might have seemed logical or even necessary, but Jackson again gave notice that he was not an ordinary general.

By this time he had made an assessment of his opposition which suggested another alternative – one which required risk-taking, but which offered the attraction of preserving his freedom of action. Retaining the opportunity for initiative was extremely important to Jackson. He kept Johnson west of Staunton in the Allegheny passes and moved the Valley Army around the south end of the Massanutten Mountains to a position in Swift Run Gap in the Blue Ridge. To those not sensitive to the intricacies of an operational-level mind at work, this must have seemed like a foolish plan, for it removed all Confederate forces from Banks' direct path to the most important Union terrain objective in the southern Shenandoah – Staunton!

Jackson's assessment of his enemy was correct. Banks was too timid to seize the opportunity to move into Staunton unmolested, for he feared exposing his flank to Jackson who sat in a classic flanking position. From that position Stonewall had his cake and was eating it too. He was effectively protecting the approach to Staunton without doing battle against a superior force; he gained time for recuperation and refitting of his army; and he put himself in a position from which he could move quickly east to support Confederate forces around Richmond, if necessary, or link up with Major General Richard Ewell who was located just east of the Blue Ridge near Gordonsville. Again, Jackson had displayed the operational acumen to accomplish by maneuver what he could not have obtained by direct action.

Brown's Gap to McDowell to Franklin

While Jackson had maneuvered Banks to a stalemate, the situation elsewhere looked grim for the Confederacy by late April. McClellan was firmly established on the Peninsula with over 100,000 men threatening Richmond from the east. McDowell's corps of about 30,000 was just north of the Rappahannock near Fredericksburg in good position to put pressure on Richmond from the north. Fremont's strength in the Alleghenies had been increased by about 7000 with the addition of Blenker's division, and an advance force under Brigadier General R. H. Milroy was putting pressure on Staunton from the west – so much so that Johnson had withdrawn to a position only a few miles west of Staunton.

General Robert E. Lee, who had assumed control of all operations in Virginia in mid-April, encouraged Jackson to attack Banks, believing the pressure on Fredericksburg (and ultimately on Richmond) would be greatly relieved if Jackson could deal a heavy blow to Banks in the valley. If nothing else were gained, such an action would preclude the reinforcement of McDowell by forces from the valley.

Again, rather than a direct attack on Banks, Jackson had a better idea. His aim was a quick strike against Fremont's Allegheny forces which, if successful, would facilitate an attack on Banks' flank from the west, an ambitious and daring plan. Jackson first put great effort into a deception operation designed to dupe the Union forces into believing that the Valley Army was headed east to assist in the defense of Richmond. Upon receiving control of Ewell's division for the operation, Jackson moved him to occupy the flanking position in Swift Run Gap. Jackson then moved out of the gap in full view of Banks' scouts and marched south toward Port Republic, then turned east through Brown's Gap in the Blue Ridge, thus leaving watchful Union eyes to draw the obvious conclusion. Once out of range of Federal observation and over the crest of the Blue Ridge, Stonewall turned his columns south to Meechum's Station on the Staunton railroad line and entrained heading west. Following a quick rail move to Staunton where he linked up with Johnson, Jackson moved his combined forces west into the Alleghenies. It is important to note that by so doing he assumed great risk, for Banks could have blocked Ewell with a small force and moved south to secure Staunton, thus trapping Jackson in the mountains between two forces of greatly superior numbers.

Jackson's quick strike against Fremont's army materialized at McDowell, Virginia, on 8 May. Before Jackson could concentrate his forces, the Federals under Brigadier Generals Milroy and Schenck launched a highly successful spoiling attack which dealt heavy losses to Jackson's lead regiments under Johnson. Under cover of darkness, the Union troops withdrew north toward Franklin without Jackson's knowledge. Jackson pressed the pursuit the next day, but effective rear guard actions, which included setting forest fires, slowed the Confederate advance and permitted the Federals to reestablish a strong position at Franklin.

Again, Jackson did not let a tactical defeat intimidate him. He had planned to move east from Franklin, after having defeated Fremont, to strike Banks' flank. But he realized the futility and danger of a major battle with a strong force in a fortified position far from his main objective. So Jackson modified his original plan and withdrew to McDowell, then east back into the Shenandoah, positioning himself for a heavy blow against Banks.

Upon reentering the Shenandoah on 17 May, Jackson had set the stage for a decisive blow against Banks with an operational maneuver of considerable risk and complexity. Although he had suffered a tactical defeat (casualties at McDowell were two to one in favor of the North) in the only major engagement in this phase of the campaign, Jackson had raised great concern in the Union command structure. His deception operation had caused a complete misreading of his intentions, so his appearance in the Alleghenies created Northern fears far beyond any logical reasoning. Jackson was beginning to prey on the psyche of the Union chain of command all the way back to Washington. The result was a hesitation in the planned Union drive on Richmond. Jackson had already begun to achieve his operational objective. He was again demonstrating the ability to look far beyond the tactical.

Additionally, his push into the Alleghenies neutralized Fremont's 20,000-man force, reducing the threat to the upper valley and to Staunton in particular, and producing favorable conditions for the deep attack. Through his actions, Stonewall had profoundly disturbed the Union high command, disrupted ongoing operations in eastern Virginia from a great distance, and in a very real sense was inside the enemy command decision cycle.

Mount Solon to Harpers Ferry (The Deep Attack)

Even though Jackson's action had been highly effective, the situation on 18 May looked increasingly dark for the Confederacy. McClellan, with over 100,000 men, was scarcely 30 miles down the Peninsula from Richmond. McDowell was poised at Fredericksburg, restrained by the disruptions created by Jackson, but fully capable of a rapid attack on Richmond. Banks had withdrawn to Strasburg, and Shields' division from his command was close to joining McDowell's force.

Lee must have been sorely tempted to call Jackson eastward to strengthen the Richmond defenses, but both Lee and Jackson showed their understanding of the operational art by rejecting the obvious ''necessity'' for increasing Confederate strength in eastern Virginia in favor of a daring maneuver – a deep attack by the Valley Army.

Jackson had already used deception and speed to mass unexpectedly against Fremont. Now he pushed his light infantry to its limits as he marched north along the Shenandoah toward Banks' position at Strasburg. With his cavalry screening to his front, Jackson created the impression of a headlong thrust at Bank's position while he turned his columns east through the New Market Gap in the Massanutten to link up with Ewell's division in the Luray Valley, a terrain compartment which runs parallel to the Shenandoah Valley. Concentrating his forces on the move, Stonewall continued north and fell upon the unsuspecting Union garrison at Front Royal. The small Federal force of about 1000 was routed, and Jackson seized the important bridges across the Shenandoah River complex.

Jackson had deceived Banks through the effective use of cavalry while using the masking effect of terrain compartments to mass against a point of enemy weakness. He was acting faster than Banks could react. The way into the Federal rear lay open.

In fact, this success created an interesting dilemma for Jackson. Clearly, the opportunity existed for a quick march to Winchester, which lay astride Banks' line of communication. Securing Winchester before Banks could react would have constituted a classic turning movement which would have forced Banks out of his strong defensive position at Strasburg. In all probability Banks would have been forced to attack Jackson on less than equal terms since Stonewall would have had the advantage of choosing good defensive terrain along Banks' communication line.

Jackson was keenly aware of the multi-leveled nature of the operational art. Even though his mission to deal Banks a strong blow would have been best served by a rapid move on Winchester, there existed the possibility that if the Valley Army executed this maneuver, Banks could move due east through Front Royal and the Manassas Gap to effect a linkup with McDowell. Even though this possibility seemed somewhat remote, its consequences were so dire that Jackson sacrificed his opportunity to fall upon Banks' line of communication. Instead he deployed his advance elements between Cedarville and Ninevah until he confirmed that Banks was withdrawing north.

Upon receiving this information from his cavalry, Jackson leaped into action, moving his infantry west at the double-time to intersect the Valley Pike at Middletown. From there he moved quickly into the exploitation, falling upon Banks' combat service support tail as it moved down the Valley Pike. He pressed the exploitation ruthlessly and relentlessly northward toward the Potomac, frustrated only by the ineptitude of his cavalry. In spite of this ineptitude, however, the results were spectacular. In retreating over 50 miles in two days (24 and 25 May), Banks' force lost 2300 men captured and enormous amounts of equipment and supplies.

As both Lee and Jackson had known, the real success of the operation could not be weighed in the battle statistics from the Shenandoah Valley. As Jackson pursued Banks and moved to occupy Harpers Ferry, the consternation in Washington grew to great proportion. Lincoln dispatched orders to McDowell to call off his attack on Richmond, planned for 25 May, and move to the Shenandoah to cut off Jackson. This respite relieved the Confederate defenders of Richmond from a precarious situation. Although the siege of Richmond was not abandoned, not for another two years would the existence of the Confederacy be so much in doubt.

As Jackson closed on Harpers Ferry in late May, his deep attack had been successful almost beyond the bounds of logic. It had achieved results completely out of proportion to the physical correlation of forces. The ultimate objective of the operational deep attack had been the enemy high command psyche, not enemy casualties or key terrain. The choice of a terrain objective (in this case Harpers Ferry) was important only to the extent that its attainment would cause psychological panic in Washington. And that it did, for Harpers Ferry was well known not only as a strategic junction of transportation arteries and for its importance to the lines of communication to the west, but also for its proximity to unprotected Union cities. The illogical fears generated by the deep attack secured results in geometric proportion to the depth of the penetration (50 miles from where Jackson had initially penetrated Banks' position a few days earlier and over 120 miles north of the Union position of three weeks prior).

Jackson's successes were not accidental. From the complexities of the mind of a master of the operational art had emerged a spectacular operation. The insight to see the potential for success on this scale was born of many years of study and analysis of military history. Stonewall had preserved his freedom of action and seized the initiative. He developed sound, timely intelligence and demonstrated the willingness to act on it. He had the audacity to plan a deep attack and the boldness and skill to ensure its proper execution. He moved with great speed, massing unexpectedly to fall upon the enemy with violence at his weakest point. He achieved superiority and then exploited relentlessly. He showed flexibility in adjusting to enemy reactions once he had penetrated the enemy's lines while never losing sight of his real objective. He had clearly gotten ''inside the decision cycle'' of the Union high command.

South to Port Republic

Lincoln had not only ordered McDowell to cut off the Valley Army by moving west, he had dispatched similar instructions to Fremont to move east out of the Alleghenies into the valley. His plan was to close the jaws of a trap behind Jackson and destroy him before the Valley Army could escape south. Stonewall had not let the euphoria of success blind his operational foresight. He carefully positioned reconnaissance elements to report the approach of forces which might threaten his ability to withdraw. Jackson had maximized the results he could achieve in the deep attack. Now he showed the good judgment to recognize that preservation of the force had become the paramount mission. Therefore, on 30 May when reports indicated the movement of Union forces to cut him off, Stonewall moved with characteristic swiftness, sending an advance guard to delay Shields (from McDowell's force) and Fremont in their move to close the trap. While his cavalry fought these delaying actions, Stonewall moved his main body over 50 miles in two days, squeezing through the jaws of the planned trap just before they could be closed. Jackson then skillfully used his cavalry both to cover his rear and to destroy bridges and emplace obstacles at key points. Of particular note is his destruction of the bridges over the South Fork of the Shenandoah River in the Luray Valley. By so doing, he denied Shields the opportunity to move quickly up the Luray Valley and preclude a move eastward by the Valley Army to reinforce the defense of Richmond, if that should become necessary.

Clearly Jackson now needed to rest his weary troops. The deep attack had drained his men, not only physically, but emotionally as well. Jackson therefore needed to occupy terrain which offered great advantages to the defender (since he was now outnumbered by at least four to one in the area) while still protecting his support base at Staunton and positioning the Valley Army for rapid movement east of the Blue Ridge. Jackson moved up the Shenandoah Valley around the Massanutten, and into the Port Republic area on 5 June, from which an impregnable position in Brown's Gap could have been established.

At this point, with Union columns approaching from two directions (around the Massanutten from the northwest and down the east bank of the South Fork from the northwest), Jackson chose to attack rather than defend. His scheme was easy to understand but would be more difficult to execute than he realized. His plan was to use his interior position to mass rapidly against each of the Union forces in succession while his cavalry screened to the northwest. Jackson intended to mass his force against Shields east of the South Fork, defeat him quickly, and then turn against Fremont to the northwest.

The result was a complete tactical failure. The concept required moving the majority of his forces across two rivers to strike Shields at 0800, then recrossing the two rivers to defeat Fremont before nightfall. Chaos ensued! The buildup of forces east of the South Fork went slowly, and units were committed piecemeal against Shields. By day's end, Jackson had barely managed a draw against Shields and had lost over 800 men. The second phase of the operation had, of course, been abandoned, and Jackson moved into Brown's gap as night fell on 9 June.

Thus the Valley Campaign ended on a sour note. Although morale and confidence had been soaring as a result of the successful deep attack, Jackson had failed to realize fully its physical and emotional toll on his men. His initial inclination to occupy a strong defensive position had been the right one. In fact, Jackson had not recognized or admitted to himself the profound physical, emotional, and mental effects of the deep attack on him personally. His plan to attack was ill-fated from its inception. Stonewall either failed to understand the tactical complexities of moving his force through the bottlenecks of a bridge and a hastily constructed man-made ford twice in a single day, concentrating, attacking, breaking contact, recrossing, and reconcentrating in the face of the enemy; or his judgment was severely impaired by the events of the preceding weeks.

Either possibility suggests a learning point for the aspiring practitioner of the operational art. In the first case the operational-level commander must recognize the fundamental differences between the operational and tactical levels. Given greater dimensions of space and time (i.e., at the operational level) Jackson's plan was potentially brilliant, certainly executable with at least a good probability of success. The considerations at the tactical level are radically different. Maneuvering forces in the face of the enemy necessitates simple, direct plans (not complex schemes of maneuver), and a detailed understanding of the time required to perform a multitude of simple tasks while under direct observation and fire.

Ironically, most contemporary US Army commanders are much better prepared to conceive operations, fight, and win at the tactical level than at the operational level. Jackson was apparently just the opposite.

The other obvious lesson from Jackson's example is that senior commanders must develop an understanding of the limits of human endurance. By the time of Port Republic, the men who had rested in Swift Run Gap six weeks before had marched almost 400 miles and fought many engagements. Senior commanders must also recognize the increased emotional and mental demands of operating deep inside enemy territory. Seizing the initiative and attacking are necessary to ultimate success, but the astute commander must recognize when *not* to attack.

Another lesson to be learned from this example is the importance of reconnaissance and security operations inside territory controlled by the enemy. Stonewall's attention to this aspect of the deep attack and good judgment in recognizing when to redeploy his forces to friendly lines were prerequisite to preservation of the force. Any commander who hopes to fight outnumbered and win should learn this lesson well.

The Relevance of Jackson's Example

An analysis of Jackson's Valley Campaign of 1862 seems to reveal that the fundamentals of Jackson's success are as relevant today for the senior leader as they were in the 19th century.

Then as now:

- The essential goal of the deep battle is most likely to be some form of interdiction, whether it be of arriving reserve or second echelon combat forces, support, the enemy commander's intentions, or his train of thought.

- Operational maneuver requires a skillful use of deception and operations security in order to allow smaller forces to concentrate against local enemy weakness with relative security.

- Highly reliable and timely intelligence is essential to the deep battle.

- Decisive deep maneuver requires the willingness to commit a relatively large percentage of the available force to maneuver into the enemy rear and the assumption of the attendant risk.

- The commander involved in deep maneuver must be prepared to bypass some enemy forces.

- At the operational level the astute commander can often accomplish through the indirect approach that which he does not have the means to achieve through direct action.

In any war with our principal adversary, the operational art would be critical. In other theaters which would not be likely to receive the bulk of resources, we, like Jackson, will have to rely on our artistry to win.

NOTES

1. A question that logically suggests itself is why the idea of the operational level of war should have become more typical of the armies of the continent of Europe than of the US Army. The institutions of the United States and Prussian armies both seem to have derived their theoretical texts for the study of warfare from the same basic source, the wars of Napoleon Bonaparte.

In the case of the Prussian army, firsthand experience of defeat by Bonaparte followed by the re-form and restructuring of their forces, which led to victory over Napoleon, provided a powerful incentive for the study of his methods. The Prussians did this principally within the context of their War Academy, the creation of which had been one of the post-Jena actions by reformers such as Clausewitz. The Prussians focused on that part of the example of Napoleon which showed that by highly skilled large-scale maneuver of forces it was possible to deal deadly blows to numerically superior enemies.

Over a protracted period of time the Prussians came to the view that it was the particular function of the army senior leadership to be prepared to perform what had been Napoleon's purely military role above the tactical level. With minds thus focused, the Prussian general staff sought to develop a high degree of skill in the conduct of large operations. Over the decades they sought to do this through the media of intensive theoretical study of past experience, operational testing of plans through war-gaming, and the widespread use of staff rides at the campaign level. With this focus they acquired and retained a great dexterity in this art, the operational art. From the example of the Prussian and later German armies, all European development of operational art, including that of the Soviets, is derived.

In the case of the American experience, the importation of Napoleonic ideas came about largely through the vehicle of the writings of Jomini as interpreted first by Dennis H. Mahan and later by Henry W. Halleck. Mahan's teaching at West Point, and indeed the whole corpus of his writing, tended to stress Jomini's division of the study of warfare into: (1) Strategy; (2) Engineering; (3) Logistics; and (4) Tactics. Jomini also mentioned the existence of something he called "Grand Tactics" by which he apparently meant the maneuver of large forces to accomplish large ends. This would seem to be a different formulation and expression of the same basic concept which led to the idea of the operational level in the collective mind of the

Prussian general staff. This Jominian vision of warfare was transmitted directly to the minds of the future chieftains of the US Army in the section rooms of West Point in the 1840s and 1850s.

That Jackson had absorbed some of this at West Point may be inferred from a letter he wrote to his sister from Jalapa, Mexico, during the Mexican War. He critiqued the conduct of operations by Generals Scott and Taylor:

> General Scott is by far the most talented and scientific, and, his comprehensive mind embraces not only different objects and ends but their several and combined bearings with regard to the ultimate object . . . . General Taylor is a plain, honest, sound minded, straight forward & undesiring man (the noblest work of God), if you knew him you would certainly like him. But he wants comprehensive view of a means to an end.

Jackson explained to his sister that victories should be obtained ''without so reducing our army as to be unable to follow up the successes.'' He told her that Taylor did not meet this requirement well in Northern Mexico where he was ''deceaved (sic) at Monterey he thought that their (sic) would be no fighting their (sic) and consequently did not prepare himself to take Ampudia's army prisoners or else make it a total reck (sic) with the loss of its arms and the saving of his own array.'' He thought Taylor did not follow up at Buena Vista as he should have done. ''In fine, General Taylor can not look beyond the gaining of a battle.''(Lenoir Chambers, *Stonewall Jackson, The Legend and the Man.*)

2. This paper does not seek to make a historical contribution, per se. The Valley Campaign cannot be satisfactorily analyzed by using the existing correspondence and record. This is due in large measure to Jackson's extreme concern with operations security. He seldom discussed his aims, objectives, and methods even with his closest advisors, and he edited from after-action reports anything that he believed might have the slightest usefulness to the enemy (Jedediah Hotchkiss, *Make Me A Map of the Valley*). Therefore, the authors have drawn conclusions based not only upon the available historical record, but upon their collective military experience and judgment after a careful, on-site inspection of the terrain.

This article appeared in the winter 1985 issue of *Parameters*.

Plan of Attack of First Army, 12 September 1918

Haudiomont

0   5   10   15 Miles

N

V Corps

Heights

Fr. 15 D.I.C.

16 September Plain

Fr. 2 D.C.P.

XXX

Mad Creek

Woëvre

of the

Rembercourt-sur-Mad

Moselle

Meuse

Fr. 26

XXX

Vigneulles

Fr. II C.A.C.

FRENCH

12 Sept.

XXX

12 Sept.

Thiaucourt

de

Rupt

XXX

Nonsard

Meuse

5

90

82

St. Mihiel

Montsec

XXX

2

Pont-à-Mousson

River

Loupmont

1

42

89

Limey

I Corps

Fr. 26

Fr. 39

Marvoisin

Seicheprey

IV Corps

River

Source: American Battle Monuments Commission,
American Armies and Battlefields in Europe
(Washington, 1938), p. 109.

———— Front Line Actually Reached

–XXX· Corps Boundary   ⌐⌐⌐⌐⌐ Jump-off Line, 12 Sept. (A.M.)

Numerals indicate divisions. Arrows indicate direction and weight of attacks.

5

St. Mihiel:
The Birth of an American Army

by DONALD SMYTHE

The year 1918 was in its final months. The United States had been at war for a year and a half, but until now efforts by the American Expeditionary Forces had been of limited significance on the western front. Not until October 1917 had its troops gone on line, and then only at the battalion level, in a quiet sector, as part of a French division. Not until January 1918 had one of its own divisions taken over a section of the front, again in a quiet sector. And not until May 1918 had it engaged in an offensive operation, and then on a limited scale – some 4000 men, a reinforced regiment, at Cantigny.

During the summer of 1918, American contributions to the Allied effort increased. The 2d and 3d Divisions helped block the German advance at Belleau Wood and Château-Thierry in June. The 3d Division earned the sobriquet ''The Rock of the Marne'' for its heroic stand at that river in July. The 1st and 2d Divisions helped spearhead the Allied counteroffensive in July against the Marne salient near Soissons, while other US divisions subsequently helped collapse the salient completely in July and August. But almost without exception, these divisions operated as part of Allied corps. No US army yet existed.

All that changed on 10 August when the American First Army, under the command of General John J. Pershing, became operational. Its first assignment was to reduce the St. Mihiel salient, a huge triangle jutting into Allied lines on the southern part of the front. The salient cut the Paris-Nancy railway and served as a possible jump-off point for a German flanking attack against Verdun to the west or Nancy to the east. It also served as an effective German bulwark against any Allied advance toward Metz or the vital Briey iron mines.

Reducing the salient had long been an American dream. Pershing had spoken of it to General Henri Philippe Pétain, head of the French Army, on first meeting him in June 1917. And then, in the fall of that year, a strategic study by GHQ staff officers recommended that it be the first US operation. Colonel Fox Conner, AEF Chief of Operations, confirmed this view in

February 1918. Finally, on 24 June 1918, when General Ferdinand Foch, Allied generalissimo, met Pershing, Pétain, and Sir Douglas Haig, the British commander, to plan future offensives, Foch assigned reduction of the salient to the Americans.[1]

At the end of August, however, just two weeks before the St. Mihiel attack was to take place, Foch suddenly proposed that the main American effort be directed not east against the salient, but north in the direction of Mezieres and Sedan, in an attack that eventually would become known as the Meuse-Argonne Operation.[2]

A reluctant Pershing agreed to this proposal and thus committed himself to what was really too large an undertaking. An untested, and in many ways untrained, American Army was to engage in a great battle (St. Mihiel), disengage itself, and move 60 miles to another great battle (Meuse-Argonne) – all within the space of about two weeks, under a First Army staff that Pershing admitted was not perfect and, as of 2 September, had no inkling that the Meuse-Argonne Operation was even being contemplated. Army staffs normally required two to three months to produce a fully articulated battle plan with all its technical annexes. This staff – and again it must be emphasized that the staff was new, inexperienced, and untested – would have about three weeks. It was a formidable commitment, if not an impossible one, and it is not clear that Pershing should have undertaken it. Two of his four army corps had just been organized, while the army staff had no experience yet working as a team.

The alternative, however, was to leave the St. Mihiel salient bulging in the Allied lines, menacing the flank and rear of any army operating west of the Meuse River. Its reduction would eliminate the last German salient on the western front. Besides – and perhaps this was the major consideration – the Americans were all set to go.[3]

The St. Mihiel salient was approximately 25 miles across and 16 miles deep, with its apex at St. Mihiel and its base anchored at Haudiomont and Pont-à-Mousson. It had been a quiet zone for most of four years. The Germans had settled down, planted vegetable gardens, and fathered children by local women.

They had also had time to construct some formidable defensive works: four or five zones with elaborately constructed trenches, shelters, barbed-wire entanglements, machine-gun nests, and artillery emplacements. The barbed wire seemed endless; in one place it ran 13 rows, some as deep as a room. A measure of the salient's strength, perhaps, was that after two strong but futile attacks in 1915 the French had been content to then leave it alone. Pershing called it "a great field fortress."[4]

To be sure, it had some weaknesses. Like all salients, it was vulnerable to converging attacks from the sides. Perhaps because the salient had been quiet for so long, the Germans manned it with second- or third-class troops. Of the eight and one-half divisions assigned to its defense, one had recently arrived from Russia and was, by the Germans' own admission, "not reliable."

Another was "completely worn out." A German noncom wrote home, "The men are so embittered that they have no interest in anything and they only want the war to end, no matter how."[5]

Despite these German shortcomings, considerable pessimism existed in the Allied high command concerning the coming US attack. Sir Henry Wilson, Chief of the Imperial General Staff, told Lloyd Griscom, Pershing's liaison officer with the British, that he viewed the "premature" formation of the American Army with "great concern." Although the doughboys themselves were brave, American staff officers suffered from "incapacity and inexperience." One of two things would surely happen: the Americans would encounter heavy resistance and be stopped with "cruel losses," as the French had been; or, encountering light resistance, they would pursue and fall into a trap. Since the Americans were sure to make a mess of it, jeopardizing the cause, Wilson sent a special messenger to Foch to persuade him to cancel the operation. Foch refused to, although he did admit that the American Army was "inexperienced and immature."[6]

Planning for the St. Mihiel operation, which was scheduled for 12 September 1918, went forward, both at First Army headquarters and at AEF GHQ. Because Pershing was busy as commander of both headquarters, he delegated considerable responsibility to the First Army Chief of Staff, Lieutenant Colonel Hugh Drum, a brilliant 38-year-old officer of wide staff experience who had been on Pershing's staff at Fort Sam Houston before the war. Fox Conner, AEF Operations Chief, loaned the First Army Lieutenant Colonel George C. Marshall, Jr., who had a reputation for working hard, being on top of things, and doing well whatever he was assigned to do. Marshall, then 37 years old, was a graduate of the Command and General Staff School at Fort Leavenworth, as were Conner and Drum. They understood the same language and worked well together.[7]

The material buildup for the St. Mihiel operation had begun in August and was formidable: 3010 guns; 40,000 tons of ammunition; 65 evacuation trains; 21,000 beds for the sick and wounded; 15 miles of reconstructed roads using 100,000 tons of crushed stone; 45 miles of standard-gauge and 250 miles of light railway; 19 railhead depots for distributing food, clothing, and equipment; 120 water points that furnished 1,200,000 gallons a day; and a 38-circuit central switchboard with separate nets for command, supply, artillery, air service, utilities, and other functional areas. Maps alone for the operation weighed 15 tons.[8]

Much of what was furnished had to be borrowed from the French and British, since priority shipments of infantry and machine gunners during the spring and summer from the United States had thrown the American Army thoroughly out of balance in matters of artillery, transportation, and needed services. Not one of the 3010 guns was of American manufacture, nor were any of the 267 tanks. The French provided virtually all the transportation and nearly half the artillerymen, tank crews, and airplanes. The air force, under

Colonel Billy Mitchell, had 1400 planes – the largest air armada ever assembled to that time – but not one was American-built.[9]

To use this mass of material, some two thirds of a million men – 550,000 Americans and 110,000 Frenchmen – moved into position around the salient. The Americans gathered from all parts of the front: from the British Expeditionary Force, from the Château-Thierry area, from the Vosges – all joining Americans who had been stationed near the salient. Finally, 18 months after the nation had declared war, and more than a year after beginning its training and service with various other Allied units, the American Army was coming into being as a living, working organism.[10]

Massing the subordinate elements of this new army for battle was difficult, for movement had to take place secretly and at night. In the dark, the roads swarmed with men, animals, trucks, guns, caissons, tanks, and every kind of impedimenta. During the day, the men hid in woods or billets and tried to catch what sleep they could. At night, they were on the road again, without lights, struggling forward in the direction of the salient. The American Army was moving up.

Or, rather, slogging up. The mud was incredible, and the continuing rain kept making more of it. Elmer Sherwood, a 42d (Rainbow) Division veteran, speculated that the only vehicles making their usual speed were the airplanes. Another soldier suggested that the American high command ought to substitute "submarines for tanks, ducks for carrier-pigeons, and alligators for soldiers." Grimy, slimy, wet, and cold, the troops cursed the mud; it got into clothes, hair, food, drink, and equipment. It was one of the agonies long remembered – sunny France![11]

The Order of Battle, from right to left, was as follows: the US I Corps (Hunter Liggett) with the 82d, 90th, 5th, and 2d Divisions. Then came the US IV Corps (Joseph T. Dickman) with the 89th, 42d, and 1st Divisions. The two corps lined up on the south face of the salient.

At the apex was the French II Colonial Corps with three French divisions (39th, 26th, and 2d Dismounted Cavalry).

On the west face of the salient was the US V Corps (George H. Cameron) with the 26th Division, part of the 4th, and the French 15th Colonial.

Against the German salient, then, Pershing was sending four corps, composed of four French and eight and one-half US divisions.[12]

Strategically, the most important corps were those of Dickman and Cameron. Entrusted with the veteran 1st and 42d Divisions, Dickman was to hit from the south face and drive hard for Vigneulles, where he was to be met by Cameron driving in with the veteran 26th Division from the west face. The juncture of the two US forces would close the salient and bag the Germans inside it.

The attack on the south face by the IV Corps (Dickman) was designated as the primary attack, and that on the west face by the V Corps (Cameron) three hours later was to be the secondary attack. Supporting attacks would be delivered on the right shoulder by the I Corps (Liggett) and at the apex by the French corps.

Pershing was gambling not only on the new and untried First Army staff, but on two new corps commanders and four untested divisions. The new corps commanders were Dickman and Cameron, both promoted from divisional command after the Aisne-Marne campaign in July; they had been given less than a month to organize their headquarters and prepare for battle.

The four new divisions were the 5th, 82d, 89th, and 90th. Two of them, the 5th and 89th, were commanded by West Point classmates of Pershing, John E. McMahon and William M. Wright, while the 90th was headed by Henry T. Allen, who had been with Pershing in the Punitive Expedition in Mexico in 1916. These three divisions had received front-line training, either in the Vosges or near the salient. William P. Burnham's 82d, however, which had trained in the rear with the British, had no front-line experience. And none of the four, of course, had seen active combat operations yet.

The other five divisions were workhorses that Pershing knew he could depend upon. The 1st and 2d had spearheaded the Soissons counteroffensive on 18 July, as mentioned, and were ranked "excellent" with regard to training, equipment, and morale. The 4th, 26th, and 42d had seen hard fighting in the drive from Château-Thierry to the Vesle River. They too ranked high.

The 1st Division was under the capable Charles P. Summerall, a commander without peer; the 2d was under John A. Lejeune, former commander of its Marine Brigade; the 4th was under John L. Hines, Pershing's adjutant during the Punitive Expedition, who had come with him to Europe on the *Baltic*; the 42d was under Charles T. Menoher, another of Pershing's West Point classmates, and the 26th was under Clarence R. Edwards. Although Edwards was beloved by his men, many officers on Pershing's staff had serious doubts about his competence. Lejeune and Hines were new commanders, replacing James G. Harbord, who had gone to head the Services of Supply, and Cameron, who had moved up to command the V Corps.[13]

In using the 1st, 2d, 4th, 26th, and 42d Divisions, Pershing was calling upon the best he had. Hoping to ensure the success of the St. Mihiel operation, he was leaving the cupboard quite bare of experienced front-line troops for the Meuse-Argonne operation, scheduled for two weeks later. He knew the risk, but there was little he could do about it. The decision to employ these experienced divisions had been made before Foch had suddenly sprung the Meuse-Argonne operation on him on 30 August. By that time all five divisions were so thoroughly committed to St. Mihiel that they could not be withdrawn from the operation.[14]

In planning the attack, the First Army had counted on borrowing 300 heavy tanks from the British and 500 light tanks from the French, but when the time came the British could not spare the "heavies" and the French could furnish only 267 "lights," about which they were pessimistic. The muddy terrain, they said, would probably bog down the machines, which were none too reliable, and the deepest German trenches were eight feet across, a distance two feet wider than the tanks were able to span.

Brigadier General Samuel D. Rockenbach, AEF Chief of Tank Corps, and Lieutenant Colonel George S. Patton, Jr., a tank brigade commander, were nevertheless convinced that the tanks could advance, provided that the mud didn't get worse. Even though the small Renaults could not cross the deepest German trenches, they could effect initial surprise, crush the wire, and lead the infantry up to the first line of trenches. Then, if the trenches were too wide, the tanks could cross with the aid of pioneers. "You are going to have a walkover," Rockenbach assured Pershing.[15]

On 10 September, two days before the attack, Pershing held a conference with his corps commanders and key members of their staffs concerning the preliminary artillery bombardment. Liggett and Dickman, hopeful of achieving tactical surprise, wanted no artillery preparation, unless continued rain inhibited the use of tanks. Cameron wanted a four-hour barrage. Major General Edward F. McGlachlin, Jr., First Army Chief of Artillery, was undecided, but inclined toward a 22-hour barrage. Lieutenant Colonels George C. Marshall, Jr., and Walter S. Grant, both on loan to First Army from AEF GHQ, urged an 18-hour preparation.[16]

Pershing postponed a decision. It had been raining off and on all day, sometimes quite hard. That night he decided on no artillery preparation, then reversed himself the next morning, 11 September, and ordered a four-hour preparation on the southern face and a seven-hour bombardment on the western. The preparation fire would disconcert the enemy, give a psychological boost to the attackers, and insure that the wire was damaged if the tanks weren't able to get to it.

It kept raining on 11 September. Pershing wrote in his diary, "Luck seems to be against us." He worked at his headquarters all day, waiting for the attack; all his corps commanders said they were ready and confident of success.[17]

The night of 11 September was jet black with steady rain. The artillery was in position, in some cases almost hub to hub, ominously silent. The troops were moved into the front lines at the last possible minute to achieve surprise. Sergeant William L. Langer, carrying ammunition in the trenches, found them practically empty at 2000 hours, but a short time later they were crowded with infantrymen, waiting apprehensively for the dawn.

Precisely at 0100 hours on 12 September, thousands of cannon fired simultaneously. Light belched from their muzzles, flaming out so frequently up and down the line that one soldier read the *Stars and Stripes* newspaper by the glare. Sergeant Langer compared the noise "to what one hears beneath a wooden bridge when a heavy vehicle passes overhead."[18]

Watching the preliminary bombardment, Pershing found the scene both "picturesque and terrible." He exulted that now, at last, after 18 months of effort, an American army was a living reality, "fighting under its own flag." Yet how many men would die on that day – American, French, German.[19]

In the trenches, cold, wet, and miserable men huddled over their rifles, shocked by the thunder of cannon, gazing with frightened fascination at the weirdly illuminated landscape, lit up as they had never seen it before. "Will I still be alive a few hours from now?" each must have wondered.

The artillery fire was directed at German command posts, rail lines and junctions, trenches, and wire. It was not terribly effective, but it did, as Pershing had hoped, give a psychological boost to the waiting infantrymen, especially those who had not heard so much artillery before.

At 0500 hours the whistles blew. All along the front, men took a tight grip on their rifles, clambered up the wood ladders out of the trenches, and went "over the top."

Watching from a commanding height at old Fort Gironville, Pershing could not see clearly because of the drizzling rain and mist, but he followed the advance by watching the explosions of the rolling barrage. He hoped that the infantry was right behind.[20]

The first thing they encountered was the barbed wire. The artillery had taken out some of it, but not much, because of the shortness of the preliminary bombardment. But trained teams of pioneers and engineers were in the lead, armed with axes, wire cutters, and bangalore torpedoes (long tin or sheet-iron tubes containing TNT). Fortunately, German counterbarrage fire was weak, giving them time to cut holes in the wire.

The infantry rushed through the gaps or, where there were none, used American ingenuity to pass. Leading platoons carried chickenwire, which, thrown across the top of the German wire, formed a bridge. Where chickenwire was lacking and the German wire was thick and low, the doughboys simply vaulted up on top of it and ran across, somewhat like a kid crossing a stream by jumping from rock to rock.[21]

The advance went well, especially on the south face, paced by the veteran 1st, 2d, and 42d Divisions, to which Pershing had assigned the open terrain so they could flank the wooded area, which had been assigned to the four new divisions.

"Get forward, there," Wild Bill Donovan yelled to his Rainbow Division men; "what the hell do you think this is, a wake?"[22]

It was almost exactly that for Terry de la Mesa Allen of the 90th Division. Shot in the mouth, teeth missing, blood running down his face, he helped wipe out a machine-gun nest before loss of blood sent him to a first-aid station. In World War II Allen would command the 1st Division in North Africa and Sicily.

Some incidents were bizarre. Sergeant Harry J. Adams of the 89th Division saw a German run into a dugout at Bouillonville. The American had only two shots left in his pistol, so he fired them both through the door and called for the man to surrender. The door opened, and the German came out, followed by another, and another, and another, and another, and another – some 300 in all! Amazed, Adams marched the whole contingent back toward the rear, covering them with his empty pistol. Americans who saw them coming thought at first it was a German counterattack.

Other incidents seemed equally unbelievable. The 2d Division captured prisoners from 57 different German units – an impossible melange. It was found that they were from all over the western front, sent to Thiaucourt to attend a machine-gun school there.[23]

Much of the ease with which the Americans advanced was due to an earlier German decision to evacuate the salient, orders having been given to that effect on 10 September. Some materiel had already been withdrawn, and more was in the process of moving when the Americans struck.

The attack thus caught the Germans embarrassingly *in via*. There were units that had practically no artillery in position, and those that did were almost out of ammunition. The German defenders were certainly not of a diehard type, as Sergeant Adams discovered when he marched in his 300 prisoners with an empty pistol. Thus it was Pershing's luck to attack a salient that the Germans were just about to hand over to him anyway, capturing without heavy losses positions which if stoutly defended would have heaped up American corpses. A wag described St. Mihiel as the battle "where the Americans relieved the Germans."[24]

By the afternoon, troops on the southern face of the salient had reached their objectives; by evening, they were one day ahead of schedule. On the west face, progress was slower, the 26th Division being delayed by the failure of the French 15th Colonial to keep up on its left. Some of its own units on the right of the line, however, had projected a long finger into the German lines pointing toward Vigneulles; through that town ran the main road of escape out of the salient. Pershing picked up the phone and ordered Cameron and Dickman to move toward Vigneulles "with all possible speed."

Pushing hard under "Hiking Hiram" Bearss, a regiment of the 26th Division reached Vigneulles at 0215 hours; some four hours later a regiment of the 1st Division closed from the east. The main road out of the salient was now cut; the mouth of the bag was squeezed shut.

On 13 September the advance continued from the south and west, wiping out the salient and stopping at the line agreed upon by Pershing at his 2 September conference with Foch. Local operations continued until the 16th, consolidating positions for defense, while the First Army prepared to pull out and head for the Meuse-Argonne operation. It had captured 450 guns and 16,000 prisoners, at a cost of only 7000 casualties.

The operation reduced the salient, restored 200 square miles of French territory, freed the Paris-Nancy railroad, opened water transportation on the Meuse, and secured the right flank of the First Army for its coming operation in the Meuse-Argonne. It also paved the way for a possible future attack against

Metz, the Briey-Longwy industrial complex, and a crucial railroad supplying the Germans to the northwest.[25]

Finally, and perhaps most important, it demonstrated that the American Army was able to successfully handle an operation of some magnitude. As the British *Manchester Guardian* put it:

It is as swift and neat an operation as any in the war, and perhaps the most heartening of all its features is the proof it gives that the precision, skill, and imagination of American leadership is not inferior to the spirit of the troops.[26]

Actually, American success came a bit too easily at St. Mihiel, engendering perhaps an unwarranted optimism and confidence similar to that which afflicted the South after the first Battle of Bull Run. Knowing that the salient was to be evacuated anyway, German soldiers abandoned their positions more readily than they might otherwise have done. Even as it was, they delayed the First Army long enough to allow most of the defenders to escape before the jaws of the pincers closed.[27]

On the afternoon of 13 September, Pétain came to Pershing's headquarters and together they visited the town of St. Mihiel. Ecstatic at their deliverance after four years of German occupation, the people – mostly women, children, and old men – crowded around them waving little French flags. Graciously, Pétain explained to the people that although the French had taken the city, they served as part of the American First Army, whose soldiers had made victory possible by their attacks on the shoulders of the salient.

Tremendously elated by the victory, Pershing felt that it vindicated his insistence on building a separate American army. "We gave 'em a damn good licking, didn't we?" he remarked. On the evening of 13 September, when receiving the congratulations of Dennis Nolan, AEF Chief of Intelligence, Pershing rose from his desk and, pacing the floor, gave the most eloquent tribute to the American soldier that Nolan had ever heard. Going back into history, Pershing remarked

how wave after wave of Europeans, dissatisfied with conditions in Europe, came to [America] to seek liberty; how . . . those who came had the willpower and the spirit to seek opportunity in a new world rather than put up with unbearable conditions in the old; that those who came for that reason were superior in initiative to those, their relatives, who had remained and submitted to the conditions; that in addition to this initial superiority in initiative they had developed, and their children had developed, under a form of government and in a land of great opportunity where individual initiative was protected and rewarded . . . .

As a consequence,

we had developed a type of manhood superior in initiative to that existing abroad, which given approximately equal training and discipline, developed a superior soldier to that existing abroad.[28]

Flushed with success, with an American army in being and growing daily more important, Pershing faced the future not only with confidence but with higher aspirations. With American soldiers flooding into France, the day would not be far off when the American Army would be larger than either the French or the British. "And when that time comes," he told George Van Horn Moseley, AEF Supply Chief, "an American should command the Allied Army."[29]

The St. Mihiel victory left Pershing in a jaunty mood. When the British Prime Minister, David Lloyd George, telegraphed his congratulations from a sickbed, saying that the news was better than any physic, Pershing answered: "It shall be the endeavor of the American Army to supply you with occasional doses of the same sort of medicine as needed."[30]

The witty Harbord, who had once commanded the 2d Division, pointed out in his congratulatory message that nearly 300 years before on the same date, 13 September, Oliver Cromwell had led his Ironsides into battle quoting Psalm 68. It seemed remarkably apropos to Pershing's recent success: "Let God arise and let His enemies be scattered: let them also that hate Him. Like as the smoke vanishes so shalt thou drive them away." Pershing answered: "Your old division might well be termed The Ironsides, though I doubt whether they went to battle quoting Psalm 68."[31]

Public German reaction to the American victory was of the sour-grapes variety. Newspapers and the official German communique pointed out that Germany had planned to evacuate the salient anyway, and that the troops had retired in good order to previously prepared positions.[32] Privately, however, the German High Command was considerably upset. Though intending to evacuate, they had not wished to do so until absolutely necessary. And although most of the defenders had gotten out, considerable stores had been either captured or destroyed in place to preclude seizure. General Max von Gallwitz, the Army Group Commander, had warned Lieutenant General Fuchs, commanding Army Detachment C opposite Pershing, "not to concede an easy success, particularly since we are dealing with Americans." Despite that warning, in 48 hours the Americans had wiped out a four-year salient twice unsuccessfully attacked by the French.[33]

Eric von Ludendorff, who functioned as the supreme German commander, was terribly disturbed. A German officer who visited him the night of 12 September found him "so overcome by the events of the day as to be unable to carry on a clear and comprehensive discussion." Field Marshal Paul von Hindenburg, the titular German Commander in Chief, called 12 September a "severe defeat" which rendered Gallwitz's situation "critical."[34]

In later years a number of people believed that the Americans might have achieved an even greater victory had the First Army been allowed to keep moving east. Douglas MacArthur was among them. On the night of 13-14 September, MacArthur, a brigade commander in the 42d Division, stole through the enemy lines in the direction of Mars-la-Tour and, ten miles to the east, studied the key German fortress at Metz through binoculars. From this reconnaissance and from interrogation of prisoners, he concluded that Metz was "practically defenseless," its garrison having been temporarily withdrawn to fight on other fronts. MacArthur immediately requested that he be permitted to attack Metz with his brigade, promising to be in the city hall "by nightfall."[35]

The request was denied. The St. Mihiel offensive was a limited operation and had already achieved its objective. Further advance ran the risk of over-involving the American Army, already committed to a new and even greater operation on a different front some two weeks hence.

MacArthur believed that this failure to push on toward Metz was "one of the great mistakes of the war." Although at the time Pershing believed that he had no choice other than to keep St. Mihiel a limited operation in order to be on schedule for the Meuse-Argonne attack, he would come to share MacArthur's view.[36]

Hunter Liggett, however, put the matter in a different light. Liggett claimed that taking Metz was possible "only on the supposition that our army was a well-oiled, fully coordinated machine, which it was not as yet." Even doing its damnedest, the First Army "had an excellent chance of spending the greater part of the winter mired in the mud of the Woëvre, flanked both to the east and the west."[37]

Liggett, the I Corps commander in this operation, and later First Army commander, knew what he was talking about when he said that the Army was not well oiled and coordinated. American infantry fired at their own planes. Further, when encountering machine-gun nests, many seemed to have no sense of how to take cover. Instead of hugging the ground and crawling forward, they charged recklessly across open spaces or fell back walking bolt upright.

Artillery fire was delayed and slow to adjust during the rolling barrages, holding up the infantry, and then the artillery was slow in displacing cannon forward, so that the infantry outstripped it during the advance. Despite the fact that the terrain furnished excellent observation posts, the artillery fired by map rather than by direct observation, using ammunition extravagantly and inefficiently.

Discipline was lax. When halted, men tended to get out of ranks and disperse, becoming stragglers. Pilfering of prisoners was almost universal. Animals were misused, abused, or not used at all. During traffic jams, instead of dismounting and resting both horses and men, the riders slouched in their saddles for hours. Animal-drawn ambulances, vitally needed at the front for transportation over muddy roads that were impassable for motor transport, were used in one division for evacuating field hospitals in the rear. And when telephone lines went dead, instead of using a horse relay system that would have provided quick, practical service over roads impassable to vehicles, commanders simply remained out of touch.

Command headquarters were too far to the rear and inadequately marked.

One staff officer carrying an important message wandered for hours before he could find either one of a division's two brigade headquarters, although he was not far from either.

Divisions issued wordy orders, full of contingent clauses and appendices, repeating information available in standard manuals and prescribing detailed formations, even down to battalion level. Most subordinate commanders and their staffs* probably never even read them.[38]

The traffic jams were monumental. Patton's gas trucks took 32 hours to cover nine miles on 13 September. Two days later Georges Clemenceau, the French Premier, was caught in a jam so huge that it confirmed all his fears about US incapacity to handle large forces. "I had warned them beforehand," he wrote in his memoirs:

They wanted an American Army. They had it. Any one who saw, as I saw, the hopeless congestion at Thiaucourt will bear witness that they may congratulate themselves on not having had it sooner.[39]

Indeed, the very day MacArthur recommended a further advance, his division's Chief of Staff was complaining that because of logistical problems the men were not being adequately fed and clothed.[40]

Far from being impressed by the American effort, many felt that it revealed serious deficiences that boded ill for the future. "The Americans have not yet had sufficient experience," said a German intelligence report, "and are accordingly not to be feared in a great offensive. Up to this time our men have had too high an opinion of the Americans."[41]

The decision to terminate the St. Mihiel offensive as planned was undoubtedly sound. Apart from the fact that striking out toward Metz might have enmeshed the First Army in a fight from which it could not readily disentangle itself in time to meet its Meuse-Argonne commitment, and apart from the fact that Pershing had already, with Pétain's permission, pushed beyond Foch's original boundaries for a "limited offensive," the American Army was as yet new and largely untested. It was better to take one sure step with success than to attempt to run before one was ready, and stumble.

NOTES

1. Ferdinand Foch, "La Victoire Finale," *Le Figaro* (Paris), 30 September 1928; Douglas W. Johnston, *Battlefields of the World War – Western and Southern Fronts: A Study in Military Geography* (New York: Oxford Univ. Press, 1921), pp. 402-03; Harvey A. DeWeerd, *President Wilson Fights His War: World War I and the American Intervention* (New York: Macmillan, 1968), p. 330; Edward M. Coffman, *The War To End All Wars: The American Military Experience* (New York: Oxford Univ. Press, 1968), pp. 263-64; US Department of the Army, Historical Division, *United States Army in the World War, 1917-1919,* 17 vols. (Washington: Department of the Army, 1948), II, 211 (cited hereinafter as *USAWW*).

2. Foch to Pershing, 30 August 1918, and Notes on Foch-Pershing conversation, 30 August 1918, Pershing Papers, Box 50, Library of Congress.

3. Foch to Pershing, 1 September 1918, Pershing Papers, Box 75; Pershing diary, 2 September 1918, Pershing Papers, Box 4; *USAWW*, II, 589-92; Coffman, pp. 271-72.

4. Hanson E. Ely, lecture, "Training Management & Instructional Methods," Ft. Belvoir, Va.,

1937, p. 3; John J. Pershing, *My Experiences in the World War*, 2 vols. (New York: Frederick A. Stokes, 1931), II, pp. 262-63; James G. Harbord, *The American Army in France, 1917-1919* (Boston: Little, Brown, 1936), p. 421.

5. Victor Keller, "A German Reply to General Pershing's War Story," *The New York Times*, 3 May 1931, p. 2C; George H. English, Jr., *History of the 89th Division, U.S.A.* (Denver: Smith-Brooks, 1920), pp. 129-30; Hanson E. Ely, "Lecture to Students of the Army Center of Artillery Studies," 10 March 1919, Hanson E. Ely Papers, in possession of his daughter, Mrs. Judy Ely Glocker, Jacksonville, Fla.

6. Willis Thornton, *Newton D. Baker and His Books* (Cleveland: Press of Western Reserve Univ., 1954), p. 432; Lloyd C. Griscom to Edward M. House, 21 September 1918, Pershing Papers, Box 85, Library of Congress; James L. Collins Diary, 15 September 1918, James L. Collins Papers, US Army Military History Institute, Carlisle Barracks, Pa.; Raymond Recouly, *Foch: My Conversations with the Marshal*, trans. Joyce Davis (New York: D. Appleton, 1929), p. 22; Stephen Roskill, *Hankey: Man of Secrets,* 3 vols. (New York: St. Martin's Press, 1971), I, 596; Newton D. Baker to James G. Harbord, 10 April 1935, James G. Harbord Papers, Library of Congress.

7. George C. Marshall, *Memoirs of My Services in the World War, 1917-1918* (Boston: Houghton Mifflin, 1976), pp. 124-28; Coffman, pp. 266-69.

8. Dennis E. Nolan to John J. Pershing, n.d., Pershing Papers, Box 352; Pershing, II, 260; Harbord, p. 414.

9. Pershing, II, 260-61; D. Clayton James. *The Years of MacArthur*, 2 vols. (Boston: Houghton Mifflin, 1979), I, 198; William Mitchell, *Memoirs of World War I* (New York: Random House, 1960), pp. 234-48. See also William Mitchell, "The Air Service at St. Mihiel," *World's Work,* 38 (August 1919).

10. Coffman, pp. 277-78; Pershing, II, 260-61.

11. Elmer Sherwood, *Diary of a Rainbow Veteran* (Terre Haute, Ind.: Moore-Langen, 1919), p. 120; William H. Amerine, *Alabama's Own in France* (New York: Eaton and Gettinger, 1919), p. 173.

12. Pershing, II, 265-66.

13. Ibid., II, 226, 265; Coffman, pp. 273-76; Robert L. Bullard, *Fighting Generals: Illustrated Biographical Sketches of Seven Major Generals in World War I* (Ann Arbor, Mich.: J. W. Edwards, 1944), pp. 1-10.

14. Hugh A. Drum to John J. Pershing, 24 September 1930, Pershing Papers, Box 354.

15. Samuel D. Rockenbach to John J. Pershing, 21 January 1924, Pershing Papers, Box 352; Blumenson, *The Patton Papers*, 2 vols. (Boston: Houghton Mifflin, 1972), I, 568-69, 574, 581-82; Pershing, II, 261; Samuel D. Rockenbach, "Tanks," December 1926, p. 8, Pershing Papers, Box 352.

16. John J. Pershing Diary, 10 September 1918, Pershing Papers, Box 4; Edward F. McGlachlin, Jr., to Hugh A. Drum, 10 September 1918, G-3 Files, AEF, 122.04, Box 3385, Record Group 120, National Archives; Marshall, pp. 134-36.

17. John J. Pershing Diary, 10-11 September 1918, Pershing Papers, Box 4; Pershing, II, 265; Coffman, p. 278; Francis P. Duffy, *Father Duffy's Story* (New York: George H. Doran, 1919), pp. 233-34.

18. Harbord, p. 422; William L. Langer, *Gas and Flame in World War I* (New York: Knopf, 1965), p. 32; DeWeerd, p. 335.

19. Pershing, II, 267.

20. Ibid., II, 266-67; Coffman, pp. 278-79.

21. George C. Marshall, "Accomplishments of the AEF," 20 April 1919, AGO 370.24EE, Record Group 94, National Archives: Paul H. Clark to General Headquarters, Letter 199, 15 September 1918, Paul H. Clark Papers, Library of Congress.

22. Duffy, p. 236; Pershing, II, 268.

23. Coffman, pp. 280-81; Hunter Liggett, *A.E.F.: Ten Years Ago in France* (New York: Dodd, Mead, 1928), pp. 153-54.

24. John J. Pershing to Joseph T. Dickman, 4 April 1926, Pershing Papers, Box 64; Maxime Weygand, *Memoirs* (Paris: Flammarion, 1953), I, 610-11; B. H. Liddell Hart, *The Real War, 1914-1918* (Boston: Little, Brown, 1930), pp. 485-86.

25. James L. Collins Diary, 12 September 1918, James L. Collins Papers; Film M-50, "Flashes of Action," Record Group 111, National Archives; Coffman, pp. 282-83; Pershing, II, 269-72.

26. Press Release #224, 28 September 1918, James L. Collins Papers.

27. *Chicago News*, 9 March 1931, Pershing Papers, Box 359; Coffman, p. 283.

28. George P. Eller interview, New York City, 28 December 1960; Ralph A. Curtin interview, Washington, D.C., 17 July 1963; Dennis E. Nolan to James Harbord, 10 February 1934, James G. Harbord Papers, New York Historical Society; "Greetings to America's General on His Birthday Anniversary," *Army and Navy Journal*, 8 September 1934, p. 40. By coincidence the victory came on 13 September, Pershing's birthday. Noting that Pershing would be 58 on the 13th, one female admirer pointed out that the two digits (5 and 8) added up to 13, an unlucky number for Kaiser Wilhelm, whose name had 13 letters in it.

29. George Van Horn Moseley interview, Washington, D.C., 13 September 1960.

30. David Lloyd George to John J. Pershing, 14 September 1918, and Pershing to Lloyd George, 17 September 1918, Pershing Papers, Box 81.

31. James G. Harbord to John J. Pershing, 13 September 1918, and Pershing to Harbord, 19 September 1918, James G. Harbord Papers, Library of Congress.

32. Press Review #224, 28 September 1918, and Summary of Information #166, 14 September 1918, James L. Collins Papers.

33. Summary of Information #250, 11 January 1919, p. 11, James L. Collins Papers; Coffman, p. 283.

34. S. T. Williamson, "The War that Was Fought behind the War," *The New York Times*, 22 March 1931, pp. 46-49; *USAWW*, VIII, 312.

35. Douglas MacArthur, *Reminiscences* (New York: McGraw-Hill, 1964), pp. 63-64.

36. Ibid., p. 64; Pershing, II, 270.

37. Liggett, p. 159.

38. "Candid Comment on the American Soldier of 1917-1918 by the Germans," [1919], pp. 6-10, James L. Collins Papers; Willey Howell, "Second Section, General Staff, First Army, in St. Mihiel and Meuse-Argonne Operations," 6 January 1919, p. 13, Folder 191-58, First Army Historical File, Box 76, Record Group 120, National Archives (cited hereafter as Howell Report); "Notes on Recent Operations #3, 1918, pp. 8-12, James L. Collins Papers; Notes by AEF Inspector General, n.d., pp. 1, 23-24, 26, and 28, Pershing Papers, Box 352; George C. Marshall, "Profiting by War Experience," *Infantry Journal*, 18 (January 1921), 36.

39. Blumenson, I, 593; Robert C. Walton, *Over There: European Reactions to Americans in World War I* (Itasca, Ill.: F. E. Peacock, 1971), p. 193; Georges Clemenceau, *Grandeur and Misery of Victory* (New York: Harcourt, Brace, 1930), pp. 75-76; Jean Martet, *Clemenceau* (London: Longmans, Green, 1930), p. 87.

40. B. H. Liddell Hart *Reputations: Ten Years After* (Boston: Little, Brown, 1918), p. 312; James, I, 210.

41. Howell Report, p. 14.

This article appeared in the June 1983 issue of *Parameters*.

6

Dien Bien Phu:
Thirty Years After

by JANOS RADVANYI

Thirty-one years ago, on 6 May 1954, hell broke loose over the valley of Dien Bien Phu. General Vo Nguyen Giap's sappers had placed their Chinese-made explosives, transported by elephants through the jungles, at the end of a tunnel dug from the Vietminh's outpost to the center of the French camp. A series of explosions blasted bunkers and French Foreign Legion paratroopers in the air. Soon thereafter the newly arrived Soviet-built mobile multiple rocket launchers, the Katyushas, a special gift of Soviet Defense Minister Radion Y. Malinovsky to Giap, pounded systematically every square foot of Dien Bien Phu. The rockets which had been used so effectively by the Red Army against the *Wehrmacht* at the Eastern Front in World War II now filled the air with terrifying whistling and tremors, destroying the remaining field fortifications. At the fall of the day, carefully coordinated Vietminh shock troops of General Giap stormed in human waves the beleaguered and exhausted Frenchmen from every direction. In 24 hours, after bitter and heroic resistance, the long siege of 36 days ended. Giap won the battle, one of the most decisive in French colonial history.

Understandably, the 30th anniversary of this occasion gave ample opportunity for the victors to celebrate. Hanoi and Ho Chi Minh City, as well as other cities and villages in Vietnam, Laos, and occupied Cambodia, were decorated with red banners and flowers. Victory celebrations were held everywhere. Speakers at mass meetings reminded the population of the growing danger of ''neo-colonialism and Chinese aggression'' and urged them to work harder to build ''the glorious future of socialism'' in the spirit of Dien Bien Phu.

But the anniversary also brought back sad memories to victors and vanquished alike. The estimated 60,000 attacking Vietminh troops had lost at least 8000 men and suffered 15,000 casualties, while the French had lost 3200 and suffered 4800 casualties. Moreover, of the 10,000 French POWs taken by the troops of Giap, only 3900 returned to France. Many of the rest perished from torture and disease in mosquito-infested jungle prison camps.[1]

Before the fall of Dien Bien Phu, as the storm clouds had gathered over the besieged fortress, the French government had made a last-minute, desperate plea to Washington for an emergency American air and naval assistance operation. The request triggered a heated debate in the highest circles in the nation's capital. In spite of the United States' doctrinal opposition to any form of colonialism, the policy of containment of communist expansion had led Washington to be sympathetic to the request for aid from Paris. First and foremost, Vice President Richard M. Nixon and Secretary of State John Foster Dulles seemed to be in favor of helping the French militarily. On the same wavelength, Admiral Arthur W. Radford, Chairman of the Joint Chiefs of Staff, went one step further. In his contingency plan, Admiral Radford suggested the use of three tactical atomic bombs to destroy the Vietminh's positions surrounding the bunkers of Dien Bien Phu. General Matthew B. Ridgway, former commander of the United Nations troops in Korea and the Army Chief of Staff at the time of the battle at Dien Bien Phu, made an eloquent protest against US involvement in Vietnam in general, and against the Radford plan in particular. His arguments convincingly took the relevance of the situation into account by pointing out that the use of the tactical atomic weapons would not reduce the number of ground forces required to achieve victory. US intervention with air and naval forces would not bring victory, he added, nor was intervention with combat forces in Indochina militarily desirable.[2]

In the midst of diverse plans, advice, and reports, the wearied President Eisenhower remained uncommitted. His only consent was to the initiation of negotiations with the allies for a "United Action Plan" to rescue the French. This move, in turn, ended in fiasco; the British simply were absolutely not interested. Prime Minister Winston Churchill bluntly told Admiral Radford that if his countrymen had not been willing to fight to save India for themselves, why expect them to be willing to fight to save Indochina for France?

Even the French themselves turned a cold shoulder to the "United Action Plan." Indeed, they were seeking quick military assistance to avoid imminent defeat and humiliation at Dien Bien Phu, not some kind of collective defense that could lead in the long run to the internationalization of the war, and result in their loss of control of the war.

Then, with the fall of Dien Bien Phu on 7 May, this diplomatic crisis came to an abrupt end, and the "United Action Plan" was laid to rest in the archives. Both official London and official Washington were relieved.[3]

As was the custom, President Eisenhower sent a message to the President of France, René Coty, and to the Chief of State of Vietnam, Bao Dai, praising the valiant French and Vietnamese defenders of the fortress of Dien Bien Phu and repeating the free world's determination to remain "faithful to the cause for which they fought."[4] But as expected, the message did not make the French forget the American President's indecision. Nor could they forgive the British callousness. Thus, understandably, once France capitulated at Dien Bien Phu and the conflict shifted to the Geneva Conference, relations between France and the United States were at low ebb. Differences between the United States and the United Kingdom also became acute, since Washington considered London to have been the prime obstacle to its much-heralded ''United Action Plan.'' In addition, there was a complete Western misreading of communist intentions, and of Ho Chi Minh's real strength and power base, as well as of the extent to which the Soviets and Chinese were interested in assisting the Vietminh.

Nobody in the West, apparently, was aware of the fact that by the early spring of 1954, the Vietminh had already made contingency plans and preparations to retreat to the Chinese border, as Mao Tse-tung had done during the Long March to northern China in the 1930s. Probably nobody in the West knew that Ho and his Prime Minister, Pham Van Dong, were asking desperately for Chinese military intervention against the French forces in Vietnam at the preparatory meeting in Moscow before the Geneva Conference.[5]

Neither Paris nor Washington realized that the losses of the People's Liberation Army in the Korean War were so heavy that China was simply not in a position to start a new venture in Indochina.[6] Washington and Paris truly expected that the Korean truce agreement of 1953 would release Chinese troops to attack French Indochina, and that Chinese intervention was imminent. As a sacred myth, the West strongly believed that fierce nationalism could drive the Vietminh to make appalling sacrifices under any circumstances for their cause. And the misconceptions of the situation held by the West went on and on.

Meanwhile, all three interested parties on the communist side, Moscow, Peking, and Hanoi, were concerned about possible American intervention in Vietnam or a Korean-type united action by the Western powers. Khrushchev, Mao Tse-tung, and Ho Chi Minh probably remembered that President Eisenhower had used the nuclear threat at the end of the Korean conflict to achieve the long-delayed armistice.[7] The probability of this and other conventional types of American military actions surfaced at the worst possible time, since the post-Stalin leadership in the Soviet Union was preoccupied with grave internal problems at home and for tactical reasons embraced a policy of peaceful coexistence abroad.

And China, while rejecting the Vietminh's request for military intervention, had turned to more pressing domestic issues and had declared a policy of detente in Asia. Thus it became evident that if Ho Chi Minh were to be rescued, a temporary cease-fire or preferably a negotiated political settlement was necessary. This rather clear-cut position on the part of the communists, however, did not preclude their determination to strengthen their bargaining position in Geneva.[8]

The crucial decision as to where and when to strike and whether to withdraw and regroup was entirely a Vietnamese decision. The independent-minded Ho Chi Minh and his Lao Dong (Vietnamese Workers' Party) Politburo seldom asked advice in strategic matters from Peking, and never from Moscow. Thus the decision to strike the French expeditionary forces at Dien Bien Phu had come as a surprise to everyone in the Kremlin, where the Soviets were preoccupied with pressing the Vietnamese for negotiations.[9] Meanwhile, the Chinese were in a better position to learn about the actual military planning of Giap, since Chinese military advisers had been stationed at the military headquarters of the Vietminh.

In the spring of 1959, I visited Hanoi as a member of a Hungarian party and government delegation, at which time I had the opportunity to get some firsthand information on the decision. It was there that I learned also the dramatic story of the fall of Dien Bien Phu, as retold by the general who conceived and masterminded the plan, Vo Nguyen Giap.

During that visit our delegation toured the Museum of the Revolution in Hanoi, with General Giap as our guide. Giap led us through the 30 halls of the museum, drawing our attention to photographs and memorabilia that dramatized the long efforts of Ho Chi Minh and his close collaborators, Pham Van Dong, Le Duan, and Giap himself.

In the central hall of the museum was a papier-mâché model of the Dien Bien Phu battlefield. When we arrived at this display, General Giap stepped to a lectern on one side of the model, bade the Hungarians be seated on wooden benches facing him, and like a university professor, launched into a lecture with the aid of a long bamboo pointer. The battle of Dien Bien Phu, he told us, was the last desperate exertion of the Vietminh army. Its forces were on the verge of complete exhaustion. Their supply of rice was running out. Apathy had spread among the populace to such an extent that it was difficult to draft new fighters. Years of jungle warfare had sent morale in the fighting units plunging to the depths.

On this note, the Supreme War Council met, remained in session for several days, and finally came to the decision that the impossible must be attempted: a surprise assault, a decisive battle. The mountain-girded valley of Dien Bien Phu was chosen as the scene of the battle on the assumption that General Henri Eugene Navarre, the commander of the French expeditionary forces, would consider that well-fortified stronghold an unlikely target of attack. This decision revealed that Giap and his colleagues knew something of the strategic thinking of the French military school. As Giap explained to us, they knew the French very well and were convinced that the postwar French military leadership had not drawn a lesson from its defeat at that other "impregnable" fortress, the Maginot Line. The calculations proved correct, said the general.

The French did not foresee the move because it was doubtless impossible for them to imagine how units and materiel could be brought to the scene through the dense surrounding jungles in the numbers and strength necessary to wage a battle. It was indeed a difficult undertaking, said Giap. First, a detailed reconnoitering of the terrain had to be effected in a relatively short time; second, the transportation of the forces had to be organized. The first objective was carried out by soldiers on bicycles and on foot who carried no load; to each soldier was assigned one coolie to carry ammunition and rice rations for both. The problem of transporting artillery batteries was solved with elephants and buffaloes. The general even gave the elephants military grades of rank, he told us.

When his forces had reached the target area, Giap had ordered a general rest of three days. During this period political officers circulated among the troops, trying to raise morale. ''The French are not gods,'' the men were told time and again. The agitation was sorely needed, Giap observed, because the soldiers were truly terrified.

The first phase of the battle was conducted in typical guerrilla warfare fashion. The Vietminh attacked by night, each time blowing up one or two pillboxes reached via tunnels dug during the day. At first Giap even permitted the French resupply transport aircraft to come and go undisturbed, and the French command concluded that the pillbox demolitions were just another series of partisan attacks. It was only later that the Vietminh brought up artillery and kept the only runway on the Dien Bien Phu airfield under constant fire. At this juncture the French tried to resupply their base by parachute drops, but the parachuted packages were captured. Meanwhile, the Vietminh batteries moved frequently, so that by the time the French artillery registered their old positions they were concentrated elsewhere. Giap's forces increased their pressure systematically until they were attacking the base day and night from all sides. Cut off from the outside world, and without supplies, the French military command recognized the hopelessness of its situation and surrendered.

What Giap had highlighted to us had not been incorporated in his book, *Dien Bien Phu*; neither was it reported in Western accounts following the battle. Only Soviet party leader Khrushchev revealed in his memoirs how desperate Ho Chi Minh's situation had been before the battle.[10] It is equally important to remember that Giap did not acknowledge in his book the substantial Chinese aid, especially the heavy artillery pieces that were instrumental in breaking the French defense line. On the other hand, he did not blame the Russians for failing to give all-out military support to the Vietminh in its life and death struggle.

But at the time, we were deeply impressed by the general's presentation.

The rest is well known. One day after the fall of Dien Bien Phu, on 8 May 1954, an international conference convened in Geneva, chaired by the USSR and the United Kingdom, with France, Vietnam, the Vietminh, the United States, and the Chinese People's Republic participating. Cambodia and Laos were also represented. A major military victory behind them, the communists started to negotiate from a position of strength. Yet three months' behind-the-scene bargaining was needed until the parties were able to work out a solution of the eight-year-old Franco-Vietminh war, an accord which provided for the temporary division of Vietnam into two parts, North and South, with a common boundary along the 17th parallel, and with a demilitarized zone on each side of the parallel. All parties agreed that Vietnam would be reunited by national plebiscite in two years. The French agreed to remove their troops from the North, now controlled entirely by Ho Chi Minh, within 300 days; Ho promised to withdraw his Vietminh units from the South. Finally, all parties consented to the creation of an International Control Commission, comprised of contingents from Canada, India, and Poland, to supervise the movement of all armed forces and the release of prisoners of war, and to oversee control of the frontiers, ports, and airfields. Separate agreements were reached on the cessation of hostilities in Cambodia and in Laos.[11]

With the signing of the Geneva Accord, real peace was still a far cry away. For Ho Chi Minh, Giap, and their comrades in the Lao Dong Politburo, diplomatic negotiation and agreements were considered as part of a process for preparing for further fighting. The Vietminh influence in the South was to be preserved, and additional southern cadres in North Vietnam were to be trained. By 1960 Ho Chi Minh spoke openly of the formation of a "united front" for the "liberation" of South Vietnam. In a matter of months Ho's united front grew into the National Front for the Liberation of South Vietnam (NLF); in the same period the nucleus of the Liberation Army of South Vietnam appeared on the scene.

Basically following the Vietminh tactic of appealing to Vietnamese nationalism, the NLF guerrillas soon made significant political and military advances. Moreover, now learning from the experiences of the Franco-Vietminh war, the Ho Chi Minh leadership made great effort to assure substantial military and economic aid from both the Soviet bloc countries and China.

As the ground war in Vietnam expanded with American involvement, not only Washington, but Moscow and Peking allowed themselves to become chained to the fortune of small and relatively insignificant powers in Southeast Asia. And the war grew even worse. The bombings intensified as American planes hit new targets in the North. The ground war in the South heightened as both sides increased their forces and expanded their range of action. Interestingly enough, the "spirit of Dien Bien Phu" still was with Ho Chi Minh and General Giap. In 1968, to put all bets on one horse as they had done in 1954, the master strategist Giap dared to guarantee that the important American Marine base and airstrip at Khe Sanh, on the road linking the Vietnamese coast to Laos, would become another Dien Bien Phu. Militarily, however, the battle of Khe Sanh and the rest of the Tet Offensive turned out to be a near disaster for Hanoi.[12]

As negotiation for a peaceful solution came to the fore, the North Vietnamese emphasized, as they had before the Geneva Conference, the strategy of "fighting while talking." And the final Paris settlement of 1973, "An Agreement Ending the War and Restoring the Peace in Vietnam," was violated by Ho Chi Minh's successor, Le Duan, the same as the Geneva

Agreement had been. His "silent partner," Soviet Party Chief and President Brezhnev, a guarantor of the Paris Agreement, was even sending the Kremlin's best military mind, General Victor Kulikov, to assist Giap and his protégé, General Van Tien Dung, in the final invasion and conquest of South Vietnam.

Today, more than 30 years after Dien Bien Phu, the 72-year-old, gray-haired Giap is no longer the *nui la*, the volcano under the snow, as once his countrymen called him. Virtually retired from public life, he surfaced again as historical necessity dictated. But his appearance should remind us that as staunch Marxist-Leninists, the Hanoi leadership considers diplomacy only a preparatory stage for fighting and believes that "war is simply a continuation of politics by others means."[13]

NOTES

1. For details of French and Vietminh losses, see Bernard B. Fall, *Hell in a Very Small Place: The Siege of Dien Bien Phu* (New York: J. B. Lippincott, 1967), pp. 483-87.
2. Army position paper to the National Security Council, *Pentagon Papers*, The Senator Gravel Edition (Boston: Beacon Press, 1971), I, 92.
3. For a first hand account of the 1954 crisis in Indochina, see Richard Nixon, *The Memoirs of Richard Nixon* (New York: Grosset & Dunlop, 1978), pp. 150-55.
4. *Pentagon Papers*, I, 106.
5. N. S. Khrushchev, *Khrushchev Remembers* (Boston, Toronto: Little, Brown, 1970), p. 481.
6. Ibid., p. 482. See also David Rees, *Korea: The Limited War* (New York: St. Martin's Press, 1964), p. 461, appendix C. According to a UN release (10/23/53) it was estimated that the casualties of the Chinese communist forces during the Korean War totaled 900,000 while the North Korean casualties were about 520,000.
7. Janos Radvanyi, *Hungary and the Super Powers* (Stanford, Calif.: Hoover Institution Press, 1972), p. 11.
8. For details of the Soviet position concerning the Geneva peace talks see Janos Radvanyi, *Delusion and Reality* (South Bend, Ind.: Gateway Editions, 1978), pp. 6-7; for details of the Chinese position, George McTurnan Kahin and John W. Lewis, *The United States in Vietnam* (New York: Dell, 1969), pp. 271-72.
9. As early as the spring of 1959, Soviet-Vietnamese relations cooled off, and Khrushchev often complained in private that Ho Chi Minh was uninterested in seeking Moscow's advice in military matters. He maintained that the decision to strike the French at Dien Bien Phu surprised him and the rest of the Soviet Politburo. Personal recollection.
10. Khrushchev, p. 482.
11. For details of the Geneva Conference, see *The Pentagon Papers*, I, 108-78; for the text of the Geneva Agreements, see Kahin and Lewis, pp. 422-50.
12. William C. Westmoreland, *A Soldier Reports* (Garden City, N. Y.: Doubleday, 1976), pp. 332-33; and Radvanyi, *Delusions and Reality*, pp. 241-43.
13. V. I. Lenin, *The Collected Works of Lenin* (New York: International Publishers, 1919), XXIX, 219. It is well known that Lenin was a keen student of Clausewitz.

This article appeared in the summer 1985 issue of *Parameters*.

III. ASPECTS OF THE GREAT CAPTAINS

7

Napoleon on the Art of Command

by JAY LUVAAS

"My son should read and meditate often about history," Napoleon asserted to one of the generals sharing his last days on St. Helena: "this is the only true philosophy. And he should read and meditate about the wars of the Great Captains; that is the only way to study war."[1]

Although much has been written about Napoleon as a general, analyzing in elaborate detail his tactical and strategical maneuvers from the Italian campaign of 1796 to the repulse of the Imperial Guard at Waterloo, surprisingly little attention has been paid to what Napoleon thought and *wrote* about leadership. His 78 maxims, which were extracted from his dictations on St. Helena several years after his death, contain practical advice on what a general should do in planning marches, fighting battles, and conducting sieges, but only three or four maxims have to do with leadership per se, ending with the startling revelation that "generals in chief are guided by their own experience or genius."[2]

When Napoleon advised his son to study the campaigns of the Great Captains, it was not so much to discover the principles of war as it was to see how these had been applied. Only by imitating these great models, that is, by understanding the basis for their decisions and studying the reasons for their success, could the modern officer hope to approach them.

Had Napoleon wished to instruct his son on the fine points of military leadership, however, he could have found no better way than to make available a selection of his own letters and papers, which contain a wealth of information and insights on the art of command. His letters to his brother Joseph and his stepson Eugene are especially revealing, for here Napoleon clearly was trying to educate members of his family to become good military leaders. To his marshals and other subordinates he said in effect, "do it," and sometimes when he was impatient of delay, Napoleon would invoke a convenient "principle" to lend infallible authority to his wishes. (This may be one reason why Napoleon often was ambivalent about the so-called "principles of war," asserting that genius acts by inspiration, that what is good in one case is bad in another, and that when a soldier becomes accustomed to affairs he tends to scorn all theories.)[3] To his brother and stepson, however, Napoleon went to great lengths to explain *why* and *how* they should execute his wishes, in the process revealing many of his secrets of leadership.

Although he did not express himself in the analytical terms of the famed Prussian theorist on war, Karl von Clausewitz, Napoleon would have agreed that good leadership was a combination of two kinds of qualities – qualities of the intellect, which are trained and cultivated; and those of temperament, which can be improved by determination and self-discipline. Good military leadership therefore is a blend of the two, the product of superior insight and will, and rarely, according to Napoleon, do all of the qualities that produce a great general combine in a single individual. When this happy combination does occur, the result is a military genius, "a gift from heaven."[4]

Of those intellectual qualities essential for high command, Napoleon would probably have placed calculation at the head of his list. "I am used to thinking three or four months in advance about what I must do, and I calculate on the worst," he explained to Joseph. "In war nothing is achieved except by calculation. Everything that is not soundly planned in its details yields no result."[5] "If I take so many precautions it is because it is my custom to leave nothing to chance."[6] A plan of campaign was faulty in Napoleon's eyes unless it anticipated everything that the enemy might do and provided the means for outmaneuvering him.[7] Napoleon recognized, of course, that in all affairs one must leave something to circumstances: the best of plans can fail as a result of what Clausewitz called friction, that is, "the factors that distinguish real war from war on paper," those "countless minor incidents" a general never could foresee.[8] Conversely, sometimes even poor plans succeeded through a freak of fortune.[9]

To be a good general, Napoleon once commented to one of his military entourage on St. Helena, "you need to know mathematics. That is useful in a thousand circumstances to correct ideas. Perhaps I owe my success to my mathematical ideas; a general must never make a picture for himself. That is the worst thing of all."[10] Toward the end of his career Napoleon sometimes was guilty of "making pictures," but in his early days he had the ability to penetrate to the heart of a question and to see the entire situation clearly.

If there were two intellectual qualities that set Napoleon apart from most men, it was his prodigious memory and his infinite capacity for mastering detail. "A very curious thing about me is my memory," he told Gourgaud. "As a young man I knew the logarithms of more than thirty to forty numbers. I knew, in France, not only the names of the officers of all the regiments, but the places where the regiments were recruited and had gained distinction."[11]

Napoleon constantly fretted in letters to his generals about the need for them to pay strict attention to their muster rolls.

The good condition of my armies comes from the fact that I devote an hour or two every day to them, and when I am sent the returns of my troops and my ships each month, which fills twenty large volumes, I set every other occupation aside to read them in detail in order to discern the difference that exists from one month to another. I take greater pleasure in this reading than a young lady would get from reading a novel.[12]

Napoleon kept a critical eye on every detail of military intelligence, the movement and supply of troops, and army organization and administration. Woe to the subordinate general who failed to provide the date, place, and even the hour where a dispatch had been penned, or who did not provide information in sufficient detail. "The direction of military affairs is only half the work of a general,"[13] Napoleon insisted. Obviously, the other half involved a detailed knowledge of all parts of the military machine. In large measure, Napoleon's own mastery over men was possible because of his mastery of information, for as he explained to one of the generals sharing his captivity: "All that I am, everything that I have been I owe to the work habits that I have acquired from my boyhood."[14] There can be no doubt that Napoleon, had he been spared to supervise the military education of his own son, would have driven this point home time and again, and with all the forces at his command.

In Napoleon's case, a trained memory was reinforced by an absorbing interest in the minutiae of military activity. One cannot read his dictations on St. Helena without being impressed by the facts at his fingertips – how much dirt a soldier could dig in a specified time; minute details of tactics, and organization, and logistics; the smallest facts from his own campaigns and those of the other Great Captains. When asked one day how, after so many years, he could recollect the names and numbers of the units engaged in one of his early combats, Napoleon responded: "Madam, this is a lover's recollection of his former mistresses."[15]

Brilliance was not essential for a general, at least not so far as Napoleon was concerned. "Too much intellect is not necessary in war," he once reminded his brother Jerome. What was essential was precision, a strong personality, and the ability to keep things in a clear perspective.[16] Probably the most desirable attribute of all, or so he told Las Cases, "is that a man's judgment should be . . . above the common level."[17] Success in war depends on prudence, good conduct, and experience.[18]

By prudence Napoleon did not mean that a good general should be cautious in the conduct of operations. *Au contraire*: a good general "must be slow in deliberation and quick in execution."[19] Whenever Napoleon used the term prudence, what he intended to convey was careful management and presence of mind.

We have now slipped over into what Clausewitz called "moral qualities," and what Napoleon undoubtedly had in mind at the time he urged that his son should read and re-read the campaigns of the Great Captains. "But all that . . . he will learn will be of little use to him," Napoleon warned, "if he does not have the sacred fire in the depths of his heart, this driving ambition which alone can enable one to perform great deeds.''[20]

The moral quality that Napoleon most admired was boldness; here again, he would have agreed with Clausewitz, who asserted that ''a distinguished commander without boldness is unthinkable.''[21] Napoleon saw boldness as *the* common denominator among the Great Captains. Alexander succeeded because ''everything was profoundly calculated, boldly executed, and wisely managed.''[22] Hannibal was bolder still,[23] and Caesar was ''a man of great genius and great boldness.''[24] Napoleon did not consider Gustavus Adolphus in a league with the others, if only because his early death meant that he must be judged on the basis of only a few campaigns, but he was impressed by the ''boldness and swift movements'' of the Swedish king's last campaigns.[25]

Clausewitz in one of his more discerning passages observed that ''boldness grows less common in the higher ranks . . . . Nearly every general known to us from history as mediocre, even vacillating, was noted for dash and determination as a junior officer.''[26]

Napoleon probably would have concurred, for he once described Turenne as ''the only general whose boldness had increased with the years and experience.'' Napoleon, it should be added, preferred Turenne for another, more personal reason. ''I like him all the more because he acts exactly as I would have done in his position . . . . He is a man who, had he come near me at Wagram, would have understood everything at once.'' From St. Helena he mused: ''If I had had a man like Turenne to assist me in my campaigns, I would have been master of the world.''[27]

In Napoleon's comments about Prince Eugene, we again read of a ''very bold march crowned by the most brilliant successes,''[28] and while he often criticized the tactics and strategy of the Great Frederick, he had only praise for the ''bold resolutions'' that had enabled Frederick to survive the Seven Years' War and emerge with his state – and his army – intact.[29]

Frederick possessed great moral boldness . . . . What distinguishes him most is not the skill of his maneuvers, but his boldness. He carried off what I never dared attempt. He abandoned his line of operation and aften acted as if he had no knowledge of the military art. Always superior to his enemies in numbers at the beginning of a campaign, he is regularly inferior to them on the field of battle.

''I may be daring,'' Napoleon concluded, ''but Frederick was much more so.''[30] He was especially great ''at the most critical moments,'' which was the highest praise that Napoleon could bestow.[31]

A general was expected to be brave, but Napoleon insisted that bravery be tempered by good judgment. If courage was the predominating quality of a general, he would be apt to ''rashly embark in enterprises above his conceptions.'' On the other hand, if a general lacked character or courage he probably would not venture to carry out his ideas.[32]

Marshal Ney, ''the bravest of the brave,'' was a case in point. ''He was good when it came to leading 10,000 men,'' Napoleon acknowledged, ''but beyond that he was a real fool." Always the first under fire, Ney was inclined to forget those troops who were not under his immediate supervision.[33] Murat was another who was brave in action but in other respects had "neither vigor nor character."[34] Napoleon distinguished between the bravery that a commander must display and that required of a division commander, and neither, he wrote, should be the same as the bravery of a captain of grenadiers.[35]

When he mentioned courage, Napoleon had also in mind moral courage – what he liked to call "two o'clock in the morning courage." When bad news comes to a person at that hour, it is dark, he is alone, and his spirits are at low ebb; it requires a special brand of courage at such a time to make the necessary decision. Such courage is spontaneous rather than conscious, but it enables a general to exercise his judgment and make decisions despite the unexpected or the unfortunate surprises.[36]

Firmness – what Clausewitz would call perseverance – was another requisite for good generalship. "The most essential quality of a general is firmness of character and the resolution to conquer at any price."[37]

The foremost quality of a commander is to have a cool head, receiving accurate impressions of what is happening without ever getting excited, or dazzled, or intoxicated by good or bad news. The successive or simultaneous sensations that the commander received during the course of a day are classified in the mind and occupy only as much attention as they deserve, for good sense and judgment flow from the comparison of several sensations taken into equal consideration. There are men who, by the moral and physical composition, distort a picture of everything. No matter how much knowledge, intellect, courage and other good qualities they might have, nature has not called them to command armies or to direct the great operations of war.[38]

The worst error a general can make is to distort what he sees or hears. Merely because some partisan has captured an enemy picket is no reason for the general to believe that the entire army is on hand. "My great talent," he told Gourgaud, "the one that distinguishes me the most, is to see the entire picture distinctly."[39]

Because of the variety of intellectual and moral factors, Napoleon recognized that "in the profession of war, like that of letters, each man has his style." Messena might excel in sharp, prolonged attacks, but for defensive purposes Jourdan would be preferable.[40] Reynier, a topographical engineer, was known as a man of sound advice, but he was a loner, cold and silent by nature and not very communicative. Obviously, he was no man to electrify or dominate soldiers. Lannes was "wise, prudent and bold," a man of little formal education but great natural ability and a man of imperturbable *sang froid*. Moreau was personally brave but knew nothing of grand tactics. Desaix, on the other hand, understood *la grand guerre* almost as well as Napoleon – or so Napoleon claimed after he had been sent into exile.[41]

It follows, therefore, that generals were not to be treated as interchangeable parts. Each was particularly well suited for some kinds of tasks, but as Napoleon wrote on more than one occasion, a great general – by which he may well have meant a complete general – "is no common thing."[42]

Because Napoleon never bothered to write a book of practical advice to his son, of the kind written by several contemporaries in France and England,[43] we can only surmise some of the things he might have said. Nevertheless, many of his strong convictions snap to attention and salute as one reads his published correspondence. The following excerpts probably should be considered for promotion to the level of maxims, to serve as pithy aphorisms on the art of command.

There are no precise or determined rules; everything depends on the character that nature has given to the general, on his qualities, his shortcomings, on the nature of the troops, on the range of firearms, on the season and on a thousand other circumstances which are never the same.[44]

War is a serious sport, in which one can endanger his reputation and his country: a rational man must feel and know whether or not he is cut out for this profession.[45]

The honor of a general consists in obeying, in keeping subalterns under his orders on the honest path, in maintaining good discipline, devoting oneself solely to the interests of the State and the sovereign, and in scorning completely his private interests.[46]

In war one sees his own troubles and not those of the enemy.[47]

In war the commander alone understands the importance of certain things. He alone, by his will and superior insight, can conquer and overcome all difficulties.[48]

Hold no council of war, but accept the views of each, one by one . . . . The secret is to make each alike . . . believe that he has your confidence.[49]

Take nobody into your confidence, not even your chief of staff.[50]

Soldiers must never be witnesses to the discussions of the commanders.[51]

Generals always make requests – it is in the nature of things. There is not a one who cannot be counted upon for that. It is quite natural that the man who is entrusted with only one task thinks only about it, and the more men he has the better guarantee he has for success.[52]

One always has enough troops when he knows how to use them.[53]

Once you have made up your mind, stick to it; there is no longer any *if* or *but* . . .[54]

War is waged only with vigor, decision and unshaken will; one must not grope or hesitate.[55]

It is at night when a commander must work: if he tires himself to no purpose during the day, fatigue overcomes him at night . . . . A commander is not expected to sleep.[56]

Give your orders so that they cannot be disobeyed.[57]

It is not enough to give orders, they must be obeyed.[58]

In military operations, hours determine success and campaigns.[59]

The loss of time is irretrievable in war: the excuses that are advanced are always bad ones, for operations go wrong only through delays.[60]

You must be slow in deliberation and quick in execution.[61]

Intelligent and fearless generals assure the success of affairs.[62]

I may be accused of rashness, but not of sluggishness.[63]

It is by vigor and energy that one spares his troops, earns their esteem, and forces some of it on the reprobates.[64]

You must not needlessly fatigue troops.[65]

You must avoid countermanding orders: unless the soldier can see a good reason for benefit, he becomes discouraged and loses confidence.[66]

Pay no attention to those who would keep you far from fire: you want to prove yourself a man of courage. If there are opportunities, expose yourself conspicuously. As for real danger, it is everywhere in war.[67]

In war the foremost principle of the commander is to disguise what he does, to see if he has the means of overcoming the obstacles, and to do everything to surmount them when he is resolved.[68]

True wisdom for a general is in vigorous determination.[69]

In war everything is perception – perception about the enemy, perception about one's own soldiers. After a battle is lost, the difference between victor and vanquished is very little; it is, however, incommensurable with perception, for two or three cavalry squadrons are enough to produce a great effect.[70]

If one constantly feels humanity he cannot wage war. I do not understand war with perfume.[71]

An army of lions commanded by a deer will never be an army of lions.[72]

Whether these or other maxims still apply today is for others to determine. The point is, they applied in Napoleon's day. At least they reflected his experience, and for that reason alone they reveal much about Napoleon and his philosophy of command.

NOTES

1. "Extraits des récits de la captivité," *Correspondance de Napoléon ler* (32 vols.; Paris: 1858-70), XXXII, 379.
2. There are many editions of Napoleon's maxims: this quotation is from the translation by L. E. Henry, *Napoleon's War Maxims* (London: 1899), p. 39. In *The Mind of Napoleon,* J. Christopher Herold includes a conversation recorded by Las Cases and a letter from Napoleon to one of his generals on the subject of command, and additional insights can be inferred from extracts of Napoleon's views of the Great Captains. (See Ibid., pp. 220-21, 224-30.) The comprehensive collection of Napoleon's thoughts on military topics assembled by Lieutenant Colonel Ernest Picard devotes only three out of 575 pages to the heading "Qualities of Command." *Préceptes et jugements de Napoléon* (Paris: 1913), pp. 214-17.
3. Napoleon to Joseph, 4 May 1807, *Corres.,* No. 12530, XV, 188; General Gourgaud, *Sainte-Hélène, Journal inédit* (2 vols.; Paris: 1899), II, 20.
4. Comte de Montholon, *Récits de la captivité de l'empereur; Napoléon a Sainte-Hélène* (2 vols.; Paris: 1847), II, 240-41; Carl von Clausewitz, *On War,* ed. and trans. Michael Howard and Peter Paret (Princeton, N.J.: Princeton Univ. Press, 1976), pp. 190-92.
5. Napoleon to Joseph, 18 September 1806, *Corres.,* No. 10809, XIII, 210; XII, 442.
6. Napoleon to Marshal Murat, 14 March 1808, *Corres.,* No. 13652, XVI, 418.
7. "Ulm-Moreau," *Corres,* XXX, 409.
8. Clausewitz, *On War,* p. 119.
9. To Vice Admiral Decres, 16 June 1805, *Corres.,* No. 8897, X, 529; "Notes sur l'art de la guerre," XXXI, 417.
10. Gourgaud, *Journal,* II, 460.
11. Ibid., p. 109.
12. Napoleon to Joseph, 20 August 1806, *Corres.,* No. 10672, XIII, 87.
13. Napoleon to Eugene, 20 June 1809, *Corres.,* No. 15388, XIX, 140; to Berthier, 28 June 1805, No. 8957, X, 571; to Murat, 12 October 1805, No. 9372, XI, 316.
14. Montholon, *Récits,* I, 321.
15. Count de Las Cases, *Memoirs of the Life, Exile and Conversations of the Emperor Napoleon* (4 vols.; London: 1836), II, 349.
16. Napoleon to Jerome, 2 May 1804, *Corres.,* No. 8832, X, 474; to Jerome, No. 12511, XV, 178.
17. Las Cases, *Memoirs,* I, 251.

18. "Note sur la situation actuelle de l'Espagne," 5 August 1808, *Corres.,* No. 14245, XVII, 429.
19. Napoleon to Eugene, 21 August 1806, *Corres.,* No. 10681, XIII, 9.
20. Corres., XXXII, 379.
21. Clausewitz, *On War*, p. 21.
22. Las Cases, *Memoirs*, IV, 140-41.
23. "Notes sur l'art de la guerre, *Corres.,* XXXI, 349.
24. Gourgaud, *Journal*, II, 162.
25. "Notes sur l'art de la guerre," *Corres.,* XXXI, 354.
26. Clausewitz, *On War*, p. 191.
27. Gourgard, *Journal*, II, 135-37.
28. "Notes sur l'art de la guerre," *Corres.,* XXXI, 355.
29. "Précis des guerres de Frédéric II," *Corres.,* XXXII, 238-39.
30. Gourgard, *Journal*, II, 17, 20, 33-34.
31. "Précis des guerres de Frédéric II," *Corres.,* XXXII, 238.
32. Las Cases, *Memoirs*, I, 250-51.
33. "Campagne de 1815," *Corres.,* XXXI, 206-07; Gourgard, *Journal*, I, 585.
34. Napoleon to Murat, 26 January 1813, *Léonce de Brotonne, Lettres inédites de Napoléon Ier* (Paris: 1898), No. 1033, p. 423.
35. "Campagne de 1815," *Corres.,* XXXI, 207.
36. Las Cases, *Memoirs*, I, 251.
37. Montholon, *Récits.*, II, 240-41; Gourgard, Journal, II, 426.
38. "Précis des guerres de Frédéric II," *Corres.,* XXXII, 182-83.
39. Gourgaud, *Journal*, II, 460.
40. Napoleon to Joseph, 6 June 1806, *Corres.,* No. 10325, XII, 440.
41. "Notes-Moreau," *Corres.,* XXX, 496; "Notes sur l'art de la guerre," Ibid., XXXI, 380; Montholon, *Récits*, I, 176.
42. Gourgaud, *Journal*, II, 423-24.
43. See *A Series of Letters recently written by a General Officer* to his son . . . (2 vols.; Salem: 1804). This American edition was from the second English edition, which bears a striking resemblance to M. le Baron D'A . . . , *Conseils d'un Militaire a son Fils* (Paris: 1874).
44. "Notes sur l'art de la guerre," *Corres.,* XXXI, 365.
45. Napoleon to Eugene, 30 April 1809, *Corres.,* No. 15144, XVIII, 525.
46. Napoleon to Marshal Berthier, 8 June 1811, *Corres.,* No. 17782, XXII, 215.
47. Napoleon to Eugene, 30 April 1809, *Corres.,* No. 15144, XVIII, 525.
48. "Observations sur les campagnes de 1796 et 1797," *Corres.,* XXIX, 341.
49. Napoleon to Joseph, 12 January 1806, *Corres.,* No. 9665, XI, 535.
50. Napoleon to Jerome, 26 May 1812, *Corres.,* No. 18727, XXIII, 436.
51. Napoleon to Marshal De Moncey, 31 March 1805, *Corres.,* No. 8507, X, 279.
52. Napoleon to Joseph, 4 March 1809, *Corres.,* No. 14846, XVIII, 308.
53. Napoleon to Joseph, 26 June 1806, *Corres.,* No. 10416, XII, 489.
54. Napoleon to Marshal Marmont, 18 February 1812, *Corres.,* No. 18503, XXIII, 229.
55. Napoleon to General Bertrand, 6 June 1813, *Corres.,* 20090, XXV, 363.
56. Napoleon conversation with Gourgaud, *Journal*, II, 159.
57. Napoleon to Marshal Berthier, 29 March 1811, *Corres.,* No. 17529, XXI, 521.
58. Napoleon to Eugene, 11 June 1806, *Corres.,* No. 10350, XII, 270.
59. Napoleon to Admiral Mazarredo, 20 March 1800, *Corres.,* No. 4689, VI, 199.
60. Napoleon to Joseph, 20 March 1806, *Corres.,* No. 9997, XII, 204.
61. Napoleon to Eugene, 21 August 1806, *Corres.,* No 10681, XIII, 96.
62. Napoleon to Marshal Mortier, 29 November 1806, *Corres.,* No. 113255, XIII, 588.
63. Napoleon to the Executive Director, 6 May 1796, *Corres.,* No. 337, I, 237.
64. Napoleon to Joseph, 28 July 1806, *Corres.,* No. 10558, XIII, 9.
65. Napoleon to Eugene, 29 July 1806, *Corres.,* No. 10563, XIII, 13.
66. Napoleon to Eugene, 5 August 1806, *Corres.,* No. 10699, XIII, 38.
67. Napoleon to Joseph, 2 February 1806, *Corres.,* No. 9738, XI, 573.
68. Napoleon to Marshal Berthier, 9 April 1810, *Corres.,* No. 16372, XX, 284.
69. "Précis des guerres de Frédéric II," *Corres.,* XXXII, 209.
70. Napoleon to Joseph, 22 September 1808, *Corres.,* No. 14343, XVII, 526.

71. Napoleon conversation with Gourgaud, *Journal*, II, 449.
72. "Campagnes d'Egypte et de Syrie," *Corres.*, XXX, 176.

This article appeared in the summer 1985 issue of *Parameters*.

8

The Military Ethics of General William T. Sherman: A Reassessment

by JOHN W. BRINSFIELD

The morality of General William Tecumseh Sherman's military campaigns – what he did and what he allowed his subordinate commanders and troops to do – has been extensively debated for more than a century. Sherman's critics charge that as a commander Sherman employed such terrorist tactics as licensing the random execution of noncombatants, destroying and pillaging private property, and even plotting Indian genocide. According to Sherman's detractors, his troops during both the Civil War and the Indian Wars, protected by the moral indifference of their commander, were guilty of murder, theft, arson, rape,[1] and the desecration of cemeteries and burial grounds.[2]

During the Atlanta campaign, for example, General W. P. Howard of the Georgia State Militia reported to Governor Joseph Brown that "the crowning act of their wickedness and villainy . . . was in removing the dead from vaults in the cemetery, robbing coffins of their silver name plates and tippings, and then depositing their own dead in the vaults."[3] Confederate General John B. Hood criticized Sherman's decision to evacuate the population of Atlanta in September 1864, writing to Sherman that his action "transcends, in studied and ingenious cruelty, all acts ever before brought to my attention in the dark history of war."[4] General Richard Taylor, son of President Zachary Taylor, wrote in 1879 that "Sherman and Sheridan, spattered with Southern blood, were throwbacks to a barbarous age."[5] Jefferson Davis, whose *Rise and Fall of the Confederate Government* provoked a newspaper debate with Sherman, wrote of the March to the Sea: "The arson of the dwelling-houses of noncombatants and the robbery of their property, extending even to the trinkets worn by women, made the devastation as relentless as savage instincts could suggest."[6] Mrs. Davis evidently did not feel that her husband had put the matter strongly enough. She offered her own moral assessment of Sherman in the *Army-Navy Journal* of 10 May 1884: "He was an inhuman monster – what he did not use he destroyed."[7]

Sherman was not slow to defend himself and his army from these piecemeal attacks. Over the course of 20 years, from 1864 to 1884, Sherman wrote letters, testified in court, gave speeches, and published his memoirs in an effort to set the record straight. In a letter to Captain J. H. Lee in 1881, Sherman explained his motivation:

> We must speak and write else Europe will be left to infer that we conquered not by courage, skill, and patriotic devotion, but by brute force and cruelty. The reverse was the fact, the Rebels were notoriously more cruel than our men. We never could work up our men to the terrible earnestness of the Southern forces. Their murdering of Union fugitives, burning of Lawrence, Chambersburg, Paducah and etc. were all right in their eyes, and if we burned an old cotton gin or shed it was barbarism. I am tired of such perversion, and will resent it always.[8]

Sherman denied that he had ever favored wanton destruction of human life in any instance; rather, he had acted throughout his military career to punish those who did not obey the law.[9] In the course of most of his major campaigns, Sherman said he preferred to conserve life and generally offered the enemy the opportunity to surrender before he set about his tasks of destruction.[10]

Sherman's problem throughout the Civil War was how to reconcile the brutal nature of modern war with the ethical values he had learned as a West Point cadet, as an Army officer, in his intermittent study of law from 1839 to 1859, and as a practicing attorney. While his primary interest as a general was undeniably directed toward strategy and tactics, there was still part of his intellectual heritage from five generations of Sherman judges that demanded a correlation between the conduct of war on one hand and the laws of warfare on the other.

In the 19th century there were many schools of classical ethics. Francis Lieber, in his 1838 edition of *A Manual of Political Ethics,* pointed out that essentially all of the schools dealt with two concepts: morals and ethics. Moral philosophy answered the question *What must I do?* Ethics answered the question *Why must I do it?*

The ethical school that most attracted Sherman was not the metaphysical or theological but the pragmatic and utilitarian, as befitted the profession of a soldier and the avocation of a lawyer. Law was a perfect sanction for Sherman's utilitarian military ethic because the law books recognized that every punishment should be proportionate to the crime. If rebellion was the highest crime against an organized society, both utilitarian ethics and the law of nations sanctioned extreme measures – such as devastation by fire and sword – as permissible expedients.

To truly understand the ethics – the rationale – for Sherman's punitive expeditions in the Civil War and after, one must approach his ideas from the standpoint of their chronological development. Sherman himself noted that his military ethics before 1862 were different than they were after that year. The detailed development of Sherman's thought from his first course in moral philosophy at West Point through the end of his military career would be a lengthy task. Nevertheless, a few comments may shed some new light on his concept of the ethics of war and support the thesis that Sherman's philosophy of war was not totally devoid of ethical and legal principle.

Ethical Education at West Point: 1839-40

The two courses that seem to have contributed most to Sherman's early ethical thought were both taught in his senior, or "first-class," year at West Point. After his summer encampment preceding that year, Sherman wrote to his brother John in August 1839:

> The encampment is now over and we are once more in Barracks and tomorrow will commence our studies . . . . This year's course of study is by far the most important of the four as well as the most interesting embracing as it does – Engineering – both Civil and Military – the construction of fortifications as well as the manner of attacking and defending them, Mineralology, and Geology, Rhetoric, Moral Philosophy, International and Common Law, Artillery and Infantry tactics.[11]

Sherman enjoyed his course in fortifications from Professor D. H. Mahan, who was probably his favorite instructor.[12] Mahan not only taught Sherman the value of the spade but also offered his opinion that the way to defeat the Indians in Florida was to destroy their food supplies.[13]

One book that Professor Mahan frequently referenced in his course was Baron Simon Francois Gay de Vernon's *Treatise on the Science of War and Fortification*, which had an appendix by Lieutenant J. M. O'Connor summarizing the thought of Jomini and Henry Lloyd on grand strategy. De Vernon's *Science of War* had been replaced as a textbook at West Point in 1836, but Sherman checked it out of the library in 1840 anyway.[14] It is interesting that the first chapter of O'Connor's translation of the *Science of War* offers a kind of Hobbesian analysis of society. "In the original state," the text reads, "mankind possessed mere animal sensibility, which results when a state of war between nations occurs and treaties and conventions are broken." In the condition of bestiality to which men revert in war, all civilization breaks down and even "churches may be used as redoubts."[15]

Sherman was not impressed with Jomini, whose work he said was "too dull, prosaic and didactic," but he was drawn to Mahan and to the general notion that obedience to law was the prerequisite for avoiding the chaos of war.[16] By the end of 1864, Professor Mahan stated this view even more directly by noting that "there are times in a nation's existence when the safety of the State is the highest law."[17]

The second course, which probably contributed even more to the development of Sherman's ethical thought, was a course in moral philosophy taught by Chaplain Jasper Adams. Chaplain Adams was an Episcopal clergyman who had been successively a professor of mathematics at Brown University, president of Charleston College in South Carolina, and president of Geneva College in New York before coming to West Point. He was not one of Sherman's favorites on the faculty; indeed, Sherman remarked that during his four years at West Point he was not "a Sunday School cadet."[18] But the subject matter covered in "the Chaplain's Course," as it was titled in the USMA Regulations of 1839, did capture Sherman's imagination: Adams taught moral philosophy, the law of nations, and constitutional law in the course the cadets called simply "ethics."[19]

Sherman was not the first cadet to be captivated by the readings in the Chaplain's Course. From 1816 when the regulations of the Military Academy specified that "a course of ethics shall include natural and political law," to 1874 when the Law Department was formed at West Point, nine different chaplains taught law to the cadets using a series of textbooks ranging from Vattel's *Law of Nations* (published in 1758) to Woolsey's *Introduction to the Study of International Law* (published in 1860). Robert E. Lee told Bishop Joseph Wilmer of Albemarle County, Virginia, that had he not read Rawle's *A View of the Constitution* in Chaplain Warner's course, he would never have left the Union.[20] General Erasmus D. Keyes said he "learned more from Professor Warner in the section room than from any other teacher," and Stonewall Jackson, as a cadet in 1845, wrote to his sister Laura that his class in ethics was "preferable to any other in the course."[21] Walter L. Fleming, a professor of history at Louisiana State University at the turn of the century and an expert on early education at West Point, went so far as to state that the Chaplain's Course was one of the most important at the Academy in light of the history of the Civil War.[22] In fact, one could make a pretty good case for the thesis that the textbooks in the Chaplain's Course contained many of the operative strategic and ethical concepts of the Civil War and that these concepts, including retaliation, blockade, emancipation, and unconditional surrender, were discussed at West Point more than 20 years before the first shot was fired at Fort Sumter.

The reason so many cadets were interested in the Chaplain's Course was that it combined the study of humanities and law, which were offered nowhere else in the curriculum. In Adams' course cadets recited for two hours a day from William Paley's *Moral and Political Philosophy* and from James Kent's *Commentaries on American Law*. As Adams informed Superintendent Richard Delafield in February 1840:

An exact knowledge of these textbooks is held to be of the greatest importance, long and patient examinations are held upon them, and the relative standing of the Cadets in the Academy is made to depend on their acquaintance with them. Not only so, but their future rank in the army, and consequently their prospects in life, are made to depend on the degree of their acquaintance with them.[23]

Adams did not approve of Paley's book because it taught "the young men that they have no conscience, diminishes their respect for truth, and perplexes, if it does not confound the distinction between right and wrong."[24] A petition by Adams to replace Paley's text was denied by the academic board, however, in part because he had already changed textbooks three times in two years and had been warned by Joel R. Poinsett, President Van Buren's Secretary of War, "to be more careful."[25]

The content of Paley's *Moral and Political Philosophy* is fascinating and worth a dissertation in itself because the textbook was studied by Jefferson Davis, Robert E. Lee, A. S. Johnston, J. E. Johnston, P. G. T. Beauregard, Ulysses Grant, and Sherman. Paley's work presents advice for daily living coupled with some reflections on the origin of government, on crime and punishment, on duty, and on the justice of warfare.

In essence Paley took a utilitarian approach to life, for "the obligation of every law depends upon its ultimate utility."[26] Rules "derive their force not from their internal reasonableness or justice but from their establishment."[27] God is the ultimate lawmaker,

a Being whose knowledge penetrates every concealment, from the operation of whose will not art or flight can escape, and in whose hands punishment is sure; such a Being may conduct the moral government of his creation in the best and wisest manner by pronouncing a law that every crime shall finally receive a punishment proportioned to the guilt which it contains, abstracted from any foreign consideration whatever [and] by carrying this law into strict execution.[28]

It is God's will that all men should be happy, and happiness is generally the greatest good for the greatest number.[29] Therefore, one asks about any moral question, "Does it promote or diminish the general happiness?" If an action promotes happiness, it is the will of God.[30]

In spite of the utilitarian nature of Paley's work, James Kent's *Commentaries on American Law* was Sherman's favorite textbook in the Chaplain's Course. In 1829 James Kent was a professor of law at Columbia, president of the New York Historical Society, and Colonel Sylvanus Thayer's personal friend. Because Kent's book covered both the law of nations and constitutional law in one summary volume, and was thus more easily taught, it replaced the works by Vattel and Rawle that had been used intermittently from 1820 to 1832.

Kent's views of human nature and the practice of warfare were rooted in a pessimistic realism. For example, Kent begins his "Third Lecture," titled "Of the Declaration and other early measures of a state of war," by contrasting Bacon's statement that "war is one of the highest trials of right . . . put upon the justice of God by an appeal to arms," with Hobbes' view that "continual war is a natural instinct of man in a savage state."[31] Kent believed that man, without the social compact, reverted to a primitive level. War was "a dissolution of all moralities" and was fought between "all the individuals of the one, and all the individuals of which the other nation is composed."[32] Retaliation was allowed in such a total war to restrain the enemy from further excess.[33]

One of the best protective measures against such chaos was a strong central government. Kent observed that "the history of the federal government of Greece, Germany, Switzerland, and Holland afford melancholy examples of destructive civil war springing from the disobedience of the separate members."[34] Therefore, Kent believed, "Disobedience to the laws of the union must either be submitted to by the government to its own disgrace or those laws must be enforced by arms."[35]

Coupled with Kent's "total war" theory and his unionist sentiments was his strong aversion to slavery. Kent's solution to the slavery problem was not Christian persuasion, as Paley had suggested, but violent, though legal, confrontation. Kent noted bluntly, "Pirates can be exterminated without declaration of war and the African slave trade is declared to be piracy by the statute laws of England and the United States."[36]

Sherman's class was examined in moral philosophy as well as other subjects in January 1840. Typically, examination periods lasted for 17 days, from eight o'clock in the morning to dusk; each cadet was examined orally by the entire faculty and sometimes by members of the Board of Visitors.[37] Cadet Sherman wrote, "The results were favorable toward me as usual."[38] He placed sixth in his class in moral philosophy, better than cadets Grant, Stuart, and Davis but not as well as Lee or Jackson placed in their classes.[39] Had it not been for Sherman's average of 150 demerits a year for problems in conduct, he would have graduated fourth rather than sixth in his class.

The academic curriculum was not the only place that military ethics and discipline were emphasized, of course. The code of honor, compulsory attendance at chapel, and the USMA Regulations of 1839 all contributed to an ethical awareness. Article I, paragraph 52, of the Articles of War, which were appended to the USMA Regulations, caught Sherman's eye. That paragraph made it a capital offense for a soldier to quit his post in order to plunder or pillage. After 1862 Sherman said he ignored this "old" idea.[40]

From Florida to Tennessee: The Transformation

From the time that Lieutenant Sherman joined the 3d Artillery Regiment in September 1840 until the Civil War began, he never really saw a battlefield. He was one of the few major commanders in the Civil War who had no combat experience in the Mexican War. His letters to his brothers and sisters from Fort Pierce, Florida, in 1841 show a relatively conservative view of military ethics. He discussed the treaties broken by the Indians and the suffering of their women and children, which was borne "with fortitude."[41] In his single engagement against the Seminoles, Sherman rode alone into an Indian village after instructing his troops to "revenge" him if he were killed. He talked the Indians out of their weapons and marched them back to Fort Pierce.[42] It was a bloodless victory that Sherman would try to repeat at Atlanta in 1864 and at Fort Laramie in 1867, but with less success.

Sherman did study law during his Army assignments in Florida and South Carolina. It was perhaps natural that he considered law as a possible second profession, as did Stonewall Jackson and J. E. B. Stuart. Yet he practiced law for only one year at Leavenworth, Kansas, before the Civil War began. Years earlier, Sherman had written to his brother John that although "everybody" in his class studied law at West Point, he did not believe he was enough of an orator to make it his profession.[43] He preferred the thought of retiring to a good farm in Iowa.

Sherman's career from his Army resignation in 1853 to the beginning of the Civil War appears to have had a marked effect on his outlook on life, but an analysis of his psychological development in the face of personal banking and business failures exceeds the scope of this discussion. Certainly his decision to abandon his post as superintendent of the Louisiana State Seminary and Military Academy in order to stay in the Union "as long as a fragment" of the "Old Constitution" survived was a monumental decision for him.[44] The turning point in Sherman's concept of military ethics, however, came between his service in Virgina in 1861 and his service in Tennessee in 1862.

Sherman's attitude in 1861 toward pillage and destruction can be seen in a letter to his wife, Ellen, after the first Battle of Bull Run:

Then for the first time I saw the carnage of battle, men lying in every conceivable shape and mangled in a horrid way . . . . No curse could be greater than invasion by a voluntary army. No Goths or Vandals ever had less respect for the lives and property of friend and foes . . . .[45]

These comments were not directed at just any volunteer army but at his own in particular. Sherman wrote to his wife in August 1861:

Our soldiers are the most destructive men that I have ever known. It may be that other volunteers are just as bad, indeed the complaint is universal, and I see no alternative but to let it take its course . . . . My only hope now is that a common sense of decency may be inspired into the minds of this soldiery to respect life and property.[46]

Even though Sherman had given up making "any friends in Virginia," he did try to maintain some discipline among his troops, who were "straggling for water, blackberries, or any thing on the way they fancied."[47]

Sherman's determination to keep his troops in line was further manifested during his service in Kentucky in the winter of 1861-62. He issued strict orders preventing his soldiers from taking any fresh food on the march, from sleeping in any vacant houses, and even from using Kentucky fence rails for firewood.[48] As a result, one regiment under his command, the Thirty-third Indiana, had more than half of its men in the hospital and suffered 62 deaths in a single month from exposure and from insufficient rations. When two citizens of Lexington, Kentucky, asked Sherman in October 1861 if he would arrest Southern sympathizers as a "retaliatory" measure, Sherman replied that he would arrest no one merely for holding an opinion as long as that person committed no overt criminal act.[49]

In carrying out these policies Sherman was obeying the orders of the War Department for operations in the border states. In spite of the fact that Jefferson Davis had written a personal letter to Abraham Lincoln on 6 July 1861 threatening random retaliatory executions of Union prisoners in Richmond if Confederate sailors captured by the Federal Navy were hanged as pirates, the War Department, through General Henry Halleck, had been holding to a very strict policy respecting the sanctity of private property and individual constitutional rights, and it continued to do so until mid-1862.[50] Sherman soon discovered, however, that the enemy did not operate under such constraints:

I would not let our men burn fence rails for fire or gather fruit or vegetables though hungry . . . . We at that time were restrained, tied by a deep-seated reverence for law and property. The rebels first introduced terror as a part of their system . . . . Buell had to move at a snail's pace with his vast wagon trains . . . . Bragg moved rapidly, living on the country. No military mind could endure this long, and we were forced in self-defense to imitate their example.[51]

The genesis of Sherman's conversion from a proponent of warfare by the rules of courtesy to warfare by the rules of survival, therefore, was not the result of a deliberate policy rooted in intellectual theory. It was a reaction to the conditions he encountered in the field. Twenty years after the Civil War, Sherman reflected on his shift in thinking:

I know that in the beginning, I, too, had the old West Point notion that pillage was a capital crime, and punished it by shooting . . . . This was a one-sided game of war, and many of us . . . ceased to quarrel with our own men about such minor things, and went in to subdue the enemy, leaving minor depredations to be charged up to the account of the rebels who had forced us into the war, and who deserved all they got and more.[52]

From his observations in 1862 in Kentucky and Tennessee, it was a short step for Sherman to begin to rationalize his changing views of warfare in terms of the darker side of the West Point curriculum of his cadet years and to see the conduct of war as involving, to a large measure, retaliation, punishment, revenge, and devastation.

Sherman was not alone in these observations, of course. Independently of Sherman, Colonel Ulysses S. Grant wrote in 1861 of his men of the Twenty-first Illinois on a march from Camp Yates to Missouri: "The same number of men never marched through a thickly settled country like this committing fewer depredations."[53] Yet Grant told his wife, Julia, "The people are inclined to carry on a guerrilla warfare that must eventuate in retaliation, and when it does commence it will be hard to control."[54]

By the summer of 1862 both the US Congress and the Lincoln Administration had become convinced that more stringent measures were necessary to subdue the rebels, who had fought so fiercely in the Peninsula Campaign and at Shiloh. On 13 July Brigadier General Steinwehr ordered Major William Steadman to arrest five citizens of Page County, Virginia, to be held as hostages and to suffer death in the event that any of Steinwehr's troops were killed by "bushwackers."[55] On 17 July Congress passed the famous Seizure Act, which provided for the confiscation or condemnation of all personal property belonging to persons engaged in rebellion.[56]

The Confederate government responded in kind by issuing General Order Number 54 on 1 August 1862, declaring the adoption of "just measures of retribution and retaliation as shall seem adequate to repress and punish these barbarities." Among other measures ordered by General Samuel Cooper, the Confederate States Inspector General, was the warning that the Confederate government would hang Union officers then held as prisoners of war in "a number equal to the number of our own citizens thus murdered by the enemy."[57]

In retaliation for increasing guerrilla activities in Mississippi and the number of ''murders'' committed by ''Southern irregulars,'' Union General Henry Halleck, on 2 August 1862, ordered General Grant at Corinth, Mississippi, to

clean out West Tennessee and North Mississippi of all organized enemies. If necessary, take up all active sympathizers, and either hold them as prisoners or put them beyond our lines. Handle that class without gloves, and take their property for public use. As soon as the corn gets fit for forage get all the supplies you can from the rebels in Mississippi. It is time that they should begin to feel the presence of war on our side.[58]

Within four days of the receipt of this order, General W. L. Elliott, Rosecrans' chief of staff at Corinth, ordered General James D. Morgan at Tuscumbia to move rebel women and children beyond his lines, seize their property, and burn their homes.[59]

At Memphis, Sherman reflected on this development in a letter to Secretary Chase, dated 11 August 1862, in words reminiscent of Kent's ''total war'' theory:

The Government of the United States may now safely proceed on the proper rule that all in the South are enemies of all in the North; and not only are they unfriendly, but all who can procure arms now bear them as organized regiments or as guerillas. There is not a garrison in Tennessee where a man can go beyond the sight of the flagstaff without being shot or captured.[60]

Grant, in turn, reflected later that the ''Constitution was therefore in abeyance for the time being, so far as it in any way affected the progress and termination of the war.''[61]

With constitutional interpretation replaced by congressional law and the principle of military necessity, Sherman was free to suppress rebellion with almost any amount of force necessary. On 1 October 1862 he wrote to his brother John:

Even on the Mississippi the boats are fired on daily. I have been compelled to burn down one town and resort to retaliation. For after eighteen months of war the enemy is actually united, armed, and determined . . . . [The] northern people have to unlearn all their experience of the past thirty years and be born again before they will see the truth.[62]

The truth, for Sherman, was that by arming all of its citizens, the South, not the North, had plunged the nation into total war. If the Union was to survive, the people of the North would have to adjust themselves to fight on the terms that the South, Sherman charged, had dictated.

On 4 October 1862, Sherman underscored this belief in a letter to Major General Grant at Jackson, Tennessee. Sherman told Grant,

Guerrillas have twice attacked boats near Randolph – the forest Queen and J. J. Roe – on both of which were many lady and children passengers. The attacks were wanton and cruel. I caused Randolph to be destroyed, and have given public notice that a repetition will justify any measures of retaliation such as loading the boats with their captive guerrillas as targets (I always have a lot on hand), and expelling families from the comforts of Memphis, whose husbands and brothers go to make up those guerrillas.[63]

Evidently this "new" turn of events in Memphis – and in his own command, for that matter – took Grant by surprise. On 18 October, when Sherman proposed to "expell ten secession families for every boat fired on," thereby visiting "on the neighborhood summary punishment," Grant sent a one-sentence endorsement to General Halleck:

> Respectfully forwarded to headquarters of the Army for information of the General-in-Chief, embodying as it does a policy, which I approve but have given no order for, in regard to treatment of rebel families as punishment to prevent firing in to boats.[64]

Five days later, Colonel William S. Hillyer, Grant's aide-de-camp, wrote Sherman: "The general heartily approves your course in expelling secession families as a punishment and preventive example for guerrillas firing into boats."[65] For the first time in the Civil War, Sherman had a commander who understood the concept of retaliation to restrain the enemy, who had witnessed the effects of total war in Texas, and who, for that matter, was also once a student of the same West Point curriculum.

From Atlanta to the Sea: The Application

That Sherman, Grant, and Sheridan translated the will of Congress and the ideas of President Lincoln into a war of devastation aimed at total victory is not a fact requiring detailed proof. Sherman himself estimated that his March to the Sea cost the State of Georgia 15,000 first-rate mules, 5000 head of cattle, and 2000 horses, in addition to 34,979 Confederate casualties.[66] The question is not, however, what homes, towns, railroads, colleges, churches, or government buildings were destroyed. After all, Grant had instructed Sherman to "get into the interior of the enemy's country as far as you can, inflicting all the damage you can against their war resources."[67] The question is, to what extent did Sherman leave the West Point ideas behind in his quest for victory?

Sherman maintained in 1864 that he tried on many occasions to persuade his enemies to surrender and thereby to end the destruction his army was causing in the South:

> I contended at first, when we took Vicksburg, by all the rules of civilized warfare, they should have surrendered, and allowed us to restore Federal power in the land. But they did not. I claim also when we took Atlanta, that they were bound by every rule of civilized warfare to surrender their cause . . . .[68]

During the Georgia and Carolina campaigns, Sherman certainly used his authority under the law of nations, congressional law, Army regulations, and the directives of Lincoln and Grant to offer generous terms of surrender that were not only in accord with the precepts of Vattel but also in the finest Napoleonic tradition.[69] Yet, when he submitted to Governor Brown of Georgia an offer to "spare the State, and in our passage across it confine the troops to the main roads and . . . moreover, pay for all the corn and food we needed,'' the Georgia Legislature rejected Sherman's proposal, called for a levy en masse of all white males aged 16 to 45, released the prisoners from the state penitentiary, and even pressed all ministers not actively serving a church or synagogue into the Confederate forces.[70] In light of this response, Sherman told Colonel Joshua Hill, one of the emissaries to Governor Brown, ''There is nothing left for me to do but to proceed.''[71]

Of the conduct of his troops during the March to the Sea, Sherman wrote in 1875:

No doubt many acts of pillage, robbery, and violence were committed by these parties of foragers, usually called 'bummers'; for I have since heard of jewelry taken from women, and the plunder of articles that never reached the commissary; but these acts were exceptional and incidental. I never heard of any cases of murder or rape; and no army could have carried along sufficient foraging for a march of three hundred miles; so that foraging in some shape was necessary.[72]

When Sherman arrived in Savannah he placed the city, including its schools and churches, under his protection with the warning ''If any person shall abuse these privileges by communicating with the enemy, or doing any act of hostility to the Government of the United States, he or she will be punished with the utmost rigor of the law.''[73] Sherman claimed that the disposal of property in and around Savannah was in accord with the ''laws of nations and the practice of civilized governments.''[74]

Sherman's campaign in the Carolinas was marked with charges of pillage and arson, just as had been the case in Georgia. The ethical maxim he had recommended to his commanders on the March to the Sea was the principle of retaliation by degree and that principle was to be pursued, in effect, throughout his military career:

In districts and neighborhoods where the army is unmolested, no destruction of (private) property should be permitted; but should guerrillas or bush wackers molest our march, or should the inhabitants burn bridges, obstruct roads, or otherwise manifest local hostility, then army commanders should order and enforce a devastation more or less relentless, according to the measure of such hostility.[75]

Sherman kept the responsibility for damages squarely on the shoulders of the Southern leadership. If they cooperated with him, he could be generous; if they opposed him, he was unrelenting in punishment.

Sherman's conduct in allegedly burning Columbia out of sheer malice and revenge for South Carolina's part in starting the Civil War seemed to his generation to mark the apex of his cruelty. Yet Sherman told the veterans of the Army of the Potomac in 1881, ''I saw with my own eyes cotton bales which had been set on fire by the Confederate cavalry. Without Logan's troops not a house would have escaped.''[76] If there were a few troops who got out of hand it was because, Sherman claimed, they found whiskey in the town the Confederates had made a liquor depot. Furthermore, the fire spread because ''God Almighty started the wind that carried it.''[77] ''If I had made up my mind to burn Columbia, I would have burnt it with no more feeling than I would a common prairie dog village," Sherman testified, "but I did not do it."[78]

Sherman noted in 1881 that after 329 pages of testimony in 23 legal cases brought against him, an international commission of judges disallowed the claim that "Columbia was wantonly fired by General Sherman."[79] What he did at Columbia, as reflected partly in his pocket diary, was to deliberately destroy only the public buildings. Then he left behind 500 beef cattle and 100 muskets for the citizens "to arm a guard to maintain order after we should leave the neighborhood."[80] Sherman consistently maintained, "Personally, I had not malice or desire to destroy that city or its inhabitants."[81]

The proof of such personal intent to avoid wanton injury in the Carolinas is in Sherman's continuing offer of peaceful terms to his enemies. In public and largely for propaganda purposes, Sherman would threaten to turn his army loose; in his words, the soldiers were "burning to avenge the national wrong which they attach to large cities which have been so prominent in dragging our country into civil war."[82] Thus he emphasized on one occasion that he would make North Carolina "howl"; but he also told his cavalry commander, General Kilpatrick, to deal "as moderately and fairly by North Carolinians as possible, and fan the flame of discord already subsisting between them and their proud cousins of South Carolina."[83] Finally, to General Joseph E. Johnston, Sherman wrote on 14 April 1865:

I am fully empowered to arrange with you any terms for the suspension of further hostilities between the armies commanded by you and those commanded by myself. . . . General Stoneman is under my command, and my order will suspend any devastation or destruction contemplated by him. I will add that I really desire to save the people of North Carolina the damage they would sustain by the march of this army through the central or western parts of the State.[84]

Sherman's comment to Johnston is not at variance with his famous letter of 12 September 1864 to Atlanta Mayor James M. Calhoun, in which Sherman promised, "When peace does come, you may call on me for any thing. Then will I share with you the last cracker, and watch with you to shield your homes and families against danger from every quarter."[85]

An Integrated Theory

With the surrender of Johnston's Army in North Carolina under terms other than those generously proposed, General Sherman's combat experience came to an end.[86] He had evolved an ethical theory of warfare, however, that would influence the conduct of the Indian Wars in the West for the next 20 years.

Sherman believed that society without law was chaotic. In 1860 he wrote, perhaps reflecting some of the old West Point ideas he had studied two decades before:

The law is or should be our king; we should obey it, not because it meets our approval but because it is the law and because obedience in some shape is necessary to every system of civilized government. For years this tendency to anarchy had gone on till now every state and country and town . . . makes and enforces the local prejudices as the law of the land. This is the real trouble, it is not slavery, it is the democratic spirit which substitutes mere opinions for law.[87]

The South violated the law first, Sherman believed. Southerners willingly participated in the 1860 election, but "because that election did not result as they wanted, they refused to abide by the result and appealed to war."[88] That decision, according to Sherman, was folly, madness, treason, and "a crime against civilization."[89] It left the South free to treat with foreign powers against the interests of the United States as a whole.

Sherman came to believe that the civil war the South was waging was a rebellion; therefore, under Vattel's old definition, the unjust and lawless rebels were subject to severe punishment.[90] Further, Sherman's theory of punishment leaned heavily on the ideas of collective responsibility and retaliation to prevent further cruelty by the enemy.[91] He instructed General Edwards R. S. Canby, for example, to hold Southern civilians accountable for guerrilla outrages, "for if they fire on boats with women and children in [them], we can fire and burn houses with women and children."[92] This was possible, of course, because warfare was waged between "all the individuals" on one side and "all the individuals" on the other. Eventually the enemy would tire and peace would return.

Sherman realized that war was not an end in itself, but a means to an end. "The legitimate object of war is a more perfect peace" under the authority of a lawful, democratic government.[93] Toward that end Sherman believed that warfare must be waged on a psychological as well as a military level. Thus many of Sherman's public statements during the Georgia campaign were designed to make the enemy "fear and dread us" and may have accounted for the fact that Sherman's armies suffered fewer campaign casualties in 1864 than his Confederate opponents.[94] General Grant, as a matter of fact, characterized Sherman's occupation of Atlanta as a "political campaign."[95]

On another level, however, Sherman saw war in somewhat metaphysical terms. He told the graduating class at West Point in 1876 that "wars are only the means to an end – not necessarily inhuman, barbarous, abhorred by God." Indeed, he suggested that "war is of divine origin," like lightning which strikes the just and the unjust alike. "We were born in war, baptized in war, and we have had wars of aggression and defence," Sherman told the cadets, but there is still "a Divinity that shapes our ends."[96]

How could war be of divine origin? Sherman wrote to Major Henry Turner two years after his West Point address:

I believe God governs this world, with all its life, animal, vegetable and human, by invariable laws, resulting in the greatest good, though sometimes working seeming hardships. The idea of a vocation from God seems to me irreligious and I would look for the inspiration of a vocation in the opposite quarter (the Devil). When anybody assumes 'vocation' their reason and all sense ceases and man becomes simply a blind animal. My idea of God is that he has given man reason, and he had no right to disregard it.[97]

Presumably the abandonment of reason brought on war, which was its own punishment in Sherman's view. Since punishment for the crime of unrestrained passion is part of the invariable law of God, war is punishment of divine origin which affects both the guilty and the innocent. The best one could do in such circumstances was to end the war as quickly and as justly as possible.

Sherman, in his Civil War years, did not abandon his attachment to the law or to some of the ethical concepts he may have learned at West Point. Rather, he placed the laws of warfare on a continuum of expediency. The important thing was not the means but the end, and to this point Sherman was clearly a utilitarian thinker. What the South learned to fear was not Sherman's aggression nor his lack of mercy. It was his revenge.

Yet Sherman's job was not to philosophize, but to destroy the roots of serious rebellion, Southern and Indian, and he spent his entire military career to that end. His doctrines of collective responsibility and retaliation were rationalizations for ending a destructive war. They should be fully understandable rationalizations to those who are heirs not only of Atlanta and Columbia, but also of Dresden, Hiroshima, and Nagasaki.

In the last analysis, Sherman may have contributed something relatively important in the field of military ethics. Foreseeing the death and destruction that war would bring, he wept on hearing of the secession of South Carolina in 1860.[98] Nineteen years later, he would tell a Michigan audience: "It is only those who have neither fired a shot nor heard the shrieks and groans of the wounded who cry aloud for blood, more vengeance, more desolation. War is hell."[99] Yet even in hell Sherman tried to show that when circumstances allowed, there should be a regard if not for chivalry at least for the laws of nations. He was not the author of either the theory or the ethics of total war, but, in his generation, he may have been the leading intellectual apologist for both. To that extent he was not a total warrior completely devoid of principle.

NOTES

1. John B. Walters, *Merchant of Terror: General Sherman and Total War* (New York: Bobbs-Merrill, 1973), pp. 137-38, 200.
2. Cited in Elizabeth H. McCallie, *The Atlanta Campaign* (Atlanta: The Atlanta Historical Society, 1939), p. 26.
3. Ibid.
4. John B. Hood, *Advance and Retreat* (New Orleans: G. T. Beauregard, 1880), p. 230.
5. Cited in Thomas C. Leonard, *Above the Battle* (New York: Oxford Univ. Press, 1978), p. 13.
6. Jefferson Davis, *The Rise and Fall of the Confederate Government* (New York: D. Appleton and Co., 1881), II, 570.
7. "J. Davis' Opinion," *Army-Navy Journal*, 10 May 1884.
8. W. T. Sherman to Captain J. H. Lee of Spottswood, N.J., 14 June 1881, in The Papers of William T. Sherman, Letterbook 95, USMA Archives Microfilm Collection. (Hereinafter cited as Sherman Papers.)
9. Robert G. Athearn, *William Tecumseh Sherman and the Settlement of the West* (Norman: Univ. of Oklahoma Press, 1956), pp. 69-70; and Lloyd Lewis, *Sherman: Fighting Prophet* (New York: Harcourt, Brace, 1932), p. 597.
10. Athearn, pp. 69-70; and Lewis, p. 598.
11. W. T. Sherman to John Sherman, 31 August 1839, Sherman Papers.

12. William T. Sherman, *Memoirs* (Bloomington: Indiana Univ. Press, 1957), II, 396.

13. George P. Winton, Jr., "Ante-Bellum Military Instruction of West Point Officers and Its Influence upon Confederate Military Organization and Operations," (Ph.D. dissertation, Univ. of South Carolina, 1972), p. 46.

14. USMA Library, "Entry of Books Issued to Cadets on Saturday Afternoons 1840-1843," in the USMA Archives, shows that Cadet Sherman checked out the *Science of War*, two volumes with plates, on 2 March 1840.

15. John Michael O'Connor, trans., *Vernon's Science of War and Fortification* (New York: J. Seymour, 1817), I, 10, 362.

16. William C. Brown, "General Sherman and the Infantry and Cavalry School," *Journal of the United States Cavalry Association*, 16 (July 1905), 124.

17. D. H. Mahan to the Hon. Gouverneur Kemble, 26 September 1864, in Edward Holden's *Library Manual*, II, 59, USMA Archives.

18. Lewis, p. 56.

19. USMA Academic Board Minutes, 5 November 1838, USMA Archives.

20. Cited in Wilbur Thomas, *General George H. Thomas* (New York: Exposition Press, 1964), p. 63. See also Douglas S. Freeman, *R. E. Lee: A Biography* (New York: Scribner's Sons, 1934), I, 78-79.

21. E. D. Keyes, *Fifty Years Observation of Men and Events* (New York: Scribner's Sons, 1884), p. 77; and Thomas Jackson Arnold, *Early Life and Letters of Stonewall Jackson* (Richmond Va.: Dietz Press, 1957), p. 73.

22. Walter L. Fleming, "Jefferson Davis at West Point," *Metropolitan Magazine*, 1908, p. 282.

23. Jasper Adams to Major R. Delafield, 3 February 1840, in the Jasper Adams Papers, USMA Archives, Drawer F.

24. Ibid.

25. USMA Academic Board Minutes, 28 October 1839 and 15 November 1839, USMA Archives.

26. William Paley, *The Principles of Moral and Political Philosophy* (Boston: West and Richardson, 1815) p. 463.

27. Ibid., p. 465.

28. Ibid., pp. 386-87.

29. Ibid., p. 64.

30. Ibid.

31. James Kent, *Commentaries on American Law* (New York: O. Halsted, 1826), I, 45.

32. Ibid., I, 53.

33. Ibid., I, 89.

34. Ibid., I, 199.

35. Ibid.

36. Ibid., I, 179.

37. Jasper Adams to Major R. Delafield, 3 February 1840, in the Jasper Adams Papers, USMA Archives, Drawer F.

38. W. T. Sherman to John Sherman, 14 January 1840, Sherman Papers.

39. Lee placed second in "Natural and National Law and Ethics" in 1829; Jackson was fifth in 1846. Grant was below average in ethics, and Sheridan had to spend a fifth year at West Point because of problems in conduct. It is interesting to note that Sherman, Grant, and Sheridan all graduated from West Point as cadet privates due to excess demerits.

40. Lewis, p. 442.

41. W. T. Sherman to "My dear Sister," 16 January 1841, Sherman Papers.

42. Lewis, p. 68.

43. W. T. Sherman to John Sherman, 7 March 1840, Sherman Papers.

44. Photographs of Sherman's letter of resignation dated 18 January 1861 are in the USMA Library.

45. Walters, pp. 20-21.

46. Ibid, p. 22.

47. Ibid., p. 21; and W. T. Sherman, *Memoirs*, II, 181.

48. Lewis, p. 188.

49. *The War of Rebellion: A Compilation of the Official Records of the Union and Confederate Armies* (Washington: GPO, 1887), series 2, vol. 2, p. 814. (Hereinafter cited as *Official Records*).

50. Jefferson Davis, *Rise and Fall of the Confederate Government*, II, 11; *Official Records*, series 1, vol. 17, part 2, pp. 16-17.
51. W. T. Sherman to James Guthrie, 14 August 1864, cited in Lewis, p. 398.
52. Lewis, p. 442.
53. William S. McFeely, *Grant* (New York: W. W. Norton, 1981), p. 81.
54. Ibid., p. 79.
55. Thomas Jordan, *General Orders from Adjutant and Inspector General's Office, C.S. Army in 1862* (Charleston, S.C.: Evans and Cogswell, 1863), p. 66.
56. John F. Callan, *The Military Laws of the United States* (Philadelphia: George W. Childs, 1863), p. 521.
57. Jordan, p. 68.
58. *Official Records*, series 1, vo. 17, part 2, p. 150.
59. Ibid., pp. 154-55.
60. Walters, pp. 57-58.
61. U. S. Grant, *Personal Memoirs of U. S. Grant* (London: Sampson Law, Marston, Searle and Rivington, 1886), II, 507.
62. W. T. Sherman to John Sherman, 1 October 1862, in the USMA Library, LAC 11541 [Library of American Civilization, on microfiche], p. 166.
63. *Official Records*, series 1, vol. 17, part 2, pp. 261-62.
64. Ibid., p. 280.
65. Ibid., p. 307.
66. W. T. Sherman, *Memoirs*, II, 132, 208.
67. Cited in Archer Jones, "Jomini and the Strategy of the American Civil War, A Reinterpretation," *Military Affairs,* 34 (December 1970), 130.
68. Lewis, p. 424.
69. Vattel held that "the right to make war ceases upon the offer of just terms." Charles G. Fenwick, ed., *The Law of Nations* (Washington: Carnegie Institute, 1916), p. 254.
70. W. T. Sherman, *Memoirs*, II, 138; and Charles C. Jones, *The Siege of Savannah* (Albany, N.Y.: Joel Munsell, 1874), p. 13.
71. Lewis, p. 423.
72. W. T. Sherman, *Memoirs*, II, 182-83.
73. Ibid., II, 233.
74. Ibid., II, 267.
75. Ibid., II, 175.
76. W. T. Sherman, "Address to the Army of the Potomac," *Army-Navy Journal*, 11 June 1881, p. 945.
77. Lewis, pp. 506-07.
78. Ibid., p. 508.
79. W. T. Sherman, "Address to the Army of the Potomac," p. 945.
80. W. T. Sherman, *Memoirs*, II, 287.
81. Ibid., II, 286.
82. Ibid., II, 211.
83. Lewis, pp. 509, 514.
84. W. T. Sherman, *Memoirs*, II, 347.
85. Ibid., II, 127.
86. Sherman proposed that the Confederate armies deposit their arms in their own state arsenals, that the officers and legislatures of the several states be recognized by the executive of the United States upon taking an oath to support the Constitution, and that the people be guaranteed their political rights and franchises under a general amnesty. Sherman saw these terms as effecting the will of Abraham Lincoln. The assassination of Lincoln led to their disapproval by President Johnson and Secretary Stanton. See Philemon Tecumseh Sherman, "Address to the Society of the Army of the Tennessee," p. 20, in the USMA Archives.
87. Lewis, p. 134.
88. Lewis, p. 332.
89. Lewis, p. 138; and W. T. Sherman, *Memoirs*, II, 152, 167.
90. Philemon T. Sherman, p. 18.
91. W. T. Sherman, *Memoirs*, II, 279-80; Athearn, pp. 69-70, 131, 279; and Lewis, pp. 579-99.
92. Lewis, p. 332.

93. W. T. Sherman, *Memoirs*, xii. The quotation is the inscription on Sherman's statue in Washington. See also W. T. Sherman, *Address to the Graduating Class of the U.S. Military Academy, June 14, 1876* (New York: Van Nostrand, 1876), p. 26.

94. Cited in Archer Jones, "Jomini and the Strategy of the American Civil War," p. 130. See also Timothy H. Donovan et al., *The American Civil War* (West Point, N.Y.: USMA Department of History, 1980), p. 325.

95. McFeely, p. 188.

96. W. T. Sherman, *Address to the Graduating Class . . . June 14, 1876*, p. 29; and W. T. Sherman, *Memoirs*, II, 126.

97. Cited in Joseph T. Durkin, *General Sherman's Son* (New York: Farrar, Straus, and Cudahy, 1959), p. 53.

98. Lewis, p. 138.

99. W. T. Sherman, "An Address Before the Graduating Class of the Michigan Military Academy, June 19, 1879," in *Bartlett's Familiar Quotations*, ed. Christopher Morley (New York: Little, Brown, 1957), p. 366.

This article appeared in the summer 1982 issue of *Parameters*.

9

MacArthur's Lapses from an Envelopment Strategy in 1945

by D. CLAYTON JAMES

The strategy which General of the Army Douglas MacArthur adopted in 1945 in the southwest Pacific campaign has received scant attention from historians. Symbolic of this neglect is the omission in the American Army's series on the Pacific conflict of a sequel to Louis Morton's *Strategy and Command: The First Two Years*, whose coverage ends in late 1943. The treatment of MacArthur's late-war strategy in most college-level textbooks on recent American or military history ranges from no mention whatsoever to propagation of a host of myths. This essay challenges three of those myths still widely believed: (1) That after the Joint Chiefs of Staff finally authorized an invasion of Luzon, the directive was subsequently implemented by MacArthur in the manner envisioned by his superiors; (2) that having gained credit, often justifiable, for brilliant moves bypassing strong Japanese forces, MacArthur continued to the war's end his policy of bypassing and thus neutralizing the enemy forces in his theater's rear areas, rather than attacking them; and (3) that during the final weeks preceding Japan's capitulation, the next major invasion that MacArthur had in mind was Operation Olympic, the landing on Japan's southernmost island, Kyushu, which was set for November 1945.[1]

Although MacArthur had proclaimed upon arriving in Australia in March 1942 that he would return to liberate the Philippines, the Joint Chiefs had not given much thought then to a long-range plan to defeat Japan, much less to a counteroffensive led by him. Indeed, the development of a plan that would most directly and rapidly bring about Japan's surrender did not become a seriously debated issue until well into 1943 when the Allied buildup in the Pacific warranted such consideration. The Joint Chiefs were flexible in their thinking at first and weighed a wide assortment of strategic alternatives for dealing with Japan. In no small measure because of pressures from MacArthur and Fleet Admiral Ernest J. King to give priority to the axis of advance each favored – respectively, the New Guinea-Philippines axis from the south and the central Pacific route from the east – the Joint Chiefs gradually narrowed down the alternatives to the seizure of either Luzon or Formosa as prerequisite to an invasion of Japan. King had long objected to continuing a major offensive via the southwest Pacific axis, and by late spring 1944 Generals George C. Marshall and Henry H. Arnold were also increasingly critical of the liabilities of an attack on Luzon. Marshall felt that MacArthur's Luzon plan would be "the slow way" and "would take a very much longer time than to make the cut across" from the Marianas to Formosa.[2] MacArthur argued that the Formosa plan was militarily "unsound" whereas political, humanitarian, and strategic considerations "demand the reoccupation of the Philippines."[3] Through studies extending over a year and a half the Joint Chiefs and their committees had been steadfastly concerned with determining which plan would be the most logistically feasible, the most economical in manpower and materiel losses, and the most strategically decisive in producing the fall of Japan. They arrived at the decision in favor of MacArthur's proposal with reluctance and trepidation. By late September 1944, Admirals King, Chester W. Nimitz, and their planners admitted that the Formosa invasion was not practical in the near future due to insurmountable logistical difficulties. On 3 October the Joint Chiefs issued a directive authorizing the Luzon operation.

At the Yalta Conference in February 1945, while MacArthur's armies were fighting on Leyte and Luzon, the Joint Chiefs assured their British counterparts that they had no intention of committing United States forces to reconquer the rest of the Philippines (such as Mindanao, Panay, Negros, Palawan, Bohol, and Cebu) and the Netherlands East Indies. For several months, however, MacArthur had been working on his Victor Plan for the seizure of the remainder of the Philippines and his Oboe Plan for the invasion of the East Indies rather than leave the two large island groupings to wilt on the vine. In fact, he had decided as early as September 1944 to send Lieutenant General Robert L. Eichelberger's Eighth Army to seize the rest of the Philippines as soon as General Walter Krueger's Sixth Army was securely entrenched on Luzon. A few weeks after the Lingayen beachhead on Luzon was established in January 1945, and while the Sixth Army was suffering severe losses in battles for Manila and other strong points on Luzon, MacArthur unleashed the Eighth Army in the reconquest of the Philippines to the south. By the time the Joint Chiefs changed their minds and issued a directive in April authorizing operations in the Philippines below Luzon, MacArthur's forces already had undertaken eight of the eleven major amphibious operations which proved necessary to secure that territory. Astoundingly, the Joint Chiefs resigned themselves to MacArthur's fait accompli and raised no objections to the eight operations conducted prior to their directive. Pondering the "mystery how and whence . . . MacArthur derived his authority to use United States forces to liberate one Philippine island after another" at a time when he "had no specific directive for anything subsequent to Luzon," Rear Admiral Samuel Eliot Morison, the distinguished naval historian, concludes that "the J.C.S. simply permitted MacArthur to do as he pleased, up to a point."[4]

A variety of factors underlay MacArthur's motivation in attacking the previously bypassed Philippine islands. The Philippine political faction of Manuel Roxas, which had MacArthur's backing, was eager to have the areas south of Luzon liberated before the Philippine Congress convened in June, because political sentiments there were predominantly against President Sergio Osmeña. As it turned out, the freed southern congressmen helped the Roxas faction to attain majorities in the Philippine Senate and House. Also, MacArthur felt a strong duty to free the entire archipelago lest the bypassed enemy troops turn with vengeance upon hapless American prisoners and Filipinos, as had occurred in the Palawan massacre of December 1944.[5] Moreover, use of the Eighth Army, Seventh Fleet, and Thirteenth Air Force in these operations blocked their transfer by the Joint Chiefs to Nimitz's theater in the central Pacific, a possibility had they remained idle for long. In addition, MacArthur wanted the central and southern Philippines in order to establish air bases to cover his projected Borneo operations and to train and stage the expected huge influx of units from Europe for the invasion of Japan.

MacArthur's dispatch of the Eighth Army to the Japanese-held Philippine islands south of Luzon and his transfer there of three Sixth Army divisions had a crippling impact on Luzon operations. Especially in the hard-fought battles at Wawa Dam, Villa Verde Trail, and Balete Pass, the lack of adequate troops and firepower was sorely felt by the Sixth Army. Operating against perhaps the ablest Japanese ground commander, General Yamashita, and the largest enemy army that American soldiers met during the Pacific war, the Sixth Army found itself locked in a costly, drawn-out, and frustrating campaign on Luzon, with Yamashita cornered but still fighting with over 50,000 troops when the war ended. MacArthur would have been wiser to have used the Eighth Army primarily to expedite the reconquest of Luzon, for few bases set up in the central and southern islands proved of value later and the beleaguered enemy garrisons south of Luzon were so isolated that they posed no threat to MacArthur's lines of communication or his future moves. The United States Army's official history states frankly that, for the most part, the southern campaigns "had no strategic importance" but "were designed for the purpose of liberating Filipinos, reestablishing lawful government, and destroying Japanese forces."[6] This was fortunately not general knowledge to the hard-pressed men of the Sixth Army during their bloody campaign on Luzon.

Continuing in the spring of 1945 to send his forces on tangents south of Luzon, MacArthur disregarded advice from Washington planners and the Australian high command in embarking on an invasion of Borneo. In early 1944 the Joint Chiefs had ordered staff studies on a possible seizure of petroleum-rich Borneo, but the idea was dropped because the undertaking would have drained MacArthur's resources, so powerful was the enemy's estimated strength in the Greater Sundas. Yet MacArthur offered a plan to the Joint Chiefs in February 1945 for an invasion of North Borneo by the Australian I Corps. He maintained that "90 days after the beginning of such an expedition it would be possible to begin operations for the production of crude expedition it would be possible to begin operations for the production of crude oil,"[7] but the Army-Navy Petroleum Board in Washington countered that it would take a year or more. Nevertheless, at Yalta later that month the Combined Chiefs authorized him to invade "British Borneo," that is, Sarawak, Brunei, and North Borneo, if an invasion of Japan did not become possible before the end of 1945. Prime Minister John Curtin and General Thomas Blamey of Australia protested his proposed use of their nation's forces in Borneo, criticizing mainly the command arrangement and strategic wisdom of the plan. MacArthur, however, finally won them to a grudging acceptance of his scheme.

In March he came forth with his six-phase Oboe Plan, calling for the invasions, in order, of Dutch Borneo, Java, the rest of the Netherlands East Indies, and finally British Borneo. Interestingly, though his superiors had told him to go ahead with contingency plans for only an attack on British Borneo, his Oboe Plan relegated it to last among the East Indies operations he intended to stage. Without much enthusiasm for the idea, the Joints Chiefs in April approved a revised version of Oboe that included only landings at Tarakan (May), Brunei Bay (June), and Balikpapan (July). These operations along the eastern and western coasts of Borneo were successfully executed, with MacArthur providing strong American air, naval, and logistical support for the Australian I Corps.

While the American Eighth Army and the Australian I Corps were following MacArthur's southward tangents in 1945, the Australian First Army was committed to annihilating the bypassed enemy forces in Northeast New Guinea, Bougainville, and New Britain. MacArthur had informed Blamey in July 1944 that soon his First Army was to "assume the responsibility for the continued neutralization of the ememy in Australian and British territory and mandates in the [Southwest Pacific Area]."[8] Upon the arrival of the Australians that autumn, six American divisions were released to join the operations in the Philippines. Until March 1945 the First Army generally confined its role to passively guarding perimeters around the remaining enemy units in the theater's rear areas. But at a meeting with MacArthur in Manila that month, Blamey learned of the plans for the Eighth Army in the Philippines south of Luzon, which the Australian commander concluded were based on "political rather than military grounds." Forthwith Blamey began to press for, and obtained, authorization for his First Army to go on the offensive. He shrewdly argued his case, citing the Eighth Army's action as precedent: "Just as it is necessary to destroy the Japanese in the Philippines, so it is necessary that we should destroy the enemy in Australian territories where the conditions are favourable for such action and so liberate the natives from Japanese domination."[9]

Australian casualties from combat and diseases were alarmingly heavy as

Blamey's troops attacked the trapped enemy forces in the dense jungles of New Guinea, Bougainville, and New Britain during the ensuing months. Why MacArthur, who had taken such pride in the lives saved earlier by bypassing these Japanese units, reversed himself and allowed Blamey to nullify the strategic value of the previous envelopments is not fully known, but probably was related to pressure on him from the Australian Government and public to either use the First Army in combat or send it home. The Australian Army's official chronicle is blunt in judging MacArthur's ''complex of decisions, some contradictory and some illogical,'' in 1945 which resulted in the Australian I Corps, ''well equipped and with powerful air and naval support . . . fighting battles of doubtful value in Borneo,'' while units of the First Army in the regions to the east ''were fighting long and bitter campaigns (whose value was doubted) in which they were short of air and naval support, and suffered . . . a poverty of ships and landing craft.''[10]

The generous assistance that MacArthur provided the Australians in Borneo was directly related to his scheme to develop bases there for an invasion of Java – a plan that he had never dismissed despite its rejection in the first Oboe Plan he had presented to the Joint Chiefs. General Eichelberger, Eighth Army commander, said that MacArthur confided to him in late spring that ''if the Navy idea of piddling around for a long time before doing anything against the Japanese homeland carries through, he still wants me to go into Java rather than have my troops sit around and stagnate.''[11] Based on the evidence of similar comments in interviews with other officers close to MacArthur, together with the still tentative and confused preparations for Operation Olympic (Kyushu invasion) by early August as well as MacArthur's previous record of success in persuading or ignoring the Joint Chiefs, it is highly probable that he would have sent the Eighth Army into Java about September. In an understatement the Australian offical history says, ''In retrospect the wisdom of embarking upon this third thrust – westward against Japanese forces isolated in the Indies – seems doubtful.''[12] It was fortunate for the lives of the Allied troops and for MacArthur's reputation that the war ended before he got his way on the Java plan, for that attack could have produced not only a tragic bloodbath in Java but also a logistical paralysis for the impending invasion of Kyushu.

If before the zenith of the Luzon-versus-Formosa debate in 1944 the Joint Chiefs had been able to foresee the tangential moves south of Luzon that MacArthur would launch, they surely would have terminated his offensive after the conquest of Netherlands New Guinea. It is regrettable that MacArthur's strategy in 1945 has gotten little scholarly notice, but it is tragic that the decisionmakers in the White House and Pentagon contemplating the North Korean invasion of the South, in June 1950, did not recall his behavior pattern of five years before. Perhaps some of them had begun to notice by April

1951 that there were similarities between MacArthur's strategic concepts and his attitude toward his superiors during the last stages of the Pacific war and during the first nine months of the Korean conflict.

NOTES

1. This essay is based mainly upon a synthesis of data in D. Clayton James, *The Years of MacArthur*, Vol. II, *1941-1945* (Boston: Houghton Mifflin, 1975), especially chaps. 9, 12, 13, 16, and 17. The footnotes for the relevant passages in these chapters, in turn, cite the primary and secondary materials used in the research. Hereafter in the notes of this essay sources will be cited only when actually quoted.
2. Henry L. Stimson, Diary, 22 June 1944, Yale University Library, New Haven, Conn.
3. Douglas MacArthur to George C. Marshall, 18 June 1944. Records of War Department Operations Division, Executive File, Record Group 165, National Archives, Washington D.C.
4. Samuel E. Morison, *History of United States Naval Operations in World War II*, Vol. XIII, *The Liberation of the Philippines: Luzon, Mindanao, and Visaya, 1944-1945* (Boston: Little, Brown, 1959) p. 214.
5. On Palawan, a Philippine island southwest of Luzon, Japanese guards at a prisoner of war camp panicked on 14 December 1944 when news came that MacArthur's forces were approaching (Mindoro was invaded 15 December). The guards poured gasoline on 149 American prisoners, set them afire, and machine-gunned the survivors (miraculously, nine managed to escape).
6. Robert R. Smith, *Triumph in the Philippines*, one of several works constituting *United States Army in World War II: The War in the Pacific*, volume 2 of the official history published by the Office of the Chief of Military History (Washington: Department of the Army, 1963), pp. 584-55.
7. MacArthur to Marshall, 5 February 1945, Operations Division, Executive File.
8. MacArthur to Thomas Blamey, 12 July 1944, Records of General Headquarters, Southwest Pacific Area, Record Group 3, MacArthur Memorial Bureau of Archives, Norfolk, Va.
9. Blamey, Appreciation [Report] on Operations of the AMF [Australian Military Forces] in New Guinea, New Britain, and the Solomon Islands, 18 May 1945, quoted in Gavin Long, *The Final Campaigns. Australia in the War of 1939-1945*, Series I (Canberra: Australian War Memorial, 1963), p. 609.
10. Long, p. 547.
11. Robert L. Eichelberger to "Miss Em" [his wife], 28 April 1945, Robert L. Eichelberger Papers, Duke University Library, Durham, N.C.
12. Long, p. 547.

This article appeared in the June 1980 issue of *Parameters*.

10

Clients of ULTRA: American Captains

by HAROLD C. DEUTSCH

The United States was a late entrant into World War II, 27 months after Adolf Hitler invaded Poland. The coming of war in Europe had only slight effect on the American defense posture, including, of course, the area of intelligence. It was not anti-war sentiment alone that operated against involvement but an optimistic estimate of the resources of the belligerents. This engendered such confidence in Allied victory that few could perceive either a moral obligation or a compelling national interest favoring American intervention. The disaster in France of May-June 1940 produced a shock that made eventual involvement conceivable. Closely in line with this was the rapidly worsening state of relations with Japan. Accordingly, vastly expanded ground, naval, and air programs were launched nearly a year after war had begun to inundate Europe and continued to grow during the following 18 months.

Among the branches of the armed services involved in this overhaul was a perennial stepchild of military establishments, intelligence. Past neglect, however, did not mean special consideration now. Only the intercept and cryptanalytical departments had enjoyed a certain kudos during the interwar years. The beginning of the 1930s had witnessed a national sensation with the revelation that breaking Japanese codes had played an important part in American diplomatic success at the 1922 Washington Arms Conference.[1] Informed military and government circles were further impressed by the remarkable work of William Friedman and his associates for Army intelligence. About 1935 they had begun to concentrate on Japanese cipher machines and only two years later scored their first major triumph in the solution of the Red machine. An even greater achievement was scored in September 1940 with the breaking of the infinitely more difficult Purple machine after 18 months of frantic team effort led by Frank B. Rowlett. If there is anyone who merits, the accolade "the man who broke Purple," it was he rather than Friedman, who was ill and incapacitated during much of this period.[2] MAGIC thus took a vital place beside ULTRA as a first-line war winner.[3]

Strictly speaking, the terms ULTRA and MAGIC should apply only to the exploitation of information derived from intercepted messages transmitted by the Enigma, Red, and Purple machines. However, both popular and historical usage have served to broaden these concepts and to apply them widely to interception and cryptanalysis of high-level wireless communications, at times even to wireless communications generally. As employed in this article, ULTRA will refer essentially to Enigma traffic and MAGIC, more broadly, to work of Americans on high-level wireless signals of the Japanese in the Pacific conflict.

Despite much debate, it remains uncertain just when American cryptanalysts were first initiated into the mysteries of the Enigma by the British. Their own labors had been almost exclusively centered on forms of Japanese communications. Though some attention had been given to German and Italian codes, this had been rather haphazard and had achieved no substantial breakthroughs. Guesses on just when London drew the veil guarding the triumphs of Bletchley Park vary from the period of first scientific exchanges in the late summer and autumn of 1940 to meetings between cryptographic specialists early in 1942.[4]

In any event, there is no evidence even to hint that American military leaders destined for the European Theater of Operations were apprised, before leaving, of the intelligence windfall that awaited them in the form of ULTRA. Most of the principal American commanders shared with their British colleagues an initial discomfort, heavily mixed with skepticism, when finally confronted with this startling information. It was too sensational, too breathtaking to pass easily for real. Of course, there was also the traditional professional military bias against intelligence, tainted as it perforce is with the ungentlemanly game of espionage.

US Clients of ULTRA in Europe

Almost alone, Dwight D. Eisenhower did not share the prejudice and distaste for intelligence. No doubt his own personal conversion to the cult of ULTRA also owed much to the impressiveness and solemnity of his initiation by Winston Churchill.[5] At any rate, as will be seen later, he was to show little reluctance to venture one of history's great gambles, the invasion of Normandy, in association with a deception that relied heavily on controls demanding multiple exploitation of ULTRA. Like most British commanders, his principal lieutenants held back at first. The less-imaginative Bradley for a time was enrolled in the "too-good-to-be-true" brotherhood. Only the success of the deception on the invasion made him into a complete convert. Patton courteously told his briefer. "I do not go much for this sort of thing." Mark Clark carried his lack of enthusiasm to the point of rudeness, interrupting Group Captain F. W. Winterbottom's explanations by leaving him in the middle of them with an excuse of having much to do.

In a sense, Eisenhower, albeit in less despotic fashion, acted something like the part of his mentor, Churchill, in constraining his subordinates to make at least a show of respect for what ULTRA was saying to them. British commanders, acutely aware that the Prime Minister was also reading ULTRA items that came to them via the Special Liaison Units, knew that their professional lives depended on close attention. In time, of course, neither British nor American military leaders required much urging to become zealous worshippers at the shrine of ULTRA. Day after day the proof of the pudding lay in the eating. At Mortain, Bradley won what was perhaps the most clear-cut ULTRA victory in the European Theater. Any final doubts Patton may have entertained vanished after ULTRA had guided him around the western German flank via Avranches. He has been characterized as having been one of the most effective users of ULTRA.

Clark's role as one of ULTRA's clients is a subject of much controversy. Winterbottom never forgave him the slight put upon him, and British authors, in particular, have tended to be rough on him.[6] As the ULTRA sensation spread in the mid-1970s, he countered mounting criticism by stressing his own high estimate of its contributions to decision-making.[7] Yet each phase of the war in Italy regarding which he has been widely criticized (the crisis during the landing at Salerno; failing to oblige General Lucas to strike inland from the beachhead at Anzio; and the dash to Rome after the collapse of the Gustav Line) is claimed to be an instance where closer attention to intelligence yielded by ULTRA would have reduced losses or enhanced success. The only instance where Clark holds ULTRA to have determined his decision is an alibi for staying put at Anzio. Learning of German concentrations aimed to contain or erase the beachhead, he avers that these made it too precarious to stick to the original scenario of aiming for the Alban Hills. Yet each of the German units involved had been identified by Army group G-2 *before* the landing was determined, and their moves to central Italy had been fully anticipated.[8]

It is ever a risk to anticipate too confidently an ultimate verdict of history, but it seems likely to be a mixed one in judging the effectiveness of the use of ULTRA by American military leaders. Like their British counterparts, they were in the main disinclined to engage in adventurous moves, the Rommel-like *volte-face*, changing dispositions instantly on the basis of new information. This, of course, does not apply to defensive situations.

The reasons for holding back this way on the British side are not of concern here. As for those which moved Americans, German military figures with whom one conversed after the war, when pressed, would confess astonishment at what they thought a lack of daring and constant leaning toward safer courses. Almost always, Patton would be cited as an exception.

Explanations which spring to mind include a certain awe of German opponents who already have so much war experience and who could lean on a prestigious staff tradition. Caution was further advised by the need of gaining experience in the handling of large formations and problems associated with the use of unblooded troops. Failure to exploit the successful landing at Anzio is a case in point.

One instance where ULTRA information facilitated a major advance is that of the 7th Army after its landing in southern France. The decision here for an immediate leap forward was based on ULTRA's revelation that the routes in question were not to be defended. This, however, can scarcely be defined as an "offensive" in the usual sense. It was the 7th Army, also, that later was a major beneficiary of intelligence in a defensive sense in being able to wreck the German New Year's offensive of 1945.

This last experience helped to convince the gifted ULTRA guardian of the 7th Army, Major Donald S. Bussey, that ULTRA's "primary value lay in static/defensive situations," a feature which he believed to be largely true of intelligence generally.[9] Defensive dispositions can often change with comparative facility; the offensive demands more in the way of planning and preparation. This would seem to be especially true in operational terms, where the American reticence concerning bold, offensive strokes as evidenced in the ETO would most clearly manifest itself.

The picture assumes a different aspect when it touches on strategy. There is a considerable tendency among students of ULTRA to underestimate its effect on strategic decision-making as well as on the execution of strategic plans. Obviously (except perhaps negatively in compelling the abandonment of plans already made), it is highly unlikely that strategy would be much affected by isolated items of information. On the other hand, the steady accumulation of data and development of insights gained from intercepted messages over a considerable period are indispensable aids to decision-making. Often most important, the types of control inherent in ULTRA for keeping track of an enemy's comprehension of what was toward were vital to the success of strategic deception.

Consideration of this leads directly to an appraisal of American performance in the area of deception. A wealth of new insight on this problem may be anticipated once Michael Howard's long-delayed fourth volume of the epoch-making *British Intelligence in the Second World War* has been released for publication. This volume was completed several years ago and only awaits authorization from government quarters.[10] Though concentrating, of course, on the British side of Allied intelligence gathering and exploitation, it perforce must frequently skirt on what the Americans were doing. As matters now stand, the evidence shows the Americans lagging sadly behind their allies. British concern referred not only to displays of ineptitude but to what seemed to be a lack of interest in the art itself. So greatly was London troubled that it twice alerted the American Joint Chiefs of Staff to the lack of coordination. The first plea was addressed to Washington in June 1942 and appeared to fall on deaf ears. This proved to be the more troubling as combined operations in the Mediterranean expanded. Toward the end of 1943, therefore, the British Joint Service Chiefs delivered to the JCS a veritable bombshell in the form of a massive report on the serious gap between American and British performance.[11]

This dramatic move had so sobering an effect that the JCS adopted measures to assure both greater effort and cooperation on the American side. Two other major developments further strengthened this resolve during the following months. The first of these was a long-delayed British decision to reveal to their allies the secret of the Double X system, through which they were manipulating the entire German intelligence network on their island. Even more of a clincher was the triumph of *Operation Fortitude*, which, in its consequences, must be counted among the most far-reaching military deceptions of history. Thereby the Germans were hoodwinked into believing that the invasion was scheduled for the Pas de Calais rather than Normandy. Once the landing was effected, they were led to expect a further move across the Straits of Dover.

Eisenhower took a strong personal interest in the orchestration of the stratagems that sparked the great deception. In appraising the role of ULTRA, there seems cause for speculation on whether its availability helped greatly to determine the choice of Normandy for the invasion. The argument hinges on the point that it was ULTRA, together with the closely intertwined Double X operation, which inspired confidence that the deception could proceed without a hitch. Particularly the follow-through of keeping the Germans on tenterhooks in expectation of a second landing would have been meaningless if the reverse course had been chosen; the Germans could never have been induced to believe that after landing in the Pas de Calais, the Allies would venture a supporting move in remote Normandy. This is not to suggest that Eisenhower and those of his associates who were ULTRA-initiated founded their calculations from the first on the rock of ULTRA. Rather, a necessarily unrecorded and probably unspoken awareness of the importance of ULTRA as a guide and control element must have played an increasing role as plans progressed. Any proposal other than the one adopted would perforce have collided with obstacles which ULTRA could not deal with so effectively.

Discussion of the performance of American captains in the ETO with respect to the utilization of ULTRA should include attention to what they owed the talented officers who presided over what was, almost everywhere, a smooth and sophisticated operation. In the first two years after the American entry, commanders relied entirely on British Special Liaison Units for this function.[12] Only in November 1943 was there an agreement on assigning American Special Security Officers to field commanders.[13]

There followed one of the most extraordinary selection processes that occurred during World War II. The officers (captains or majors) attached as SSO's to army groups and army commands were, without exception, former civilians who had distinguished themselves in such fields as law, business, or the academic world. They were men who stood out for such qualities as tact, lack of awe in the face of rank or position, knowledge of men, and whenever appropriate, a readiness for self-effacement. In the latter sense, they could be classed as unknowing disciples of the brilliant Frank B. Rowlett, who on the wall of his office displayed a plaque proclaiming what should ever be the credo of the intelligence officer and might well be that of public servants generally: ''There is no limit to what a man can accomplish if he does not care who gets the credit for it.''

The usual setup at an army command included access to ULTRA on the part of the commander-in-chief, the chief of staff, the chief of operations, and the chief of intelligence. In some instances the principal order of battle specialist was also admitted to this charmed circle. The function of an SSO greatly transcended those of a transmission belt between Bletchley Park and field commanders. He was expected to familiarize himself as thoroughly as possible with situations in his army sector so as to promote speedy recognition of the potential exploitations of items of information. On the basis of such insight, he was to be prepared to advise when it was appropriate or desired.

Another major responsibility of the SSO was guardianship over security. At times over-eager superiors would strain at the leash, itching to use ULTRA information in ways that endangered the source. If such moves could not be prevented or occurred without prior knowledge on the part of the SSO, it was his duty to report the circumstances to London. One SSO made such reports on five different occasions.[14] Though commanders were not officially aware of this surveillance, they could sense enough of it usually to accept with grace the ULTRA-discipline expected of them.

ULTRA and MAGIC in the Pacific

In appraising the performance of American military leaders in using signal intelligence, it deserves notice that in the Pacific they could count on both built-in and growing advantages. Compared with the ETO, where opponents initially won almost every inning in the intercept war, the contest in the Pacific was from the beginning one-sided in American favor. Neither the Germans nor the Japanese were ever able to make meaningful headway toward solution of the Sigaba, a machine that in time became the workhorse of American communications.[15] Relatively speaking, Japanese commanders continued to stumble in the dark, whereas their American rivals could count on constant advances in both intercept and cryptanalytical services. As against the situation in Europe, where the shrinking of German territorial control correspondingly lessened use of wireless communication, the increasing isolation of Japanese island garrisons made codes and ciphers that much more vulnerable.

Douglas MacArthur, like Dwight Eisenhower, seems to have been free of the all-too-common military scorn of intelligence. Against this, he had such faith in his judgments that once formed, he did not easily change his mind on the basis of new information or arguments. Because of this quality, the more sycophantic elements in his entourage shrank from disturbing him with information that conflicted with such predispositions. This state of affairs worsened with time and produced its most fateful consequences during the Korean War, when MacArthur, after penetrating the north, disrelished the prospect, moving rapidly toward certainty, of Chinese intervention. Throughout this crucial period his G-2, Major General Charles A. Willoughby, appears to have systematically screened out reports that spelled out this unwelcome threat.[16]

Three signal intelligence organizations, American or American-controlled, presented a sometimes badly divided front in the Pacific intercept war. In Washington, the War Department's Special Branch very naturally aspired to coordinate American signals intelligence throughout the world. This function was to be exercised in large part by the SSOs, who were being readied to implement the April 1943 accord with the British. Eisenhower and MacArthur were notified routinely of their approaching assignment to all front commands. For Eisenhower this meant no more than the simple substitution of American SSOs for British Special Liaison Units. Not entirely without reason, MacArthur saw in the continuation of the SSOs as members of Special Branch an extension of leading strings to his headquarters. It required a mission of the deputy chief of Special Branch, Colonel Carter Clarke, to induce him to accept them in the Southwest Pacific Area (SWPA). He was determined, however, to keep them fenced in. They were never integrated nor even admitted into the headquarters intelligence operation, the Central Bureau Brisbane (CBB); did not receive the daily intelligence bulletin; and were all too often subjected to shabby personal treatment. Both in the move of MacArthur's headquarters to Hollandia and the invasion of Leyte, they were left behind and had to seek ways to hitch a ride in follow-up transportation.[17]

MacArthur's further dealings with Special Branch demonstrated all too frequently the ''localitis'' which was a perpetual lament of General Marshall. As CBB progressed in solving Japanese army signals, this knowledge was withheld both from the SSOs and from Special Branch itself. Washington only gained access to the highest-level Japanese cipher when Australian cryptanalysts in New Delhi solved it and relayed the information.

One need not go far for an explanation of MacArthur's interest in keeping Special Branch in the dark on the penetration of Japanese military traffic. No doubt confidence in his own huge signals intelligence establishment (by the end of the war CBB had grown to over 4000 persons) promoted a feeling that he had little to gain from a flow of exchanges with Washington. A more positive motivation must have sprung from his well-known propensity to promote the impression that any success gained within the sphere of his command was the outcome of his judgment or intuition. Like Montgomery, he was loath to let it be known, especially in higher headquarters, that a victory had anything to do with ''reading the enemy's mail.''[18]

MacArthur's suspicions and obsession with self-assertion influenced similar relations with the other great signals intelligence center in the Pacific – that of the Navy at Pearl Harbor. Under the impression that this facility had withheld information from him, he directed that Navy representatives should not be admitted to CBB. Yet CBB had as much to gain from a close cooperative relationship as Pearl Harbor, which produced MAGIC material of the first order. Fortunately MacArthur's usually complacent chief of staff, Major General Richard K. Sutherland, who was closer to these matters than his commander, ventured behind his back to make arrangements by which products of Navy signals intelligence continued to flow to SWPA.

Even in combined operations, the Navy from time to time suffered severely from usually careless, rather than malicious, withholding of information by SWPA. A particularly serious instance concerned Admiral Marc Mitcher's Fast Carrier Force as it approached to cover the landing at Hollandia. Mitcher was left so completely in the dark by Willoughby on this occasion that his chief of staff, Captain Arleigh Burke, saw no solution but to make a personal aerial reconnaissance.[19] In part, Willoughby's neglect may have been associated with a serious intelligence failure on his part with respect both to the estimate of Japanese forces at Hollandia and the topography of the beach area.

From the standpoint of building a sound, coordinated intercept and crypt-analytical operation in the Pacific, the verdict of history appears likely to be that MacArthur and his immediately involved subordinates (Sutherland, Willoughby, and the chief of signals, Brigadier General Spencer B. Akin) did scarcely more to help than to hinder. This is not to imply that the three great operating centers (Special Branch in Washington, Pearl Harbor, and CBB) did not have much to say to each other. About a third of all communications between MacArthur and Admirals Nimitz and Halsey had to do with intercept information.[20] But when such cooperation was endangered or broke down, the responsibility usually lay with SWPA, and all too often with its commander personally. If further evidence of the intrusion of the personal equation into these matters were required, it could be found in the famed episode of Admiral Yamamoto's death. When the commander of Japan's Combined Fleet was waylaid and gunned down over Bougainville, it required no less than the intervention of the JCS to prevent MacArthur from publicizing it as a triumph of his command, though at the probable sacrifice of the intercept bonanza that had been so laboriously put together.[21]

If the SWPA command had a questionable record in the matter of its contribution to erecting the best possible signals intelligence in the Pacific, where can it be said to stand in relation to utilizing the *products* of ULTRA and MAGIC? Unquestionably, they had much to do both with individual successes and the steady advance northward. Summing up the benefits of ULTRA and MAGIC for the entire war period, SWPA's G-3 (Operations), Major General Stephen A. Chamberlain, holds that the Pacific war was shortened by three years! In specific instances it was a key factor in such spectacular victories as the Battle of the Bismarck Sea, the destruction of the airfields at Wewak, and the bloody repulse of the Japanese at Aitape. In other instances (Kokoda, Biak, Peleliu) it was used so inexpertly as to exact disproportionate sacrifices of American lives. It is difficult to escape the conclusion that Willoughby all too frequently failed to appreciate how vital intelligence items could best be used in the conduct of operations.[22]

The record of the use of communications intelligence in the Pacific by the US Navy is not free from errors, oversight, and the usual growing pains. The defeat at Savo Island (8-9 August 1942), for example, has been called the worst in American naval history. But seen as a whole, the picture shows much that is exciting and sometimes inspiring. It produced the single victory of World War II that can be advanced as a respectable candidate among the decisive battles of history.[23] American naval intelligence also scored heavily in more drawn-out aspects of the intercept war by playing the major role in the submarine success story. Probably only the airplane can rival the submarine as an instrument in the steady attrition of the power of Japan.[24] ULTRA and MAGIC were indispensable for what was accomplished by both.

The vital role of cryptanalysis in the staging of the Battle of Midway is eloquently related in many publications and requires no further elucidation. What does perhaps deserve additional comment is the uniqueness of the roles of Admiral Chester A. Nimitz and his Fleet Intelligence Officer, the later Admiral Edwin Layton. The former stands almost alone in staking so much on the basis of information derived from intercepts at a time when naval authorities in Washington were highly skeptical.[25] Layton stands out as a chief of intelligence who had an unfailing appreciation of what could be gleaned from wireless sources and for the professional integrity that gained and maintained for him the confidence of his chief. Together they deserve a major portion of the credit for the brilliant record of the Navy in turning the tide in the Pacific with a dramatic beginning only a few months after the disaster of Pearl Harbor had seemed to eliminate it as a significant factor for at least a year to come.

Those who relish pricking "the bubble reputation" may look forward to a never-ending field day in reassessing the performance of Allied leaders in the light of the intrusion of the ULTRA and MAGIC factor. There is no getting around that ULTRA and MAGIC presented British and American commanders, as it were on a silver platter, a veritable bonanza of openings to surprise, mislead, deceive, frustrate, logistically starve, or disrupt the plans of their opponents. Revelations on the workings of ULTRA and MAGIC, as they flow from declassification teams into archives, threaten to erode, at times perhaps deal heavy blows to, the reputations of specific Allied generals, and occasionally of Allied leadership generally. More rarely, the renown of those who possessed the vision to discern the vistas opened to them by ULTRA and MAGIC merits enhancement. In effect, American captains, like their colleagues and adversaries of many lands, must from this new perspective once again submit themselves to the scrutiny of history.

NOTES

1. The year 1931 witnessed the publication of Herbert O. Yardley's *The American Black Chamber.*
2. Only eight Purple machines were produced and were confined strictly to signals exchanged

with the most important embassies. Interview with Frank B. Rowlett, 16 March 1983. The measure of their employment thus differs profoundly from that of the Enigma, of which around 100,000 rolled off German assembly lines. Particularly remarkable about the solution of Purple is that it was accomplished solely by cryptanalysis and from intercepts so limited in number. Also, there was no awareness as yet of the prior breaking of the Enigma as a result of Polish/French/British strivings. If this had been known, it would have encouraged and spurred on the project. Both the Red and Purple machines were constructed on principles wholly different from those of the Enigma. Interview with Frank B. Rowlett.

3. As ULTRA is frequently written in capital letters, it is logical to do so also for MAGIC.

4. Debates upon the various theses (there are at least four) about the timing of the revelations of ULTRA to Americans need not concern us in this essay but will be analyzed by the author elsewhere.

5. Inviting Eisenhower to Chequers for the weekend, Churchill introduced him to the ULTRA secret by exacting a prior oath that he would never expose himself to capture by flying over enemy-held territory or approaching closely to the front.

6. Thus Ronald Lewin, *ULTRA Goes to War* (New York: McGraw-Hill, 1978) on the situations enumerated below.

7. In a letter of 6 August 1980 to Jack E. Ingram of which a copy is available to the writer, Clark protests that he "sought" ULTRA and that "anyone who did not accept it would have been crazy, for it was like reading the enemy's mail." Though stressing that ULTRA material reaching his headquarters often did not pertain to his command area, Clark states that, "When we were in trouble at Anzio the intercepts helped us tremendously."

8. Lewin, *ULTRA Goes to War*, p. 86.

9. Donald S. Bussey, "ULTRA and the Seventh Army." Also conversations with Colonel Bussey.

10. It appears a safe assumption that this postponement of publication reflects the public furor over the Anthony Blunt affair, in which a highly honored art historian was identified as the recruiter in chief for Soviet intelligence at Cambridge University in the 1930s. There is a reluctance, we hope a temporary one, to publicize certain aspects of World War II intelligence history.

11. It was highly unusual for British or American military authorities to criticize one another in official documents.

12. British Special Liaison Units attached to American commands were selected and dedicated men who had to perform their duties more or less under crossfire. The presence of a mysterious and, it seemed, somewhat privileged foreigner within an American intelligence unit at times inspired jealousy and even suspicion. The reports of inspectors who visited headquarters in the Mediterranean wherever ULTRA had clients repeatedly dwell on such situations.

13. The agreement of 29 November 1943 was concluded between Group Captain F. W. Winterbottom on the British side and Major General George V. Strong and Colonel Alfred T. McCormack on the American.

14. Bussey, "ULTRA and the Seventh Army," and conversations with Colonel Bussey.

15. The Sigaba was by far the most sophisticated communications device of World War II. One item: whereas the Enigma contained either three or four rotors within the machine and the far more formidable *Geheimschreiber* ten, the Sigaba featured 15.

16. Colonel Eric H. F. Svensson, then on Willoughby's staff (apparently as chief of counter-intelligence) was utterly convinced that all indications pointed to an impending Chinese intervention. Finding himself unable to penetrate to MacArthur via Willoughby, he, in his desperation, thought of waylaying the commander in the hallway. As related by Colonel Donald P. Shaw, then on the staff of Colonel Svensson.

17. During the invasion of Leyte, the SSO, Major John Gunn, had to hitch a boat ride in the tail end of the expeditionary force and wander disconsolately along the beach on which he was dumped hoping to be taken in by some kindly mess. Ronald Lewin, *The American Magic: Ciphers and the Defeat of Japan* (New York: Farrar Straus Giroux, 1980), pp. 267-70.

18. Montgomery was similarly inclined to reserve credit for any success to himself. He resented having even Churchill read the same ULTRA reports that reached him and that made clear how much he owed to them.

19. As communicated to Ronald Lewin by Admiral Burke *(The American Magic*, p. 232) and spelled out further to the writer by the Admiral in a conversation of 28 March 1983. In Burke's view, Willoughby lacked the insight to determine well the intelligence that fitted the needs of its

clients and how an item could affect current operations. Burke and his pilot had a narrow escape, their plane being hit by gunfire and barely making it back to the carrier, a wing falling off as they landed on the deck.

20. As related to the writer by members of the National Security Agency staff engaged in the declassification of intercept material.

21. MacArthur's resentment at what he probably saw as "meddling" is demonstrated in the acid tone of his postwar reference to the incident: "Washington lauded it as one of the most important bags of the war, but labelled it top secret and forbade publication."

22. This was the conclusion of the later Admiral Arleigh Burke after prolonged experience with these phases of the Pacific War. Conversation with Admiral Burke, 28 March 1983.

23. It is interesting and significant from the standpoint of appraising the role of sea power in World War II that the other "battle" which is sometimes put forward as having been decisive is that of the Atlantic. It is questionable, of course, whether one can validly compare the weight of a single encounter with that of a series of operations that endured over years.

24. By the termination of the war in the Pacific, the Japanese merchant fleet had been reduced to seven percent of its original strength plus what had been produced or captured during the conflict. Well over 60 percent of these losses had been accounted for by the submarine, which in the later phases of the war went out almost solely on specific missions rather than on search and destroy cruises.

25. Admiral King, the chief of naval operations, was a rather inflexible, irascible man who did not adjust easily to the sensational upgrading of the role of wireless intelligence that was developing in the Pacific command.

This article appeared in the summer 1985 issue of *Parameters*.

11

MacArthur's Fireman: Robert L. Eichelberger

by JOHN F. SHORTAL

To millions of people the name Douglas MacArthur evokes the image of a brilliant, confident, and supremely successful combat commander. In the 41 years that have elapsed since the last campaign of World War II, his victories have come to be viewed as quick, smooth, and simple operations against an impoverished foe. However, hindsight has obscured the tenacity of the Japanese and the immense difficulties MacArthur encountered in the Southwest Pacific. Not all of his victories were quick and easy; the Japanese did not quit upon request. In three major campaigns – Buna in December 1942, Biak in June 1944, and Manila in January 1945 – MacArthur suffered initial setbacks from the Japanese. In each case, he was forced to call in a fireman to rally American troops and salvage desperate tactical situations. MacArthur always used the same fireman to handle his most difficult missions, Lieutenant General Robert Lawrence Eichelberger. In each case, Eichelberger's combination of tactical innovation, commonsense training, and personal leadership produced dramatic results.

MacArthur was a legendary field commander. Robert Eichelberger, on the other hand, did not fit the Hollywood image of a general. He was not young, handsome, or tough-talking. He did not wear specially designed uniforms or use theatrics calculated to impress his troops. Rather, by 1944 he was a 58-year-old man who, although in excellent physical condition, was slightly overweight and concerned about his waistline.[1] What Eichelberger did have going for him was an iron will, a strong concept of duty, a warm sense of humor,[2] and an innovative tactical ability. He never failed to conquer any assigned objective.

The story of MacArthur's problem at Buna is well known. His first offensive of the war was in grave jeopardy in November 1942, when an insufficiently trained American division had been stymied and demoralized by the Japanese. Douglas MacArthur, whose pride had been severely wounded in the recent Philippines campaign, had no other reserves in the theater. Furthermore, the poor performance of this division caused the Australians to question the fighting abilities of American soldiers. To salvage this desperate tactical situation and to breathe new life into the American soldiers at Buna, MacArthur summoned Eichelberger from Australia. On the evening of 30 November 1942, MacArthur issued one of the most famous operations orders in American military history. He said:

Bob, I'm putting you in command at Buna. Relieve Harding. I am sending you in, Bob, and I want you to remove all officers who won't fight. Relieve Regimental and Battalion commanders; if necessary, put Sergeants in charge of Battalions and Corporals in charge of companies – anyone who will fight. Time is of the essence; the Japs may land reinforcements any night . . . . I want you to take Buna, or not come back alive.[3]

Thirty-two days later this American division, whose fighting capabilities had been questioned, conquered Buna. The capture of Buna was MacArthur's first ground victory of World War II. It was a closely fought battle in which he was forced to take on an enemy who held all the advantages in equipment, training, and experience. MacArthur had few troops at his disposal, and the much-discussed industrial capacity of the United States had not yet manifested itself in this theater.[4] The margin between victory and defeat at Buna was the dynamic and inspirational leadership of Robert Eichelberger. An eyewitness later described Eichelberger's contribution as follows:

You were sent at the eleventh hour to salvage an impossible situation without any assistance except your own intelligence and your own force of character . . . . While I was with you I was convinced that if the troops under your command did not go into Buna, you would have unhesitatingly gone in there alone.[5]

Although Buna is the most well-known example of MacArthur's use of Eichelberger's formidable leadership talents, it was not the only one.

MacArthur's Second Problem: Biak

The conclusion of the Buna campaign in January 1943 secured the eastern portion of New Guinea for the Allies. In order to carry the Allied offensive into the Philippines, MacArthur had to isolate the powerful Japanese base at Rabaul and then move up the northern coast of New Guinea. Throughout 1943, MacArthur conducted a series of brilliant operations which cut the Japanese line of communication to Rabaul. This enabled him to neutralize completely the Japanese forces at this location without conducting a bloody frontal assault. However, by January 1944 MacArthur had moved only 240 miles north of Buna and still had 2240 miles to go before reaching Manila.[6] In order to bring the war to a more rapid conclusion, MacArthur decided to conduct a series of deeper amphibious envelopments up the northern coast of New Guinea.[7]

By late May 1944 MacArthur had moved up the northern coast of New Guinea as far as the Island of Biak, which was within bomber range of the Philippines (800 miles), and within fighter range of the Japanese airfields on Palau.[8] MacArthur had cut through the Japanese defenses with skill. The amphibious envelopments at Saidor (2 January), Aitape and Hollandia (22 April), and Wakde (17 May) were great successes. George C. Marshall even called the Hollandia operation a "model of strategic and tactical maneuvers."[9]

At Biak, unfortunately, MacArthur's luck ran out. Biak was important because the Japanese had built three airfields on the island, and MacArthur hoped to use these airfields to launch bombing missions against Japanese bases in the Philippines. Since he expected the task force to have seized and built up at least one airfield by 10 June, he had promised to support Admiral Nimitz's operation at Saipan in the Marianas on 15 June 1944 with aircraft from these airfields.[10]

At 0715 hours on 27 May 1944, Major General Horace Fuller and two regiments (186th and 162nd Infantry) of the 41st Division landed at Biak. The Japanese offered no resistance at the beaches, and the initial landings were a complete success.[11] General Fuller's plan called for the 162nd Regiment to move along the beach road, which ran at the base of a steep cliff, to the three airfields. Meanwhile, the 186th Regiment would move on a parallel route through the mountains.[12] In the first two days General Fuller's forces moved quickly, covering eight miles along the beach road, which brought them within 1000 yards of the first airfield (Mokmer Drome).[13] Unfortunately, MacArthur's staff had seriously underestimated the Japanese defensive capability on the island. Instead of the 4380 Japanese troops they had anticipated, more than 11,000 Japanese soldiers were at Biak. In December 1943, the Japanese high command had sent the veteran 222nd Infantry Regiment of the 36th Division to Biak. This unit was commanded by Colonel Naoyuki Kuzume and reinforced with elements of the 221st Infantry and the 2nd Development Unit.[14] Colonel Kuzume was described in an American after-action report as "a soldier of the highest calibre and a tactician compelling respect."[15] For five months he had carefully prepared his defenses.

Colonel Kuzume had astutely assessed the Allied objective as the three airfields along the southern coast of Biak. Therefore, he skillfully emplaced his forces in the coral ridges above the coastal road which ran from Mandom to the Mokmer airfield. He also positioned troops in the compartmented ridge systems 1000 yards north-northwest of the Mokmer airfield. The terrain, including many caves, complemented the interlocking ridge network which not only dominated the coastal road and three airfields, but provided concealed emplacements for the enemy's artillery, mortars, and machine guns.[16]

On 29 May, Colonel Kuzume counterattacked three times with two battalions of infantry supported by tanks and artillery fire against the 162nd Infantry positions. In the four-hour fight, the American forces neutralized eight Japanese tanks and destroyed the better part of a Japanese battalion. However, the Japanese were successful in driving the 162nd Infantry back two miles east of the Mokmer airfield and forcing them onto the defensive.[17] General Fuller requested and received the 163rd Infantry Regiment to reinforce his task force. With this support, General Fuller was again able to mount an offensive and by 8 June had finally seized his first airfield, Mokmer. However, the Air Corps could not use the field because Japanese gunfire completely controlled it.[18]

On 14 June 1944, the tactical situation of General Fuller's Hurricane Task Force was bleak. In 19 days of combat they had succeeded in seizing only a single Japanese airfield, one that could not be used by Allied air forces. Furthermore, Admiral Nimitz's forces would go ashore at Saipan on 15 June without Southwest Pacific air support because the Hurricane Task Force had failed in its principal mission.[19]

The Biak operation had become a personal embarrassment to MacArthur; he had been caught in exaggerations to the Joint Chiefs of Staff and to the American public. On 28 May, after General Fuller's initial success, General MacArthur had announced that the impending fall of Biak "marks the practical end of the New Guinea campaign." On 1 June, MacArthur's communique announced that Japanese resistance "was collapsing." On 3 June, MacArthur's communique optimistically announced that "mopping up was proceeding on Biak."[20] However, at the same time that MacArthur was announcing to the world the imminent successful conclusion of the campaign, the Australian press was relaying a totally different story. Spencer Davis reported in *Australia Newsweek* that "obviously, it would require additional reinforcements to achieve the resounding victory proclaimed ten days ago by General MacArthur."[21]

MacArthur, aware of the discrepancy between the actual tactical situation and his communiques, became increasingly concerned as time went on. On 5 June he told General Krueger (the 6th Army Commander and General Fuller's immediate superior): "I am becoming concerned at the failure to secure the Biak airfields . . . is the advance being pushed with sufficient determination? Our negligible ground losses would seem to indicate a failure to do so." On 14 June, MacArthur cabled General Krueger: "The situation on Biak is unsatisfactory. The strategic purpose of the operation is being jeopardized by the failure to establish without delay an operating field for aircraft."[22]

During the first two weeks of June 1944, as the tactical situation stagnated, MacArthur continued to press General Krueger for results. General Krueger recalled that he "dispatched several radiograms to the task force commander directing him to speed up the operation. But it was easier to order this than get it done for . . . the troops were faced by great difficulties."[23]

With the tactical situation stalemated, victory having been proclaimed two weeks earlier and the invasion of Saipan scheduled for the next day, MacArthur and Krueger called for their most able field commander to salvage the situation and put out this fire before it consumed their reputations. At 1800 hours on 14 June 1944, General Krueger summoned General Eichelberger to an emergency conference at his headquarters. At this conference General Krueger "explained that after continuous fighting, coupled with extremely unfriendly terrain, intense heat and scarcity of water, the infantry units within the task force were beginning to tire to a critical degree."[24] General Krueger then told Eichelberger to take command at Biak the following morning.

At 0830 hours on 15 June, Eichelberger and a small staff departed for Biak. They arrived at General Fuller's headquarters at 1230 that day.[25] Eichelberger spent the first two and one-half days at the front familiarizing himself with the tactical situation and the fighting capabilities of his own forces. On 16 June he went to the regimental command posts of the 186th and 162nd Infantry Regiments to assess personally the morale and effectiveness of those units. On 17 June, he observed the conduct of the two units under fire.[26] Eichelberger radioed General Krueger: "Today I have been with General Doe and 186 and 162 Infantry. With the possible exception of the first Bn 162 Inf the troops are not nearly as exhausted as I had expected and I believe they can be made to fight with energy."[27]

On 17 June General Krueger, still under pressure from General MacArthur, radioed Eichelberger to "launch your attack . . . promptly and press it home with the utmost vigor."[28] Eichelberger, however, had a plan for defeating the Japanese and was not going to be pressured into prematurely launching his attack because of MacArthur's and Krueger's embarrassment over previous communiques. Therefore, on 17 June Eichelberger sent this succinct message to General Krueger, outlining his plan of attack:

Having arrived here forty-eight hours ago in almost complete ignorance of the situation, I have spent two days at the front. Tomorrow [Sunday], I have called off all fighting and troops will be reorganized. On Monday, I propose to put three battalions in the rear of the Japanese, and on Tuesday I propose to take the other two airields.[39]

After clearly informing General Krueger of his plan and his pace, Eichelberger took two additional actions on 17 June. First, he ordered a reinforced rifle company to occupy Hill 320, which was the dominating terrain feature in the area north of the three airfields, thus providing an excellent observation point.[30] Second, Eichelberger issued his instructions for the 19 June attack. He would not try to directly seize the airfields nor conduct a frontal attack against the Japanese positions. Instead, he would envelop the enemy by going around the Japanese southern flank and seizing the ridgeline north of Mokmer airfield from the rear.[31] Eichelberger's objectives were to eliminate the Japanese ability to fire on Mokmer airfield and to obtain favorable terrain from which to launch future advances.[32] Eichelberger later credited the Japanese with giving him the solution for cracking their defenses. He had carefully examined all their operations in World War II and believed that the Japanese tactics in Malaya would provide the method of ending the stalemate on Biak. In Malaya, each time the British forces prepared a defensive line, the Japanese enveloped it. Once the British discovered that the Japanese were in their rear, the whole defensive line collapsed and the British withdrew to establish another. This process was repeated down the entire peninsula. Eichelberger believed that at Biak the "Japanese troops [would], just like occidental troops, take a very dim and unhappy view of enemy forces in their rear."[33]

On 18 June, Eichelberger repeated a lesson he had learned at Buna and rested his troops before the major attack. As the soldiers rested, Eichelberger gave his subordinate commanders time to reorganize their forces and to ensure that "everybody could find out what they were doing."[34] Eichelberger also sent out patrols to reconnoiter the Japanese positions, and by evening on 18 June his troops were, in the words of an eyewitness, "ready to move hard and fast."[35]

On the morning of 19 June, the 41st Division launched a coordinated attack and moved hard and fast to accomplish Eichelberger's objectives. The 3rd Battalion, 163rd Infantry, and two battalions (2nd and 3rd) of the 186th Infantry Regiment "had enveloped the rear of the Japanese in the west caves and could prevent their reinforcement or escape."[36] Furthermore, this attack secured the Mokmer airfield from hostile ground attack.

Even though the attack on 19 June was a complete success, the situation demanded that Eichelberger continue to press his troops forward. He ordered an attack on 20 June to seize the remaining two airfields, Borokoe and Sorido, and to destroy the Japanese who were emplaced in the west caves (by the 162nd Infantry). By 1030 hours on 20 June, Eichelberger had seized the Borokoe and Sorido airfields.[37] The Hurricane Task Force's original mission had been accomplished. Eichelberger continued to press the attack against the Japanese who were neutralized in caves even though the airfields were secured.

On the night of 21-22 June, the Japanese commander, Colonel Kuzume, recognized defeat. He destroyed the regimental colors and all official documents and then ordered all able-bodied soldiers to attempt a breakout. The Japanese tried three times to break through the lines of the 186th Infantry. At 2100 hours, and then at 2400 hours on 21 June, the Japanese attacked and were repulsed. At 0400 hours on 22 June, the Japanese tried for the final time. All three attacks failed.[38] The last Japanese resistance in the caves was finally mopped up on 27 June.

Eichelberger departed Biak at 0900 hours on 28 June. It had taken him only five days to seize the three Japanese airfields and to break the enemy's main line of defense. It is worth noting that he accomplished this at a cost of only 400 Americans killed, compared to the 4700 Japanese killed in action.[39] Eichelberger credited his success "to profanity, flattery, offers of rewards, threats, and lady luck."[40] The tactical situation had been solved quickly, and MacArthur's reputation had not been tarnished. MacArthur could move on to his cherished operations in the Philippines without concern for Biak. After this operation, MacArthur rewarded Eichelberger with the command of the new Eighth Army.

MacArthur's Third Problem: Manila

MacArthur successfully returned to the Philippines on 20 October 1944 when the Sixth United States Army landed on the island of Leyte. On 9

January 1945, MacArthur landed the same Sixth Army, commanded by Lieutenant General Walter Krueger, at Lingayen Gulf on the main island of Luzon. In 12 months, MacArthur had moved 2000 miles closer to Japan and had commenced the liberation of the Philippines. With the exception of Biak, all these operations had proceeded like clockwork.

The objective of the Sixth Army forces that landed at Lingayen Gulf was the City of Manila, 120 miles to the south. The assault troops at Lingayen Gulf consisted of the I and XIV Corps and the 40th, 37th, 6th and 43rd Divisions.[41] General Krueger and his forces encountered no opposition on the beaches and little in the initial advance; however, terrain and logistical problems did slow the pace.[42] On 12 January 1945, only three days after Sixth Army had landed on Luzon, General MacArthur summoned General Krueger to his headquarters to complain of the slow progress. MacArthur believed that since the Sixth Army casualties were light, they had encountered little resistance and could pick up the tempo of their attack. MacArthur was unimpressed with Krueger's arguments for additional troops with which to conduct the dash for Manila.[43]

MacArthur, who felt the Japanese would not defend Manila, had correctly assessed the intentions of the Japanese commander on Luzon, General Tomoyuki Yamashita. Yamashita, with 275,000 Japanese troops on Luzon, realized that he could not possibly hope to defend the entire island. He knew that he could not confront the overwhelming forces MacArthur could bring to bear against him in the important region of the Central Plains and Manila Bay.[44] Therefore, he planned a fighting withdrawal into the mountainous strongholds in northern Luzon, which would tie up large amounts of allied shipping, troops, and aircraft. He hoped that this defense would delay the inevitable invasion of the Japanese homeland.[45] General Yamashita specifically ordered Lieutenant General Shizuo Yokoyama, the Eighth Division Commander, not to defend Manila but rather to evacuate the city.[46] However, due to bureaucratic disagreements between the Japanese army and navy, Vice Admiral Denshichi Okochi, the naval commander in Manila, decided to conduct a full-scale defense of the city against Yamashita's wishes.[47] Admiral Okochi's decision later caused a great deal of friction between General MacArthur and General Krueger.

By mid-January 1945, as the Sixth Army moved on Manila at a snail's pace, MacArthur grew more and more obsessed with the capture of the city. Manila Bay was of vital importance, but MacArthur's reasons were more than simply logistical and strategic.[48] It was almost as if his personal military reputation depended on liberating the city as quickly as possible. Therefore, throughout the month of January, the slow progress of the Sixth Army was a great irritant to General MacArthur. On 23 January, a newspaper correspondent, Lee Van Atta, informed Eichelberger that "General MacArthur had been laying down the law to Krueger about the slow advance at Lingayen and that he had given him an ultimatum to be in Manila by the 5th of February."[49] On 30 January

1945, General MacArthur personally went to the front to investigate the reason for the Sixth Army's slow advance. According to the official Army historian for his campaign, MacArthur found the pace of the advance "much too leisurely."[50] MacArthur then informed General Krueger that the 37th Division had demonstrated "a noticeable lack of drive and aggressive initiative."[51] General MacArthur in frustration said that the Sixth Army was "mentally incapable but if given tremendous forces they [were] able to advance ponderously and slowly to victory."[52]

This standard of performance was unacceptable to MacArthur and, as had become the routine when his reputation was at stake, he called on Eichelberger. To speed up the pace of operations on Luzon, MacArthur directed Eichelberger to conduct an amphibious landing on 31 January at Nasugbu, 45 miles southwest of Manila. The assault troops for this operation were the 11th Airborne Division, commanded by Major General Joseph Swing, and the 511th Parachute Regimental Combat Team.[53] MacArthur intended the Nasugbu landing to be a "reconnaissance in force to test the enemy defenses in southern Luzon."[54] Eichelberger was directed to land only one regimental combat team (188th Glider Regiment) initially. However, he was given the discretion to land the 187th Glider Regiment and to push north toward Manila if he met no opposition. In addition, Eichelberger had the authority to airdrop the 511th Parachute Regiment to exploit success, if the situation warranted it.[55] General MacArthur hoped that this operation would divert Japanese forces from north of Manila and prohibit them from concentrating all their defenses against the Sixth Army.[56]

At 0815 hours on 13 January 1945, Eichelberger landed his first assault force (the 188th Regimental Combat Team) at Nasugbu Beach. This regiment encountered light resistance from the Japanese and by 0945 had seized the town of Nasugbu and the Nasugbu airport.[57] At 1030 hours Eichelberger, aboard the USS *Spencer*, made the decision to exploit the initial success of the 188th Regimental Combat Team. He ordered General Swing to land the rest of the 11th Airborne Division and to push on as rapidly as possible toward Manila. By noon the rest of the division had landed and was driving inland.[58]

Eichelberger went ashore at 1300 hours and immediately proceeded to the front to confer with General Swing.[59] Eichelberger, who was not without personal ambition, had as his objective to drive rapidly toward the capture of Manila.[60] Eichelberger later reflected that this operation was successful because "speed was emphasized and contact once gained was maintained until the enemy was either dispersed or annihilated." Eichelberger's tactics, which demanded rapid penetration by his infantry in order to avoid the stalemate that would ensue if the Japanese had time to establish their defenses, had been developed at Buna and Biak, where he had found that the infantry had a tendency to go slow and wait for the artillery to defeat the enemy.[61]

Eichelberger's emphasis on speed was rewarded when lead elements of the 188th Regiment seized the important Palico River bridge, eight miles inland, at 1430. The 11th Airborne Division's after-action report stated that "the Palico River Bridge had been prepared for demolition, but the Japanese were surprised by the rapid advance of our troops, and were caught on the far side of the bridge. Our fire prevented them from reaching the bridge and they withdrew toward Tagaytay Ridge."[62] This bridge was important because it allowed Eichelberger's forces to use the Nasugbu-Tagaytay road, which was an all-weather highway, and considerably shortened their supply line.[63]

After the bridge was seized, Eichelberger ordered General Swing to continue the advance through the night because he believed that the "enemy troops were confused and retreating," and a halt at dark would have permitted them to reorganize.[64] At midnight, the 187th Regiment passed through the 188th and continued the advance toward Manila. The 11th Airborne Division pushed on throughout the night. The following morning Eichelberger went to the front to inspect and exhort his men and soon found himself moving with the lead company in the advance.[65] His emphasis on speed had paid great dividends in his first 28 hours ashore. The 11th Airborne Division not only had established a port and an airfield in this time, but also had penetrated the main line of Japanese resistance and had advanced 19 miles.[66] To exploit this success, Eichelberger alerted the 511th Parachute Regiment to be prepared for an airborne drop in the vicinity of Tagaytay Ridge.[67]

By 2 February 1945, the 11th Airborne Division had fought its way through two Japanese defensive positions and by dusk had reached the third and most powerful Japanese position in the vicinity of Tagaytay Ridge.[68] Tagaytay Ridge was the most important military position held by the Japanese in southern Luzon. It was a formidable obstacle because its 2400-foot height dominated all the terrain in the region. Also, there was a two-lane concrete highway which led from Tagaytay Ridge straight down (30 miles) into Manila.[69] Therefore, as General Eichelberger and General Swing personally moved forward with the lead elements on 2 February, Eichelberger made the decision to envelop the Japanese positions on Tagaytay Ridge by air-dropping the 511th Parachute Regiment behind the Japanese. The Japanese would then be in a crossfire between the US elements.[70]

At 0730 on 3 February 1945, the 188th Regimental Combat Team assaulted the highest hill on Tagaytay Ridge, known as Shorty Hill. At 0815 the 511th Parachute Regiment jumped behind the Japanese position on Tagaytay Ridge.[71] Eichelberger was again under fire as he observed the critical assault from two directions, which finally reduced the Japanese positions on Tagaytay Ridge. By 1300 hours the Japanese positions had been destroyed and the 511th Parachute Regiment had linked up with the 188th Regiment. As soon as Tagaytay Ridge was secure, patrols were sent down the highway toward Manila.[72]

In accordance with General Eichelberger's tactical emphasis on speed, General Swing loaded the 511th Parachute Regiment on trucks on the night of 3-4 February and ordered them to proceed "toward Manila until resistance was encountered."[73] The rest of the division followed on foot.[74] The Eighth Army after-action report describes the success of this tactic: "So rapid was our advance that the enemy had neither the time nor the presence of mind to detonate mines they had previously prepared along the route of march. Consequently, demolished bridges did not slow our advance until we reached [the town of] Imus."[75]

At 1000 hours on 4 February 1945, Eichelberger had reached Imus and was moving with the forwardmost elements of the 511th Parachute Regiment. The main highway bridge at Imus had been destroyed by the Japanese, and an alternate crossing bridge, 500 yards to the west, was heavily defended. However, the 511th with Eichelberger leading soon found a small crossing site and destroyed the Japanese positions from the rear.[76] Eichelberger's emphasis on speed in this action almost cost him his life, as he recorded in his diary: "[I] moved forward to the south end of the bridge and was pinned down by sniper fire which could not be located."[77]

After this action the 511th Parachute Regiment pushed on toward Manila. Eichelberger again positioned himself at the most dangerous and crucial point of the operation, as evidenced by the following diary entry: "I continued on down the road keeping abreast of the leading elements until [we] reached Las Pinas."[78] The speed of this attack continued to surprise the Japanese. The 11th Airborne after-action report stated that "once again the Japanese were found asleep, and the Las Pinas bridge was secured before the demolitions were set off."[79] The 511th had reached the southern suburbs of Manila and continued their drive until 2130 hours, when they were halted by well-prepared Japanese positions at the Paranque bridge. By 4 February the 11th Airborne had traveled 45 miles and had reached Manila.[80]

During this operation Eichelberger seemed to be everywhere at once. After the 511th Parachute Regiment crossed the Las Pinas bridge, Eichelberger found that the truck shuttling system was not functioning properly; therefore, he "returned to Tagaytay Ridge to do what [he] could about speeding up this advance."[81] The next morning Eichelberger again displayed great personal courage and moved with the advance elements of the 511th Parachute Regiment across the Paranque bridge. However, this was the end of the rapid movement by the Eighth Army. The Americans had reached the Genko-Line which had been designed to protect Manila from an attack from the south.[82] The Genko-Line was held by the Japanese 3rd Naval Battalion. Robert Ross Smith, the US Army official historian for this campaign, described the 3rd Naval Battalion positions as "the strongest in the Manila area, having the virtue of being long established. Reinforced concrete pillboxes abounded at street intersections in the suburban area south of the city limits, many of them covered with dirt long enough to have natural camouflage."[83] Against these positions, the 11th Airborne was able to move only 2000 yards in two days.[84]

On 7 February 1945, Eichelberger received word from MacArthur that the 11th Airborne would soon come under the Sixth Army control. Eichelberger departed Luzon before Manila was captured, on 9 February 1945, in order to prepare for the southern Philippines campaign.[85]

MacArthur had two reasons for ordering Eichelberger to conduct the Nasugbu landing and Eichelberger had successfully accomplished both of them. The official objective was "to disrupt the Japanese lines of communication [and] create a diversion to support the main landing at Lingayen [by Sixth Army]."[86] However, Eichelberger understood that MacArthur had another motive: "I realize that placing me with a small force south of Manila was the MacArthur way of stirring up Krueger into action and speed. He succeeded when the newspapermen reported that troops that had been able to go only yards a day had begun to go miles after hearing that I was en route."[87] Eichelberger's estimate of the Sixth Army was verified by an eyewitness; Major General William C. Dunckel wrote Eichelberger: "When you were pushing on Manila so rapidly, I visited Sixth Army Headquarters and found them greatly agitated over the fact that you would be in Manila before they were, and I believe to this day that we could have saved more of Manila if they had given you the means to come in by way of Nasugbu."[88] The result of MacArthur's prodding of General Krueger, Eighth Army's siphoning of Japanese troops from the north of Manila, and General Krueger's jealousy of Eichelberger was that by 4 February 1945 the Sixth Army had two divisions, the 1st Cavalry Division and the 37th Division, on the outskirts of Manila.[89]

In 104 hours, Eichelberger had pushed his troops 45 miles from Nasugbu to Manila. He had once again salvaged the tactical situation for MacArthur.

In the 41 years that have elapsed since World War II, the difficulties encountered by MacArthur in the Southwest Pacific have been glossed over and in some cases all but forgotten. His victories have been made to seem automatic. This is terribly unfair to the soldiers who fought for MacArthur. He had problems in the Southwest Pacific and his victories were far from automatic. In three cases, Buna, Biak, and Manila, his reputation as a brilliant strategist was almost tarnished. In each case he called on Lieutenant General Robert Eichelberger to salvage the situation. Eichelberger never failed him. A combination of innovative tactics, personal courage, and commonsense leadership made Eichelberger an effective, trusted field commander.

NOTES

1. Eichelberger was 6-1 and weighed 190 pounds. R. Eichelberger to E. Eichelberger, 13 January 1944 and 3 April 1945. Contained in the Eichelberger papers, Duke University, Durham, North Carolina.
2. Fred Brown to R. Eichelberger, 4 August 1961. Eichelberger Papers, Duke University; Jay Luvaas, *Dear Miss Em: General Eichelberger's War in the Pacific, 1942-1945* (Westport, Conn.: Greenwood Press, 1972), p. xiv.
3. Robert Eichelberger and Milton MacKaye, *Our Jungle Road To Tokyo* (Washington: Zenger, 1949), pp. 21-23. The division was the 32nd Infantry.
4. Ibid., pp. 18-19.
5. Luvaas, p. 58; D. Edwards to R. Eichelberger, 11 January 1943; Eichelberger Papers.
6. Eichelberger and MacKaye, p. 101.
7. Ibid.

8. Eichelberger and MacKaye, p. 138; Harold Riegelman, *Caves of Biak: An American Officer's Experience in the Southwest Pacific* (New York: Dial, 1955), p. 137.

9. D. Clayton James, *The Years of MacArthur, Vol. II, 1941-1945* (Boston: Houghton-Mifflin, 1975), p. 453.

10. George Kenney, *General Kenney Reports: A Personal History of the Pacific War* (New York: Duell, Sloan and Pearle, 1949), p. 289; James, p. 459; Luvaas, p. 125.

11. R. G. 407-201-2: B. 3028, "G-2 Summary of the Biak Operation: 27 May-29 June 1944," p. 2, Federal Research Center, Suitland, Md., hereinafter cited as "G-2 Summary of Biak."

12. James, p. 458.

13. Spencer Davis, "Slaughter on Biak," *Australia Newsweek*, 12 June 1944; Eichelberger Papers.

14. "G-2 Summary of Biak," pp. 2-4, 7-9; Robert Ross Smith, *Approach to the Philippines* (Washington: Dept. of the Army, Office of the Chief of Military History, 1953), p. 299.

15. "G-2 Summary of Biak," p. 9.

16. Ibid., p. 4.

17. Ibid., p. 5; Davis; Eichelberger Papers.

18. Eichelberger and MacKaye, p. 139; Smith, *Approach*, p. 325.

19. Smith, *Approach*, p. 341.

20. James, p. 459.

21. Davis; Eichelberger Papers.

22. James, pp. 459-60.

23. Walter Krueger, *From Down Under to Nippon* (Washington: Combat Forces Press, 1953), p. 101.

24. Allied Forces, Southwest Pacific Area, "I Corps History of the Biak Operation," p. 3; Eichelberger Diary, 14 June 1944; Eichelberger Papers.

25. Eichelberger Diary, 15 June 1944; Eichelberger Papers.

26. Ibid., 16-17 June 1944.

27. R. Eichelberger to W. Krueger, 16 June 1944; Eichelberger Papers.

28. W. Krueger to R. Eichelberger, 17 June 1944; Eichelberger Papers.

29. Eichelberger and MacKaye, p. 146.

30. Allied Forces, "History of the Biak Operation," pp. 5-6; Eichelberger Papers.

31. Ibid.

32. Smith, *Approach*, pp. 368-69.

33. Eichelberger and MacKaye, p. 146.

34. R. Eichelberger to E. Eichelberger, 19 June 1944; Eichelberger Papers.

35. Riegelman, p. 142.

36. Smith, *Approach*, p. 372.

37. Eichelberger Diary, 19 June 1944; Allied Forces, "History of the Biak Operation," p. 8; Eichelberger Papers.

38. R. G. 407: 341-INF(186)-0.1 B.10641, pp. 25-26, Federal Records Center, Suitland, Md.; Allied Forces, "History of the Biak Operation," p. 12; Eichelberger Papers.

39. James, p. 460.

40. R. Eichelberger to E. Eichelberger, 3 June 1944, in Luvaas, p. 135.

41. Krueger, p. 218.

42. Ibid, p. 225.

43. Ibid., pp. 227-28.

44. Robert Ross Smith, *Triumph in the Philippines* (Washington: Dept. of the Army, Office of the Chief of Military History, 1963), p. 94.

45. James, p. 625.

46. Smith, *Triumph*, pp. 96-97.

47. Ibid., pp. 240-41.

48. James, p. 631.

49. Eichelberger Diary, 23 January 1945; Eichelberger Papers.

50. Smith, *Triumph*, p. 212.

51. Ibid.

52. Eichelberger Diary, 23 March 1945; Eichelberger Papers.

53. "Report of the Commanding General, Eighth Army, on the Nasugbu and Bataan Operations," p. 9. Robert Eichelberger, "The Amphibious Eighth," p. 4, both contained in the Eichelberger Papers.

54. "Report After Action with the Enemy Operation Eikevi, Luzon Campaign, 31 January-30 June 1945," p. 3. R. G. 407: 7.311-0.3 Box 7583, National Records Center, Suitland, Md. Hereinafter cited as "Operation Shoestring."

55. Smith, *Triumph*, p. 14; "C.G. Report on Nasugbu and Bataan," p. 14; Eichelberger Papers.

56. Eichelberger, "Amphibious Eighth," p. 4; Eichelberger Papers.

57. "Operation Shoestring," p. 1.

58. Ibid.; Eichelberger and MacKaye, p. 190.

59. Eichelberger Diary, 31 January 1945; Eichelberger Papers.

60. "Report of C.G. Nasugbu and Bataan," foreword; Eichelberger Papers.

61. Ibid.; R. Eichelberger to E. Eichelberger, 20 June 1944, Luvaas, p. 133.

62. "Operation Shoestring," p. 1.

63. "Report of C.G. Nasugbu and Bataan," pp. 6, 16; Eichelberger Papers.

64. Eichelberger and MacKaye, p. 190.

65. R. Eichelberger to E. Eichelberger, 2 February 1945, Luvaas, p. 208; "Operation Shoestring," p. 2.

66. "Operation Shoestring," p. 2.

67. "Report of the C.G. Nasugbu and Bataan," p. 16; Eichelberger Papers.

68. Ibid.; "Operation Shoestring," p. 2.

69. Eichelberger and MacKaye, p. 194; "C.G. Report on Nasugbu and Bataan," p. 6; Eichelberger Papers.

70. "Operation Shoestring," p. 2.

71. Ibid., p. 3.

72. Edward M. Flanagan, *The Angels: A History of the 11th Airborne Division, 1943-1946* (Washington: Infantry Journal Press, 1948), p. 76; Eichelberger Diary, 3 February 1945, Eichelberger Papers.

73. "Operation Shoestring," p.3.

74. Ibid.

75. "Report of the C.G. Nasugbu and Bataan, p. 22; Eichelberger Papers.

76. Ibid.; Eichelberger Diary, 4 February 1945; Eichelberger Papers.

77. Eichelberger Diary, 4 February 1945; Eichelberger Papers.

78. Ibid.

79. "Operation Shoestring," p. 4.

80. Ibid.; "C.G. Report Nasugbu and Bataan," p. 22; Eichelberger Papers.

81. Eichelberger Diary, 4 February 1945, Eichelberger Papers.

82. "Operation Shoestring," pp. 4-5; "C.G. Report Nasugbu and Bataan," p. 24; Eichelberger Papers.

83. Smith, *Triumph*, p. 265.

84. Ibid.

85. Eichelberger Diary, 7-9 February 1945; Eichelberger Papers.

86. "Report of C.G. Nasugbu and Bataan," foreword; Eichelberger Papers.

87. Eichelberger Dictations, 4 November 1960; Eichelberger Papers.

88. Major General Bill Dunckel to R. Eichelberger, 3 March 1945; Eichelberger Papers; James, p. 634.

89. James, pp. 632-33.

This article appeared in the autumn 1986 issue of *Parameters*.

IV. CIVIL-MILITARY RELATIONS

12

'Your Authority in France Will Be Supreme': The Baker–Pershing Relationship in World War I

by DONALD SMYTHE

During World War I, President Woodrow Wilson had little direct contact with General John J. Pershing. The President met the general only once in that period, on 24 May 1917, four days before Pershing sailed for Europe. Their brief meeting was cordial, but Wilson frankly surprised Pershing by talking very little about the war and giving no particular instructions.[1]

The administration dealt with its field commander mainly through its Secretary of War, Newton D. Baker, who gave Pershing unqualified support. Baker is reputed to have said to him: ''I will give you only two orders – one to go to France and the other to come home. In the meantime your authority in France will be supreme.''[2] It certainly was. As George C. Marshall, Jr. remarked to Pershing after the war:

> Though we have a hundred more wars, I do not think we will ever be so lucky in the choice of a Secretary. I cannot conceive of any future field commander ever being accorded the support you received.[3]

Amalgamation

Baker's support of Pershing was shown most especially in the amalgamation controversy with the Allies, which began in December 1917 and continued to the following summer. To the hard-pressed British and French, amalgamation made good sense. The American buildup was terribly slow. Nine months after declaring war, the United States had only 175,000 troops in France. Of four combat divisions, only one had been in the front lines, and that only on a battalion level and in a quiet sector.[4]

But with Russia out of the war, many German divisions released from the east would soon be on the Western Front, giving the enemy an estimated 60-percent manpower advantage. Italy was still reeling after the Caporetto debacle in October. England had just ended the catastrophic campaign of Ypres and

139

Passchendaele. France, hardly recovered from the failure of the Nivelle offensive and the army mutinies the previous spring, had reached her manpower limit. Thus, with strong German offensives expected in the spring, the war might well be lost before America could organize and train its own army.[5]

Accordingly, from December 1917 on, the Allies made strong attempts to amalgamate American companies or battalions into Allied units, with the understanding that when the emergency had passed they could be recalled for service in American divisions. They contended that raw American recruits would train better and faster if associated with British and French veterans. American commanders and staffs were inexperienced and less apt to use competently the magnificent American manpower than their Allied counterparts, who had been tried and tested by more than three years of war. Furthermore, the trans-Atlantic transport problem was such that by the time America brought over the support troops and impedimenta to sustain a separate army, the war might well be lost.[6]

Concerned, President Wilson talked the matter over with Secretary Baker, who cabled Pershing on 18 December:

Both English and French are pressing upon the President their desires to have your forces amalgamated with theirs by regiments and companies, and both express the belief in impending heavy drive by Germans somewhere along the lines of the Western Front. We do not desire loss of identity of our forces but regard that as secondary to the meeting of any critical situation by the most helpful use possible of the troops at your command.[7]

In effect, then, the administration was willing to consent to amalgamation if the situation were sufficiently "critical." But it reserved judgment on that matter, not to itself, but to its overseas commander, Pershing, who was on the spot and who could more accurately assess the situation. The President, Baker told Pershing, "desires you to have full authority to use the forces at your command as you deem wise," although he did suggest consultation with French and British counterparts.[8]

Pershing did consult, but he was strongly opposed to amalgamation, except in extreme emergency and then only temporarily. "No people with a grain of national pride would consent to furnish men to build up the army of another nation," he said.[9]

In addition, he contended that no matter what the Allies said, they would not easily permit him to reclaim amalgamated American troops (a contention borne out by subsequent experience); that Americans would have language difficulties in serving with the French; and that Americans would inevitably resent any British or French mistake which got large numbers of American troops killed. In addition, the Allies seemed to be training more for trench than for open warfare, which he advocated.[10]

On 1 January 1918, Pershing cabled Baker:

Do not think emergency now exists that would warrant our putting companies or battalions into British or French divisions, and would not do so except in grave crisis.[11]

That crisis occurred on 21 March 1918, when the Germans launched a massive offensive against the British. Suddenly the Western Front, which since October 1914 had scarcely moved 10 miles in either direction, had a hole in it 40 miles deep and 40 wide.[12]

Six days later, on 27 March, the military representatives of the Supreme War Council unanimously passed Joint Note Number 18, which stated:

> It is highly desirable that the American Government should assist the Allied armies as soon as possible by permitting, in principle, the temporary service of American units in Allied army corps and divisions . . . . In execution of the foregoing, and until otherwise directed by the Supreme War Council, only American infantry and machine-gun units . . . [should] be brought to France.[13]

The text was written by an American, General Tasker H. Bliss, and passed over Pershing's objections. The following day, Secretary Baker, who happened to be in Europe, also overruled Pershing and recommended to the President that he approve Joint Note Number 18 "in view of the present critical situation."[14]

One should note that the decision by Bliss and Baker to give priority shipment to infantry and machine-gun units necessarily postponed organization and training of complete American divisions and thus made impossible the formation of an independent American army, at least for the time. Pershing is frequently presented in American history books as a great white knight battling the evil Europeans in their scheming machinations to prevent the formation of an American army, but the situation was not so black and white. Bliss and Baker supported the Europeans, as did General Leonard Wood, Admiral William S. Sims, and Colonel Edward M. House – all Americans and all as patriotic as Pershing. As House said:

> Pershing's feeling that an American army under his command should be established and made as formidable as possible is understandable. Nevertheless, the thing to be done now is to stop the Germans and to stop them it is evident that we must put in every man that is available.[15]

A case can be made that Pershing was myopic and narrow in his view of the crisis. David Lloyd George, the British Prime Minister, felt that Pershing was impervious to "intelligence and common sense," preferring to build up a separate American army even if it meant losing the war.[16]

One should note also that Joint Note Number 18 made no specific mention of the number of infantry and machine-gun units that were to be shipped, nor of the length of time that they would be given preferential shipment. Later Lloyd George filled in the details by asking that 120,000 be shipped each month for the next four months (April, May, June, and July 1918). On 19 April, after returning to America and consulting with the President, Baker approved the request. On that date, he handed Lord Reading, the British High Commissioner in America, a memorandum stating that his decision was made because of "the exigencies of the present military situation."[17]

When Pershing read the 19 April memorandum later, he exclaimed, "If this isn't amalgamation what is it?''[18] Even though Baker specified that the troops, when transported to Europe, were to be under Pershing's direction and trained and used at his discretion, what else could he do with them except feed them into Allied ranks in an emergency? It was either that or sit out the war. He lacked the auxiliary and supply services to build up separate American divisions, much less separate corps and armies.[19]

By some inexplicable quirk, the administration failed to inform Pershing of Baker's important memorandum until 26 April, one week after it had been given to Lord Reading.[20] Although Pershing heard a rumor of it through the British liaison officer at his headquarters at Chaumont, he disbelieved it, feeling there must have been some mistake.[21] Hence, when the British in London produced a cable from Reading quoting Baker's memorandum of 19 April, Pershing insisted that Reading must have misunderstood Baker (Pershing was in London from 22 to 24 April to confer about shipping). Such a concession about amalgamation could not possibly have been made, he contended, and he would not be bound by it.[22]

Although the British gnashed their teeth at Pershing's refusal and were sure he was wrong, they decided to come to terms with him. Even under the 19 April memorandum, he had something they very much wanted – discretion to decide where American troops went after they arrived in Europe. Thus far the British could expect only 60,000, and those only during the month of April under an earlier agreement made by Baker and Pershing.[23]

Accordingly, Lord Alfred Milner, the British War Minister, signed an agreement with Pershing on 24 April (the London Agreement), whereby during the month of May infantry and machine-gun units of six divisions would be brought over for training and service with the British. Artillery personnel were to be brought over next, and should any surplus shipping be available, it would bring over whatever Pershing wanted to balance out his forces.[24]

When Pershing returned to Chaumont, he was startled to receive a copy of Baker's memorandum of 19 April, promising priority shipment of 120,000 infantry and machine-gunners a month from April through July. Only then did he realize how far off base he had been in London. Whereas Baker had committed himself to a priority shipment of 480,000 infantry and machine-gunners stretched over four months, Pershing had allowed the British only 126,000, and this only for the month of May, exacting a promise that the British bring over artillery personnel and other troops "immediately thereafter."[25]

The question now was, Which agreement would the United States honor?

By all rights, it should have been the Baker memorandum of 19 April, made by Pershing's superior, the Secretary of War. But once Baker learned of the 24 April London Agreement, he decided to support it, perhaps thinking that if the British were willing to agree to it, things were not as bad as they had seemed. Furthermore, Pershing was on the scene. His London Agreement preserved

American freedom of action, kept future options open, and did not so drastically postpone the formation of a separate American army.[26]

The fact that two separate and contradictory agreements had been made brought home to Secretary Baker the inevitable confusion of trying to carry on negotiations simultaneously on both sides of the Atlantic. Accordingly, he strongly recommended to President Wilson that any future arrangements be made only by Pershing, "so that we would have one agreement made at one place, rather than several agreements made in several places which were more or less irreconcilable in some of their terms." To their great vexation, the British and French Ambassadors were told that Baker would make no further agreements with them concerning troop shipments; on this question the man to see was Pershing.[27]

Pershing was to have subsequent battles over the amalgamation question, but his hand was strengthened by knowing that he had the backing of the Secretary of War, to whose judgment the President of the United States would ordinarily defer. George C. Marshall, Jr. was right when he told Pershing: "Though we have a hundred more wars, . . . I cannot conceive of any future field commander ever being accorded the support you received."[28]

The Goethals Proposal

A second instance in which Baker supported Pershing was the logistic crisis during the summer of 1918, which led to the so-called Goethals Proposal. Because of priority shipments given to infantry and machine-gunners in the spring, producing a consequent lack of supply troops, the American Expeditionary Force (AEF) began to fall progressively behind in moving supplies from the ships, through the ports, and to the troops inland. A massive bottleneck was building up at the ports.[29]

In Washington the feeling grew that Pershing was trying to do too much, attempting to wear too many hats. Sir William Wiseman, a British agent there who had the ear of both Colonel House and President Wilson, warned that the AEF was heading for a supply crisis and that something must be done about it.[30]

Secretary Baker agreed and decided to appoint as logistical chief in Europe General George W. Goethals, an engineer who had carried the construction of the Panama Canal through to completion and a man with an international reputation as an administrator. On 6 July Baker wrote Pershing that he planned to send Goethals to Europe to handle supplies and that, in order to free Pershing to devote full time to training and fighting his army, Goethals would be in a coordinate, rather than subordinate, position to Pershing.[31]

Pershing gagged on the letter, which arrived 26 July. To him an independent supply chief violated a fundamental military principle – unity of command. In all the major armies the field commander also controlled the supply lines. Only thus could military operations and their logistical support be properly coordinated.[32]

Fortunately for Pershing, Baker's proposal was only a suggestion. As always, the Secretary was extraordinarily deferential to his field commander. "Will take no action until we are in perfect accord," he promised. "My whole purpose in this matter is to get all of the data before you and rather to aid you to come to a right conclusion than to impose my own."[33]

To tell the truth, Pershing knew that his supply organization needed shaking up.[34] On 27 July, the day after receiving Baker's letter, Pershing relieved the Services of Supply commander and appointed Major General James G. Harbord, a trusted subordinate, in his stead. That same day he sent off a confidential cable to the Secretary of War marked "RUSH RUSH RUSH RUSH." The supply system, he said,

includes transportation up to the trenches and is intimately interwoven with our whole organization. The whole must remain absolutely under one head. Any division of responsibility or coordinate control in any sense would be fatal. The man who fights the armies must control their supply through subordinates responsible to him alone. The responsibility is then fixed and the possibility of conflicting authority avoided. This military principle is vital and cannot be violated without inviting failure. It is the very principle which we all urged upon the Allies when we got a supreme commander . . . . I very earnestly urge upon you Mr. Secretary that no variation from this principle be permitted.[35]

Later that day Pershing sent another cable, asking Baker to postpone a decision until a letter on the subject could reach him. He also urged the Secretary to visit Europe again "just as soon as possible." Pershing was obviously worried by what he considered a threat, in the person of Goethals with coordinate authority, to his AEF organization.[36]

The following day Pershing wrote a letter repeating his arguments, especially that of unity of command and responsibility.[37] Still later that day he wrote again, suggesting that if Baker felt strongly on the matter, Goethals could be sent to Europe to look things over, but with no promise of command. Pershing could ascertain his attitude and decide if he would fit in. He was insistent, however, that it must be as a subordinate.[38]

Two cables and two letters within 48 hours! The Secretary had touched a sensitive nerve.

Baker realized this and decided to drop the Goethals idea. He was won over by Pershing's arguments against divided authority and realized that Goethals, while extremely competent, was not an easy man to work with, whereas Harbord worked well with Pershing and had his entire confidence. Urged on by Baker and House, whom Pershing had contacted, the President decided that "nothing would be done contrary to Pershing's wishes."[39] Rarely has an overseas commander received greater support from his superiors.

The Armistice

The only time during the war when Pershing overreached himself with his superiors concerned the armistice. On 25 October 1918, Marshal Foch called a conference of the Allied commanders to determine, not whether an armistice should be granted, but – assuming one was – what the precise terms should be.[40]

Since Foch had not called the meeting to discuss alternatives, Pershing did not bring up the question of surrender. He felt strongly about it, however, and had serious reservations about granting any armistice at all. Such was the Allies' progress that he felt they were justified in demanding unconditional surrender.[41]

On 25 October Pershing cabled the War Department, reporting the meeting and summarizing the proposed armistice terms. Baker's reply, dated 27 October, gave the President's reaction to the terms and added this significant sentence:

The President . . . is relying upon your counsel and advice in this matter and . . . will be glad to have you feel entirely free to bring to his attention any consideration he may have overlooked.[42]

Baker and the President were thinking about modifications in the armistice terms. Pershing took the message to mean he was authorized to suggest modification of the basic approach, that is, to proposed surrender rather than an armistice.

In retrospect, it is clear that Pershing should have proposed his idea of unconditional surrender directly to the War Department and awaited a decision. But events were moving swiftly in Europe. The Supreme War Council was scheduled to meet on 30 October, and Pershing did not receive Baker's message of 27 October until the day before. Colonel House was in Europe, but as bad luck would have it, Pershing was unable to talk to him, being confined to his room with a bad case of the grippe.[43]

On Wednesday, 30 October, the first day that Pershing was back in circulation, he met Colonel House five minutes before the Supreme War Council met and gave him a copy of a document he had sent to it that very day, summarizing his arguments against an armistice and calling for unconditional surrender. A copy was simultaneously sent to the War Department.[44]

House was dismayed by the document. While Pershing was quite within his rights to suggest specific armistice terms when requested, he was obviously out of place in suggesting that the war should not be terminated at all, or should eventually be terminated one way rather than another – especially when unasked. President Wilson had determined on an armistice, as had other Allied leaders. Pershing was meddling where he did not belong. He was that worst of all things: a general mixing in politics.[45]

Pershing's document produced consternation in Washington. Baker told the President: ''He is obviously on record one way with you and another way with the Supreme War Council! It is really tragic.''[46]

Baker was wrong in thinking that Pershing's 25 October and 30 October documents contradicted each other. The first one, as Foch said in opening the meeting that day, addressed what the armistice terms should be if there were an armistice. The latter addressed simply whether there should be an armistice.

Washington was right, however, in feeling that Pershing had violated instructions. He had been told in Baker's 27 October cable that if he had any other ideas, he was to communicate them to the President; he was also urged to confer with Colonel House, who was on the spot. Pershing did neither of these things. He sent his ideas on unconditional surrender directly to the Supreme War Council and let the President know about it afterwards. He did the same with House, merely handing him a carbon of his document on the way into the meeting. On both points he was clearly out of order.[47]

Called upon to explain his conduct, Pershing cited Baker's 27 October cable authorizing him to "feel entirely free" to bring up other considerations.[48] Baker was unsatisfied with this explanation. "A bad matter is made much worse by this," he said, and drew up a letter of reprimand, stressing that political matters were outside military jurisdiction. On the President's advice, however, he decided not to send it. After all, the war was almost over.[49]

With this sole exception, Pershing had his own way in Europe as far as the President and Secretary of War were concerned. "Your authority in France will be supreme," Baker had told Pershing when he went to Europe.[50] That supremacy is borne out by the record.

NOTES

1. John J. Pershing, *My Experiences in the World War* (New York: Frederick A. Stokes Company, 1931), I, 37; Ray Stannard Baker, *Woodrow Wilson: Life and Letters* (New York: Doubleday, Doran and Company, 1927-39), VII, 85; John J. Pershing jotting No. 11 (undated, but in the 1920s), Box 355, John J. Pershing Papers, Library of Congress.

2. I have made a quotation out of Baker's remark, which is reported in indirect address in Frederick Palmer, *Newton D. Baker: America at War* (New York: Dodd, Mead & Company, 1931), I, 180.

3. George C. Marshall, Jr. To Pershing, 24 November 1930, Box 354, Pershing Papers.

4. Pershing, *My Experiences*, I, 277.

5. US Department of the Army, *United States Army in the World War, 1917-1919* (Cited hereafter as *USAWW*) (Washington: US Government Printing Office, 1948), II, 88; James G. Harbord, *The American Army in France, 1917-1919* (Boston: Little, Brown, 1936), p. 185; J. F. C. Fuller, *Decisive Battles of the U.S.A.* (New York: Harper & Brothers, 1942), p. 376.

6. Thomas Lonergan, *It Might Have Been Lost* (New York: G. P. Putnam's Sons, 1929), pp. 9-10, 33; Bernard Serrigny, *Trente ans avec Petain* (Paris: Plon, 1959), pp. 167-68; Harbord, 190; David Lloyd George, *War Memoirs of David Lloyd George* (London: [n.p.], 1933-37 [also published during the same years in Boston by Little, Brown]), V, 3005-6; Charles Seymour, ed., *The Intimate Papers of Colonel House* (Boston: Houghton Mifflin, 1926-28), III, 309-10; *USAWW*, III, 4; Maurice Hankey, *The Supreme Command* (London: Allen and Unwin, 1961), II, 744; Tasker H. Bliss to Newton D. Baker, 2 February 1918, Box 74, Tasker H. Bliss Papers, Library of Congress; S. T. Williamson, "The War That Was Fought Behind the War," *The New York Times*, 22 March 1931, sec. p.9, p.1; Hugh A. Drum diary, 1-29 January 1918, Hugh A. Drum Papers, in the possession of Elliott L. Johnson, US Air Force Academy, Colorado Springs, Colorado; cable from William Graves Sharp to the Secretary of State, quoting Arthur Frazier, 30 January 1918, Edward M. House Papers, Sterling Library, Yale University; Charles de Marenches to Pershing, 14 December 1923, Box 353, Pershing Papers.

7. Baker, VII, 417.

8. *Ibid.*

9. Pershing, *My Experiences*, I, 254-55.
10. *USAWW*, II, 132.
11. *Ibid.*
12. J. F. C. Fuller, *The Conduct of War, 1789-1961* (New Brunswick, N.J.: Rutgers Univ. Press, 1961), p. 160; D. Clayton James, *The Years of MacArthur* (Boston: Houghton Mifflin, 1970-75), I, 161.
13. *USAWW*, II, 258.
14. *Ibid.*, pp. 261-62.
15. Seymour, III, 444; Frederick Maurice, "General Pershing and the A.E.F.," *Foreign Affairs*, 9 (July 1931), 602; Lloyd Griscom to Pershing, 16 July 1918, Box 85, Pershing Papers.
16. Lloyd George, V, 3018.
17. *USAWW*, II, 336-37.
18. Pershing notation penciled on Baker memorandum of 19 April 1918, in Box 19, Pershing Papers.
19. Pershing, *My Experiences*, II, 8; *USAWW*, II, 283-85 and 336-37.
20. *USAWW*, II, 351-52.
21. Dennis E. Nolan to Pershing, 7 April 1930, Box 354, Pershing Papers.
22. James G. Harbord, address at the Army War College, 11 April 1932, pp. 11-12, in James L. Collins Papers, in possession of James L. Collins, Jr., Washington, D.C.; Pershing, *My Experiences*, II, 6; Harbord, *American Army*, pp. 254, 259.
23. *USAWW*, II, 286-88, 292 and 329-30; Lonergan, p. 122; Lloyd George, V, 3044; Pershing, *My Experiences*, I, 383-84.
24. James G. Harbord, *Leaves from a War Diary* (New York; Dodd, Mead,1925), pp. 275-76; Lonergan, pp. 172-75; *USAWW*, II, 342-43; Pershing, *My Experiences*, II, 6-9; Lloyd George, V, 3051-52.
25. *USAWW*, II, 342-43.
26. Baker to Woodrow Wilson, 29 April 1918, in Box 8, Newton D. Baker Papers, Library of Congress.
27. Baker to Pershing, 6 June 1918, Box 19, Pershing Papers; Edward M. Coffman, "Conflicts in American Planning: An Aspect of World War I Strategy," *Military Review*, 43 (June 1963), 83; Gerald R. Reading, *Rufus Isaacs, First Marquess of Reading* (New York: [n.p.], 1942-45), II, 98.
28. Marshall to Pershing, 24 November 1930, Box 354, Pershing Papers.
29. Newton D. Baker to James G. Harbord, 8 February 1935, James G. Harbord Papers, Library of Congress; Harbord, *American Army*, pp. 347-48; Pershing, *My Experiences*, II, 139.
30. Wiseman to House, 11 May 1918, House to Wilson, 3 June 1918, and House diary, 23 May 1918 – all in House Papers; Wiseman to Eric Drummond, 30 May 1918, William Wiseman Papers, Drawer 91, Folder 129, Sterling Library, Yale University; Peyton C. March to Pershing, 5 July 1918, Box 123, Pershing Papers; Lloyd C. Griscom to Pershing, 20 July 1918, Box 85, Pershing Papers.
31. Pershing, *My Experiences*, II, 185-86.
32. *Ibid.*, pp. 180-81; Harbord, *American Army*, p. 352.
33. Baker to Pershing, 30 July 1918, Box 19, Pershing Papers.
34. Pershing to James G. Harbord, 30 January 1935, James G. Harbord Papers, New York Historical Society; Harbord, *American Army*, p. 353; Harbord, *Leaves*, p. 339.
35. Pershing, *My Experiences*, II, 177; *USAWW*, II, 553. Later that year, during the great Meuse-Argonne campaign, Pershing stripped his Services of Supply of every available man because of a manpower crisis. He did so simply by ordering it. Had the supply services been under an independent commander, responsible not to Pershing but to Washington, it might not have been so easy (*My Experiences*, II, 180-81).
36. Pershing to Baker, 27 July 1918, Box 19, Pershing Papers.
37. Pershing, *My Experiences*, II, 190-91.
38. Pershing to Baker, 28 July 1918, Box 19, Pershing Papers.
39. Baker to Pershing, 30 July 1918, Box 19, Pershing Papers; Pershing to House, 7 August 1918, Box 97, Pershing Papers; House diary, 17 August 1918, and Gordon Auchincloss to Arthur Frazier, 21 August 1918 – both in House Papers; Wilton B. Fowler, *British-American Relations, 1917-1918: The Role of Sir William Wiseman* (Princeton: Princeton Univ. Press, 1969), p. 156.
40. Jean Jules Henri Mordacq, *Le Ministere Clemenceau; Journal d'un temoin* (Paris: [n.p.], 1930-31), II, 292-93; T. Bentley Mott, *Twenty Years as Military Attache* (New York: Oxford Univ. Press,

1937), pp. 262, 268; T. Bentley Mott to Pershing, 4 December 1929, Box 354, Pershing Papers.

41. *USAWW*, X, 29; Pershing, *My Experiences*, II, 368-69.
42. Baker to Pershing, 27 October 1918, Box 8, Baker Papers; Pershing, *My Experiences*, II, 360.
43. Pershing diary, 26-30 October 1918, Box 4, Pershing Papers; House diary, 27 October 1918, House Papers; Gordon Auchincloss diary, 29 October 1918, Drawer 55, File 84, Gordon Auchincloss Papers, Sterling Library, Yale University; Pershing, *My Experiences*, II, 364; Charles G. Dawes, *A Journal of the Great War* (Boston: Houghton Mifflin, 1921), I, 195-96.
44. *USAWW*, X, 29; Pershing diary, 30 October 1918, Box 4, Pershing Papers; Auchincloss diary, 30 October 1918, Drawer 55, File 84, Auchincloss Papers.
45. Auchincloss diary, 30 October 1918, Drawer 55, File 84, Auchincloss Papers; Arthur Frazier to Pershing, 16 November 1938, Box 78, Pershing Papers.
46. Baker to Wilson, 31 October 1918, Series II, Reel 101, Woodrow Wilson Papers, Library of Congress; Robert Lansing diary, 31 October 1918, Box 65, Robert Lansing Papers, Library of Congress.
47. Pershing, *My Experiences*, II, 364-65.
48. Baker, *Wilson*, VIII, 561; Pershing cable No. 1869, 4 November 1918, Series II, Box 187, Wilson Papers; Pershing diary, 3 November 1918, Box 4, Pershing Papers.
49. Arthur Walworth, *Woodrow Wilson* (New York: Longmans Green, 1958), II, 192; Baker to Wilson, 5 November 1918, and Wilson to Baker, 7 November 1918 – both in Series II, Box 187, Wilson Papers. The Baker letter of reprimand to Pershing, 5 November 1918, can no longer be found in either the Baker or Wilson Papers, but I am indebted to Dr. Bullitt Lowry of North Texas State University for furnishing me a copy of the letter which he copied years ago from Box 8 of the Baker Papers.
50. Palmer, I, 180. See n. 2. above.

This article appeared in the September 1979 issue of *Parameters*.

13

The 1949 Revolt of the Admirals

by KEITH D. McFARLAND

The word "mutiny" usually brings thoughts of a group of crude, unkempt men of the sea deposing an evil captain whose tyranny they found insufferable. But this stereotype of a mutiny rarely holds true in real life. Certainly it didn't in the case of the most unusual mutiny in the history of the United States Navy. That rebellion against authority took place not at some distant time, but just 32 years ago. It took place not at some uncharted spot in an ocean halfway around the world, but in Pentagon offices and congressional hearing rooms. The "crew" was not rabble, but an elite group of decorated admirals who had devoted their lives to the Navy and their country. And the "captain" was not a crazed despot; he was President Harry S. Truman, and his "Executive Officer" was Secretary of Defense Louis A. Johnson. Known as "The Revolt of the Admirals," this event was a flagrant peacetime challenge hurled by top-ranking military men at the civilian leadership of the military.

Rather than an outgrowth of a new problem, the 1949 Revolt of the Admirals was a flare-up of the feud between the advocates of land-based airpower and those of sea-based airpower. From the days of Billy Mitchell on, both sides were convinced that their particular arm provided the most sound basis on which to build the nation's defense. While the unity of purpose in World War II would seem to have reduced interservice rivalry, such was not the case. In fact, in many ways the war actually increased tensions as the Army, Navy, and Army Air Corps continually bickered over missions, roles, and responsibilities. Such disputes and obvious need for unified procurement activities led to serious consideration of military unification, but it was agreed that the midst of war was the wrong time for any drastic change in the command setup, and the question of unification was placed on the shelf until the war was over.[1]

No sooner had the fighting overseas come to an end than it was replaced by a domestic conflict which the press called "The Battle of the Potomac."[2] This conflict was a bitter clash between the Army and the Navy, wrangling over their respective unification plans. The Army, which accepted as a foregone conclusion that the Air Corps would emerge as a separate service, favored a true merger of the armed forces with control exercised by a single cabinet officer. The Navy, on the other hand, accepted only reluctantly the idea of a separate Air Force and strongly opposed a merger with the Army, instead preferring a setup that would coordinate the separate services. Throughout the fall of 1945 and the following year the battle raged. By January 1947 the Administration and both services had a plan they could accept, and after lengthy congressional hearings the National Security Act of 1947 was passed and signed into law on 26 July.

What the act provided for was not a unified command, but a coordinated national military establishment made up of three equal executive departments – Army, Navy, and Air Force – with each headed by a secretary with cabinet status. Military input was to be provided by the Joint Chiefs of Staff, consisting of the Army and Air Force Chiefs of Staff and the Chief of Naval Operations. Provision was made for a Secretary of Defense, but the position was weakened by providing only for coordination and supervisory activities. Clearly, the Navy view of a coordinated rather than a unified command had prevailed.[3]

President Truman's choice to become the first Secretary of Defense was Secretary of the Navy James Forrestal, a man who had played a major role in setting up the new national military establishment.[4] As the new Secretary attempted to implement the provisions of the National Security Act, a task that would have been difficult even in tranquil times, he was hampered in 1947 and 1948 by the challenge of the Cold War, which placed great pressure on the military establishment. At the same time, the President was pressing for major reductions in the defense budget; thus, competition among the services for the limited funds became increasingly intense. In an attempt to secure a greater portion of the tight budget and thus assure the future well-being of their respective services, the three civilian secretaries and their top military advisers intensified their contention over the missions and responsibilities they felt were needed to improve their positions.

When Truman signed the National Security Act, he also issued Executive Order 9877 setting forth the roles and missions of each military service. Because that document was vague on a number of points, however, Forrestal had to work with the secretaries to clarify responsibilities. Although some progress was made, differences remained, especially those involving various aspects of aviation. According to the Navy, the Air Force wanted control of "anything that flew" while the Air Force contended that the Navy wanted a second air force under the guise of tactical airpower. Both services felt they should have strategic bombing capabilities. The Army wanted control over anything that walked or moved on land – a goal that worried the Navy because it might lead to the loss of the Marines.[5] As the debates continued, the Navy became increasingly concerned that the Air Force wanted its aviation and the Army wanted its amphibious responsibilities.

In late 1947 the Air Force began a campaign for a 70-group Air Force as opposed to the 55-group force advocated by the President. In this endeavor it was quite successful in gaining considerable support in Congress and among the public. Forrestal indirectly opposed the Air Force campaign by urging a balanced force concept according to which funds would be divided evenly among the three services. The idea of three equal shares was not well received when it was found how small the shares would be. Before long, officials of each of the branches of the military were publicly demanding a greater portion of the defense funds, this in spite of Secretary Forrestal's request that they not do so. That Forrestal had no real control over the civilian or military leaders of the various services soon became evident.[6]

As the months of 1948 passed, President Truman grew more concerned because the Secretary of Defense seemed to have so little control over his service chiefs. Truman thought that Forrestal's problem stemmed from too much leniency in dealing with his subordinates.[7] Before the National Security Act had been passed, Truman had said he would appoint ''the hardest, meanest so and so'' he could find to be Secretary of Defense.[8] Obviously he had not found him. By fall, the President was in the midst of his battle for reelection, and when Forrestal chose not to take part in that campaign, refusing even to provide financial support, Truman made up his mind that if he were returned to office, the Defense Secretary would have to go.[9]

In September 1948, when Truman's defeat seemed virtually certain, Louis A. Johnson, of Clarksburg, West Virginia undertook the seemingly thankless and unquestionably difficult task of serving as the Democratic National Committee's finance chairman. In essence this meant raising money for the President's campaign. Johnson, who headed the prestigious law firm of Steptoe and Johnson, did a superb job of raising funds, bringing in more than $1.5 million to finance the reelection campaign. When Truman defeated Thomas E. Dewey in the political upset of the century, the finance chairman was clearly in line for a political payoff of some sort. On 2 March 1949, the President announced that Johnson would replace Forrestal as Secretary of Defense.

That Johnson's appointment was in part politically motivated cannot be denied; however, to draw the conclusion that he was chosen only to pay a political debt ignores the fact that the well-to-do lawyer had a number of qualifications and characteristics which made him in many ways a logical choice for the position. First, Johnson was experienced in defense matters. During World War I he had seen action in France as an infantry captain, and in the Twenties and Thirties he had kept up on defense issues by his activities in the American Legion, eventually becoming its National Commander. Further, from 1937 to mid-1940 he had done an outstanding job as Franklin Roosevelt's Assistant Secretary of War. According to Robert Patterson, Secretary of War from 1945 to 1947, Johnson's efforts in preparing American industry for war were responsible for shortening World War II by 18 months. Johnson's stay at the War Department was clouded by his running feud with Secretary of War Harry H. Woodring. Indeed, their personal and ideological dispute became so disruptive that Roosevelt had to let both men go. But while Johnson was often accused of being overly aggressive and too politically oriented, even his severest critics acknowledged that he was an excellent administrator and planner who had done a commendable job in his War Department post.[10]

Truman also turned to Johnson because he was a dynamic, hard-charging man who was not afraid to knock heads when necessary. Johnson's physical size – six feet two, 220 pounds – combined with his flamboyant personality and skills as a debater to make his presence felt in any group.[11] Considering Truman's belief that Forrestal had been too accommodating of his service secretaries and military leaders, Johnson's strength seemed quite attractive. Then, too, there was Johnson's propensity for personal loyalty. One key characteristic that the West Virginian had shown during his stay in the War Department and in the years after was a fierce loyalty to the chief executive, and if there was anything Truman tended toward in his cabinet appointments it was a person who would be loyal.[12] In late 1948 the President needed a Secretary of Defense who could achieve two items of high priority: implementation of a major austerity program and true unification of the services. Truman wanted an experienced defense man who could be hard-nosed with subordinates and loyal to him. And Louis Johnson seemed to fit that bill.

Although Johnson's appointment was generally well accepted in Army and Air Force circles, such was not the case among high-ranking Navy personnel. Losing a Secretary of Defense who had formerly headed the Navy Department and had been supportive of it was alarming enough, but now that man was being replaced by an ambitious politico who was well known for his pro-Air Force views. In the late 1930s Johnson had been one of the first high-ranking national officials to openly advocate a 10,000-plane Air Corps and a strongly upgraded national aircraft productive capacity. Johnson had continued to champion the cause of the Air Corps and in early 1940 remarked to President Roosevelt that ''this country must accept the fact that airpower is not simply an auxiliary to land and sea forces. It has become a paramount factor in national defense.''[13] World War II gave support to his position. In 1949, Navy officials had no reason to believe that time had changed Johnson's views.[14] When Johnson assumed his new position, Navy leaders were looking for the worst, and they did not take long to find it.

By the time Johnson was sworn in on 28 March 1949, he was publicly committed to bring real unification and economy to the defense establishment, but just how soon he would act or how far he would go was still uncertain. The answer, however, was soon forthcoming. On 7th April, the day after Army Day, Johnson announced that henceforth all such observances by the individual services would be eliminated. The purpose was to get the services to think of themselves as one defense establishment rather than separate entities. A week later he took a much bolder step in issuing ''Consolidation Directive No. 1,'' which set forth new public information policies, including a provision that all security reviews of statements by active duty and retired personnel would henceforth be handled in the Office of the Secretary of Defense. Outspoken naval officials interpreted this as an attempt on Johnson's part to gag them, to keep them from speaking their minds.[15] At about the same time, Johnson recommended and the President approved an earlier Air Force request to cut back procurement of certain fighters and medium bombers in order to purchase three dozen B-36s instead. That the proposal had originated months before Johnson arrived on the scene and that Forrestal had approved the transaction before his departure were beside the point; the Navy saw only what it wanted to see – Johnson as a villain.[16]

As alarming as the new Secretary's actions were during his first three weeks on the job, they were just firecrackers compared to the blast he was about to set off. On 23 April, less than a month after taking office, Johnson took the step that set off the Revolt of the Admirals: he cancelled construction of the new Navy super aircraft carrier, the U.S.S. *United States*. Probably nothing else that he could have done would have been more demoralizing to the Navy, for that craft was the symbol and hope of its future.

Navy planning for a large, flush-deck carrier capable of launching planes that could deliver atomic bombs had started shortly after World War II began. The effort continued, and in early 1948 Navy Secretary John L. Sullivan announced plans to build a 1090-foot, 65,000-ton super carrier. At that time the question of whether the Navy would have a strategic bombing role was still unresolved, and the Navy believed that the prototype vessel would assure its place in that regard and, with that, a greater share of the shrinking defense pie. With the responsibilities of the service secretaries and Joint Chiefs of Staff still not clarified under the National Security Act, the Navy believed it could unilaterally make the decision to proceed with the carrier. Consequently, in March 1948 Secretary Forrestal announced to the Joint Chiefs that he and the President had approved construction. In the year that followed, plans were completed, contracts let, and on 18 April 1949 the keel was laid in Newport News, Virginia.[17]

Planning for the carrier had proceeded amid great controversy between the Navy and Air Force, the latter seeing it as an attempt to move in on its strategic bombing role. Because of the discord, and since the keel had not yet been laid when Johnson came to office, he wanted to study the issue and decide whether to proceed with the project. The matter was discussed at his first meeting with the Joint Chiefs, but only briefly, and no recommendations were made. Four days later, on 15 April, Johnson asked the Chiefs to present their individual views on the advisability of continuing construction of the carrier. In the week that followed, the Secretary conferred daily on the issue with the Army Chief of Staff, General Omar N. Bradley; the Air Force Chief of Staff, General Hoyt S. Vandenberg; and the Chief of Naval Operations, Admiral Louis E. Denfeld. The Chiefs quickly made their positions and the reasons behind them known to Johnson. Both Bradley and Vandenberg opposed construction, while Denfeld supported it.[18] Johnson briefed the President on the matter on at least a half dozen occasions, primarily to report what was taking place rather than to ask advice, for Truman saw this as Johnson's decision to make.[19] While seeking counsel from the uniformed military chiefs, Johnson chose not to discuss the matter with any of the service secretaries, even though Secretary Sullivan had requested an opportunity to do so.

By the evening of 22 April, Johnson, after reading the final drafts of the papers to be presented by the Joint Chiefs, had made up his mind to cancel. Before informing the President, he sounded out the chairmen of the House and Senate Armed Services Committees, Representative Carl Vinson and Senator Millard E. Tydings, both of whom supported the decision. The following morning, Johnson called the President and told him of the decision. Truman fully concurred. Johnson then issued the order to Secretary Sullivan directing that construction of the carrier be halted immediately. The order was simultaneously released to the press.

Secretary Sullivan, who had not been consulted on the matter, was in Texas for a speaking engagement when he learned of the decision. He immediately returned to Washington, where he prepared a scathing letter of resignation to President Truman. At the direction of Truman's secretary, Charles G. Ross, Sullivan sent the letter to Secretary of Defense Johnson instead, thus preserving the Navy Secretary's friendship with the President. Sullivan's resignation was immediately accepted, and the letter, castigating Johnson for failure to consult with the Navy on such an important matter, soon appeared in newspapers around the country.[20]

Neither such criticism as Sullivan's nor making the cancellation decision bothered Secretary Johnson; for various reasons, he actually relished the occasion. To him the carrier decision provided an opportunity to move in the direction of his two major goals – unification and economy – with one swoop. Progress toward unification would result from moving to halt an earlier unilateral decision on a weapon and getting all the services, through the Joint Chiefs, to evaluate it and make a recommendation. Economy would be effected through saving nearly $200 million by not building the craft. There was even more to be gained by Johnson in making the decision that he did: he could demonstrate to representatives of all services that he was in control and was not afraid to make hard decisions.[21]

Sullivan's resignation immediately became a *cause célèbre* for Navy brass, who hailed Sullivan as a man of principle who was willing to sacrifice his career for a just and noble purpose. But the hoopla over the Secretary's departure could not mask the setback suffered by the Navy and the victory gained by the Air Force in the continuing battle between the two services over the issue of strategic bombing responsibilities. Johnson's cancellation order seemed to confirm that the new Secretary of Defense was indeed the adversary that the Navy fully expected him to be.

In the aftermath of the cancellation, naval frustrations were at an extremely high level as many top officials, most notably aviators, concluded that the existence of their branch was at stake. In this charged atmosphere they began preparing for a battle they perceived as essential to save their service from a severe crippling at best and extinction at worst. By this time the Navy had pinpointed its three major adversaries: President Truman, whose insistence on a total military budget of under $15 billion for fiscal years 1949 and 1950 was making all the squeezing necessary; Secretary of Defense Johnson, who seemed determined to build up the Air Force at the expense of the Navy and who was taking the economy drive even further than Truman was calling for; and the Air Force, which was misrepresenting what airpower could do and what the Navy could not do in providing for the nation's defense. With the ''enemies'' identified, the questions remaining were which to attack, and how. The first of these was easily answered: the President was ruled out for political and patriotic reasons, leaving Johnson and the Air Force. And the method of attack would be propaganda, both positive, which would build up the Navy, and negative, to attack the Defense chief and the Air Force. These attacks were designed to create such an outcry that Congress and the American public would look into the question of defense strategy and then right the wrongs being committed against the Navy.

Early in 1949, Cedrick R. Worth, a former Navy commander serving as a special assistant to Under Secretary of the Navy Dan A. Kimball, prepared an anonymous document which cited 55 allegations of wrongdoing against Secretary Johnson, Secretary of the Air Force Stuart Symington, and the Air Force's B-36 program. In assembling the document, Worth used rumors and innuendoes as well as an artful sprinkling of accurate information. The essence of the document was that the controversial B-36 bomber was an ineffective and vulnerable weapon that could not live up to the claims of the Air Force, and that knowing this, Johnson and Symington had still permitted its procurement. The document alleged that the two officials had approved purchase, even after they knew the truth, because they were friends of Floyd B. Odlum, head of the corporation that controlled Consolidated-Vultee Aircraft, the supplier of the plane; because Johnson had been a director of Consolidated-Vultee until he resigned to take his Defense post; and because Odlum had pumped, at Johnson's insistence, nearly $6 million into the President's 1948 campaign.[22]

Worth's document found its way into the hands of Representative James E. Van Zandt, a Naval Reserve officer and a member of the House Armed Services Committee. In an impassioned speech on the floor of the House, Van Zandt revealed the charges and called for a congressional investigation. The allegations were so sensational and received so much publicity that the House Armed Services Committee voted, on 9 June, to investigate the charges, learn where they came from, determine the capabilities of the B-36, examine the roles and missions of the services, and determine whether the decision to cancel the super carrier had been sound. The hearings thus called for were to be held in two phases, the first in August and the second in October.

The Revolt of the Admirals, which had first been characterized by behind-the-scenes grumbling in the aftermath of the carrier cancellation, came out into the open for the first time in the August hearings before the House committee. That phase of the investigation, formally called the "Investigation of the B-36 Bomber Program," began on 9 August and concluded on 25 August. During that period both the Air Force and the Navy made elaborate presentations, during which 35 witnesses representing all branches of the service, the Congress, and private corporations testified. The Air Force went first, and it presented most thoroughly the procurement and evaluation history of the B-36. The detail and precision with which the Air Force presented its case discredited most of the anonymous charges.[23]

In the latter part of this phase of the inquiry, the committee examined the charges of political and personal favoritism in the giving of contracts. Secretary Johnson set forth to the satisfaction of the committee members the nature of his past relationship with Consolidated-Vultee and destroyed the claim that Floyd Odlum had given more than $6 million to the President's campaign. Further, Johnson explained that his recommendation in April to approve the purchase of 36 additional B-36s merely reaffirmed a decision that Forrestal had made shortly before his departure, and then was made only after he received a recommendation that had gone through normal review procedures.

On 24 August, the day after the Secretary's appearance, the validity of Johnson's testimony was verified by a surprise witness – Cedrick Worth. In two days of testimony, Worth proceeded to explain that the document containing the charges was a spurious piece of work he had concocted for narrowly partisan reasons. With the author of Van Zandt's charges now identified and the allegations of irregularities in procurement now discredited, phase one of the hearings came to a close. When Worth finished testimony on 25 August, the committee recessed until 5 October, at which time it was to begin examining the capabilities of the B-36, the questions of service functions and responsibilities, and the soundness of the carrier decision.

The Navy had been caught and embarrassed. But even after having attempted a cheap shot and failed, it was not ready to give up the cause. The Air Force had come out well, showing the thoroughness of its bomber evaluation and the integrity of its procurement procedure. As for Johnson and Symington, Chairman Vinson stated that they had come through the inquiry "without the slightest blemish."[24]

By the end of August, Secretary Johnson was in a stronger position than he had been since entering his new position. This was primarily due to congressional passage in mid-August of the 1949 amendments to the National Security Act, which greatly strengthened the position of the Secretary of Defense; however, Johnson's newly conferred powers did not worry the Navy nearly as much as several of his decisions in the summer of 1949. For example, some uneasiness stemmed from Johnson's revocation and then reinstatement of Consolidation Directive No. 1, which caused some Navy officers to believe that he was playing games with their right to speak their minds on procurement and unifcations issues. When Johnson attempted, although unsuccessfully, to keep a pro-Navy article from appearing in the *Saturday Evening Post*, and then when he began publicly criticizing Navy partisans for undertaking "a campaign of terror against unification," they were sure that he was biased.[25]

Nothing bothered the Navy more, however, than Johnson's continuing efforts at economy. In July the Secretary informed the service chiefs that the budget for fiscal 1951 would be even more austere – $13 billion – and would not be divided evenly; the Navy would receive less than the Air Force and Army. A few weeks later he indicated that he would advocate cuts of all Navy components, but especially of carriers, carrier groups, and Marine aviation, the latter being targeted for a 50-percent cut.[26] Johnson believed that by eliminating waste, duplication, and unessential forces a billion dollars could be saved each year, and on 10 August he appointed a special interservice management committee, headed by Air Force General Joseph T. McNarney, to show where the cuts would be made. In early September, McNarney informed the services that in the coming fiscal year the Secretary would cut funds substantially from current levels. Cuts announced totaled $929 million, with the Air Force losing $196 million, the Army $357 million, and the Navy $376 million.[27] This time the Navy felt Johnson was going too far. Naval leaders believed that they had no choice but to fight; if they did not, Johnson would sink the Navy and knock its air arm out of the sky more effectively than any enemy force could. The B-36 charges of the previous May and the August hearings had been kid stuff; now they were really ready to rebel.

On 10 September the revolt entered a new phase when Captain John G. Crommelin, a prominent naval aviator serving on the staff of the Joint Chiefs, called in the press and issued a public statement claiming that the Navy was being systematically and intentionally destroyed by Secretary of Defense Johnson and the Joint Chiefs. Active and retired Navy men immediately came to Crommelin's defense, and Chief of Naval Operations Denfeld and Under Secretary Kimball not only moved to protect him but attempted to reward him with a favorable reassignment. Navy Secretary Francis Matthews intervened and ordered him to a less desirable post.[28] Matthews, too, was opposed to the proposed budget cuts, but he thought that he and his subordinates should take up the matter with Johnson personally, not air their grievances publicly.

During the first week of October, Johnson assured Matthews that the Navy could present its budget concerns to him. Hoping he could persuade the Defense chief to restore some of the cuts, Matthews consequently wanted to postpone the House committee hearings until January. Then, if the Navy was still dissatisfied, it could take its case to the House committee. Postponement, he argued, would provide an opportunity to solve the problems in house. The Navy Secretary convinced Denfeld of the merits of delay and appeared to have won over Chairman Vinson when a forceful and dynamic air advocate, Admiral Arthur W. Radford, Commander-in-Chief of the Pacific Fleet, returned to Washington to lead the admirals in revolt. Citing a letter from Vice

Admiral Gerald P. Bogan (with endorsements by himself and Denfeld) that claimed morale in the Navy was at an all-time low, Radford persuaded Vinson to proceed with the inquiry. After that meeting Captain Crommelin again gained notoriety by releasing the secret Bogan, Radford, and Denfeld correspondence to the press.[29]

On 5 October, the House Armed Services Committee reconvened and proceeded with the second phase of its probe – an inquiry into "The National Defense Program – Unification and Strategy." As this portion of the hearings began, the Navy set out to show that unification, especially as being implemented by Johnson and the Joint Chiefs, was not working and, indeed, was tearing the Navy apart. The first eight days of the probe belonged to the Navy, which paraded before the committee such prominent figures as Admirals Radford, William F. Halsey, Thomas C. Kinkaid, Chester W. Nimitz, William H. P. Blandy, Bogan, and Denfeld; Fleet Admiral Ernest J. King; and Captain Arleigh A. Burke (the primary planner of the Navy presentation) to set forth its case. The essence of their testimony was that the Air Force had sold the nation a bill of goods in the form of the atomic blitz theory of warfare and that the instrument of that policy, the B-36, was an ineffective weapon and "a billion-dollar blunder" on the part of the Air Force. Furthermore, they claimed that unification was not working because Secretary Johnson and the Joint Chiefs were making decisions that were properly the Navy's, the unsound carrier cancellation being a good example. Secretary Johnson was also taken to task for in effect changing congressional appropriations by implementing an economy program that prevented hundreds of millions of dollars appropriated for the military services from being spent on them. Fear was also expressed that under the present Administration the amphibious mission of the Marines might be lost to the Army.[30]

Following the Navy presentations, the Air Force had its opportunity for rebuttal. With Secretary Symington leading the way, it was quite successful; however, the real case against the Navy was not set forth by anyone associated with the Air Force, but by Army General Omar N. Bradley, recently appointed Chairman of the Joint Chiefs of Staff, a position provided for in the 1949 amendments to the National Security Act. The usually mild-mannered Bradley shocked everyone as he proceeded to blast the Navy in what was the most forceful presentation of the hearings. He criticized the Navy for being too preoccupied with the past and for failing to see that new times created a need for new military strategies. Bradley noted how the Navy had opposed unification from the beginning and had never stopped opposing it. Beyond that, he claimed, on numerous occasions naval leaders deliberately made false accusations against Johnson and the Joint Chiefs because they did not get their way. Bradley deplored the Navy's "open rebellion against the civilian control" and accused the "over-zealous enthusiasts" of being "fancy dans who won't hit the line with all they have on every play, unless they can call the signals."[31]

The next day newspapers from coast to coast carried stories on the "Fancy Dans" in the Navy.

Additional Army generals followed Bradley with the same message, and on 21 October, the last day of the hearings, Secretary Johnson was called to tell his side of the story. Johnson accused the Navy witnesses of presenting an inaccurate picture of what was taking place. He then told his side of the carrier cancellation decision, making clear that he had received considerable input from all the Chiefs, including the Navy's, before making his decision. He also went to great length to explain and justify his economy moves and to emphasize that all services, not just the Navy, were being forced to take cuts. The Secretary ended his presentation with a call for increased understanding by each of the services so that they could bring about true unification.[32] The following day the hearings ended.

That the Revolt of the Admirals had failed became apparent in a series of events which began shortly after the hearings ended. The first naval casualty was Admiral Denfeld, who was removed as Chief of Naval Operations on 28 October, just one week after the hearings. This move was initiated by Secretary Matthews and approved by Johnson and President Truman.[33] His position was filled by Admiral Forrest P. Sherman, who had chosen not to involve himself in the revolt. According to Truman these changes were necessary "to restore discipline in the Navy."[34] In the months that followed, Captain John Crommelin was "purged" and two of the testifying admirals, Blandy and Bogan, were forced into retirement by being given assignments that they found completely unacceptable. An attempt by Matthews and Johnson to punish one of the wayward officers, went awry, however. In December they tried to block the promotion of Captain Arleigh Burke, the primary architect of the Navy's presentations at the hearings; their effort was thwarted by President Truman's personal intervention, and Burke was promoted and eventually went on to distinguish himself as Chief of Naval Operations from 1955 to 1961.[35]

Two months after the hearings, the House Armed Services Committee issued the first of two reports on its inquiry. The first report dealt with the first phase of the hearings – the B-36 procurement charges. In it the committee lauded the Air Force and its handling of the B-36 program. The report cleared Secretary Johnson and Secretary Symington of any wrongdoing and expressed complete confidence in them. Two months later, on 1 March 1950, the committee issued its report on "Unification and Strategy." In it were 33 findings and conclusions which primarily pointed out the problems and complexities of unification and called for more cooperation, consultation, and education to make true unification a reality. Secretary Johnson was criticized for the manner in which the super carrier was cancelled, but the cancellation itself was upheld. He was also mildly criticized for going against the will of Congress by refusing to spend duly appropriated funds.[36] The reports gave little solace to the Navy, offering it sympathy but nothing else. The reports provided a sort of finality to what by that time was quite clear: The Revolt of the Admirals had failed.

The committee reports and removal of Admiral Denfeld were indications that the revolt had not succeeded, but there is more evidence of its failure when one asks what the admirals achieved. The answer is very little. There were no discernible changes in the military budget for fiscal 1950 or 1951, either in terms of total amount or distribution. The atomic blitz theory continued to hold sway throughout the nation. The B-36 procurement continued unabated. Strategic bombing remained the primary responsibility of the Air Force. And construction of the super carrier was not resumed. Those things that the Navy had set out to change remained virtually unaffected.[37]

For Secretary of Defense Johnson, the impact of the revolt is not clear-cut, for he emerged both a winner and a loser. On the positive side were several considerations: he established himself among the armed services, Congress, and public as a bold, forceful individual who fully intended to be master in his own house and to make unification work, regardless of the opposition to it; he emerged with his personal integrity not only intact but greatly enhanced; and he gained from Congress and the public an understanding of the difficult nature of his job and the need for unification and eliminating waste. But the revolt also extracted a price from Johnson, for it alienated some members of Congress, the press, and the public who believed that his handling of affairs and his personal manner before the committee revealed a man who was too brusque and insensitive to make unification work. Moreover, it made final his alienation from the Navy. The latter would loom large in his dismissal in September 1950, because with the coming of war in Korea the Secretary of Defense needed the complete confidence and support of all the military services.

Who, then, benefited from the revolt, if not the Navy or Secretary Johnson? The Department of Defense did not, for in airing its problems in public it revealed the turmoil that existed there. Perhaps only the Air Force emerged better off than before, because the hearings seemed to convince the public that its earlier confidence in the value of airpower as a defensive tool and offensive weapon was well warranted. About the only other positive statement that can be made about the revolt is that it might have helped clear the air among the feuding services so they could proceed with unification.

By the spring of 1950, morale of naval leaders was, not surprisingly, near rock bottom. With the failure of the admirals' revolt, the continuing economy drive of the seemingly anti-Navy Secretary of Defense, and the nation's intensifying love affair with the Air Force, the outlook for the Navy was not bright; however, events abroad were soon to change that situation. Following the outbreak of war in Korea in June 1950, it became increasingly apparent that the United States still needed conventional land and sea forces.

The Korean War did what the admirals in revolt had been unable to do, showing the nation that there was a place for the Navy and Marines in mid-

20th-century warfare. By providing gunfire support of land forces, launching air strikes from aircraft carriers, blockading the Korean coast, and transporting men and supplies, the Navy again proved its worth in combat. The Marines likewise gained new respect in Korea, with the highly successful amphibious landing at Inchon showing the need for such capability.

As the war led to increased reliance on, and respect for, the Navy, appropriations grew. A new building program was initiated in 1952. That year witnessed the laying of the keels of the first postwar aircraft carrier, the U.S.S. *Forrestal*, and the first nuclear-powered warship, the submarine U.S.S. *Nautilus*, plus authorization of the first guided-missile cruisers. In time, the nuclear-powered submarines were armed with nuclear weapons – the Polaris, Poseidon, and later Trident ballistic missiles – and for nearly two decades this naval nuclear capability has been an integral part of the nation's strategic nuclear Triad. The Navy also achieved the strategic bombing role it desired, acquiring AJ Savages, A3D Skywarriors, and A3J Vigilantes, all carrier-based aircraft capable of carrying nuclear weapons.

The Marines also prospered in the post-Korean War period; operations in Lebanon, the Dominican Republic, and Vietnam all showed a need for and the effectiveness of that fighting force. In the 1980s the Marines have taken on a new position of importance, playing a prominent role in the Rapid Deployment Joint Task Force.

As one looks back over the past 30 years, it is apparent that all the speculation about the demise of the Navy and Marines that accompanied the Revolt of the Admirals was never realized. For that the nation can be thankful.

NOTES

1. Paul Y. Hammond, *Organizing For Defense* (Princeton: Princeton Univ. Press, 1961), pp. 186-92; Frank N. Trager, "The National Security Act of 1947: Its Thirtieth Anniversary," *Air University Review,* 29 (November-December 1977), 5-7.
2. "Battle of the Potomac," *Newsweek,* 19 November 1945, p. 63.
3. Russell F. Weigley, *History of the United States Army* (New York: Macmillan, 1967), pp. 492-94.
4. Walter Millis, ed., *The Forrestal Diaries* (New York: Viking, 1951), pp. 293-95.
5. Paolo E. Coletta, "The Defense Unification Battle, 1947-1950: The Navy," *Prologue,* 7 (Spring 1975), 7.
6. Paul Y. Hammond, "Super Carriers and B-36 Bombers: Appropriations, Strategy and Politics," in *American Civil-Military Decisions,* ed. Harold Stein (Birmingham: Univ. of Alabama Press, 1963), p. 486.
7. Margaret Truman, *Harry S. Truman* (New York: William Morrow, 1973), p. 40.
8. Jonathan Daniels, *The Man of Independence* (Philadelphia: J. B. Lippincott, 1950), p. 305.
9. Arnold A. Rogow, *James Forrestal: A Study of Personality, Politics and Policy* (New York: Macmillan, 1963), p. 281; Edward T. Folliard, "Louis Johnson to Succeed Forrestal as Defense Chief," *The Washington Post,* 4 March 1949, pp. 1-2.
10. Memorandum by President Truman, 12 September 1950, General File-Louis Johnson, Eban Avers Papers, Harry S. Truman Library; Keith D. McFarland, *Harry H. Woodring: A Political Biography of F.D.R.'s Controversial Secretary of War* (Lawrence: Univ. Press of Kansas, 1975), pp. 146, 229-30; "People In The News," *The Washington Post,* 4 March 1949, p. 2.
11. Interviews with Gerald P. Nye in Washington, D.C., 13 June 1969, and with Stephen Ailes in Washington, D.C., 28 July 1977.

12. Richard F. Fenno Jr., *The President's Cabinet: An Analysis in the Period from Wilson to Eisenhower* (Cambridge: Harvard Univ. Press, 1959), p. 49.

13. Memorandum for the President from Louis Johnson, 15 May 1940, President's Secretary File: Louis Johnson, Franklin D. Roosevelt Library.

14. Robert L. Dennison, Oral History Interview, Harry S. Truman Library, p. 71.

15. "New Defense Secretary," *Army and Navy Journal*, 2 April 1949, pp. 887, 916; John G. Norris, "Johnson Says He'll Promote Armed Unity," *The Washington Post*, 29 March 1949, pp. 1-2; Hammond, "Super Carriers and B-36 Bombers," p. 493.

16. US Congress, House, Armed Services Committee, *Investigation of the B-36 Bomber Program, Hearings,* 81st Cong., 1st Sess., pp. 478-79.

17. Coletta, pp. 7-9; Walter H. Waggoner, "Keel is Laid for Super-Carrier," *The New York Times,* 19 April 1949, pp. 1, 48.

18. US Congress, House, Armed Services Committee, *The National Defense Program – Unification and Strategy, Hearings,* 81st Cong., 1st Sess., pp. 619-20.

19. Harry S. Truman, *Memoirs,* Vol. II, *Years of Trial and Hope* (Garden City: Doubleday, 1956), p. 53.

20. *Unification and Strategy, Hearings,* pp. 619-21; John L. Sullivan, Oral History Interview, Harry S. Truman Library, pp. 62-63; Walter H. Waggoner, "Sullivan Quits As Head of Navy," *The Washington Post,* 27 April 1949, pp. 1, 6.

21. Johnson later claimed that the carrier vs. B-36 controversy was "the issue that gave me a chance to run the Department. The secretary didn't have control before. This was the thing that gave me control" (Carl W. Borkland, *Men of the Pentagon: From Forrestal to McNamara* [New York: Praeger, 1966], p. 75).

22. *Investigation of the B-36 Program, Hearings,* pp. 528-55.

23. Hammond, "Super Carriers and B-36 Bombers," pp. 499-500.

24. *Investigation of the B-36 Program, Hearings,* pp. 475-80, 486, 490, 528, 628-29, 655.

25. Hammond, "Super Carriers and B-36 Bombers," p. 505; Walter H. Waggoner, "Johnson Says U.S. Must Keep Armed For Surprise Blow," *The New York Times,* 22 June 1949, p. 1; Hanson W. Baldwin, "Atomic Blitz Doubted," *The New York Times,* 25 June 1949, p. 2. The article "Admiral Talks Back to the Airman" by Daniel V. Gallery appeared in the 25 June 1949 issue of the *Saturday Evening Post.*

26. Hanson W. Baldin, "Defense Friction Eases," *The New York Times,* 28 July 1949, p. 3; "Shift Ordered In U.S. Defense," *U.S. News and World Report,* 12 August 1949, p. 22.

27. *Unification and Strategy, Hearings,* pp. 624-25.

28. "Pentagon Crippling Power of Navy," *The New York Times,* 11 September 1949, pp. 1, 47; "Navy Inquiry On B-36 To Call Crommelin," *The New York Times,* 12 September 1949, p. 3; "Halsey Champions Critic of Pentagon," *The New York Times,* 13 September 1949, pp. 1, 22; Hanson W. Baldwin, "Unification Is Hurt," *The New York Times,* 14 September 1949, p. 18; "Admirals Elevate Crommelin, But Matthews Reverses Them," *The New York Times,* 16 September 1949, pp. 1, 13.

29. Hammond, "Super Carriers and B-36 Bombers," pp. 505, 508-12.

30. *Unification and Strategy, Hearings,* pp. 39-53.

31. Ibid., pp. 515-36.

32. Ibid., pp. 621-32.

33. Louis E. Denfeld, "Reprisal: Why I Was Fired," *Collier's,* 18 March 1950, pp. 13-15; Austin Stevens, "Denfeld Removed on Truman's Orders," *The New York Times,* 28 October 1949, pp. 1, 3; Austin Stevens, "Johnson Prohibits Changes In Roles of Armed Forces," *The New York Times,* 29 October 1949, pp. 1-2.

34. Truman, *Years of Trial and Hope,* p. 53.

35. Hammond, "Super Carriers and B-36 Bombers," p. 548; "White House Denies Shift in Navy List," *The New York Times,* 15 December 1949, p. 2; Hanson W. Baldwin, "Pentagon Battle Is Far From Over," *The New York Times,* 25 December 1949, sec. 4, p. 4; "Truman Promotes 'Rebel' to Admiral," *The New York Times,* 30 December 1949, pp. 1, 12.

36. US Congress, House, *Investigation of the B-36 Bomber Program,* Report of the House Armed Services Committee on H.R. 234, 81st Cong., 2d Sess., Report 1470, pp. 20-22, 32-33; US Congress, House, *Unification and Strategy,* Report of the House Armed Services Committee, 81st Cong., 2d Sess., House Document 600, pp. 53-56.

37. Although it cannot be proven, it is possible that while the Navy lost the battle it may have

actually won the war because, by rebelling as it did, it caused Secretary Johnson, Congress, and President Truman to soften their anti-Navy tendencies.

This article appeared in the June 1981 issue of *Parameters*.

14

McNamara at the Pentagon

by DOUGLAS KINNARD

January 20th, 1961, was a cold and sunny day in Washington. As Dwight Eisenhower watched, his successor as President, John F. Kennedy, set forth his vision of the Sixties in his inaugural address. It was vigorous, activist, and optimistic. Kennedy had campaigned long and hard on the inadequacies of Eisenhower's defense and foreign policies. It was, therefore, to be expected that a more aggressive foreign policy and a larger allocation of resources to defense would be forthcoming. The rhetoric of the inaugural address gave support to these expectations.

Kennedy had offered Robert Lovett the post of either Secretary of State or Secretary of Defense, but he declined them both. Lovett did, however, recommend Robert McNamara, then president of the Ford Motor Company, for the Defense post and supported Dean Rusk as Secretary of State. Kennedy subsequently offered the two these top cabinet posts. In the course of accepting the job at Defense, McNamara had insisted on selecting his own assistants. In fact, he presented a letter to Kennedy for his signature that would put this arrangement in writing. Kennedy laughed and put the letter in his pocket, but he agreed to the arrangement.[1]

McNamara was born in San Francisco in 1916 and graduated from Berkeley in 1937. He received a Master of Business Administration degree at Harvard in 1939 and the following year joined the faculty there, specializing in the application of statistical analysis to management problems. During World War II he served as a commissioned officer in the Army Air Corps, working as a staff officer in statistical control. After the war, he and nine other Air Force statistical control experts hired themselves out to the Ford Motor Company. He rose rapidly in the firm, and when elected its president in 1960 he was the first to hold that office who was not a member of the Ford family.

Although he obviously had enormous ability and drive in order to succeed as he did at Ford, in certain respects he was not typical of automobile industry executives. Eschewing the usual habitats of that group, such as Grosse Point Shores, he preferred to live in the collegial community of Ann Arbor near the University of Michigan. Here his relaxation was more that of a college professor – discussion, books, symphonies – than of the relentlessly driving automobile executive that he was. These avocations were to stand him in good stead in the social life of Kennedy's Washington – in Camelot, if you wish – into which he fitted nicely.

There seems to be a general consensus on many of McNamara's personal characteristics: intelligent, able, decisive, self-confident, hard-driving, puritanical, and free of cynicism are terms used most frequently by his associates in describing him. He was most comfortable in dealing with a problem when he could view it in terms of figures, and he required, when possible, that papers submitted to him employ such a format. The rimless glasses and slicked-down hair helped give him a stern and formidable look, but he could be as engaging a person as anyone in Washington.

Another of his characteristics noticed by those who knew him best is less desirable in a Secretary of Defense. Apparently it was difficult for him to compromise on issues – in this sense he was an unpolitical animal, a disadvantage in the Washington jungle.

McNamara approached his new duties at Defense in the same activist spirit he had displayed at the Ford Motor Company. To describe it in his own words, "The direction of the Department of Defense demands not only a strong, responsible civilian control, but a Secretary's role that consists of active, imaginative, and decisive leadership of the establishment at large, and not the passive practice of simply refereeing the disputes of traditional and partisan factions.''[2] An example of this philosophy in action comes through clearly in his approach to management, to be discussed shortly.

After Kennedy appointed Rusk as Secretary of State, the two cabinet members got together and agreed on what they felt was the proper relationship between the Defense and State Departments. Thereafter, there was a close rapport between them. McNamara supported the conventional understanding that defense policy is derived from foreign policy. Still, if one goes back over McNamara's pronouncements in the 1960s, such as those concerning NATO or nuclear strategy, there is a curious blend of original foreign-policy import. Take for example McNamara's annual posture statements, first published in February 1963 (in support of the Fiscal Year 1964 Defense Budget). The introductory statements are 25-50 percent foreign policy – basically written in the Pentagon. State had the opportunity to comment , but it is generally agreed that the agency that writes the first draft is in charge of the situation.

McNamara's Management Approach

Of all the writings on McNamara's tenure in the Department of Defense, the majority stress his management approach.[3] It was thus that he made his major impact on defense decisionmaking. Moreover, certain aspects of this management approach were his major legacy to the Defense Department. McNamara was interested in more than simply efficient management. He wanted to achieve more effective top-management control of total defense

resource allocation by cutting across the services horizontally on such issues as force structure and competing weapon systems. That is, rather than initially settling upon individual service budgets, McNamara wished to settle first upon resources to be allocated to the various functional missions – strategic retaliatory, continental defense, general purpose forces, and so forth – and then parcel these to the individual services on the basis of the most cost-effective alternatives. We cannot here go into the full details of McNamara's management apparatus, but certain aspects should be highlighted to place his tour in the Pentagon in proper perspective.

Prior to McNamara's appointment, a Pentagon-sponsored study examined what the 1958 Defense Reorganization Act authorized the Secretary of Defense to do that he was not already doing.[4] Thomas Gates, McNamara's immediate predecessor, was impressed by the study and recommended it to McNamara. In essence, the study pointed up the fact that the Secretary's authority under the act was considerable and had not yet been exploited. McNamara therefore decided that no further legislation was needed to enhance his authority, but that management changes were. As he put it,

From the beginning in January 1961, it seemed to me that the principal problem in efficient management of the Department's resources was not the lack of management authority. The National Security Act provides the Secretary of Defense a full measure of power. The problem was rather the absence of the essential management tools needed to make sound decisions on the really crucial issues of national security.[5]

The primary management tools that McNamara initiated were the Planning-Programming-Budgeting System (PPBS) and systems analysis. PPBS was installed by Charles J. Hitch, an economist who had been with RAND and had, in 1961, coauthored with Roland N. McKean *The Economics of Defense in the Nuclear Age*. Systems analysis was developed as an analytical technique within the department under the supervision of Alain G. Enthoven, who had joined the Defense Department in 1960 as an operations research analyst. When Hitch was made Assistant Secretary (Comptroller) at the beginning of the new Administration, Enthoven became his deputy, focusing specifically on systems analysis. In 1965 he became an Assistant Secretary himself when the Systems Analysis Office was raised to that level.

PPBS provided both an information base and a control device linking together long-range planning and shorter-range budgeting through programs costed over a five-year period.[6] Although Hitch wanted to take 18 months to install the new system, McNamara decided to do it in six, so that it could be used in developing the Fiscal Year 1963 Budget – the first budget for which the new Administration was fully responsible.

The planning phase was one that had previously existed, but with a somewhat different thrust. The basic military input was the Joint Strategic Objectives Plan – known as the JSOP – developed by the Joint Chiefs of Staff. Volume I was a joint document that assessed the strategic threat to the United States in the context of its worldwide commitments. Volume II, which

contained recommended force levels to deal with the security demands developed in the preceding document, tended to be less of a joint document. Since force levels eventually determined each service's future, there was a strong tendency for this document to reflect service inputs and hence in aggregate to set forth unrealistic requirements.

The new thrust introduced into the planning phase by McNamara was to require military-economic studies, comparing alternative ways of accomplishing national security objectives based upon cost effectiveness. These studies (which were prepared in Enthoven's office, rather than as part of the JSOP) were in reality the basis for the remainder of the PPBS cycle. The instruments for implementing the studies were called Draft Presidential Memoranda, issued for each of the nine Defense Department wide mission and functional areas into which the defense budget was divided. The Memoranda were based on analysis that cut across service boundaries, affecting the way they carried out their roles and missions.

The programming phase, the bridge between planning and budgeting, began with the receipt by the Secretary of the JSOP and the nine Draft Presidential Memoranda. Actually, the planning and programming phases are somewhat difficult to separate analytically. Programming is more specific than planning and determines the resources needed to reach specific objectives. It was, moreover, the key phase in the entire process. The major programming document, consisting of information packages on individual program elements, was known as the Five-Year Defense Program.[8] After reviewing the JSOP and the individual Memoranda, the Secretary provided guidance to the services for subsequently proposing changes to the Five-Year Program.[9]

Upon receipt of program change requests, the Office of Systems Analysis again played a key role. Having previously prepared the Draft Presidential Memoranda, the office now analyzed the service recommendations for changes to the Five-Year Program.[10] The task at this point was to determine the issues, assumptions, and cost alternatives, and to suggest the questions for the Secretary to ask the service proposing a particular change.

Meanwhile, the Joint Chiefs were also reviewing the Draft Presidential Memoranda and then providing their own recommendations. McNamara, aided by Systems Analysis and other elements of his staff, then reached decisions concerning the JCS and service change requests, and towards the end of August of each year issued final Draft Presidential Memoranda as the basis for the final budgeting stage. This stage, which usually culminated in presidential decisions in late December, was not without controversy. However, in a sense the controversy during the final budget phase had been preempted by the programming stage (which had its own share of controversy).

Systems analysis was in effect the instrument by which data were compared as a means of determining the cost of various options. It also provided the means for judging the logic of the many proposals (sometimes conflicting) that

came from throughout the Department, including the services. These proposals might involve such matters as forces, hardware decisions, or training.

The foregoing, then, in general terms, describes the McNamara management approach. Probably nothing in the McNamara period caused more debate within the Department of Defense and the Congress than his management apparatus. This was especially true of Systems Analysis, manned by the so-called "Whiz Kids" who allegedly paid little attention to the professional military. The system had its supporters as well as detractors,[11] and its successes as well as its failures. The best known of the latter probably was the F111 variable-sweep-wing bomber. Plagued by developmental problems, huge cost overruns, failure to meet performance specifications, and operational difficulties, the F111 proved to be the most controversial weapon system the United States ever procured.

The best case in support of the McNamara management approach is made in the book by Enthoven and Smith previously cited. As they see it, defense policymaking was improved in two broad ways. First, strategy, force requirements, and costs were brought together in a single analysis, rather than as a result of negotiations among the services that led to arbitrary allocation of resources. The second area of improvement, according to Enthoven and Smith, lay in providing the Secretary with an independent, mainly civilian, analytical staff. This capability was necessary inasmuch as McNamara had decided on an active role rather than merely mediating between competing military claimants.

There is little question that McNamara's management system permitted him to take the initiative from the services. For example, the Draft Presidential Memoranda were a way of setting forth the assumptions and thus for all practical purposes defining the solution. There is no question that this system established an increasingly adversarial relationship between the Office of the Secretary of Defense on one hand, and the Joint Chiefs and the services on the other. Further, it eventually brought friction with elements of Congress.

Critics of McNamara's management and especially of systems analysis were many. One of the more frequent criticisms concerned the downgrading of professional military advice and influence. In effect, it was alleged, decisions were being made by civilians on military questions without proper consultation with the professionals. The following charge was typical: "The military planning end of the bridge spanned by the Five-Year Defense Program has been replaced by a body of ad hoc civilian-sponsored, directed or conducted studies and analyses to which the military contribution is largely facts and manpower operating under terms of reference established by civilian authority."[12]

Another frequently voiced criticism was that much of the analysis was designed to support preconceived solutions or decisions already made. Perhaps

this is not too surprising. Defense decisions are often, after all, highly political in their implications. The most rational solution to a problem is frequently foreclosed by a call from the White House[13] or by an influential congressman.

In retrospect, McNamara's management approach was a major innovation. It was bound to be a source of bureaucratic friction, since it diverted power from the military to the Secretary. But McNamara's major accomplishment was no mean feat: for the first time, the Secretary of Defense gained real control of the Pentagon. Though the early PPBS was primitive, it was gradually refined and has been retained as McNamara's enduring legacy to the Department of Defense. Systems analysis survived in a different way, not as an all-powerful office, but as an analytical mode of thought now prevalent throughout the Pentagon in both the service staffs and the Joint Staff.

McNamara and Vietnam

In the early days of the Kennedy Administration, McNamara was not deeply involved in the Vietnam question. In the fall of 1961, however, he became so increasingly. In December, while en route home from a NATO Ministerial Meeting in Paris, he attended the first of many meetings on Vietnam in Honolulu. The military had many questions to ask McNamara about what equipment would be provided for the South Vietnamese, about the broad policy on assistance, and so forth. McNamara's responses were positive: "We are," he said, "going to the uttermost limits of policy."[14]

When he returned to Washington, McNamara reported to Kennedy and Rusk. At this point, the Defense Secretary assumed a major supervisory role with respect to US actions in Vietnam. He became in fact the "action officer" on Vietnam for the President. From this point on, no one in the State Department was in a position to vie with him for this role, even had one wished to do so.

By early 1964, just after the Kennedy assassination, it would still have been possible to reassess the American role in Vietnam. Lyndon Johnson was a new President, and the changed political situation in Vietnam in the wake of the Diem assassination would seemingly have made a reevaluation of the US role a live option. However, 1964 was an election year in America and Johnson had assumed the Kennedy mantle. In addition, he believed in the American effort, perhaps more than Kennedy had. In any case, the reassessment did not take place.[15]

Whatever ambiguity there may have been in the degree of commitment of the United States up to this point, none was left after publication of the presidential decision embodied in National Security Action Memorandum 288 in March 1964:

We seek an independent non-Communist South Vietnam. We do not require that it serve as a Western base or as a member of a Western alliance. South Vietnam must be free, however, to accept outside assistance as required to maintain its security. This assistance should be able to take

the form not only of economic and social measures but also police and military help to root out and control insurgent elements.[16]

Beginning in the late fall of 1964, events moved rapidly in Vietnam: two days before the US election the enemy attacked the American base at Bien Hoa; on Christmas the Brinks officers' hotel in downtown Saigon was bombed. By this time, with the election over, the President was considering his options. In late January McGeorge Bundy was dispatched to Saigon to look over the situation. Then came a benchmark event that set in motion a series of actions from which there was no turning back. On the afternoon of 6 February 1965 (Washington time), there occurred the Pleiku incident in which US barracks and helicopters were subjected to surprise fire from the Viet Cong, resulting in a substantial number of casualties. After receiving recommendations by phone from Bundy and Ambassador Taylor in Saigon, Johnson decided to respond by aerial attack on North Vietnam.

In the next month Marine ground units were dispatched to the Da Nang area to provide security for the air base from which by now US aircraft were conducting air missions in South as well as North Vietnam. Apparently, at this point there was no consideration of the widespread introduction of ground troops by Washington. However, it is doubtful that anyone with experience missed the important threshold being crossed. Introduce ground combat organizations and it is a long time indeed before they can be removed from such a situation as existed in Vietnam at that time.

The announced rationale for the initial deployments of US ground units was the security of American bases and installations in South Vietnam. These were bases whose aircraft were primarily involved in Rolling Thunder, the bombing campaign against North Vietnam. By the time most of the deployments were underway, however, the rationale had shifted. In the first place, Rolling Thunder was not meeting the expectations of its proponents about bringing Hanoi to negotiations. Further, there was at the same time a deteriorating military situation in South Vietnam. Therefore, by late March the possibility of introducing large numbers of US combat troops into South Vietnam was a real one.

The watershed meeting regarding the troop buildup took place in Hawaii on 20 April, with McNamara, Bundy from State, JCS Chairman Wheeler, Sharp, Westmoreland, and Ambassador Taylor present. As a result of the conference, Westmoreland gained a commitment for 40,000 more troops, including an Army brigade, the 173d Airborne. The floodgates were about to open. Meanwhile, the situation worsened for the Army of Vietnam – with an ambush here, a defeat there, it seemed that South Vietnamese forces were coming unglued.

By late May, events in Vietnam began to take an ominous turn with reports of ARVN units melting away in battle. By early June, plans were underway to send 75,000 troops to Vietnam. By late June, Westmoreland felt the need for major reinforcements, and McNamara was dispatched to Vietnam to look into the situation. Events moved rapidly following his return. His report endorsed the view of raising the ante to 150,000 troops by the end of 1965 and the possibility of more than 300,000 troops a year hence. At a meeting in the White House all officials involved expressed support of McNamara's recommendations. The climax came on 28 July 1965 when President Johnson at a nationally televised press conference redefined US objectives in South Vietnam:

> We insist . . . that the people of South Vietnam shall have the right of choice, the right to shape their own destiny in free elections in the South, or throughout all Vietnam under international supervision, and they shall not have any government imposed upon them by force and terror so long as we can prevent it.

At this point, however, Johnson expanded the objective: "We intend to convince the Communists that we cannot be defeated by force of arms or by superior power."[17] The President was definitely laying US prestige on the line.

In his initial recommendations to the President following his return, McNamara had recommended a call-up of the Reserves. However, the bad aftertaste left by the activations during the Berlin situation in 1961 and the desire to avoid a debate with Congress persuaded Johnson to fight the war with an essentially conscript force. The President wanted to prosecute the war and build his Great Society at the same time – to have both guns and butter. A congressional debate might well have resulted in derailment of the Great Society. Johnson's decision was to send 175,000 US troops for the time being, although in the press conference he used the number 125,000 and indicated that more would be sent later.[18] Troop increase followed troop increase in following months, with each increase being called a "program." The goal was called by Westmoreland "minimum essential forces," rather than the "optimum forces" of 670,000 that he occasionally requested but that were never seriously considered.

Secretary McNamara told Westmoreland early on not to "worry about the economy of the country, the availability of forces, or public or congressional attitudes." He, Westmoreland, should ask for what he felt was necessary to achieve his objectives, and McNamara would do his best to accommodate. After the decision was made, he would pressure the Army to meet the request immediately. With no Reserves to call up, the successive levies for Vietnam threw the Army into turmoil, in time wrecking the US Army in Europe and the Army strategic reserve in the United States.

McNamara was in Vietnam in October 1966 on one of his many trips to get a fresh feel for the situation. With the mid-year elections a month away, the President wanted the best assessment of the increasingly unpopular war that he could get. This trip was important in persuading McNamara that the war was a losing proposition.[19] Although he did not openly communicate this feeling, probably out of loyalty to the President, in retrospect it seems clear that apprehensions he had already begun to entertain were strongly reinforced. We see some hint of this in his report upon his return, in which the nagging doubts of this supremely self-confident man began to emerge: "I see no way to bring the war to an end soon." Despite the high enemy casualties, McNamara reported that there "is no sign of an impending break in enemy morale and it appears that he can more than replace his losses by infiltration from North Vietnam and recruitment in South Vietnam." As for the Rolling Thunder bombing campaign in the North, McNamara judged that it had neither slowed infiltration to the South nor cracked the enemy's spirit in the North.[20]

Consequently, the Secretary's proposals to the President were designed to stabilize the US military posture in a way that could be maintained indefinitely, while at the same time stressing pacification and the improvement of the South Vietnamese armed forces. Specifically, he recommended stabilizing US ground forces at 470,000; constructing an infiltration barrier along South Vietnam's northern border; and stabilizing the Rolling Thunder bombing campaign at current levels. Clearly, McNamara had decided to try to contain the continued expansion of the war effort, reversing the approach of the preceding 18 months.

McNamara's recommendations concerning stabilization of ground force strength in the South and Rolling Thunder operations in the North brought into the open a conflict between the Joint Chiefs and the Defense Secretary over the conduct of the war. Concerning the notion of leveling off ground forces at 470,000, the Chiefs were initially guarded. However, on the bombing they were straightforward in their written reaction to McNamara's recommendation:

The Joint Chiefs of Staff do not concur in your recommendation that there should be no increase in level of bombing effort and no modification in areas and targets subject to air attack. . . . To be effective, the air campaign should be conducted with only those minimum constraints necessary to avoid indiscriminate killing of population.[21]

The controversy continued into the spring of 1967. McNamara prepared for a trip to Saigon to hear what the military there had to say – or at least discover the tenor of their thoughts, as he already knew pretty much what they would say. He himself was now thinking of a troop ceiling of somewhere between 485,000 and 500,000 in contrast to Westmoreland's "minimum" ceiling – at this point, one of 550,000. The Mideast war that broke out in early June caused a postponement of the trip, but McNamara finally reached Saigon on 7 July. On the final night of his visit, McNamara and Westmoreland worked out a compromise (to which Westmoreland apparently did not fully agree) for a new ceiling of 525,000. This was considered close to the highest level that could be sustained without mobilizing the Reserves, something the President did not wish to do.[22]

The controversy over the bombing was to follow a different and more dramatic course than had the troop-ceiling issue. While the military endorsed a significant expansion of the air campaign in the North, McNamara and many of his key civilian advisors favored a restricted campaign south of the 20th parallel. It was an important and divisive issue not only in the Pentagon, but in Congress and in the public realm. In August 1967, the issue had become public enough and controversial enough, in fact, for Senator John Stennis of the Preparedness Subcommittee of the Armed Services Committee to conduct a probe into the air war in North Vietnam.[23] McNamara had prepared a detailed analysis to show that increased escalation of bombardment would not accomplish US objectives. Indeed, he felt that de-escalation might well further the possibilities for a negotiated settlement of the war.

McNamara presented his testimony on 25 August. This was the only occasion on which McNamara took a position that, if not contrary to the President's position, probably hedged Johnson's future options. The official relationship between the President and his now "dovish" Secretary of Defense was never quite the same again, nor was McNamara's influence with the President ever as secure.

McNamara's testimony (which took the entire day) was designed to convince both extremes: to those who wanted more bombing, that it would be futile; to those who wanted none, that there was a purpose to bombing in certain areas. The air war was not a substitute for the war in the South, as some believed it could be, he stated. Still, he pointed out, it had its objectives: to reduce infiltration to the South; to raise the morale of the South Vietnamese people; and to exact a sufficient price from the North for them to conclude finally that negotiations were preferable.

Despite the gulf between his and the President's thinking, McNamara's testimony did set the stage for a diplomatic initiative on the part of the President, the so-called San Antonio formula. The key part of the formula, delivered publicly by the President in San Antonio on 29 September 1967, relaxed America's previous position somewhat in that we would no longer require advance concessions by North Vietnam nor the stopping of all military effort by the North: it asked only that their level of military activity not be raised. The initiative led to nothing at the time. However, it did help set the stage for the bombing halt that took place in the fall of 1968.

During the preceding April, McNamara had been tentatively offered the presidency of the World Bank. In a discussion about the job with the President, he received no direct reaction. In mid-October, however, the President finally asked McNamara if he was still interested and, upon receiving an affirmative reply, indicated that he would help him get the position.[24] Johnson was true to his word; the nomination went to the Bank on 22 November. When the announcement was made on the 29th, even Washington, where leaks of imminent cabinet changes are routine, was surprised. McNamara stayed on until the end of February 1968 to help with the fiscal 1969 budget, but he was now a lame duck and his power was gone. The seizure of the *Pueblo* by the North Koreans on 23 January and a few days thereafter the North Vietnamese and

Viet Cong Tet Offensive of 1968 guaranteed that he would be busy and occupied to the end.

Some Observations

When McNamara became Secretary of Defense in January 1961, the Department was more than 13 years old and had had seven previous secretaries. From a loosely decentralized arrangement in the Forrestal days, the control of the secretary had gradually tightened. Eisenhower's 1958 Reorganization Act provided for even greater central control, but the act had been basically untapped when McNamara was sworn in.

The successful, intelligent, and dynamic new Secretary was determined to be an activist in carrying out his role. Although his intellectual interests had evolved far beyond those of managing the Ford Motor Company, his basically business orientation had not permitted the development of a fully mature geopolitical world view, with the result that initially he accepted that of the new President and his immediate advisers.

With respect to his pioneering introduction of systems analysis into defense decisionmaking, a final word is in order. The early unit within the Comptroller's Office did some ground-breaking work. Later, as an independent agency, the office grew too large and the work was less well done. Furthermore, the adoption of a public adversarial role vis-à-vis the military impaired the office's credibility and perhaps lessened its effectiveness. But systems analysis as a mode of thought has proved both beneficial and lasting.

Much has been made of McNamara's accountant's approach to problems – his ease with charts and his insistence upon quantitative analysis in all areas. A note of caution is in order with respect to pressing this view of McNamara too far. The driving force in all analysis is the assumptions that lie behind it, and in arriving at these McNamara was not simply a computer. He relied on intuition and hunches as much as any human being, and it is erroneous to assume otherwise. This is not to deprecate the analytical mode, but only to stress that the ideal of totally detached and scientific analysis developed by McNamara and his team was never achieved in practice.

If we leave aside Vietnam, McNamara played a major and successful role in the development of national strategy and defense policy in the first three or four years of his tenure. Although the necessarily brief length of this article has not permitted us to trace the development of his strategic thinking, he deserves fairly high marks in this regard.[25] He attempted with moderate success to make American military power more responsive to US foreign policy and national security objectives. While rejecting a counterforce strategy, he did oversee the development of an American nuclear deterrent that could survive a USSR attack and still inflict unacceptable losses on that country. He also strengthened the command and control facilities of our strategic retaliatory forces, thus increasing the flexibility with which they could be employed.

What McNamara did not do was work out a relationship of trust with the military – the ideal example of which is the Stimson-Marshall partnership during World War II. True, McNamara worked well with JCS Chairmen Taylor and Wheeler, but more than this was needed. The JCS as a group did not receive enough direct contact with the President. One member of the Chiefs during that period told me he felt like a spectator of the war rather than a decisionmaker who was integrally involved. By law, the Joint Chiefs are, after all, the principal military advisors to the President. Of course, they work also for the Secretary of Defense, but on the life-or-death issues of national security no Secretary of Defense should insist on acting as conduit between the President and his uniformed military advisors.

McNamara served Presidents Kennedy and Johnson well. He was respected by them and was included in the small inner circles in which each liked to do his real decisionmaking. McNamara was a strong cabinet officer and at the same time a key presidential spokesman and representative in the sense that he loyally reflected the President's views to the Defense bureaucracy, to Congress, and to the public. Indeed, perhaps he was too loyal – who knows what would have happened had he vigorously articulated his misgivings about the war earlier than he did?

NOTES

1. Interview with Roswell Gilpatric.
2. Robert S. McNamara, *The Essence of Security* (New York: Harper and Row, 1968), p.x.
3. A representative sample of this literature includes Alain C. Enthoven and K. Wayne Smith, *How Much is Enough* (New York: Harper and Row, 1971); Clark A. Murdock, *Defense Policy Formation* (Albany: State Univ. of New York Press, 1974); James M. Roherty, *Decisions of Robert S. McNamara* (Coral Gables, Fla.: Univ. of Miami Press, 1970); Ralph Sanders, *The Politics of Defense Analysis* (New York: Dunellen, 1973); and Samuel A. Tucker, ed., *A Modern Design for Defense Decision* (Washington: Industrial College of the Armed Forces, 1966).
4. This was the Air University Black Book of Reorganization Papers. The Symington Task Force set up by Kennedy during his 1960 campaign also used this book. Some of the proposals were quite far-reaching, such as employing a single Chief of Staff for the armed forces. This approach was rejected by McNamara.
5. McNamara, p. 88.
6. Military forces, also an element of programming, were projected over an eight-year period.
7. I.e. Strategic Retaliatory Forces, Continental Defense Forces, General Purpose Forces, Airlift and Sealift, Reserve and Guard, Research and Development, General Support, Retired Pay, Military Assistance.
8. The Five-Year Defense Plan was comprised of summaries of each program element (for example, a particular tactical fighter being requested) together with all the supporting information on that element, such as force descriptions, procurement lists, and facilities lists.
9. The services had been provided earlier with Tentative Force Guidance tables that could also form the basis for program change requests.
10. Systems Analysis did not review all service proposals. Some were reviewed by other offices, such as Installations and Logistics, and Research and Engineering.
11. Some well known military figures who subsequent to their retirements made strongly adverse comments were General Thomas White, Air Force Chief until 1961; his successor General Curtis LeMay; and Admiral George Anderson, Chief of Naval Operations until 1963.
12. Stanley M. Barnes, "Defense Planning Processes," *United States Naval Institute Proceedings*, 90 (June 1964), 32-33. For a comparable view from a former Defense Department Comptroller,

see the address by W. J. McNeil excerpted in "This Speech Wasn't Cleared," *Army, Navy, Air Force Journal and Register*, 20 June 1964, pp. 1, 8.

13. McNamara's speech concerning the Anti-Ballistic Missile in September 1967 comes to mind. Based on analysis, a speech had been written rejecting the ABM. However, Johnson did not want to get caught during the 1968 election with an ABM "gap" comparable to the missile "gap" (invented) with which he and Kennedy had plagued the Republicans in 1960. Hence, a presidential decision was made to go for some ABM deployments. In this case, the same rejection speech was made usable merely by adding at the end of the text support for a light ABM deployment to counteract the potential Chinese threat.

14. Interview with William P. Bundy.

15. On 27 January 1964, Secretary McNamara testified before the House Armed Services Committee. The following extract from his testimony captured the tenor of feelings of the new Administration: "The survival of an independent government in South Vietnam is so important to the security of all of Southeast Asia and to the Free World that I can conceive of no alternative other than to take all necessary measures within our capability to prevent a Communist victory" ("Text of McNamara's Testimony on Southeast Asia," *The New York Times*, 30 January 1964, p. 2).

16. *The Pentagon Papers: The Defense Department History of United States Decisionmaking on Vietnam*, Senator Gravel edition (Boston: Beacon Press, 1971), II, 112.

17. "Transcript of the President's News Conference on Foreign and Domestic Affairs," *The New York Times*, 29 July 1965, p. A-12.

18. For Johnson's perspective on the early buildup decision, see Lyndon Baines Johnson, *The Vantage Point* (New York: Holt, Rinehart, and Winston, 1971), chap. 6.

19. Interview with William P. Bundy.

20. *Pentagon Papers*, IV, 348.

21. Ibid, p. 357.

22. During that same summer, Clark Clifford and General Maxwell Taylor were sent by the President to visit the other countries with troops in Vietnam (Korea, Thailand, Australia, New Zealand, and the Philippines) to solicit further contributions. The additional increment was minimal.

23. The best account of the August 1967 hearings is Philip G. Goulding, *Confirm or Deny* (New York: Harper and Row, 1970), chap. 6.

24. Henry Trewhitt, *McNamara* (New York: Harper and Row, 1971), passim.

25. For an informed, interesting, but dated and somewhat polemical account of this, see William W. Kaufmann, *The McNamara Strategy* (New York: Harper and Row, 1964).

This article appeared in the September 1980 issue of *Parameters*.

15

Benedict Arnold's Treason as Political Protest

by JAMES KIRBY MARTIN

It is a basic American habit to dismiss Benedict Arnold's act of treason as an aberration, something that only a petty, willful, self-serving person would dare to attempt, especially during the glorious age of the nation's founding. Indeed, the portrayal of Arnold as a totally dishonorable figure began within days of his fleeing the encampment at West Point on 25 September 1780. To his contemporaries, the former apothecary-merchant from Connecticut became the personification of what their Revolution was not. They viewed him as the potential arch-despoiler of all that was good in their cause. He was a man with "two faces" who has listened to "Beelzebub . . . the Devil."[1] Satan, some claimed, had bought the general with nothing more than filthy lucre. That explained why Arnold's act was "one of the blackest pieces of treachery perhaps that time itself has not before evidenced."[2] It proved that he had "practiced for a long time the most dirty, infamous measures to acquire gain." Fortunately, however, the Almighty, as the author of light, had been on the rebel side: "The discovery plainly indicates that the liberties of America are the objects of divine protection."[3]

Historians of our own time have not pushed far beyond the images wrought by Arnold's contemporaries. Certainly, the devil has been removed from the script. And few would still ascribe to divine intervention Arnold's failure to deliver up West Point (and perhaps even George Washington). Most, however, would agree that the general's behavior was an aberration, no doubt caused by serious defects of character. Willard M. Wallace, Arnold's foremost modern biographer, summarized him this way: "Utterly egocentric, he demanded that his moral standards be accepted, while, at the same time, he objected if people resented his breaking theirs . . . . Given his fierce pride and a consuming sense of grievance, the addition of a catalytic agent like the need of money created an explosion."[4]

Historians thus have generally dismissed Arnold as a historical oddity. In doing so, they have measured him through the prism of his act of treason and have concluded that serious flaws of character pervaded his personality from the date of his birth. They have repeated tales of a youthful deviant who strewed broken glass in the streets to cut up the bare feet of playing companions, who robbed birds' nests, and who deserted the British Army during the French and Indian War; of a young adult who destroyed his beloved sister Hannah's one serious attempt at matrimony by threatening to shoot her suitor, and who maliciously mistreated his first wife and perhaps infected her with syphilis; and of a middle-aged man who sent the same love letter to more than one woman when seeking a second wife, who used his position of command to line his pockets with unearned profits, and who siphoned off public funds intended for the war effort for his own ease and comfort. While a few of these charges contain some element of truth, others have no basis in fact. More important, they may very well be beside the point, since they do little more than support predispositions toward negative caricature.

Indeed, such a litany simply reinforces the conclusion that Benedict Arnold was a thoroughgoing scoundrel who did not understand the Revolution – nor its ideals. It forecloses the possibility that Arnold's actions may have reflected directly on the sorry state of relations between the Army and society in Revolutionary America. In fact, I will argue that Arnold's frustrations with the wartime polity, more than shortcomings of personal character, served as the predominant motivating force behind his act of treason. Arnold was reacting to the shortcomings of the Revolutionary effort (which he knew by intimate experience), and his plotting with the minions of Sir Henry Clinton was the product of deeply held personal grievances related directly to the lack of consistent civilian support for the war, best described as society's failure to live up to the high republican ideals of the cause. In this framework, his act of treason may be comprehended as the most excessive form of individual protest issued by any one person during the War for American Independence. If we view his act of treason as political protest, then it may very well be that Benedict Arnold was anything but an aberrant among his peers in Revolutionary America, until he took his ultimate step. At that point, he became an extremist in his method of defiance – and a very harsh social critic in the statement that he made.

We must begin by noting that the year 1775 marked the high tide of patriot enthusiasm and popular resistance to British policy. Charles Royster has employed the phrase *rage militaire* to describe the early days of Anglo-American martial determination.[5] What must be remembered is that Arnold was one of thousands who came forward with bursting enthusiasm. Having earlier been named captain of the Governor's Guards in New Haven, the future general ordered out his company upon learning of Lexington and Concord. After bullying the town fathers into issuing powder and ball, he marched off with his men to Cambridge, Massachusetts. Before leaving New Haven, Arnold and the fifty men who felt called to go forth with him signed "an agreement" on principles governing their martial stand. Since they had been "driven to the last necessity," they were "obliged to have the recourse to arms in the defense of their lives and liberties.'' The subscribers compacted to conduct themselves with decorum while in service and to respect the rights of civilians because they were "men acquainted with and feeling the most generous fondness for the liberties and inalienable rights of mankind, and who were in the course of divine providence called to the honorable service of hazarding their lives in their defense."[6] These are words of strong commitment, which indeed represent some comprehension of the Revolution and its ideals, despite the conclusion of James T. Flexner that Benedict Arnold "could kill the strong, spare the weak, succor the wounded, ... but he could not understand what the American Revolution was all about."[7]

That Arnold was anxious to defend liberty may be dismissed as the desire of an egomaniac for military glory, but that reasoning only serves to water down the level of commitment of all other patriots who rushed to Cambridge in April 1775. The illustrative point is that Arnold was typical of those 10,000 New Englanders who unhesitatingly took up arms after Lexington and Concord. He was the same person who had indignantly inquired shortly after the Boston Massacre: "Good God, are the Americans all asleep and tamely giving up their Liberties, or are they all turned philosophers, that they don't take immediate vengeance on such miscreants; I am afraid of the latter."[8] He was the same person who wrote during his legendary march to Quebec: "This detachment is designed to co-operate with General Schuyler to frustrate the unjust and arbitrary measures of the [British] ministry, and restore liberty to our brethren in Canada."[9] At the outset of war, Benedict Arnold's perceptions and actions were those of the model citizen of virtue who willingly accepted the mantle of soldier in defense of his community against the specter of tyranny.

At the end of 1776, Arnold was just as loyal and dedicated to the cause, even though there had been personal feuds and setbacks. One can point to the contention with gangling Ethan Allen at Ticonderoga; to his vituperative quarrel with Lieutenant Colonel John Brown; to his failure to seize Quebec and the severe leg wound he sustained in the attempt; to the petty criticism he endured for losing the small Champlain flotilla in standing up to Guy Carleton at Valcour Island; and to his failure to settle his public accounts satisfactorily. However, there is no evidence that Arnold was less of a committed patriot by the end of 1776. His qualities of fortitude and courage were still much in evidence. Indeed, what was different was that great numbers of rebels, who had not been through as much as Arnold, had lost that initial blush of enthusiasm – and were less interested in service and sacrifice over the long term.

Thus Arnold *was* an aberration of sorts. He was among the few citizen soldiers who remained committed in the field, whatever the personal cost. He was among those few who understood from first-hand experience that the most distressing dilemma now facing Washington was a serious shortage of manpower. Indeed, even before the British government gathered for its concentrated effort of 1776, Continental Army officers were aware that they faced an ominous problem. The sunshine patriots of 1775, those who in the beginning had rushed to the American standard, found that determined military commitment (as befitting the virtuous, property-holding citizen) was much more demanding and difficult than they had at first counted on. Great numbers refused to reenlist for the 1776 campaign. Recruiters urged them to remember "the bountiful rewards of the industry of our worthy forefathers" and asked "whether we will see our wives and children, with everything that is dear to us, subjected to the merciless rage of uncontrolled despotism." They reminded the citizenry that "we are engaged . . . in the cause of virtue, of liberty, of *God*."[10] To little avail, as it turned out. More citizen-soldiers rushed home from the war at the end of 1775 than agreed to stay out for yet another year of fighting.

If the trend of disdaining Continental service was already evident, the massive British campaign of 1776 all but buried lingering signs of the *rage militaire*. Before the year was over, Washington was pleading for "a respectable army," one built on long-term enlistments, thorough training, and acceptable standards of discipline. If the casual army life of 1775 had held little appeal for Anglo-American citizens, then that which Washington now thought mandatory held much less. What was becoming obvious to the Army's leadership was that the rhetoric of citizen virtue and moral commitment lacked deep roots. Thus, compared with the broad generality of citizens at the end of 1776, particularly in terms of their thoughts and actual service in the field, Arnold had persistently demonstrated a strong sense of virtue and commitment. The gap between him and those citizens who had eschewed long-term service would contribute materially to his (and many other officers') coming disillusionment.[11]

In 1777 Washington's Army started to take on a striking new appearance. There was a dramatic shift downward in the social origins of recruits, as the Revolutionary society turned more frequently to the downtrodden in its midst to fight the war. It was in the same year that Continental Army protest against the civilian sector assumed clearly identifiable forms. In order to put Arnold's unusual act of protest in perspective, we must take a brief look at Washington's new-modeled Army, the broken promises made to that Army, and the resulting acts of defiance directed against the civilian sector.

Only in recent years, with the advent of quantitative analysis, have scholars ascertained that the social composition of Washington's soldiers shifted dramatically after 1776.[12] The first Army, which lasted into 1776, had a middle-class character. Men (and a few women) left behind hearth and freehold farm to stand up against perceived British tyranny. Most of these enthusiasts had gone back home by the end of 1776, if not long before. (Some of them went on to perform valuable service as militia auxiliaries after that time.) As a group, they were unwilling to accept long-term service, harsh discipline, or the rigors of survival in camp and field.

At this critical juncture, as the full brunt of William Howe's army was being felt in New York and New Jersey, Washington and Congress had little choice but to turn to the "poorer sort." These new regulars came largely from the disadvantaged classes, whose actual numbers had been rising dramatically for at least two decades before the Revolution. Many, including slaves and indentured servants, were not free, and they made convenient substitutes for their masters. In regard to age, those who were not free were most often in their late teens and early twenties, although a small handful entered the ranks when they were fourteen and younger. Lack of personal property and economic standing, moreover, was not just a function of age; the families of most recruits and conscripts were also quite poor. Among post 1776 Continentals, then, poverty (and lack of opportunity) — before, during, and after the war — was a common characteristic.[13]

By the spring of 1777, it was more than clear to the rebel leadership that state manpower quotas, so long as abstract notions of virtuous citizenship were the incentive, would remain unfilled. This is not to argue that those who made up the new modeled ranks were incapable of virtue or of believing in the ideals of the cause. Certainly they were, and their actions proved it. But that is not the point.[14] What we must recall here is that respectably established citizens did not remain for the long-term fight, and officers like Benedict Arnold were well aware of that. These citizens preferred to let others be the cannon fodder in their place – essentially on a contractual basis. Their legislators and congressional delegates gave bounties and promised regular pay, decent food, clothing, and even handsome land grants after the war as rewards for service. The central fact for the Continental Army was that the civilian population did not do a very effective job of keeping its part of the contract. One need only think of the disastrous supply shortages that plagued Washington's Army for the remainder of the war to establish the obvious.

That mutual trust between soldiers and civilians deteriorated rapidly after 1776 or that rank-and-file protest grew in an atmosphere of unfulfilled promises should hardly come as a surprise. Evidence of widespread anger in the ranks over the broken contract pervades surviving records. Private Joseph Plumb Martin captured the prevailing mood when referring to camp conditions in 1780: "We therefore still kept upon the parade in groups, venting our spleen at our country and government, then at our officers, and then at ourselves for our imbecility in staying there and starving in detail for an ungrateful people who did not care what became of us, so they could enjoy themselves while we were keeping a cruel enemy from them."[15]

Common soldiers vented their spleens through such diverse means as swearing, heavy drinking, insubordination, looting, bounty jumping, and deserting. When considered as protest, these actions represent something more than simply "time-honored military vices," to employ the words of Charles Royster.[16] Such an interpretive emphasis has the effect of muting, if not losing, the impact of what these historically silent troops were explicitly stating about their sense of betrayal by civilians. Over time, moreover, acts of individual defiance took on a decidedly group-oriented quality, ultimately involving large-scale mutinies (the most prominent of which were the uprisings of the Pennsylvania and New Jersey lines in January 1781).

This is not the place for a full discussion of incidents of soldier protest. What needs to be established, however, is that individual and group acts of defiance were widespread – and they mounted to a crescendo in 1779 and 1780. While crops and other food sources were often pillaged, however, there was rarely wanton violence directed against civilians. The behavior of the Pennsylvania mutineers of early 1781 was typical on that count. The soldiery resented the indifferent way in which the civilian sector handled the contract, all of which left a legacy of bitterness that almost inevitably resulted in high levels of rank-and-file protest and defiance.[17]

The officer corps, like the rank and file, resorted to protest with increasing (and patterned) frequency after 1776. In common with ordinary soldiers, their venom gained strength from a gaping sense of civilian indifference, if not betrayal. To complicate the case of the officers, there was also the persistent and nagging fear that their demonstrable moral commitment would never be appreciated – that it would go unrecognized and unrewarded. It rankled them that so many civilians would not participate fully, on the one hand, yet stood to make financial profits from the war efforts, on the other. That civilians could benefit from their travail when they were making significant personal financial sacrifices while in service for the sustenance of the whole republican polity was an ultimate test of self-sacrifice for them. As officers made comparisons between themselves and civilians, their perception of hypocritical civilian behavior made for a potentially explosive situation.[18]

There is no way to deny that the officers, as individuals and as a group, were getting into a bad mood. By 1779 and 1780, the tone of their utterances had become particularly strident. General John Paterson wrote indignantly: "It really gives me great pain to think of our public affairs; where is the public spirit of the year 1775 ? Where are those flaming *patriots* who were ready to sacrifice their lives, their fortunes, their all, for the public ?"[19] Alexander McDougall summarized his shattered expectations during March 1779 when writing to Nathanael Greene: "I am sorry to hear of the dissipated manners of that Capital. It 'augurs' ill to America. Can the Country expect Spartan Virtue in her army, while the people are wallowing in all the luxury of Rome in her declining state. . . . The consequence is obvious."[20] Lieutenant Colonel Ebenezer Huntington was as bitter as any other officer. He wrote caustically in July 1780: "I despise my countrymen. I wish I could say I was not born in America. . . . The insults and neglects which the army have met with from the country beggars all description."[21]

Benedict Arnold, just thirteen days before fleeing to the British, expressed practically identical feelings: "It is . . . to be lamented that our army is permitted to starve in a land of plenty." He sensed "a fault somewhere" and wanted it "traced up to its authors" who "ought to be capitally punished."[22] Such comments were the product of very real frustrations with the civilian sector. They also reflected the officers' failure to gain appropriate concessions and support from society as a result of various forms of individual and group protest.

Before the end of 1777, some officers, especially those in the lesser ranks, had expressed their disgust by resigning. Here was a fundamental form of individual protest. Even more important, by the end of 1777 the officer corps had started to rally around the demand for half pay pensions. This issue did more than promote solidarity. It encapsulated frustrations — and held out the prospect that tensions could be alleviated. If the officers could get Congress to approve postwar pensions, then there would be the prospect of long term financial security in the face of short term sacrifice. There would be a tangible reward for virtuous behavior, a quality which deserved special recognition from the point of view of the officers, especially since they had come to believe (with some good evidence) that so few citizens truly measured up to Revolutionary ideals.

The Continental Congress, in its turn, seemed caught between ideology and reality. Many delegates considered the officers' demand for pensions as nothing more than blackmail. As they debated the issue in the spring of 1778, many agreed with the sentiments of James Lovell of Massachusetts, who spoke about "a wish or design to put our military officers upon the footing of (the) European." Lovell openly wondered why these citizen-soldiers had "forgotten that this *was* in its beginning a *patriotic* war."[24] Other civilian leaders worried about "a total loss of virtue in the Army," about officers who were not "actuated by the principles of patriotism and public spirit," and about the implied "idea of a standing Army in time of peace."[25] Washington, who initially opposed the notion of pensions, came around in early 1778. He was blunt with Congress. "Motives of public virtue may for a time. . . actuate men to the observance of a conduct purely disinterested," he wrote. However, days of "continual sacrifice" without attention to "private interest" had passed. Washington thus declared the officers' demand to be necessary and just.[26]

After lengthy debate (and out of some fear that the officers might carry through on threats of more resignations), Congress reluctantly passed a circumscribed pension plan in May 1778. That did not close the issue or end protest, however. The officers persisted in pressing for lifetime half-pay pensions. In July 1780, they issued their most extreme statement yet: "Exposed as" they were "to the rapacity of almost every class of the community," they demanded full pensions, or they "should be obliged by necessity to quit the service." And if "ill consequences should arise to the country, they (would) leave to the world to determine who ought to be responsible for them."[27] In October 1780, Congress finally conceded on a full postwar pension plan, should funds become available. (Ironically, the traitorous course of Benedict Arnold helped to get the central government to act favorably.) Even with that promise, the pension issue kept cropping up again, culminating in the implied threat of coup d'etat at Newburgh in 1783 –

certainly the most potentially volatile confrontation relating to civil-military differences during the wartime period.[28]

While Benedict Arnold was only at the perimeter of the group that spoke loudest for pensions (a curious note, given standard assumptions about Arnold and greed), he was at the storm center of controversies over rank. The ink had hardly dried on the first commissions of June 1775 before disputes were breaking out over why this or that person should be senior to some other. Such maneuvering for favored position certainly should not be construed exclusively as protest. But in time, individual general officers began to confront Congress over its standards for promotion – using the threat of resignation to carry home their objections to absolute and arbitrary civilian decision-making in such matters.

Because of all the turmoil over rank, Congress tried to establish appropriate guidelines governing promotions, as enumerated in its Baltimore resolution of early 1777. "In voting for general officers," the delegates pronounced, "a due regard shall be had to the line of succession, the merit of the persons proposed, and the quota of troops raised, and to be raised, by each state."[29] The question was whether Congress could be as objective in applying the guidelines as would have been hoped.

Benedict Arnold's tribulation in 1777 was only one instance of many confrontations between particular officers and Congress over rank. Because of his service in the Quebec venture, Congress recognized Arnold's merit by commissioning him a brigadier general early in 1776. A year later (on the same day that the Baltimore resolution had been promulgated), the delegates passed him over and named five other brigadiers, all junior to Arnold, to the rank of major general. Washington was prominent among those in the Army who felt strongly that Arnold did not deserve such treatment, given his outstanding record of service in the field. In explaining itself, however, Congress defended its decision by pointing out that Connecticut already had its complement of major generals, based on that state's proportion of troops in rank. In dismay and anger over what he called his besmirched honor, Arnold protested by threatening to resign. There can be no doubt that many delegates did not like Arnold personally, and they clearly came to resent the fact that he had the audacity to question congressional authority openly.[30]

Events soon took an unusual turn. Late in April 1777, Arnold, while visiting in Connecticut, rushed to the defense of his state by helping to quash a foray by British soldiers that had resulted in the sacking and burning of Danbury. Arnold personally rallied local militia, fought brilliantly (on one heated exchange his horse was shot out from under him while another bullet tore open his uniform), and was instrumental in driving the marauding British column back to the coast. Shortly thereafter, a red-faced but still proud Congress belatedly promoted Arnold to major general. To prove their superior hand, however, the delegates did not restore his seniority.

Arnold found it degrading to have to cope with such congressional reasoning

– slapping while rewarding, rewarding while slapping. Between 20 May and 14 July 1777, he wrote six letters of protest to John Hancock, then President of Congress. He specifically appealed for justice, explaining: "Honor is a sacrifice no man ought to make, as I received so I wish to transmit [it] inviolate to Posterity."[31] He had earlier written to Washington: "When I entered the service of my country my character was unimpeached. I have sacrificed my interest, ease, and happiness in her cause."[32] Congress, he believed, had called his personal character into question. Now they were offering an insult in the form of a reward. As a gentleman, he felt duty bound to remove the stain from his record.

The congressional delegates did not view Arnold's letters of protest in that light. They resented his personal meddling, considering it an infringement upon important civil prerogatives. Finally, at the end of November 1777, Congress, in acknowledging Arnold's vital role at Saratoga, awarded him the seniority that he had thought his due. But by that time, Arnold was seriously questioning why anyone should adhere to a code of selfless dedication, since from his perspective Congress and the general population were making a mockery of that tenet.

Such incidents of individual officer protest over congressional decisions abetted the deterioration of relations between the civil and military sectors.[33] To officers like Arnold, any needless tampering with rank became an attack upon one's personal honor – now seemingly more important than pure self-sacrifice in the cause. In turn, Congress, enduring unremitting pressures from all sides, did not always use good judgment. The delegates generally viewed protesting officers, in the pithy words of John Adams, as "Mastiffs, scrambling for rank and pay like apes for nuts."[34] Washington's lieutenants wanted the respect they thought due them as responsible citizens and newly emergent professional soldiers. Congress, however, treated them more as aspiring mercenaries – with all the threats to civil society that such a term implied. Washington continually worried about these tensions, writing at one point: "We should all be considered . . . as one people, embarked in one cause, in one interest; acting on the same principle and to the same end." Yet the "very jealousy" of Congress regarding the Army's proper "subordination to the supreme civil authority is a likely means to produce a contrary effect."[35]

In this setting, it cannot be emphasized enough that Benedict Arnold was not alone in his protest. He was one among many high-ranking officers whose enthusiasm for republican self-sacrifice had been dampened by the course of events. He was one among many who was coming to resent civilian indifference and perceived congressional arrogance. In Arnold's correspondence, the preservation of personal honor, above all else, had begun to take on central meaning; purity of concern for the cause and the preservation of liberty, reminiscent of 1775, was losing its importance.[36] Even in early 1778, Arnold was typical of other general officers. He was not yet psychologically ready to break from his peers and become an extremist in terms of methods of protest

We must ask, then, what led the former Connecticut merchant to his rendezvous with disaster, when other officers, many of whom were just as disillusioned (and at times more outspoken), never gave second thought to going over to the enemy. No doubt there were highly individualized factors in Arnold's case. There were his battlefield wounds that left him half-crippled – a physical reminder of unappreciated sacrifice; his mishandling of his military governorship in Philadelphia and the assault on his personal character by Joseph Reed's Supreme Executive Council; and his marriage to Peggy Shippen, which fed his continuing desire for money, a luxurious lifestyle, and acceptance in the best social circles. Dwelling on these factors would serve to explain part of the pattern. However, there is a neglected dimension, given that Arnold, in his changing perceptions regarding the attainability of republican ideals, was more alike than different from his fellow general officers in 1777 and 1778.

The differences between Arnold and the rest become clearer by considering modes of protest. While the bulk of officers focused their discontent by joining hand-in-hand in the pension drive, Arnold remained at the perimeter, as we have seen. Indeed, Arnold's correspondence rarely reveals much interest in linking with his associates in the pension dispute.[37] Perhaps that is because he perceived collective protest on this issue as nothing more than a fool's errand, given Congress's lack of financial authority. Then again, it may be that he consciously chose to express his protest in individual rather than collective terms. If that is the case, then perhaps we have found a key reason why he eventually selected the traitor's course.

In 1778, Arnold, acting as an individual, did take up the pension cause indirectly when he decided to become the self-appointed champion of the deceased Joseph Warren's children. "About three months ago I was informed that my late worthy friend General Warren," he wrote, "left his affairs unsettled, and that, after paying his debts, a very small matter, if anything, would remain for the education of his children." It bothered Arnold that the children of such a noted patriot had "been entirely neglected by the State" – and that citizens had not felt any obligations to provide for the offspring of one who had so prominently sacrificed his life in their defense.[38] Arnold decided to push Congress for a special pension for Warren's widow and children. (More generally, the officers had demanded the same for their families in their pension drive.) Arnold also committed his personal funds. If Congress proved to be niggardly, then he guaranteed that he would mount a private subscription campaign. Ultimately, he gave at least $500 toward the care and education of Warren's children, and he eventually badgered Congress into conceding a major general's half pay until the youngest child reached majority status.[39]

Arnold's was basically a one-man campaign. When he became sure that a special congressional pension would be forthcoming, he was genuinely pleased. However, the fact that the Massachusetts delegation remained divided on the issue infuriated him. And he could not avoid commenting about the civilian mentality: "Charity, urbanity, and the social virtues seem swallowed up in the tumult and confusion of the times, and self wholly engrosses the nabobs of the present day."[40] These words were written on 3 August 1780, just 52 days before Arnold fled from West Point.

His quest for financial justice for Warren's children served a number of personal needs. Most significant, it allowed Arnold to place himself in the role of a selfless benefactor attempting to overcome an act of civilian injustice that discredited the republic. After all, he was protesting in favor of the progeny of a fallen hero. Arnold could thus hold up to the world the hard heartedness of a community which, indeed, had failed to attain the mark of public virtue. In a certain sense, by so visibly demonstrating his concern the general was doing more than just protesting. He was mocking the cause and its civilian leadership for being so shallow in its Revolutionary commitment. At the same time, he was expressing his own disillusionment as an officer who had repeatedly "fought and bled" in the service of his country.[41]

Of equal significance, Arnold chose to challenge as an individual – not as part of the group. Certainly his plea for Warren's children was an indirect extension of the broader officer-congressional clash over pensions, but there is no evidence that he was acting as an agent of the larger movement. It would have been uncharacteristic of Arnold if he had been. He was, if anything, a confirmed individualist in his actions. That had been his trademark as a rising prewar merchant, as a commander in battle, and as an officer in endless petty conflicts with other Revolutionaries. When he protested his passover for a major general promotion in 1777, for example, he took his own case to Congress. By comparison, when the Philippe du Coudray incident occurred during the same year, Nathanael Greene, Henry Knox, and John Sullivan joined in a coordinated petition for redress before Congress.[42] That Arnold was ultimately capable of the most extreme form of personal protest, that of turning completely against a cause which he had once held so dear, should not be mind-boggling, then, given his style of direct, personal, individualized behavior in combination with the broader pattern of mounting disillusionment among the most faithful of Revolutionary military leaders.

Feelings about civilian ingratitude first began to play on Arnold with particular intensity in 1777. Initially, this change in attitude was an outgrowth of his promotion controversy. The debilitating wound that he suffered in the Saratoga campaign seemed to add to his psychological turmoil. Thus when Arnold became military commander in Philadelphia after the British evacuation in June 1778, he seemed to revel in the opportunity of slighting home-front republican purists.[43] When Joseph Reed and the Pennsylvania Constitutionalists accosted him publicly in February 1779 for alleged malfeasance in office, Arnold wrote heatedly: "I am heartily tired with my journey, and almost so with human nature. I daily discover so much baseness and ingratitude among mankind that I almost blush at being of the same species.''[44] When the general failed to get a quick court-martial hearing in an attempt to clear his name, he penned these frantic words to George Washington: ''I want no favor; I ask only justice . . . . Having made every sacrifice of fortune and blood, and become a cripple in the service of my country, I little expected to meet the ungrateful returns I have received from my countrymen; but as Congress have stamped ingratitude as a current coin, I must take it.''[45] Arnold composed these lines in early May 1779, only a few days before he sent his first treason letter to New York City.

Arnold, perhaps more than the other officers, personalized his sense of disillusionment. His grounds for grievance were straightforward in his mind. He had repeatedly displayed public virtue and moral commitment. He had attempted to be a loyal republican. The general citizenry and its leaders, however, had betrayed him and others, which meant that they, in their self-interest, had forsaken the cause – and turned it into a sham.

What it all came down to for Arnold by the summer of 1779 was that the quest for republicanism had become meaningless. As Arnold stated to Samuel Holden Parsons on 8 September 1780, the ''contracted politics and little sense'' of congressional delegates ''will not suffer them to admire or reward the virtue they cannot imitate.''[46] Without the republican ideal, the Revolution was all but lost. The ultimate form of positive, individual protest, then, would be to recognize reality and to go over to the enemy – which, after all, was the parent state. Effecting a personal reconciliation with Great Britain might, in turn, unleash a wave of similar acts, with Arnold playing the central part of the ''pied piper'' in leading a hopelessly lost populace back into the arms of an anxious and forgiving parent.

This is not meant to argue that Arnold perceived his climatic act of personal protest in purely benevolent terms. Fully disillusioned, he expected financial recompense and recognition as a hero for his act. From his perspective, if he had been naive in his enthusiasm during 1775, he now acknowledged that the world was corrupt – and that only fools, such as he believed he had been, would not think of themselves first.

Aboard the British war vessel *Vulture* in the Hudson River on 25 September 1780, Arnold sorted out his thoughts. The Revolution had apparently taught him that mankind was somehow doomed to fall short of achieving an ideal political state. ''The heart which is conscious of its own rectitude cannot attempt to palliate a step which the world may censure as wrong,'' he wrote to his former patron-in-arms, George Washington. ''I have ever acted from a principle of love to my country since the commencement of the present unhappy contest between Great Britain and the colonies. The same principle of love to my country actuates my present conduct, however it may appear inconsistent to the world, who very seldom judge right of any man's actions.''[47] If republicanism could not work, he was saying, then the only sensible course was to reestablish allegiance with Great Britain.

Arnold hoped that his act of extreme protest would ignite the collapse of the

American cause. Thus on 20 October 1780, he called upon "friends, fellow soldiers, and citizens" to "arouse and judge for yourselves – reflect on what you have lost – consider to what you are reduced, and by your courage repel the ruin that still threatens you."[48] By hindsight, we know that few citizens took his appeal seriously. Indeed, the populace had already started to employ him as a source of reinvigorated support for the cause.[49] It is a supreme irony that Arnold's act of treason backfired on him to the extent that it did. For in many ways Arnold was correct in his assessment. The cause was in desperate shape during 1779 and 1780. What he never counted on, however, was that his ultimate act of defiance would function as a rallying point for renewed determination by rebel citizens in attempting to live up to republican ideals. But that necessitated turning Benedict Arnold into the likeness of the devil. And it has been that image which has persisted in historical literature – rather than that of a man who, out of disillusionment, went too far in protesting the people's attitudes toward the military in Revolutionary America.

NOTES

The author wishes to acknowledge the valuable assistance of Amos T. Miller of the University of Houston, Richard H. Kohn and Mark Edward Lender of Rutgers University, Charles Royster of the University of Texas at Arlington, and George Athan Billias of Clark University in the preparation of this essay.

1. Words taken from a woodcut which reproduced the scene of a Philadelphia parade denouncing Arnold's treason. The parade occurred on 30 September 1780. The parade, which included noted gentlemen, Continental officers and soldiers, and the city's infantry unit, centered on a horse-drawn float. Exhibited on the platform was "an effigy of General Arnold sitting." He had "two faces, emblematical of his traitorous conduct, a mask in his left hand, and a letter in his right from Beelzebub, telling him that he had done all the mischief he could do . . . . At the back of the General was a figure of the Devil, shaking a purse of money at the general's left ear, and in his right hand a pitchfork, ready to drive him into hell as the reward due for the many crimes which the thief of gold had made him commit." Such imagery, which took strength from what might be called the ideology of evangelical republicanism, was pervasive as an explanation of Arnold's behavior. On 26 September 1780, for example, Captain Samuel Frost wrote in the Orderly Book of the Sixth Massachusetts Regiment, stationed at Tappan, New York, that "Treason of the blackest dye was yesterday discovered . . . . Such an event would have given the American cause a deadly wound, if not a fatal stab; happily the treason has been timely discovered to prevent the fatal misfortune, the providential train . . . affords the most convincing proof that the Liberties of America is [sic] the object of the Divine Protection." Orderly Book in United States Military Academy Library. Spelling in all quotations has been modernized.
2. William Tillotson to Thomas S. Lee, 28 September 1780, C. E. French Collection, Massachusetts Historical Society [hereinafter MHS].
3. Alexander Scammell to Meshech Weare, 1 October 1780, Weare Papers, MHS. Comments by Tillotson and Weare are typical of dozens of others that have survived.
4. *Traitorous Hero: The Life and Fortunes of Benedict Arnold* (New York: Books for Libraries, Inc., 1954), p. 317. This volume remains the only scholarly biography of Arnold in our time. Certainly as revealing is Isaac N. Arnold, *The Life of Benedict Arnold* (Chicago: Jansen, McClung, 1880).
5. Charles Royster, *A Revolutionary People at War: The Continental Army and American Character, 1775-1783* (Chapel Hill: Univ. of North Carolina Press, 1980), pp. 25-53.
6. 24 April 1775, Peter Force, ed., *American Archives*, 4th Sers. (6 vols.; Washington: GPO, 1837-46), pp. 383-84.
7. James T. Flexner *The Traitor and the Spy: Benedict Arnold and John André* (New York: Harcourt,

Brace, 1953; new ed., Boston: Little, Brown, 1975), p. xiii. While Flexner did research his subject, his story often embroiders upon the factual record, which may explain why professional historians treat the Wallace biography with more respect.

8. Arnold to B. Douglas, 19 June 1770, *Historical Magazine*, 1st Sers. (1857), I, 119.

9. Arnold to John Manir or Captain William Gregory, 13 October 1775, in Force, *American Archives*, 4th Sers., III, 1062. Arnold was not given to political introspection with pen in hand.But surviving glimpses of his thoughts establish him as a committed republican.

10. "To the American Soldiery," Cambridge, 14 November 1775, in *ibid.*, III, 1557-59. See also "To the Worthy Officers and Soldiers in the American Army," Cambridge, 24 November 1775, in *ibid.*, III, 1667-68.

11. On paper, the Continental Army consisted of 46,197 soldiers (including militia and troops under Philip Schuyler in the Northern Department) during September 1776; and the total for October 1776 was 48,017. By comparison, Washington had 10,003 troops in May 1777; and the Northern Department totaled 5193 in July and 8300 in August 1777. It is safe to conclude that the overall manpower pool had dropped by at least 50 to 60 percent, if not more, between the summer of 1776 and the summer of 1777. See Charles H. Lesser, ed., *The Sinews of Independence: Monthly Strength Reports of the Continental Army* (Chicago: Univ. of Chicago Press, 1976), pp. 32-49.

12. Mark Edward Lender, "The Social Structure of the New Jersey Brigade: The Continental Line as an American Standing Army," in *The Military in America: From the Colonial Era to the Present*, ed. Peter Karsten (New York: The Free Press, 1980), pp. 27-44; John R. Sellers, "The Common Soldier in the American Revolution," *Military History of the American Revolution: Proceedings of the Sixth Military History Symposium, USAF Academy*, ed. S. J. Underdal (Washington: GPO, 1976), pp. 151-61; Sellers, "The Origins and Careers of the New England Soldier: Noncommissioned Officers and Privates in the Massachusetts Continental Line" (paper delivered at the American Historical Association Convention, 1972); and Edward C. Papenfuse and Gregory A. Stiverson, "General Smallwood's Recruits: The Peacetime Career of the Revolutionary War Private," *William and Mary Quarterly*, 3rd Sers., 30 (January 1973), 117-32.

13. It was not just that these soldiers were young and, therefore, not yet in their prime earning years. Their families were also quite poor, which suggests a limited range of economic opportunity, unless one was possessed of unusual individual talent. Lender, for instance, found that 46 percent of the Jersey soldiery or their families (for those underage) owned no taxable property whatsoever. Fifty-seven percent of the Jersey Continentals were landless, not an attractive condition in that state's largely agricultural economy. Sellers' case studies reveal distinctly similar patterns; and among the Maryland troops of 1782, half of those with traceable wealth, according to Papenfuse and Stiverson, came from family units holding less than £45 in assessed wealth. Leaning upon the poor and underprivileged in society for long-term fighting was already a well-engrained American tradition. See the relevant sections of Gary B. Nash., *The Urban Crucible: Social Change, Political Consciousness, and the Origins of the American Revolution* (Cambridge: Harvard Univ. Press, 1979).

14. This is the point made by Charles Royster in the appendix to *Revolutionary People at War*, pp. 373-78. It is my contention that Royster has construed the Lender-Sellers-Papenfuse-Stiverson studies more narrowly than necessarily should have been the case. From my reading, these studies question an all-pervasive ideological force as posited in the rather deterministic explanations of Bernard Bailyn and others. At some point, such generalizations must be comprehended as tendencies rather than as absolutes. For a balanced statement, see Robert Middlekauff, "Why Men Fought in the American Revolution," *Huntington Library Quarterly*, 43 (Spring 1980), 135-48.

15. George F. Scheer, ed., *Private Yankee Doodle: Being a Narrative of the Adventures, Dangers and Sufferings of a Revolutionary Soldier* (Boston: Little, Brown, 1962), p. 186.

16. Royster, p. 71.

17. The patterns of individual and group protest, both of the rank and file and of the officer corps, are discussed more fully in James Kirby Martin and Mark Edward Lender, *'A Respectable Army': The Military Origins of the Republic, 1763-1789* (Chicago: AHM, forthcoming), *passim*. See also James Kirby Martin, "A 'Most Undisciplined and Profligate Crew': Protest and Defiance in the Continental Ranks, 1776-1783," which will appear in *Arms and Independence: The Military Character of the American Revolution*, ed. Ronald Hoffman (Charlottesville: Univ. of

Virginia Press, forthcoming).

18. Although differing somewhat in emphasis, important secondary studies of officers' attitudes include Royster, pp. 82-95, 197-218, 295-330, 343-60; Richard H. Kohn, "American General, of the Revolution: Subordination and Restraint," in *Reconsiderations of the Revolutionary War: Selected Essays*, ed. Don Higginbotham (Westport, Conn.: Greenwood Press, 1978), pp. 104-23; and Jonathan Gregory Rossie, *The Politics of Command in the American Revolution* (Syracuse: Syracuse Univ. Press, 1975), *passim*.

19. Paterson to William Heath, 31 March 1780, *The Heath Papers*, MHS *Collections*, 7th Sers. (5 vols.; Boston: MHS, 1898-1907), V, 44-45.

20. McDougall to Nathanael Greene, 24 March 1779, Greene Papers, American Philosophical Society, Philadelphia.

21. Huntington to Andrew Huntington, 7 July 1780, "Letters of Ebenezer Huntington, 1774-1781," *American Historical Review*, 5 (February 1900), 725-26.

22. Arnold to Nathanael Greene, 12 September 1780, Peter Force Transcripts, Library of Congress.

23. See in particular "Remarks on Plan of Field Officers for Remodeling the Army," November 1777, in John C. Fitzpatrick, ed., *The Writings of George Washington* (39 vols.; Washington: GPO, 1931-44), X, 125-26. See also George Washington "To the Committee of Congress with the Army," Valley Forge, 29 January 1778, in *ibid.*, 362-65, 400-03.

24. Lovell to Samuel Adams, 13 January 1778, Edmund C. Burnett, ed., *Letters of Members of the Continental Congress* (8 vols.; Washington: Carnegie Institution of Washington, 1921-36), III, 31-33.

25. Henry Laurens to James Duane, York, 7 April 1778, in *ibid.*, III, 153-55; and Thomas Burke to Richard Caswell, York, 9 April 1778, in *ibid.*, III, 160-63.

26. "To the Committee of Congress with the Army," 29 January 1778, in Fitzpatrick, *Writings of Washington*, X, 363.

27. The pensions promised by Congress in 1778 had a seven-year limitation ("Memorial of General Officers," 11 July 1780, quoted in Roger J. Champagne, *Alexander McDougall and the American Revolution in New York* [Schenectady: Union College Press, 1975], p. 160). Champagne's study, while featuring McDougall, represents the best published attempt to piece together the pension controversy in the years 1778-80.

28. See in particular Richard H. Kohn, "The Inside History of the Newburgh Conspiracy: America and the *Coup d'Etat*," *William and Mary Quarterly*, 3rd Sers., 27 (April 1970), 187-220. One should also look at the criticisms of this presentation along with Kohn's replies in Paul David Nelson, "Horatio Gates at Newburgh, 1783: A Misunderstood Role," *William and Mary Quarterly*, 3rd Sers., 29 (January 1972), 143-58, and C. Edward Skeen, "The Newburgh Conspiracy Reconsidered," *William and Mary Quarterly*, 3rd Sers., 31 (April 1974), 273-98.

29. 19 February 1777, Worthington C. Ford *et al.*, eds., *Journals of the Continental Congress* (34 vols.; Washington: GPO, 1904-37), VII, 133. For additional commentary, see "Abstract of Debates" by Thomas Burke, in Burnett, *Letters of Members*, II, 262.

30. Some of this anti-Arnold sentiment reflected upon his personal disputes with John Brown and Moses Hazen in which Arnold had accused Brown of plundering officers' baggage and Hazen of disobedience and possible theft of goods seized from Canadians for the support of the American army retreating from Canada. Ultimately, a military court of enquiry cleared Hazen and rebuked Arnold for having cast aspersions on the former's character. Brown never got the hearing he wanted, but both men carried their cases to Congress, insisting that it was Arnold who was the thief. None of this helped Arnold's reputation, and it no doubt influenced Congress's decision to pass over him on 19 February 1777. Typical of direct lobbying against Arnold is John Brown to Theodore Sedgwick, 6 December 1776, Sedgwick Papers, MHS. In this letter Brown wrote: "And now in my turn I think proper to transmit to Congress, the Petition Complaint Answers & Evasions of General Gates, and demand General Arnold to be arrested and brought to trial on said complaint." All of this, according to Brown, was for Sedgwick's "amusement."

31. Arnold to Hancock, 11 July 1777, Papers of the Continental Congress, National Archives. See also Arnold to Hancock, 20 May, 10 June, 13 June, 12 July, and 14 July 1777.

32. Arnold to Washington, 11 March 1777, Jared Sparks, ed., *Correspondence of the American Revolution . . .* (4 vols.; Boston: Little, Brown, 1853), I, 353-56.

33. See note 18. A good example of such protest is found in a letter from William Maxwell to John

Hancock, 28 August 1776, Papers of the Continental Congress, National Archives. Maxwell presumed "that Col. St. Clair's friends will not pretend . . . he has served his country with more zeal than your memorialist has done; but what will the continent think, where a younger officer is preferred, but that the older one is not fit for it." Maxwell also noted that he "would have quit the service immediately but that the present alarming state of his country requires his presence in the field." Congress elevated Maxwell to a brigadier generalship in October 1776. Such individual protest, whether from Arnold, Maxwell, or others, did have a ritualistic cast to it.

34. Quoted in Kohn, "American Generals," pp. 118-19.
35. Washington to John Bannister, 21 April 1778, Fitzpatrick, *Writings of Washington*, XI, 290-92.
36. It is impossible to pick a precise date when Arnold started putting more emphasis upon personal honor than on the pursuit of liberty for the community. My reading of his extant letters would suggest that his change in outlook clearly appears during the period of the promotion controversy in 1777.
37. In July 1778, Arnold related to Nathanael Greene that he was in ill health and tied up with his duties as military commander of Philadelphia. The implication was that he was too busy to get involved. See Arnold to Greene, 25 July 1778, Henry Huntington Library, San Marino, Calif.
38. Arnold to Mercy Scollay, 15 July 1778, MHS. See also Mercy Scollay to Benedict Arnold, 5 August 1778, and Benedict Arnold to Dr. David Townshend, 6 August 1778, MHS.
39. Arnold, *Life of Arnold*, 216-21 attributes Arnold's apparent good deed to a "heart . . . warm with gratitude and generosity." While this may have been the case, there can be no doubt that the general had found a perfect pedestal on which to display civilian ingratitude.
40. Arnold to Mercy Scollay, in *ibid.*, 218-19. In this letter Arnold made passing reference to the officers' pension drive, referring to widows and orphans. That he tied his ad hoc campaign to the broader effort is interesting. Besides seeking to embarrass Congress, it may be that Arnold wanted to believe that his efforts would result in gains for families of the slain more generally. This was a curious concern for a man about to commit treason.
41. As Arnold became more disillusioned, he took to repeating the "fought and bled" phrase with regularity. At the least, he was emphasizing his self-sacrifice in the face of attacks on his character and honor. A good example may be found in a letter he wrote to Timothy Matlack (from which the quotation is taken) while in Philadelphia, 6 October 1778, Joseph Reed Papers, New-York Historical Society. In this case, Arnold was defending the actions of his aide, David Franks, who had sent Matlack's son to fetch a barber. The son, William, complained that this duty was unbecoming a militia sergeant. For further details of an incident that would eventually become a public charge against Arnold by the Joseph Reed group in Pennyslvania, see Timothy Matlack to Arnold, October 1778, Joseph Reed Papers, New-York Historical Society.
42. Kohn, "American Generals" pp. 112-20. See also Don Higginbotham, *The War of American Independence: Military Attitudes, Policies and Practice, 1763-1789* (New York: Macmillan, 1971), pp. 214-16.
43. For more detail on Arnold's controversy, see Wallace, *Traitorous Hero*, pp. 170-92; Robert L. Brunhouse, *The Counter-Revolution in Pennsylvania, 1776-1790* (Harrisburg: Pennsylvania Historical Commission, 1942), pp. 64-68; and H. James Henderson, *Party Politics in the Continental Congress* (New York: McGraw-Hill, 1974), pp. 231-37.
44. Arnold to Margaret Shippen, 8 February 1779, Arnold, *Life of Arnold*, pp. 230-31.
45. Arnold to Washington, 5 May 1779, Sparks, ed., *Correspondence American Revolution*, II, 290-92. For the chronology, see Carl Van Doren, *Secret History of the American Revolution . . .* (New York: Viking Press, 1941), pp. 191-95.
46. Peter Force Transcripts, Library of Congress.
47. "On Board the *Vulture*," 25 September 1780, David Franks papers, American Jewish Archives, Cincinnati, Ohio.
48. "To the Officers and Soldiers of the Continental Army . . . ," Arnold, *Life of Arnold*, pp. 332-34.
49. This theme is developed in Charles Royster, "'The Nature of Treason': Revolutionary Virtue and American Reactions to Benedict Arnold," *William and Mary Quarterly*, 3rd Sers., 36 (April 1979), 163-93.

This article appeared in the September 1981 issue of *Parameters*.

V. HISTORY AS A PRELUDE TO DOCTRINE

16

Indians and Insurrectos: The US Army's Experience with Insurgency

by JOHN M. GATES

Both during the Vietnam War and after, students of 19th-century American military history frequently claimed to see important similarities between whatever campaign they happened to be surveying and the conflict in Indochina. In his 1976 Harmon Memorial lecture, Robert M. Utley, a distinguished historian of the Indian-fighting Army, drew attention to the "parallels with frontier warfare" in the so-called "limited wars" of the nuclear age. Jack Bauer, in his study of the Mexican War, implied much the same thing in a reference to General Scott's operation to secure his line of supply from attack by Mexican guerrillas. Scott's problems, wrote Bauer, were "as complex and difficult as any faced by modern American soldiers who think the problem unique to mainland Asia." I concluded my own book with the observation that a study of the Army's Philippine campaign might provide insight into the solution of similar problems in the 20th century. Underlying all such observations seems to be a belief that the Army had failed to learn as much as it could or should have from its 19th-century counterinsurgency experience.[1]

Utley blamed the leaders of "the Indian-fighting generations," civilian and military alike, for the failure of 20th-century counterinsurgency doctrine to "reflect the lessons" of the 19th-century experience. As he observed in his lecture, "Military leaders looked upon Indian warfare as a fleeting bother. Today's conflict or tomorrow's would be the last, and to develop a special system for it seemed hardly worthwhile."[2] Alternatively, one might argue that 19th-century experience was absent from 20th-century doctrine because of a lack of attention on the Army's part to its own history of counterguerrilla operations. Only nine lines are devoted to the guerrilla war in the Philippines in the *American Military History* volume of the Army Historical Series, for example.

Probably both interpretations are correct. In the 19th and 20th centuries alike, the Army's leaders do appear to have given insufficient attention to the problems of fighting unconventional wars, but there may be a third and even more important reason why no doctrine of counterinsurgency emerged from the campaigns of the 19th century to serve the purposes of those of the 20th. The Army's efforts against such diverse enemies as the Mexicans, Confederates, Indians, and Filipinos took place in such different contexts and over such a long span of time that whatever common elements might have been present were either too obvious to merit discussion by the officers involved at the time or too hidden from their view to be discerned.

In the Mexican War, American soldiers faced guerrillas in the context of an international war fought between two governments, each of which acknowledged the existence and legitimacy of the other. Although the contest was quite one-sided and the Mexican government weak and frequently in disarray, the war was a conventional one in which the uniformed forces of each party, fighting in regular formations and pitched battles, carried the major burden of effort on each side. Mexican guerrillas were never more than an annoyance to US forces. The Americans could not ignore them, but the outcome of the war was not dependent on their actions. The Army did an excellent job of keeping Mexican guerrillas under control and preventing them from interdicting American supply lines. It also managed to convince the Mexican population at large that a people's war against the American Army was both unwise and unnecessary. For the United States, however, success in the war came, as one would expect, from the repeated defeat of Mexico's regular forces and the deep penetration of an American Army into the interior of Mexico, seizing the nation's capital as well as its principal port.

As in Mexico, guerrilla activity during the American Civil War drew troops away from front-line units to guard supply lines and garrison posts to the rear, but the war itself was decided by the fortunes of the uniformed forces locked in mortal combat on such battlefields as Shiloh, Antietam, and Gettysburg. Even more important was the wearing down of the Confederacy by the North's overwhelming superiority in both human and material resources, particularly when Sherman projected those resources into the heart of the Confederacy or when Grant threw them relentlessly against Lee's hard-pressed forces in Virginia. As it evolved in the context of the Civil War, guerrilla activity never amounted to more than harassment. Although Virgil Carrington Jones has argued persuasively that "gray ghosts and rebel raiders" operating in northern and western Virginia prevented Grant from implementing his plans for an attack against Richmond for the better part of a year, thus prolonging the war, Jones made no case whatever that such guerrilla activity was in any way decisive. In the end, Grant defeated Lee, and the South surrendered. Only a full-scale people's war, something as abhorrent to many Southern leaders as it was to the Northerners opposing them, might have had a truly significant effect on events, but that did not happen. The Army's operations against Civil War guerrillas remained, as in Mexico, a sideshow to the real war fought by regular units on the battlefield.

One important difference between the war in Mexico and that in the United

States did exist. In Mexico, the United States government did not seek to conquer the entire country, only to make the Mexican government acquiesce in its demands regarding westward expansion into a sparsely populated Mexican territory hundreds of miles from the Mexican heartland. Not threatened by permanent conquest, Mexicans had little incentive to embark on a war of national liberation comparable to that which they launched a decade later against the forces of Maximilian. When the Mexican government admitted defeat, the American Army quickly withdrew, leaving the two belligerents at peace, at least with each other.

The Civil War, however, was not an international conflict between two sovereign states, despite Southern claims to the contrary. Instead, as a war of secession (or rebellion), it raised, for Army officers, significant problems that had not existed in Mexico. Union commanders, for example, were unsure of the treatment to be accorded to prisoners who, under civilian laws, might well be guilty of treason. A more important, though related, problem stemmed from the necessity to fight the war in such a way that reunion could be accomplished. If a people's war of resistance comparable to that faced by Napoleon in Spain had emerged in the South, a lasting peace might never have been achieved. Thus, the political problems presented by Confederate guerrillas were much more complex than those facing the Army in the Mexican War.

The Indian Wars present the greatest problem for anyone seeking to generalize about the Army's guerrilla war experience. Although the Indians of North America used guerrilla tactics, they were not really engaged in a guerrilla war. Unlike the guerrillas of Mexico or the Confederacy, they were not part-time soldiers hidden by a friendly but sedentary population. Nor did they act in support of an existing regular army. Instead, they were a primitive people under attack by a host of forces, many of which they only partially understood, and they responded with violence in a sporadic fashion, with no strategic concept to guide their actions. Often they resisted because they had no other acceptable choice, but they fought as nomads or from insecure bases and not, as the Mexicans and Confederates, hidden in the arms of a larger population living behind the lines of their enemies. In the terms of Mao's analogy, the Indian warriors were fish without a sea, easily identified as enemies, if not so readily hunted down.

In his well-known survey of primitive war, anthropologist H. H. Turney-High listed five attributes of what he called "true war": the presence of "tactical operations," "definite command and control," the "ability to conduct a campaign for the reduction of enemy resistance if the first battle fails," a clear motive that is the motive of the group rather than that of an individual member, and "an adequate supply."[3] Applying his criteria to the Indians of North America, one sees that they rarely engaged in "true war." Although most Indian groups possessed a rudimentary knowledge of tactics, they usually lacked discipline and commanders able to exert military control over warriors in the heat of battle. In some tribes, such as the Osage, battle had evolved as a religious ritual in which, according to ethnographer Francis Lee Flesche, the pre-battle ceremonies and songs could take longer than the battle itself. In most tribes, participation in battle was usually voluntary, making either total mobilization or total war impossible. Similarly inhibiting were the lack of a clear objective, which distinguishes the more complex and longer phenomenon of "true war" from simply a successful battle, and the absence of the ability to sustain a campaign with adequate supplies. Although Indian scouting and intelligence gathering were often superb by Army standards, Indians also relied upon magic to divine enemy intentions or make plans, and the absence of methodical planning was yet another negative feature of the Indian approach to battle. The Indians, widely known for their stealth and ferocity, demonstrated those characteristics in a context that was significantly different from that of a guerrilla war so often attributed to them.

When Indians fought against the Army they fought as warriors. Although tactically they fought as guerrillas, and often displayed tremendous skill in the process, strategically they were not guerrillas. They were not attempting to wear down the enemy by harassment, nor were they in a position to create secure base areas or win over the civilian population living in the heartland of the Army they confronted. They fought as they did because it was the only way they knew to fight, and their success in keeping in the field as long as they did resulted as much from the Army's meager size as from the Indian's prowess as warriors.

Much of the Army's work on the frontier was that of a constabulary. It served eviction notices on Indians and then forcibly removed them when required. If "imprisoned" Indians "broke out" of the reservations, the Army found them and coerced them back. Failing in the latter, it would attempt the equivalent of an arrest, an armed attack to force the Indians to surrender. Indians who raided white settlers, Army posts, or peaceful reservation-Indians engaged in criminal activity, in white eyes at least; and the Army's task was that of the police officer, to track down the guilty parties and bring them back for punishment. Because of the numbers involved those activities sometimes looked like war, and in a few instances, when entire tribes rose up in arms to fight against the intrusion of the white, it was. Most of the time, however, it was routine though difficult police work.

As the US Army's only military activity between the 19th century's infrequent real wars, the so-called Indian Wars have received far more attention than they deserve. At best, except for a few significant successes, such as that against Custer at the Little Big Horn, the Indians were little more than a nuisance. In the final analysis, one must agree with Robert Utley that the Army was only

one of many groups that pushed the frontier westward and doomed the Indian. Other frontiersmen – trappers, traders, miners, stockmen, farmers, railroad builders, merchants – share largely in the process. They, rather than the soldiers, deprived the Indian of the land and the sustenance that left him no alternative but to submit.[4]

The pressure of an expanding white civilization, not the campaigns of the Army, was the primary reason for the end of Indian resistance. The Indian Wars are both the most extensive and also the least relevant of the Army's 19th-century experiences fighting "guerrillas."

The Army's confrontation with guerrillas in the Philippines differed markedly from all its previous experiences, being much more comparable to the guerrilla wars of national liberation waged after World War II than to any of the Army's earlier campaigns. Unlike the Mexican or the Civil War, the war's outcome would not be decided by the clash of regular forces, and the outcome was not, as in the Indian conflicts, certain from the start. In the Philippines, the United States was engaged in a war of conquest, although Americans both at the time and later have seen fit to hide their actions by referring to the enemy as insurgents, or worse. There could be no insurrection, however, because the United States did not control the Islands when the Philippine American War began in 1899. The fighting that ensued took place between two organized forces, one representing the government of the United States and the other representing the revolutionary government of the Philippine Republic under the leadership of Emilio Aguinaldo. The conflict began as a conventional war, pitting American regulars and volunteers against the Philippine army that had seized control of the Islands from Spain. Although beginning as a guerrilla force, the army surrounding the Americans in Manila had adopted conventional organization and tactics, planning to engage the American forces in regular combat and hoping to gain international recognition for the Philippine Republic as a result.

When their attempts at regular warfare ended in disaster, the Filipinos shifted to a guerrilla strategy aimed at making an occupation of the Philippines too costly for the Americans and achieving by a political solution what they had failed to achieve through a more conventional military approach. The problems presented by the Filipino strategy were greater than any faced by the Army in its previous confrontations with Indians or true guerrillas. Bent on conquest of the entire Philippines, the United States could not achieve peace and accomplish withdrawal by arranging a partial cession of territory as it had done in Mexico. And because the value of the Islands as a colony resided, at least in part, in the population, policies of removal or extermination were also inappropriate, even had they been acceptable on moral grounds – and, of course, they were not. Filipino numbers and the colonial nature of the conflict thus precluded a solution based on the experience of the Indian Wars. Finally, the Filipino leadership, unlike that of the South in the Civil War, had no reservations about calling their followers into the field in a people's war of prolonged guerrilla struggle. From the Army's point of view, however, the Philippine situation, like that of the Civil War, demanded that the war be fought and ended in a way that would help create a lasting peace.

The tremendous differences in the contexts of the Army's guerrilla war experiences make generalizations difficult, but not impossible. Some uniformities can be discerned, although frequently they are not nearly so important as the differences, a point to be doubly emphasized when one attempts to compare any of the Army's guerrilla war experiences with the war in Vietnam.

The most obvious uniformity is that of guerrilla technique; General George Crook's observation that Apaches "only fight with regular soldiers when they choose and when the advantages are all on their side" might just as easily have been made about Mexican, Confederate, or Philippine guerrillas.[5] And a Confederate guerrilla leader spoke in terms readily understandable to the other guerrillas confronting the Army during the century when he described his mission against the Yankees as

to hang about their camps and shoot down every sentinel, picket, courier and wagon driver we can find; to watch opportunities for attacking convoys and forage trains, and thus render the country so unsafe that they will not dare to move except in large bodies.[6]

Whether in Mexico, the Shenandoah Valley, the Great Plains, or the Philippines, guerrillas behaved much the same: fleeing from strength, attacking weakness, preying upon small isolated garrisons and poorly defended supply trains, killing the lone sentry or the unwary patrol, living off the land with the aid of their people – and terrorizing those who refused to cooperate or joined with the enemy.

A secondary uniformity, only slightly less obvious than the first, can be seen in the Army's response to the threat posed by Indian and guerrilla bands. The actions taken to counter them were remarkably similar from place to place over time. Whether the enemy was Mexican, Confederate, Indian, or Filipino, the Army responded eventually with many of the same general techniques of counterguerrilla warfare. To protect supply lines, commanders increased the size of the guard assigned to supply trains and strengthened garrisons along their routes of march. To facilitate operations against marauding bands and to provide security to populated areas, commanders garrisoned towns and built forts. To hunt down enemy units and force them to disband or be destroyed, the Army sent highly mobile, self-contained units into the field to pursue them relentlessly. Often at a disadvantage because of their unfamiliarity with the terrain or the local population, Army officers enlisted the support of indigenous inhabitants whenever possible. In Mexico, for example, Lieutenant Colonel Ethan Hitchcock obtained the aid of robber Manuel Dominguez and his band, and in the American southwest General George Crook formed units of friendly Apaches to help him find and fight renegades such as Geronimo. In perhaps the most celebrated use of indigenous collaborators, Frederick Funston used a force of Filipino scouts to capture Aguinaldo in his own headquarters in 1901.

The Army was relatively successful in developing methods to deal with the problems presented by hostile Indians and guerrilla bands in the field. A more difficult set of problems emerged, however, regarding the treatment to be accorded guerrilla combatants who had been captured, particularly part-time guerrillas, and the noncombatant population from which the guerrillas derived support. Throughout the 19th century one sees tension between two general policies, one rooted in severity and the other more humane. The frustrations of guerrilla warfare, the ease with which guerrilla bands eluded regular troops when aided by a friendly population, the atrocities committed by irregulars, and a common assumption that guerrillas were not legitimate combatants all worked to push commanders in the field toward a policy of reprisal. But recognition by these officers that their enemies were frequently doing nothing that they themselves would not do in a similar situation, the need to fight and terminate conflicts in a fashion that would bring a lasting peace, and the desire to keep one's humanity even in the midst of barbarous war all supported policies of conciliation aimed at winning over the opposition by good works rather than fear.

Nineteenth-century customs and laws of war reflected, rather than resolved, these tensions. Although the United States had yet to promulgate any official statement on the laws of war to guide officers during the Mexican War and the early years of the Civil War, by February 1863 Professor Francis Lieber, a noted authority on international law, had drafted a code that was summarized and distributed to the Army on 24 April of that year as General Order No. 100, "Instructions for the Government of Armies of the United States in the Field."[7] It became the cornerstone of the growing body of international law upon which current practices rest, and by the time of the Philippine-American War it had become the final word for American Army officers on the laws of war.

General Order 100 manifested the tension between the two different approaches to pacification. On the assumption that "sharp wars are brief," the order asserted that "the more vigorously wars are pursued the better it is for humanity." In an 1862 commentary written for General Halleck on the status of guerrilla parties in the laws and customs of war, Lieber concluded that "armed bands" rising "in a district fairly occupied by military force, or in the rear of an army," were "universally considered" to be "brigands, and not prisoners of war" when captured. He also observed that such groups were "particularly dangerous because they could easily evade pursuit, and by laying down their arms become insidious enemies."[8] His negative view of guerrillas was carried over into General Order 100. Although item 81 of the order stated that properly uniformed "partisans" were entitled to be treated as true prisoners of war, item 82 stated that guerrillas who fought without commissions or on a part-time basis, returning intermittently to their homes to hide among the civilian population, were to be treated "summarily as highway robbers or pirates." Similarly, so-called "armed prowlers" were also denied the privileges of prisoners of war, and all who rose up against a conquering army were "war rebels," subject to death if captured. As item 4 noted, "To save the country is paramount to all other considerations."

At the same time that it condemned the guerrilla and sanctioned reprisals, however, General Order 100 also recognized that the conduct of officers administering martial law should "be strictly guided by the principles of justice, honor, and humanity." Although military necessity might justify destruction, even of innocent civilians, it did not sanction "cruelty . . . revenge . . . [or] torture." General Order 100 reminded officers that men who took up arms did not cease "to be moral beings, responsible to one another and to God." Unarmed citizens were "to be spared in person, property, and honor as much as the exigencies of war will admit." Retaliation, deemed "the sternest feature of war," was to be used with care, "only as a means of protective retribution" and "never . . . as a measure of mere revenge." As item 28 observed:

Unjust or inconsiderate retaliation removes the belligerents farther and farther from the mitigating rules of regular war, and by rapid steps leads them nearer to the internecine wars of savages.

Lieber knew that in war the barrier between civilization and barbarism was exceedingly thin, and he provided few opportunities for conscientious soldiers to breach it.

Even before the development of the guidelines set forth in General Order 100, the Army's campaigns against guerrillas had demonstrated both the severity and the humanity evident in Lieber's work. In Mexico, for example, captured guerrillas had been treated as criminals, either killed upon capture or after trial by military commissions. The Army also resorted to more general and collective punishments, including the destruction of villages suspected of harboring irregulars and the assessment of fines against municipalities and their officials to compensate for the destruction done by Mexican guerrilla bands. At the same time, General Scott and other commanders attempted to convince Mexicans that if they remained at peace, the United States would neither interfere with their customs and religion nor subject them to exploitation.

Civil War soldiers appear to have been guided by the experience of the Mexican War, and many Union officers began the war with the hope that by treating the Confederates leniently they could achieve a swift peace. In the first months of the war, the Army attempted to enforce a conciliatory policy aimed at protecting both the private property and constitutional rights of Confederate civilians. In the winter of 1861, for example,Sherman complained that his men suffered from exposure and short rations while the slaveholders of Kentucky ate fresh food in the warmth of their homes, and Grant said of his march to Missouri that "the same number of men never marched through a thickly settled country like this committing fewer depredations."[9]

The frustrations of trying to counter Southern guerrillas, however, soon led many officers to treat Southerners more severely. In Virginia, for example, General John Pope levied contributions on communities to compensate for damage done by guerrillas. He also decreed that male civilians within his lines take an oath of allegiance or be expelled, threatening them with death if they returned. When Confederate irregulars fired upon Union boats from the banks of the Mississippi, Sherman retaliated by burning a nearby town, and he told Grant that he had

given public notice that a repetition will justify any measures of retaliation such as loading the boats with their captive guerrillas as targets . . . and expelling families from the comforts of Memphis, whose husbands and brothers go to make up those guerrillas.[10]

In Missouri, following the 1863 raid on Lawrence, Kansas, by the band of William Quantrill, General Thomas J. Ewing ordered the population removed from four counties and their crops and property destroyed or confiscated. Endorsing his actions, his commanding officer, General John Schofield, observed that "nothing short of total devastation of the districts which are made the haunts of guerrillas will be sufficient to put a stop to the evil."[11] The following year, in Virginia, Grant demonstrated his agreement. Frustrated by Mosby's guerrillas, he ordered Sheridan to send a division "through Loudoun County to destroy and carry off the crops, animals, Negroes, and all men under fifty years of age capable of bearing arms" in an attempt to destroy Mosby's band. "Where any of Mosby's men are caught," Grant told Sheridan, "hang them without trial."[12] Only Mosby's retaliatory execution of some Union soldiers prevented Sheridan from carrying out Grant's order to the letter.

A special case, clearly different from the wars already described, the campaigns against the Indians displayed the same tension between severity and humanity, although in a different context. Officers were frequently appalled by Indian outrages such as those described by Sheridan in an 1870 report to Sherman:

Men, women, and children . . . murdered . . . in the most fiendish manner; the men usually scalped and multilated, their [   ] cut off and placed in their mouth [Sheridan's omission]; women ravished sometimes fifty and sixty times in succession, then killed and scalped, sticks stuck in their persons, before and after death.

At times, however, the officers bent on the destruction of a people they saw as brutal savages also expressed a degree of understanding and even admiration. Colonel Henry B. Carrington, who viewed the mutilated bodies of the soldiers killed in the 1866 Fetterman massacre, could still say that had he been a red man, he "should have fought as bitterly, if not as brutally, as the Indian fought." And General Nelson Miles praised the Indians' "courage, skill, sagacity, endurance, fortitude, and self sacrifice," as well as their "dignity, hospitality, and gentleness."[13]

Historian Richard Ellis has concluded that commanders such as O. O. Howard, George Crook, and John Pope were "sincere and benevolent men performing a difficult job."[14] Pope observed in 1875 that only "with painful reluctance" did the Army

take the field against Indians who only leave their reservations because they are starved there, and who must hunt food for themselves and their families or see them perish with hunger.[15]

Many officers recognized, as did Crook, that hostilities could be prevented if only the Indians were treated with "justice, truth, honesty, and common sense."[16] But such a humane policy was impossible for the American nation of the 19th century, bent on expansion and development. Soldiers recognized that they had little control over the fate of the Indians; instead, they believed the Indian to be doomed to "extinction" by forces "silently at work beyond all human control."[17] Given such assumptions, Sherman's remark in 1868 that "the more we can kill this year, the less will have to be killed next war" takes on the quality of statement of fact, rather than that of a cruel, unfeeling comment by a soldier committed to waging total war.[18]

The pattern in the Philippines at the century's end had much in common with events both in Mexico and in the Civil War. Many of the officers in the islands – such as General Elwell S. Otis, in command when the war began, and General Arthur MacArthur, his successor – were convinced that the swiftest way to end the war and pacify the population was to demonstrate the benefits of American colonial government; and the Army put considerable effort into establishing municipal governments, schools, and public works projects. Rejecting the concept of total war implied in Sherman's March to the Sea, most officers in the Philippines, at least initially, seemed to accept the idea put forth by Captain John Bigelow, Jr., in his *Principles of Strategy* that "the maintenance of a military despotism in the rear of an invading army must generally prove a waste of power."[19]

As the frustrations of the guerrilla war increased, however, officers began to either urge upon their superiors in Manila a policy of greater severity or engage in harsh reprisals without waiting for official sanction. As Colonel Robert L. Bullard wrote in his diary in August 1900:

It seems that ultimately we shall be driven to the Spanish method of dreadful general punishments on a whole community for the acts of its outlaws which the community systematically shields and hides.[20]

A few months later General Lloyd Wheaton urged "swift methods of destruction" to bring a "speedy termination to all resistance," claiming it was "no use going with a sword in one hand, a pacifist pamphlet in the other hand and trailing the model of a schoolhouse after."[21] Fortunately, General MacArthur recognized the value of the reform programs being implemented by the Army as well as the efforts being made to prevent excesses in the campaign against the guerrillas. Even he was frustrated, however, and, by the end of 1900, sanctioned the enforcement of the most severe sections of General Order 100. In areas where guerrillas and their supporters proved most intransigent, such as Batangas Province, the Army even resorted to population relocation and a scorched-earth policy comparable to that of General Ewing in western Missouri. On the island of Samar the line between retaliation and revenge became blurred beyond recognition for some soldiers.

Atrocities have taken place in virtually all wars, but the frustrations of guerrilla warfare, in which the enemy's acts of terror and brutality often add to the anger generated by the difficulty of campaigning, create an environment particularly conducive to the commission of war crimes. In almost all such wars one can discover numerous incidents in which counterinsurgents resorted to acts of counterterror, punishment, or revenge that fell clearly outside the relatively severe actions sanctioned by 19th-century laws of war.

During the Civil War, reprisals sometimes went well beyond these sanctioned by the laws of warfare. Robert Gould Shaw, for example, witnessed the "wanton destruction" of Darien, Georgia, in 1863, an act that made him ashamed to be an officer of the Union force that committed the act.[22] According to Shaw, the city was destroyed for no apparent reason other than his commander's desire to subject the Southerners to the hardships of war. As described by Shaw, it was an act of pure revenge and a war crime. In other instances, when the enemy was perceived as savage, the Army's actions could be even more severe, as exemplified by Custer's 1868 attack of Black Kettle's Cheyenne camp on the bank of the Washita. The men of the 7th Cavalry destroyed numerous Indians (including women and children), the camp's tepees (thus denying the survivors food and winter robes), and 875 Indian ponies.

Stories of atrocities would become the hallmark of the Philippine campaign. No history of that war is complete without a description of the "water cure," in which unwilling suspects were seized and their stomachs forcibly filled with water until they revealed the hiding place of guerrillas, of supplies, or of arms – or, as happened on occasion, until they died. The more frustrating the campaign became, the more frequently the Americans crossed the line separating the harsh reprisals sanctioned by General Order 100 from such crimes of war as torture and wanton destruction.

Although often quite harsh, the Army's 19th-century response to problems of guerrilla warfare was, in general, based upon the existing laws of war. Widely publicized, of course, have been the deviations from those laws that took place. In virtually every conflict, officers and men alike committed atrocities, such as shooting prisoners or noncombatants, or torturing people suspected of withholding information. Significantly, despite the tendency of those committing such acts and of their supporters to plead the extenuating circumstances of barbarous guerrilla war as a defense, few people accepted their argument that no crime or breach of the laws of war had been committed.

The conclusion that American soldiers in the 19th century made an effort to fight guerrillas within the context of a set of legal and moral restraints would not be particularly significant were it not for the tremendous contrast presented by current counterinsurgency campaigns. In places as remote from each other as El Salvador and Afghanistan, one sees an acceptance of widespread and seemingly indiscriminate terror against civilians as a primary technique for dealing not only with insurgents and their supporters, but with the uncommitted as well. At present, the laws of war are frequently ignored, and war against potential as well as actual insurgents is fought with a barbarity associated more with the likes of Attila the Hun than the soldiers of supposedly civilized nations.

For American soldiers not yet directly involved in this wholesale assault on the laws of war and humanity, the contrast between the attitude of many American officers in the 19th century and that evident in a number of foreign armies at present, particularly in Latin America, highlights a moral problem of immense proportions. That American officers are not unaware of the problem has been demonstrated by events such as the 1980 West Point symposium on "War and Morality." At that gathering, Professor Michael Walzer spoke of "two kinds of military responsibility," and his approach to the subject had much more in common with the views held by most 19th-century military officers than those exhibited by many of the world's soldiers currently engaged in counter-guerrilla warfare. In language that Francis Lieber would have readily endorsed, Walzer observed that the military officer "as a moral agent" has a responsibility beyond that upward to the officers over him and downward to the soldiers under him. He also has a responsibility "outward – to all those people whose lives his activities affect."[23] In the 19th century, Walzer's second kind of military responsibility was accepted by American officers as they attempted to defeat guerrillas without sinking to the level of barbarity that is now deemed "indispensable."[24]

Today, if US Army officers fail to give careful attention to the moral problems inherent in warfare against determined guerrilla forces, they may find themselves drawn more into the inhumane form of contemporary counterinsurgency practiced by communists and capitalists alike. To avoid such a fate, they must continue to ask themselves what at first glance seems to be a very 19th-century question. In countering insurgents, they must ask – in the moral sense of these words (a sense not commonly brought to bear in gauging the potential effectiveness of military operations) – what response is *right*, *good*, and *proper*. To do less is to risk the loss of their humanity as well as any claim to be defending a government based upon the rule of law.

NOTES

1. Robert M. Utley, "The Contribution of the Frontier to the American Military Tradition," in James P. Tate, ed., *The American Military on the Frontier* (Washington: Office of Air Force History, US Air Force, 1978), p. 13; Jack Bauer, *The Mexican War, 1846-1848* (New York: Macmillan, 1974), p. 332; John M. Gates, *Schoolbooks and Krags: The United States Army in the Philippines, 1898-1902* (Westport, Conn: Greenwood, 1973), p. 289.

2. Utley, "The Contribution of the Frontier to the American Military Tradition," p. 9.

3. Harry Holbert Turney-High, *Primitive War: Its Practice and Concepts* (Columbia: Univ. of South Carolina Press, 1949), p. 30.

4. Robert M. Utley, *Frontier Regulars: The United States Army and the Indian, 1866-1891* (New York: Macmillan, 1973) p. 411.

5. George Crook, "The Apache Problem," *Journal of the Military Service Institution of the United States,* 7 (October 1886), 263.

6. Bruce Catton in Virgil Carrington Jones, *Gray Ghosts and Rebel Raiders* (New York: Holt, 1956), p. ix.

7. See *The War of the Rebellion: A Compilation of the Official Records of the Union and Confederate Armies* (Washington: GPO, 1880-1901), Series III, Vol. 3, pp. 148-64, for a copy of General Order 100.

8. Francis Lieber, ''Guerrilla parties considered with reference to the laws and usages of war,'' *The War of the Rebellion*, Series III, Vol. 2, pp. 308-09.

9. John M. Brinsfield, ''The Military Ethics of General William T. Sherman: A Reassessment,'' *Parameters*, 12 (June 1982), 41-42.

10. Ibid.

11. Charles R. Mink, ''General Orders, No. 11: The Forced Evacuation of Civilians During the Civil War,'' *Military Affairs*, 34 (December 1970), 134.

12. David J. Ozolek, ''Retribution at Front Royal,'' *Military Review*, 61 (September 1981), 69.

13. Thomas C. Leonard, *Above the Battle: War making in America from Appomattox to Versailles* (New York: Oxford Univ. Press, 1978), pp. 48 and 51.

14. Richard N. Ellis, ''The Humanitarian Generals,'' *Western Historical Quarterly*, 3 (April 1972), 178.

15. Odie B. Faulk, *The Geronimo Campaign* (New York: Oxford Univ. Press, 1969), p. 26.

16. Leonard, p. 49.

17. Ibid., p. 55.

18. Russell F. Weigley, *The American Way of War: A History of United States Military Strategy and Policy* (New York: Macmillan, 1973), p. 160.

19. John Bigelow, *The Principles of Strategy*, rev. ed. (Philadelphia: J. B. Lippincott, 1894), pp. 263-64.

20. Robert Lee Bullard, Diary, 17 August 1900, Robert Lee Bullard Papers, Library of Congress, Washington, D.C.

21. Wheaton's endorsement, 11 January 1901, on J. M. Thompson to Adjutant General, 4 January 1901, ''Diary of Events, 12-30 Jan., 1901'' AGO 369140, Records of the Adjutant General's Office, Record Group 94, National Archives, Washington, D.C.

22. Robert Gould Shaw in Henry Steele Commager, ed., *The Blue and the Gray: The Story of the Civil War as Told by Participants* (Indianapolis: Bobbs-Merrill, 1950), p. 497.

23. Michael Walzer, ''Two Kinds of Military Responsibility,'' *Parameters*, 11 (March 1981), 45.

24. ''Indispensable'' was the word used by a French colonel to describe the importance of torture in the Algerian campaign. See Peter Paret, *French Revolutionary Warfare from Indochina to Algeria: The Analysis of a Political and Military Doctrine* (New York: Praeger, 1964), p. 69.

This article appeared in the March 1983 issue of *Parameters*.

17

Ambivalent Warfare: The Tactical Doctrine of the AEF in World War I

by JAMES W. RAINEY

Close adherence is urged to the central idea that the essential principles of war have not changed, that the rifle and the bayonet remain the supreme weapons of the infantry soldier and that the ultimate success of the army depends upon their proper use in open warfare.

– John J. Pershing, 19 October 1917[1]

The Commander in Chief of the American Expeditionary Forces issued the above dictum as a statement of doctrinal principle intended to guide the training of his forces for combat on the Western Front. Under Allied pressure to mold his force and commit it to battle as soon as possible, Pershing did not have the luxury of time to engage in any lengthy study of combat doctrine or to test his theories in field exercises. He perceived his task to be an either/or proposition: adopt the principle of position warfare that had characterized combat on the Western Front since 1914, or stand pat with the tactical doctrine espoused in the American Army's combat bible, the *Infantry Drill Regulations*.

The tactical doctrine specified by the IDR and similar publications had been developed by others, and these methods of fighting were grounded in American military tradition. During the period of American involvement in the war, the Army hierarchy would publish further doctrinal literature. Nevertheless, it remained Pershing's self-appointed task to interpret the existing doctrine and to order his units to adopt this refined doctrine. His influence in this regard was pervasive and reached across the ocean to influence the training of Army units in America under the direction of the War Department.

But Pershing's intended *modus operandi* for his AEF raises interesting questions, the most fundamental being the degree to which American tactical doctrine would be in harmony with the nature of the warfare of the Western Front. Had Pershing truly found a unique solution to the tactical stalemate of the trenches, or did he adopt a doctrine that was unworkably at odds with the reality of the battlefield? What was the basis of his doctrinal theory, and was it thought out with any degree of intellectual honesty? Was it clearly stated, and

211

did Pershing construct his units in conformity with the doctrine they were expected to execute? What was the effect of Pershing's actions on the preparation of the AEF for battle?

This article intends to offer evidence to support the conclusion that the tactical doctrine of the AEF was fraught with inconsistencies. Such inconsistencies resulted in an army not fully prepared for the combat it faced on the Western Front.

Black Jack Pershing believed that three years of trench, or position, warfare had conditioned the British and French armies to a defensive mentality and an acceptance of a war of attrition. All they knew, he argued, was how to attack from trench to trench, to surge forward, drive the Germans out of their trenches, occupy them, and await the inevitable counterattack, all the while wearing down the enemy in an indecisive war of attrition. But in Pershing's estimation, Allied offensives had led to nothing more than local territorial gains at the expense of millions of casualties. Pershing reasoned that the Allies believed warfare had changed, that the awesome killing effect of the machine gun mandated a positional war of attrition, and that open warfare, the clash of units in a war of movement, was obsolete.[2]

Pershing wanted to field an army wedded to the spirit of aggressiveness. He did not foresee this occurring if the AEF adopted the tactics of trench warfare: "[We] must contemplate the assumption of a vigorous offensive. This purpose will be emphasized . . . until it becomes a settled habit of thought."[3]

Pershing therefore elected not to adopt the tenets of position warfare. He forcefully believed that the Germans could be beaten only by driving them out of their trenches and into the open, where the qualitative superiority of the American infantry marksman could be employed most effectively in a war of movement and pursuit:

It was my opinion that the victory could not be won by the costly process of attrition, but it must be won by driving the enemy out into the open and engaging him in a war of movement . . . [We] took decided issue with the Allies and, without neglecting thorough preparation for trench fighting, undertook to train mainly for open combat, with the object from the start of vigorously forcing the offensive.[4]

Pershing placed primary reliance in open warfare on the infantry soldier, believing that the rifle and bayonet would be the dominant weapons in a war of movement. The Allies, he perceived, had "all but given up the use of the rifle," the average Allied soldier relying on machine guns, hand and rifle grenades, and trench mortars as his principal weapons. Pershing worried that American soldiers, through association with Allied troops, would develop this same tendency and hence would be doomed to the trenches, and he constantly exhorted his officers to guard against allowing their troops to adopt Allied habits. AEF leaders must instill in their troops a high degree of confidence in the rifle and the bayonet.[5]

Reliance upon the infantry rifleman in open warfare continued unchanged as the principle of American combat doctrine advocated by Pershing throughout the war. Pershing insisted that his units achieve the skills to fight according to this principle. Pershing quarreled with any proposed doctrinal changes if they contradicted his strong belief that the American infantryman, trained in the proper application of rifle firepower, would be the ultimate tool of victory.

The detailed doctrinal principles to which Pershing consistently referred in his divisional training programs were those contained in the Army's IDR. The edition of these regulations in use at the time of America's entry into World War I was that of 1911, as amended to 1917.[6] According to the IDR, the key to success in battle lay in achieving fire superiority when attacking an enemy deployed either in prepared positions or in the open: "Attacking troops must first gain fire superiority in order to reach the hostile position. Over open ground attack is possible only when the attacking force has a decided fire superiority."[7]

Achieving fire superiority would enable the attacking force to come close enough to the enemy position to execute the charge. Artillery fire would be used to "aid . . . the infantry in gaining fire superiority,"[8] but "in the advance by rushes, sufficient rifles must be kept constantly in action to keep down the enemy's fire." After the enemy's position had been penetrated and he had been routed, formed bodies of troops following the assaulting force were to engage in a "vigorous" pursuit in order to "reap the full fruits of victory."[9] This section of the IDR also contained the caveat that "few modifications enter into the problem of attacking fortifications . . . If the distance is short and other conditions [unspecified] are favorable, the charge may be made without fire preparation." This caveat appeared in the 1911 and the amended 1917 editions of the IDR.[10]

The 1911 edition of the IDR does not evince much appreciation of the lethality of the machine gun. This is not surprising, since the American Army had not suffered the impact of these weapons in large-scale combat. The regulations state that "machine guns must be considered as weapons of emergency . . . of great value at critical, though infrequent, periods of an engagement." Attacking units possessing machine guns were advised not to employ them "until the attack is well advanced. Machine guns should not be assigned to the firing line of an attack." When attacking a hostile force armed with machine guns, and when the attacker did not possess artillery support, "infantry itself must silence them before it can advance. An infantry command that must depend upon itself for protection against machine guns should concentrate a large number of rifles on each gun in turn and until it has silenced it."[11]

While it may be understandable to find these precepts in a 1911 manual of American tactical doctrine, it is most surprising to note identical statements in the revised 1917 edition of the IDR, after the killing effect of the machine gun had been demonstrated during three years of battle on the Western Front.[12] It would be too simple an assumption to ascribe this to a lack of appreciation by American military leaders of the lethality of machine gun fire. Likewise, it would be naive to assume that American military leaders were unaware of the degree of sophistication that warfare had attained by 1917. What then explains the indicated lack of study in the IDR of methods other than reliance on traditional American ''musketry'' to carry the offensive against an entrenched foe armed with automatic weapons? Why did Pershing insist on an essentially ''conservative approach to war'' when modern weapons had made the traditional American methods of open warfare anachronistic?[13]

The American military experience was not lacking in examples of the difficulties encountered when offensive forces attempt to dislodge enemy troops ensconced behind fortifications. The American Civil War was replete with incidents in which entrenched defenders armed with rifles demonstrated their primacy over attacking troops. While some of these lessons may have passed out of the Army's consciousness during its postwar frontier experience, American military leaders had continued to study the evolution of warfare through observation of foreign conflicts. Lieutenant Francis V. Greene observed the events of the 1877-78 Russo-Turkish War and recorded his perceptions in a letter to General William Tecumseh Sherman in March 1878. Impressed by the strength and staying power of the defense as displayed during that war, Greene offered the judgment that ''99 out of 100 division generals will fail to carry trenches by assault.'' Captain Carl Reichman, observing the 1904-05 Russo-Japanese War, described in the July 1906 edition of *The Infantry Journal* the battle of Liaoyang, during which four and a half Japanese divisions supported by 240 guns assaulted an entrenched Russian corps of 15,000 men and 80 guns: ''The I Siberian Corps repulsed all attacks. This will convey some idea of the strength of the defensive.''[14]

Pershing's contacts with machine guns had been considerable before 1917, and his tactical theories regarding the weapons trace their roots to these experiences. Like Reichman, an observer of the Russo-Japanese War, Pershing viewed the Japanese use of entrenchments supported by machine guns. He reported that ''[machine] guns are inconvenient of transportation, but . . . increase the morale of the troops. In a defensive position [the machine gun] can be used without disadvantage.'' Pershing understood that the Japanese classed machine guns with artillery as indirect fire support weapons. He noted with some trepidation the reluctance of infantry to advance in the face of machine gun fire, but Pershing was at the same time buoyed by the sight of spirited Japanese infantrymen nevertheless succeeding in battle. The precautionary advice of a French military attaché who observed that too much reliance on machine guns sapped aggressiveness was absorbed by Pershing.[15]

Observing Japanese Army maneuvers in 1907, Pershing witnessed the tactical refinements the Japanese had made in the use of machine guns to furnish direct fire support to advancing troops. He mused that these innovations were changing the nature of combat, and he criticized Japanese infantry for attacking machine guns in too close order.[16]

Pershing had conducted several training exercises that included the participation of machine gun elements, and thereby gained practical experience in their capabilities and limitations. These exercises included mock combats at Fort McKinley in the Philippines in 1907 and invasion maneuvers near Manila in 1910. As commander of the 8th Brigade at El Paso, Texas, in 1914, he directed a tactical problem in the attack and defense of that city with forces on both sides armed with supporting machine guns.[17]

During the Mexican Punitive Expedition in 1916, Pershing commanded troops in operations where machine guns were used on both sides. In one incident Pershing dispatched a force of six cavalry troops and one machine gun platoon to attack the Villistas at Ojos Azules. Upon meeting the enemy, the cavalry troops formed and executed the classic mounted charge, while "somewhere back in the dust trailed the Machine Gun Platoon." Another time, two of Pershing's cavalry troops executed a dismounted attack against an enemy force armed with a machine gun. Stung by the enemy's firepower, several officers were killed and the American troops broke off the action. But Pershing happily observed that even in defeat his troopers had killed 30 and wounded 40 Mexicans with accurate rifle fire.[18]

The AEF commander's faith in the efficacy of the infantryman against modern weaponry, in view of his certain understanding of the capabilities of machine guns, suggests a man-at-arms who was the captive of tradition. Pershing's attitude during World War I regarding the machine gun and methods to defeat it is evidence that he was having difficulty reconciling the realities of modern warfare with his military heritage. His professional psyche was bound to a faith in American marksmen, be they the masses of riflemen employed by Grant in his bloody battles of attrition or the more individualistic marksmen of Pershing's own experiences. This heritage contained Pershing's interpretation of American combat doctrine.

A recent assessment of the AEF experience argues that Pershing "overlooked" the facts of long-range artillery and machine gun fire when he pronounced that victory was to be secured by engaging the Germans in a war of movement on open terrain.[19] "Overlooked" is perhaps too imprecise a term to apply to Pershing's theorizing; ambivalence is a better descriptive, in the sense that Pershing's belief in the myth that American infantrymen could routinely overcome machine guns and the *reality* of combat on the Western Front presented the AEF with the existence of mutually conflicting theoretical guidance. Unfortunately, such ambivalence extended to other aspects of Pershing's doctrine.

But evidence suggests that others within the American Army were more cognizant than Pershing of the effects of modern weaponry and appreciated that the nature of warfare on the Western Front was alien to the American

Army's experiences in post-Civil War fluid open combat. The forces of American military tradition still had an effect on many besides Pershing, but through an examination of the evidence one gains the sense that American tactical thought was maturing and attempting to reconcile the dichotomous influences of tradition and change.

Pershing's staff met on 11 July 1917 with a War Department board of officers sent to France to determine the most appropriate tactical organization and equipment for the American combat divison. In one finding the "Baker Board," so called after its senior member, Colonel Chauncey B. Baker, determined that one of the division's artillery regiments should be equipped with 3.8-inch or 4.7-inch howitzers. Pershing's staff argued against this conclusion, stating their preference for 6-inch (155 mm) guns. The rationale of Pershing's Operations Section was twofold. First, 155 mm guns were readily available from French resources; hence, American units could be armed at a rapid pace. Second, the heavier 155 mm guns, while less mobile, would provide greater firepower. Firepower was the choice of these AEF officers over mobility for warfare on the Western Front because of "the belief that the present war would not assume the form of a war of any considerable movement."[20]

AEF staff officer Lieutenant Colonel John H. Parker submitted a report to Pershing on 7 August 1917 concerning Parker's visit to a French automatic weapons training center. Parker, who in previous reports had trumpeted himself as the AEF's premier machine gun theoretician, candidly observed:

We are both convinced we have been shown . . . the day of the rifleman is done. He was a good horse while he lasted, but his day is over . . . The rifleman is passing out and the bayonet is fast becoming as obsolete as the crossbow.[21]

While Parker's remark did not endear him to his commander-in-chief, it is suggestive of the difficulties that Pershing's staff was having in reconciling the tactical doctrine espoused by their chief with the grim reality of the Western Front.

Parker's report is also indicative of the influence of the French and British experience. Because of the scarcity of American instructors and training literature in the early stages of the American involvement, Pershing was forced to borrow trainers and training documents from his Allies. Numerous French and British publications on tactical doctrine were issued to American units. The doctrine and "lessons learned" contained in these Allied documents were not in harmony with the tactical precepts of open warfare that Pershing espoused, but by virtue of the deluge of distribution of these publications, the AEF on a wide scale was exposed to the French and British view of warfare.

On 9 August 1917, Pershing's GHQ forwarded to the commander of the American 1st Infantry Division 175 copies of a translation of the 1915 French publication "Tactical Employment of Machine Guns," "for issue to Officers of your command." This document stated that "the increase in the number of machine gun units tends to make this weapon the principal fire-arm of the infantryman."[22]

War Department Document 583, "Instructions on the Offensive Conduct of Small Units," was a French pamphlet distributed by the War Department in May 1917, and by AEF GHQ in August 1917. It contained the standard French pessimism: "Infantry of itself has no offensive power against obstacles defended by fire . . . [and] reinforcement of riflemen . . . will simply increase the losses." The War Department added a "Translation Notice" that reviewed the changes in warfare since 1914. Noted were the presence of extensive entrenchments, the power of the machine gun, and the inability of infantry forces to capture or break through modern entrenchments unless supported by massive artillery fire.[23]

By late summer 1917, War Department tactical literature reflected that a recognition of the changed nature of warfare had seeped deeply into American doctrinal thought. The War College Division of the General Staff had responded to a July 1917 Pershing recommendation regarding combat training by issuing War Department Document No. 656, "Infantry Training," the introductory paragraphs of which indicated the type of warfare for which the War Department believed American divsons should be trained:

In all of the military training of a division, under existing conditions, training for trench warfare is of paramount importance. Without neglect of the fundamentals of individual recruit instruction, every effort should be devoted to making all units from the squad and platoon upwards proficient in this kind of training. It is believed that in an intensive course of 16 weeks troops can be brought to a reasonable degree of efficiency through the squad, platoon, and company, making it possible with a minimum of training in France for them to take their places on the line. The responsibility for the instruction in trench warfare of field officers, staff officers, and higher commanders rests with special force upon the division commander.[24]

This document is not the only indicator of this trend in American tactical thought. Commenting on a British pamphlet on the use of automatic weapons which stated, "however far we push the German back he will always have behind him a series of carefully prepared positions . . . [so that] there is little chance of a return to open warfare," reviewing officers of the War College Division described these instructions as "excellent material" and "best matter I have seen."[25] In France, the AEF in March 1918 distributed yet another translated French document that clearly enunciated the realities of the Western Front. It described the German defensive doctrine of organizing defenses in depth, supported by interlocking fields of machine gun fire emanating from dispersed strong points. But to combat and defeat these "elastic" defenses, the document stated, "demands no essential modification in our offensive tactics." German defenses "can be defeated by infantry, formed in depth . . . advancing close behind the barrage." Pershing's headquarters issued these instructions "for the information and guidance of" the AEF, thereby establishing as doctrine combat procedures that were in confusing conflict with Pershing's own precepts regarding open warfare.[26]

There is evidence other than that contained in these theoretic documents that American officers realized by mid-1918 that reliance on infantrymen and traditional American musketry in open warfare would not be the most appropriate method for defeating the German Army. Pershing's staff in early 1918 conducted, at his direction, a study of the "square division" to determine if it was the type of unit best suited for the nature of warfare in which the AEF was engaged. Lieutenant Colonel Hugh Drum directed the study.

Drum's conclusions are contained in a lengthy memorandum submitted on 18 May 1918 to Colonel Fox Conner, his superior and the chief of the AEF Operations Section. Drum compared a division organized around three light regiments to the square division's two brigade/four regiment system. He allowed that the former organization offered advantages in mobility and flexibility to the commander interested in envelopment and maneuver. But Drum concluded that these tactics were not in harmony with the situation on the Western Front, where German defenses consisted of strong points arrayed in great depth, frontage, and density. To combat these defenses, Drum argued that mass concentrations rather than flexible formations were required: "In some cases the enemy's deployment may be so dense that the old time shoulder to shoulder function will be required." The square division should be retained, he noted, since "In a war of masses and protracted flanks, the offensive produces success by surprise blows, whose power is insured by great depth." The square division was the ideal formation to provide the capacity for attack in depth; its organization should not be changed "until the experience of combat shows conclusively that our basic principles are wrong." Many of the American commanders surveyed by Drum in his study supported his perception. For example, the commander of the 2d Infantry Division stated, "Since on the western front open warfare will occur only in periods, followed by long periods of trench warfare, the ideal organization is that best suited for offensive trench warfare."[27]

AEF tactics would still be based upon reliance on the infantryman, but a grudging appreciation of the evolution of warfare, it seemed, was forcing some American military leaders to conclude that those infantrymen would have to be employed not as individual marksmen in fluid open warfare, but rather in a war of mass and attrition all too reminiscent of Grant's bloody campaign from the Wilderness to Petersburg. The Army since the Civil War had remained bound to the principle of the destruction of the enemy army as the objective of warfare.[28] Drum wrote in late October 1918, "The gaining of ground counts for little, it is the ruining of his army that will end the struggle."[29] To destroy an enemy armed with weapons of 20th-century technology required neither reliance on 18th-century tactics of maneuver nor the attainment of the Napoleonic climactic battle; rather, victory demanded grasping hold of the enemy army in combat and consuming it through bloody and relentless attrition. The Catholic chaplain of the 42d Infantry Division, Father Francis P. Duffy, alluded to this reliance on Grantian tactics. Commenting on the tactical style displayed by Major General Charles Summerall, Duffy wrote, "He wanted results, no matter how many men were killed."[30]

One could argue that Pershing himself knew that the AEF would have to resort to a war of attrition. The 28,000-man square division that Pershing adopted was a behemoth more suited for sustained slugging than for a war of movement in the open. Historians are in general agreement that Pershing opted for a much larger division than the British and French employed because its increased volume of sustained rifle firepower would give the American division the capacity to carry entrenched enemy positions, a task at which the lighter Allied divisions had failed. It must be noted that Pershing had been given the option by Army Chief of Staff Tasker H. Bliss of designing the table of organization of the American division. When the Baker Board recommended that the AEF adopt a square division of two brigades with two regiments each, numbering 25,500 men, Pershing concurred. The rationale of the board was that the AEF would require a division large enough to absorb losses and still remain in action, anticipating attritional combat.[32]

One other bit of evidence suggests that Pershing was more resigned to the need to prepare the AEF for position warfare than his rhetoric on open warfare implies. Chief of Staff Bliss in September 1917 had directed that in the rifle training of individual soldiers, "special emphasis should be placed on rapid fire."[33] If one accepts that in increasing the rate of fire of a bolt action rifle there will be some decrease in accuracy, then we can understand Pershing's rationale in bombarding the War Department with statements that the soldiers he was receiving were woefully deficient in marksmanship. Now, this fact does not lead one to conclude that Pershing favored either open or position warfare, as skill with the rifle would be valuable in both. However, the fact that Pershing emphasized the need for individual marksmanship training at known distances rather than for Bliss's rapid-fire training, which taught a soldier how to shoot on the move and at moving targets, suggests that Pershing appreciated the tactical situation in which American marksmanship most likely would be employed. A War Department officer who supported Pershing's viewpoint argued:

The situation on the western front . . . is totally different from that we were taught to expect and for which we trained prior to the war. On this front the distance to practically every point on the enemy's line is as well known as the marked distance on the target range and it has become a question of hitting whatever appears at any of these known distances.[34]

But despite his awareness of the nature of modern warfare, despite his apparent realization that he would have no other choice but to plunge his divisions into a bloody war of attrition, John Pershing's rhetoric remained a captive of his own military experiences of fighting Indians on the open plains and of pursuing Moros in the Philippines and Villistas in the arid Mexican interior. He never was able to reconcile these theoretical conflicts, and this explains the paradox of his insistence on open warfare at a time when the enemy and technology had changed the rules. Two documents issued by Pershing's staff during the summer and fall of 1918 indicate that Pershing at that stage of the war clung to a wistful longing for the open warfare of his own experiences, and to reliance upon infantry marksmen for the successful prosecution of that type of combat.

In a July 1918 document, Pershing illustrated the differences in artillery support that troops could expect to encounter in trench and open warfare:

> In trench warfare [artillery fire is characterized by] a timed creeping barrage which the infantry may follow at a distance of about 100 yards; in open warfare such close co-operation between the infantry and artillery cannot be expected.[35]

Did Pershing merely accept this condition as a consequence of a war of movement, or did he want his infantry in open warfare to rely primarily upon their own weapons and not to look to the artillery as a crutch? The evidence in Pershing's doctrinal pronouncements supports the latter.

On 7 August 1918, Pershing sent the following memorandum to his chief of staff, Major General James McAndrew:

> Please have the Operations Section make a tactical study of the question of attack. It seems to me that perhaps we are losing too many men by enemy machine guns. I think this might be met by tanks or possibly by artillery. I wish a very careful study made of it.[36]

The resultant product was endorsed wholeheartedly by Pershing, and it represents the most relevant doctrinal publication issued during the war that reflects his tactical philosophy. For despite his mention of tanks and artillery as possible solutions, the result of the study reemphasizes what Pershing had been saying all along.

Published on 5 September 1918, "Combat Instructions" reiterated Pershing's interpretation of open warfare and the methods that his combat units were to employ in conducting it. Its opening statement is reflective not only of the ineffectiveness of the training conducted by the American divisions, but also of the lack of clarity of the doctrinal and training guidance issued to the AEF:

> The principles [of open warfare doctrine previously] enunciated . . . are not yet receiving due application. Attack formations of platoons, companies, and battalions are everywhere too dense and follow too rigidly the illustrations contained in the Offensive Combat of Small Units [a translation of a French training document published in January 1918]. Waves are too close together; individuals therein have too little interval. Lines are frequently seen with men almost elbow to elbow, and seldom with intervals greater than two or three paces. Columns, when used, are too long; in first line companies they should rarely have a greater depth than ten files. All formations are habitually lacking in elasticity; there is almost never any attempt to maneuver, that is, throw supports and reserves to the flanks for envelopment. Scouts, if used, are frequently only a few yards in front of the leading waves, where the only purpose they can serve is to blanket or to receive the fire of the men behind them. Subordinate officers display little appreciation of the

assumed situation and how best to meet its requirements. It is necessary, therefore, to repeat once more a few fundamental principles which must be impressed upon all concerned.[37]

Perhaps General Pershing either was not explaining his combat philosophy clearly enough to allow it to be translated into an effective training program, or no one was listening to him. It is more probable, though, that American officers and soldiers were confused by the paradoxes between Pershing's insistence in training for a style of warfare that was at odds with the conditions of the Western Front and his and the War Department's construction of an army that was ill suited to conducting a war of movement.

"Combat Instructions" contrasted trench and open warfare in terms of the manner of deployment of tactical units. Trench warfare was characterized by rigidly uniform formation, "regulation of space and time by higher command down to the smallest units," and "little initiative [by] the individual soldier." Open warfare was indicated by precisely the opposite factors, with irregular formations, scouts preceding the assaulting waves, and a high degree of "individual initiative," with primary reliance placed upon "the greatest possible use of the infantry's own fire power to enable it to get forward."[38]

The pamphlet prescribes the execution of a battalion attack under the conditions of open warfare once "the enemy's first line trenches have been entered," and recognizes the German machine gun as the primary threat to American infantry. The battalion commander is advised to use the supporting weapons at his disposal, the one-pounder gun, the light mortars, and the division trench mortars. The role of supporting artillery is discussed, and the battalion commander is reminded of the "powerful" assist artillery provides to enable the infantry "to handle local situations." However, the deleterious effect of using artillery in direct support of assaulting troops is also noted:

> The assignment of artillery to infantry units binds such artillery closely to the infantry it is supporting and gives the infantry commander a powerful combination of arms with which to handle local situations without loss of time. On the other hand, it tends to lessen the power of artillery concentration of the division as a whole, and may render the infantry unit clumsy and immobile. Moreover it demands a high degree of decision and initiative on the part of both the infantry and artillery commanders immediately involved.[39]

Machine guns in support of assaulting infantry are assigned a somewhat greater role than specified in the IDR. The machine gun was still seen as a "weapon of emergency" by Pershing, since in the initiation of an attack, "the machine gun platoons will at first usually follow in the rear of the first line companies." "Combat Instructions" states that machine guns should "concentrate [their] fire . . . on those hostile nests or strong points which are making the most trouble."[40]

"Combat Instructions" leaves no doubt, however, that Pershing still considered the infantry rifleman the sine qua non in combat, even against a semi-entrenched foe armed with machine guns. True, the battalion commander is advised to use supporting weapons, but he is reminded that when he calls upon his most effective supporting arm, the artillery, to "handle local situations," he is lessening "the power of artillery concentration of the division as a whole." True, the machine gun is commended as a valuable supporting weapon, but only to be used when the attacker meets the "most trouble." But a platoon of infantry is accorded the capability of being able "by itself . . . to capture one, or even a pair, of hostile machine guns. The capture of a nest of machine guns will probably be beyond the capacity of a platoon, and will require the company to send its support platoons to the flanks to envelop or encircle."[41]

One should not dismiss lightly the impact that these caveats made on infantry commanders. The message from Pershing is that these officers are expected to achieve success primarily by force of their own combat arm, the infantry.

Pershing so strongly believed in the validity of the combat doctrine promulgated by him that he directed his staff to prepare a revision of the War Department IDR. Although this revision did not appear until after the Armistice, its preparation was underway during the later months of the war, and it is reflective of the lack of evolution in Pershing's tactical thinking. A brief review of its salient points provides a valuable insight into Pershing's perception of the nature of combat by the end of the war.

Despite the lessons wrought by the new weapons, one finds that Pershing's professed faith in the rifle had not changed. The machine gun was still touted primarily as a defensive weapon. Its value to assaulting troops was diminished by its lack of mobility vis-à-vis the rifle or the automatic rifle.[42] The tank, perhaps the most revolutionary of the new weapons, was recognized as an important auxiliary weapon, but its value was seen as limited to the opening stages of an assault conducted during position warfare. Tanks provided an effective weapon to penetrate the enemy's initial defenses, but this advantage would be of negligible value if the tank assault was not followed up by supporting infantry. "Infantry must take immediate advantage of an opportunity to exploit a success obtained by a tank. Tanks are unable to exploit their own superiority of fire or hold a position."[43]

No, Pershing held, it was the rifle that won the war, and he steadfastly clung to this belief:

In spite of the addition of numerous auxiliary weapons to infantry units, the rifle is by far the most formidable weapon of the infantry soldier. Effective rifle fire is essential to victory and is the element which most frequently determines the issue of the battle.[44]

Throughout the literature on tactical doctrine issued by General Pershing, the consistent overriding theme is a belief in the value of open warfare over trench warfare. The latter had led only to stalemate on the Western Front. Only when the Germans were chased out into the "open," Pershing argued, could they be beaten. Only this mode of battle, he said, would end the senseless war of attrition that had cost millions of casualties.

But in studying Pershing's pronouncements on open warfare, something appears to be missing. Pershing professed disdain for position warfare and preference for open warfare on numerous occasions. He understood fully the modalities of static combat, of the attack from, and the defense of, prepared entrenchments. His staff and subordinate commanders, at Pershing's insistence, focused considerable innovative thought on means to prosecute successfully a war of position as a necessary preliminary to a war of movement. For instance, on 5 September 1918, all AEF corps commanders were ordered to send one officer from each of their divisions to observe new techniques developed by the 3d Infantry Division's 6th Engineers for passing infantry through wire entanglements. The 6th Engineers had perfected a "rug" of wire matting that could be rolled over poles laid across the wire. Troops would scurry over the "rug" and move rapidly into the enemy's entrenchments.[45]

But Pershing's tactical thought never was able to reach and pronounce a definition of those elements that constituted "open" warfare, the clash of infantry units in the open, within the context of the realities of the Western Front. AEF tactical literature is detailed in describing how to attack an entrenched enemy position, and how to continue the assault against secondary and tertiary trenches or strongpoints. But unit-to-unit combat in the open, the "pure" form of open warfare, is not defined. Yet this was the mode of warfare for which Pershing demanded that his units prepare!

This conclusion is nowhere more evident than in the new IDR. One section of this document contains detailed guidance on the conduct of position warfare. Pershing then stressed his belief in the preliminary nature of position warfare by stating, "An engagement of this kind is not the end but merely the means to an end. It has for its purpose the forcing of the enemy into the open where his masses may be decisively attacked and destroyed."[46] One then expects to find similar detailed instructions on the conduct of this next phase of battle, the open maneuver phase. But the remainder of the new IDR continues to describe the conduct of the attack against enemy strongpoints or entrenched positions. Units from platoon to brigade are provided explicit instructions on how to attack an enemy deployed in these configurations. Nowhere is there found similar guidance on the conduct of units engaged in the pursuit of an enemy in the open, "where his masses may be decisively attacked and destroyed."[47]

What, then, may we conclude from this evidence of ambivalent American tactical doctrine? One judgment might be that Black Jack Pershing really never expected that his units would engage in open warfare. Perhaps he knew that an attritional war of position was the only way to defeat the Germans, but feared to state this conclusion openly because he did not want his divisions to adopt the nonaggressive mentality that he believed was the product of trench warfare. Perhaps Pershing had concluded that "no real alternative remained to a strategy which aimed at destroying the German armies by grinding them into ruin."[48] He unwittingly admitted as much when he stated that the American objective during the Meuse-Argonne offensive was "to draw the best German divisions to our front and to consume them."[49]

We may also conclude that it was unfortunate that Pershing could not bring himself to admit this recognition of reality during the conflict. His failure to do so caused considerable consternation among the American infantrymen training to fight the battles. How could these officers prepare their units to team with their supporting arms to combat entrenched Germans when the mass of rhetoric and doctrinal literature thundered Pershing's faith in infantrymen and musketry in a fluid war of movement? The price for deviation from these dicta during training, commanders knew, was swift and certain relief by "the Chief." But the price for adherence was higher in combat, because commanders were confused by Pershing's insistence on a tactical doctrine that was totally at odds with reality. How were they to fight Germans in the open when the Germans were not about to accommodate these tactics and had to be pried out of their entrenchments only to fall back again and again into more entrenchments, as was the German tactic in the Meuse-Argonne? How were American commanders going to execute Pershing's war of movement on the terrain where he hoped to employ his divisions, the plain of the Woëvre, when this terrain was known to consist of such impedimenta to rapid movement as impervious clay soil, dotted with numerous stagnant pools, criss-crossed by small streams, and open to panoramic observation from German-dominated hills?[50] An advance across such terrain, especially in poor weather, would have been the AEF's Passchendaele. "Open warfare" is an irrelevancy when advancements in weapon technology have rendered the survival of attackers in the open a short-term prospect.

The conflict between the way Pershing ordered American units to prepare to fight and the way their instincts told them to fight is indicated in Major General Summerall's admonishment to his 1st Infantry Division after the combat at Soissons in August 1918. Summerall stated that the density of the American formations at Soissons had caused casualties. They had been trained to advance with intervals of up to ten paces between men, he reminded his troops, but commanders had rushed support troops forward prematurely to thicken front lines, a maneuver that only served to deplete reserves and offer more concise targets for German machine guns.[51] But American infantry officers knew that their arm could succeed and at the same time satisfy Black Jack Pershing only if they smothered German machine guns with American flesh.[52]

Historian Allan Millett has captured succinctly the essence of the problem caused by Pershing's insistence on training to perfect a doctrine – open warfare – that was alien to the nature of this war, imprecisely stated, and ill-suited for execution by the type of tactical units that Pershing had adopted:

> Many infantry officers, especially those who took [Pershing's] doctrine literally, did not open their tactical formations and skillfully use their supporting arms. Except for the preplanned, set-timed barrages by both artillery and machine guns, the infantry did not get the support it might have had, and it paid in casualties.[53]

Finally, we may conclude that ambivalent doctrine does not provide a firm foundation on which to train an army. Major General Hunter Liggett was perplexed as he pondered how to satisfy Pershing's orders to train the divisions of his I Corps for open warfare. Liggett, considered the best professional intellect in the AEF, groped for a solution to the very fundamental problem created by the ambivalence in American tactical doctrine. He wrote to Colonel Fox Conner on 9 April 1918:

I am enclosing a copy of a memo which I have drawn up, and which it is believed will enable Division Commanders of the 1st Corps to train upon some practical line for open warfare, offensive and defensive. I can find nothing in the mass of literature I have received which teaches this, to me essential question.

Liggett's memo was forwarded to Conner by a staff officer of I Corps who added to it a marginal note that read:

The General has been trying to figure a scheme whereby each C.O. (Regt., Brig. Div.) would have a *reserve* etc. Perhaps as a "seedling" this may grow into something.[54]

Armies that possess a settled doctrine for combat that is in harmony with the nature of the war in which they are engaged do not need to plant "seedlings" in the midst of that war. For the AEF, by April 1918 it was a little late for that.

NOTES

1. Cable 228-S, 19 October 1917, Pershing to AG, War Department, quoted in US Army, Historical Division, *United States Army in the World War, 1917-1919* [hereinafter *USA/WW*], 17 vols. (Washington: Department of the Army, 1948), XIV, 316.
2. John J. Pershing, *My Experiences in the World War,* 2 vols. (New York: Stokes, 1931), I, 151-52. Frank E. Vandiver, *Black Jack: The Life and Times of John J. Pershing,* 2 vols. (College Station: Texas A&M Univ. Press, 1977), II, 772.
3. Program of Training for the 1st Infantry Division, October 1917, quoted in *USA/WW*, XIV, 304.
4. Pershing, *Experiences*, I, 152.
5. Ibid., I, 153-54.
6. War Department, Document No. 394, *Infantry Drill Regulations, United States Army, 1911* (Washington: GPO, 19 August 1911). Eighteen changes were issued between 1911 and 1917. None of the changes pertained to the data cited in this paper. For a review of the revised document, see: US Infantry Association, *Infantry Drill Regulations, United States Army 1911, with Changes 1-18* (Philadelphia: J. B. Lippincott, 1917).
7. *IDR, 1911,* p. 100.
8. Ibid., p. 104.
9. Ibid., pp. 111-12.
10. Ibid., p. 114; *IDR, Changes 1-18*, p. 118.
11. *IDR, 1911*, pp. 123-24.
12. *IDR, Changes 1-18*, pp. 127-28.
13. Russell F. Weigley, *History of the United States Army* (New York: Macmillan, 1967), p. 391.
14. Greene's letter and Reichman's article are quoted in Russell F. Weigley, *The American Way of War: A History of United States Military Strategy and Policy* (New York: Macmillan, 1973), pp. 198-99.
15. Vandiver, I, 370-71.
16. Ibid., I, 434.
17. Ibid., I, 422-23, 486-87, 591.

18. Ibid., II, 642, 652-53, 655.
19. David M. Kennedy, *Over Here: The First World War and American Society* (New York: Oxford Univ. Press, 1980), p. 174.
20. Report of Conference between the Baker Board and the AEF Staff, 11 July 1917, quoted in *USA/WW*, I, 107, 110.
21. Parker's report contains a marginal handwritten comment by Lieutenant Colonel Paul B. Malone, Chief of the AEF Training Section, that reads: "Speak for yourself, John." National Archives, Record Group 120, Entry 268, File 13.12.
22. National Archives, Records Group 120, Entry 268, File 13.1.
23. War Department, *Instructions on the Offensive Conduct of Small Units* (Washington: GPO, 1917), pp. 5-6, 9.
24. War College Division, General Staff, US Army, War Department Document No. 656, *Infantry Training* (Washington: GPO, 27 August 1917), p. 5.
25. National Archives, Records Group 65, File 9383-204.
26. AEF, Document No. 160, *Instructions for the Offensive Combat of Small Units* (Chaumont, France: GHQ, AEF, March 1918) pp. 4-5.
27. Memo, Drum to ACofS, G3, 18 May 1918, with comments from American division commanders, quoted in *USA/WW*, II, 406-12.
28. Weigley, *American Way of War*, p. 511, n. 13.
29. Quoted in Edward M. Coffman, *The War to End All Wars: The American Military Experience in World War I* (New York: Oxford Univ. Press, 1968) p. 338.
30. Quoted in D. Clayton James, *The Years of MacArthur, 1880-1941* (Boston: Houghton Mifflin, 1970), pp. 219-22.
31. Weigley, *History of the United States Army*, p. 386; Kennedy, p. 173; Josiah N. Miller, "Development of Departmental Direction of Training and Training Policy in the United States Army Revolutionary War to 1920" (Draft manuscript, Department of the Army, Office of the Chief of Military History, n.d.), pp. 1-23.
32. John B. Wilson, "Army Lineage Series: Division and Separate Brigades" (draft manuscript, US Army Center of Military History, n.d.), pp. 3:6, 3:9, 3:12. Pershing may also have opted for a large division composed of a small number of subordinate units because such a structure would have required fewer trained officers, who were in relatively short supply.
33. Memo, Chief of Staff to AG, 17 September 1917, Subject: Small Arms Target Practice, National Archives, Records Group 165, File 7906-15.
34. Memo, LTC Morton C. Mumma to LTC Bowman, 26 November 1917, Subject: Establishing a School of Musketry at Jacksonville, Florida, National Archives, Records Group 165, File 6657-105.
35. AEF Document No. 1312, *Instructions for the Defensive Combat of Small Units, Infantry, Platoon to Regiment* (Chaumont, France: GHQ, AEF, July 1918) p. 8.
36. National Archives, Records Group 120, Box 101, Entries 16,17, 18 (Chief of Staff, GHQ, Memoranda, Cablegrams, Telegrams, 1917-19).
37. AEF Document No. 1348, *Combat Instructions* (Chaumont, France: GHQ, AEF, 5 September 1918), p. 3.
38. Ibid.
39. Ibid., p. 7.
40. Ibid., p. 3.
41. Ibid., pp. 4-5, 7.
42. AEF, *Infantry Drill Regulations (Provisional), Army Expeditionary Forces, Part 1, 1918* (Chaumont, France: GHQ, AEF, 12 December 1918), p. 80.
43. Ibid., p. 142.
44. Ibid., p. 78.
45. *USA/WW*, III, 350-51.
46. AEF, *IDR, Part I, 1918*, pp. 97-100.
47. Ibid., pp. 100-37.
48. Weigley, *American Way of War*, p. 202.
49. Leonard Ayers, *The War With Germany: A Statistical Summary* (Washington: GPO, 1919), p. 111.
50. James, p. 200.
51. National Archives, Records Group 120, Entry 1241, File 201-56.

52. Kennedy, p. 204.
53. Allan Millett, *The General: Robert L. Bullard and Officership in the United States Army, 1881-1925* (Westport, Conn.: Greenwood Press, 1975), p. 315.
54. National Archives, Records Group 120, Entry 268, File 13.

This article appeared in the September 1983 issue of *Parameters*.

18

Patton and the Concept of Mechanized Warfare

by WILLIAM J. WOOLLEY

Coming to terms with the industrial revolution caused a crisis of some sort in nearly every modern army. For most, the crisis was introduced by the machine gun, which mechanized the production of firepower. The resultant increase in the power of the defense overturned most of the Napoleonic tactical principles that had been so laboriously worked out during the previous century. But the mechanization of movement made possible by the gradual military adaptation of the principles of automotive transport threatened to revolutionize all aspects of warfare. As a result, during the decades separating the two world wars, the major source of military controversy in nearly every modern army was the issue of introducing the internal combustion engine into warfare on the ground and in the air.

On the ground the debate centered on the tank. At issue was not whether tanks should be used in warfare – all doubt on that question had vanished during the war – but how they were to be used. In nearly all major armies this controversy was ignited by the claims of a radical minority that warfare should be revolutionized by supplanting the traditional combat arms with totally new mechanized forces designed to fight the innovative mobile and strategic forms of warfare described in the works of J. F. C. Fuller and Basil Liddell Hart. These claims, in turn, aroused the opposition of a larger group which generally would allow mechanized weapons no more than a supportive and tactical role within the traditional combat arms, which were expected to fight war in a conventional manner.[1]

In the United States Army the traditionalist outlook remained particularly dominant throughout the interwar period. This dominance was not due to a repressive conservatism imposed from above: The American Army was too fragmented in its structure to allow this, and its command leadership depended more on consensus than on coercion in exercising control. The problem lay, rather, in the institutional and intellectual obstacles that stood in the way of effecting change within the Army. Given the continued disaggregated structure of the Army, significant change could not be made without the mobilization of some degree of consensus among the officer corps. While the Army had the communications networks necessary for such a mobilization (professional journals and schools reinforced by widespread webs of private correspondence), it was also necessary that officers be receptive to change and adaptive in their thinking. While most American officers in this period saw themselves as professional and progressive students of warfare, there were still many aspects of their mental outlook that made accommodation to rapid or far-reaching change difficult. A study of the changing attitudes of one officer in this period, George S. Patton, Jr., toward the issue of mechanized warfare illuminates some of the problems faced by many of the others in making the adaptations it demanded.

Actually, Patton might appear to have been a unique case in this regard. He had more exposure to tanks than almost any other American officer of his time. During the First World War he organized the American Tank School in France and then led the first American tank units in battle. In the interwar period he continued to read extensively about mechanized warfare and wrote and spoke on the subject often.[2] In 1940 he was among the first officers chosen to command a major mechanized unit in the two armored divisions finally being formed. Yet, despite the fact that he had an exposure to tanks that was longer and more extensive than that of almost any of his peers, his attitudes toward mechanization were basically traditionalist. During the 1920s and early 1930s he was one of the most outspoken defenders of the traditionalist military outlook and one of the most caustic and popular critics of the concept of mechanization. And while, by 1940, he had come to accept many of the ideas of the mechanizationists, this adaptation was a slow one which involved a complex interplay between traditionalist values and professional appraisals of the changing nature of warfare. Thus, in coming to terms with mechanization Patton was different from most of his fellow officers only in that he was somewhat more successful in making the mental adaptations necessary and much more vocal in doing so, leaving behind a wealth of articles, lecture notes, letters, and reports to mark the trail of his evolution.

In his intellectual attitudes and outlooks, George S. Patton, Jr., was truly a product of pre-industrial America.[3] He was raised in the ranching country of southern California in a wealthy family which still identified with the values of the Confederate South. His education was heavily classical in both subject and outlook and emphasized the belief that success in life was measured by the development of inner character. Patton's post-secondary education at Virginia Military Institute and West Point served mainly to reinforce this and other values already held. Moreover, by the end of his undergraduate education, Patton had managed to organize his outlooks into an ideological system that possessed a considerable internal coherence, providing him a highly stable base from which to examine any issue. Two aspects of that ideological system were extremely important in shaping his outlook toward mechanization and therefore are worth a brief look.

The first of these was a set of interrelated ideas that arose from Patton's intensive consciousness of history. As was the case with many of his fellow military professionals, Patton loved history. It was by far his best subject in secondary school[4] and at West Point he repeatedly extolled the study of history as the only path to professional success.[5] Yet, outside of flavoring his later writing with historical examples, Patton never made serious use of history in his own professional development. In fact, in the mid-1920s he declared history to be inadequate as a means of learning military leadership.[6] Instead, what history provided Patton was an intellectual underpinning for his existing values and, more important, a means of understanding his world and the changes he perceived going on within it.

Part of his orderly view came from the perspective offered by history and especially by the classical history on which Patton was raised. From this perspective Patton deduced early in life that while the character of man's activities might change over time, man's nature did not. Hence, warfare, as a human activity, was made up of both an inner essence that remained immutable over all time and outward manifestations of that essence that could be expected to change with time. As he wrote in 1927, "Our difficulties differ in manifestation but not in nature from those Alexander experienced or Caesar knew."[7] Patton used this perspective to legitimize change in his world, and especially changes in weapons, since Patton lumped all weapons in the area of manifestations. The tank, born in the trench warfare of the First World War, Patton argued repeatedly, was merely a manifestation of the moving siege towers used by Alexander the Great against Tyre in 333 B.C. Again facing problems similar to those overcome by Alexander, man had merely "reinvented" the tank.[8]

Yet this historical perspective would not legitimize everything. Weapons or doctrines devised to deal with unique situations falling outside the universal character of war were not to be considered legitimate. Nor could weapons developed to deal with one distinct military function be legitimately adopted for another. The tank, as a reintroduced siege weapon, was not automatically a legitimate weapon for cavalry. And, of course, any revolutionary doctrine such as mechanized warfare that denied the existence of a timeless and immutable central essence of warfare was, itself, illegitimate.

On a larger scale, history also provided Patton a simplified cosmology for understanding not only his own particular relationship with society but also developments within that society. The basis of this cosmology lay in his vision of Roman history. In that history he saw as the central event the Punic Wars, in his mind a clash between a young, virile, idealistic, and collectivist Roman society and a soft, materialistic, and selfishly individualistic Carthaginian society. Yet, while Rome triumphed in that struggle, its victory was only temporary, as rising materialism, complacency, and a loss of combativeness led eventually and, perhaps inevitably, to its own decadence and destruction.[9] Throughout his life Patton generalized this model, using it to explain not only the distance in sentiment between American society and its military forces, but also the effects of industrialization and prosperity on American society.[10] The result was that Patton tended to hold himself aloof from a society he saw becoming like Carthage, and especially from its industry and the fruits thereof.

The second important aspect of Patton's ideological system was his vision of war, which was human-focused rather than political. For him war was not an abstract instrument of policy but a periodic manifestation of the human character. As such, its essence was conflict between men. In war, man was central; all the rest – strategy, tactics, organization, and especially weapons – were peripheral. He stated this theme most explicity in 1926, writing,

> It is the cold glitter in the attacker's eye not the point of the questing bayonet that breaks the line. It is the fierce determination of the drive to close with the enemy not the mechanical perfection of the tank that conquers the trench. It is the cataclysmic ecstasy of conflict in the flier not the perfection of his machine gun that drops the enemy in flaming ruin.[11]

Patton repeated this message of the ascendancy of man over weapon in nearly every article or lecture he wrote. This vision of warfare affected Patton's attitude toward mechanization in two ways. First, much of the mechanizationist argument depended upon an appreciation of the capacities of the tank, placing the focus on the weapon rather than on man. Second, seeing conflict as the essential character of war tended to center Patton's interest on tactics much more than on strategy. While he became a bit more strategic in his outlook in the 1930s, Patton always saw war in terms of the climactic Napoleonic battle and therefore had less interest in the mechanizationists' more strategic vision of war.

Finally, it must be made clear that while his perceptions of history and war influenced Patton's interpretation of reality, they never blinded him. Patton had a curiosity and a desire to lead, as well as a kind of impishness, which made him quite receptive to new ideas and new things. He also had sufficient intellectual integrity to insure an honest evaluation of whatever he encountered. Last, and most important, Patton had a highly developed imagination which was vital in dealing with mechanization. While tanks had been used in the First World War, they had acted only in support of traditional military operations. The new concepts of the mechanizationists had never been tried in combat, so they could be evaluated only on the basis of imaginary constructs, an area in which most empirically-minded military professionals felt fairly uncomfortable, but in which Patton moved with great ease.[12] However, while these intellectual assets allowed Patton to be more receptive to the ideas of the mechanizationists, his firm traditionalist founding still proved a formidable obstacle to any serious transformation in his thinking, even over the distance of a long career.

Patton began that career by establishing himself firmly within the traditionalist camp, though he also demonstrated his capacity to see outside of it. Within his first four years of service he had already made a name for himself by participating successfully in the 1912 Olympics[13] and by redesigning the cavalry saber to improve its qualities as an offensive weapon.[14] Patton also had acquired an interest in the automobile. He bought a car at his first duty station and later took one apart and reassembled it. His service on General John J. Pershing's staff in the punitive expedition into Mexico in 1916 led him to see the military value of the automobile,[15] and when he applied for service on Pershing's staff in the American Expeditionary Force in 1917, he listed an understanding of gasoline engines as one of his assets.[16]

It was initially a concern for his career, however, rather than an interest in automobiles that led Patton to join the nascent Tank Corps as it was being formed in France in late 1917. Patton then was desperately seeking an escape from staff duty, which he found boring and without career potential. While he considered shifting branches in order to get command of an infantry battalion, he decided that greater chances for promotion lay with the tanks.[17] Yet once associated with tanks, Patton developed an attachment for them that

transcended career concerns, and he began early to accommodate them intellectually into his traditionalist world. Not only was the introduction of tanks legitimized by association with Alexander the Great, but Patton also developed the habit of referring to them in animalistic terms, and in his attempts at poetry he tried to give the tank service the same aura of romantic respectability enjoyed by cavalry.[18] All this culminated for Patton in several opportunities to lead his tanks in combat, an experience which he found to be "thrilling"[19] and which allowed him sufficient opportunity for traditional heroism to win the Distinguished Service Cross.

Thrilling and fulfilling as this wartime experience with tanks may have been, Patton's view of their role in combat remained unabashedly traditional. Shortly after the war he noted that "immense as the influence of mechanical devices may be, they can never of themselves decide a campaign. Their true [role] is that of assisting the infantry man . . . . They can never replace him."[20] The dreams of the enthusiasts about mechanical armies he derided as "absurd."[21] This traditionalist vision was, perhaps, reinforced by a vague fear that tanks could lead to an industrialization of warfare. Patton seemed distinctly alert to tendencies in that direction. In April 1917, he wrote to his wife, "right now I am more like Henry Ford than a soldier,"[22] a feeling that he repeated on several other occasions. He feared that peacetime would accentuate this industrial character of tank service, leaving it "very much like coast artillery with a lot of machinery that never works."[23]

Patton's attachment to the tanks kept him in the Tank Corps for nearly two years after the end of the war, during which time he campaigned actively in favor of granting the corps status as an independent combat arm.[24] This position, which was quite at variance with his wartime orthodoxy, was apparently adopted by Patton more out of expediency than from a real shift in attitude. It was the line being taken by his commanding officer and other officers in the corps, and an independent status for the corps offered Patton his best chance for promotion. His arguments along this line, however, contained little that would appeal to professionals, and he abandoned them afterward.

Patton left the Tank Corps in October 1920 in a mood of increasing pessimism regarding the future of both the country and the Army. The National Defense Act of 1920 had not only ended the independent status of the Tank Corps (and the career prospects Patton had earlier associated with service in the Tank Corps), but had also gutted the Army, indicating a rapidly developing public disaffection with its armed forces. Patton explained this development to himself in terms of the Carthaginian tendency of American society,[25] and like many of his colleagues he turned his attention to the preservation of the professional integrity of the Army. For the next eight years, his interest in tanks and mechanized warfare diminished considerably.[26] His principal concern, instead, was the problem of command and his perception that a rapid invasion of civilian attitudes was undermining the traditional heroic model of military leadership.[27] Not only were officers becoming too concerned with their own personal security in combat, but they were being taught that a scholarly approach to leadership was superior to a moral one, that "brains outrank guts."[28] In this mood, he tended to view the Army's interest in mechanization as another form of the civilian invasion of the military world. It was the public's fascination with things mechanical and its susceptibility to the "histrionic abilities" of the mechanizationists that were forcing the Army to pay what he considered to be undue consideration to the issue. Patton's response was a volley of arguments emphasizing the actual limitations of existing military vehicles and reiterating the idea that war was made by men, not machines.[29]

The year 1928 proved to be something of a turning point both for mechanization in the United States and for Patton. The successful development of several fast tank prototypes that year provided the vehicles needed by the theories of the mechanizationists, while a successful summer maneuver by an independent mechanized unit in Great Britain seemed to vindicate those theories and led the Secretary of War to commit the American Army to the development of its own experimental mechanized force.[30] Meanwhile, in May 1928 Patton was transferred to the Office of the Chief of Cavalry as head of the Plans and Training Division. The Office of the Chief of Cavalry was then much concerned with mechanization but in an ambivalent way. On the one hand the office was the political and intellectual citadel of traditionalism within the cavalry. It published *Cavalry Journal* and coordinated all lobbying efforts on behalf of the cavalry. Its major concern in this area was to counter mounting pressures in favor of supplanting horse cavalry with armored vehicles. On the other hand, the chief's office was mandated by law and by the expectations of military professionals to develop the weapons and doctrines needed by the cavalry to meet new situations.

Patton's position in the office was particularly ambiguous, since he was expected to head both enterprises.[31] His initial response to this was to seek a middle ground that would allow the cavalry the appearance and some of the advantages of mechanization without diluting its traditional character. Several years earlier he had supported the idea of attaching several troops of armored cars to a cavalry division to act in cooperation with horse units.[32] By late 1928 the cavalry was ready to accept this limited mechanization. Division maneuvers involving organic armored-car troops were held in October 1929, with Patton observing for the Chief of Cavalry.[33]

Patton initially defended this modest concession as representing the limit of mechanization necessary,[34] supporting his position with more articles and lectures on the continued value of horse cavalry. Nevertheless, by the spring of 1930 his evaluation of developments in other armies convinced him that in almost any future combat situation American cavalry could expect to encounter hostile armored vehicles.[35] A mechanization limited to armored cars capable of operating only on roads would obviously be an inadequate response to such a situation. While he agreed that the problem might be met temporarily by developing mobile .50-caliber machine guns for horse pack as antitank weapons,[36] he was rapidly becoming convinced that a more far-reaching solution was called for and that this solution involved the tank.

Earlier Patton had argued that there was no place for the tank in the cavalry, since "at present there is no tank . . . which can keep up with Cavalry."[37] However, the appearance of the new fast tank prototypes in 1928, and particularly the model developed by J. Walter Christie, caused him to reconsider. The Christie prototype was capable of rapid maneuver on either wheels or tracks, so that it seemed to offer the advantages of both the armored car and the tank. In June 1929, Patton pressed the Chief of Cavalry to purchase several Christie prototypes for experimental purposes, but without success.[38] In 1930, General Guy V. Henry, who was more flexible on the mechanization issue, became Chief of Cavalry, and with his encouragement Patton began to develop proposals that would further mechanize the cavalry. By early 1931 he was arguing that the cavalry could not hope to counter expected enemy armored vehicles unless it possessed armored vehicles of its own.[39] While Patton cautiously referred to such vehicles as "heavy armored cars," it is clear that he had Christie tanks in mind. At the same time, in his historical references the tank was increasingly referred to as the modern descendent of the armored knight, or chariot warfare.[40] By mid-1931, Patton was urging the Chief of Cavalry to employ all possible available resources to acquire heavy armored cars.[41]

Contact with the reality of current military trends was not, however, the most important force that pushed Patton toward accepting the tank. Efforts over ten years to defend traditional horse cavalry had caused him to refine considerably his traditionalist attitudes, leading him to a vision of warfare that was more mobile, strategic, and mechanized. Repeated emphasis of the cavalry's critical role in reconnaissance led Patton from his earlier tactical and battle-centered vision of war to a conception that was more campaign-oriented and strategic.[42] Similar efforts to dissociate American cavalry from the failures of European cavalry during the First World War on the grounds that Americans belonged to the dragoon rather than the cuirassier tradition of cavalry led Patton to envision cavalry less as a unit capable of shock action in battle and more as a self-contained organization that emphasized maneuver and firepower.[43]

Finally, and most important, for over ten years Patton and others had argued that one could make no judgment about the future of cavalry on the basis that it had not been used in the First World War, since that war had been of a unique character unlikely to be seen again.[44] For Patton this argument was not a matter of expediency but represented a genuine and deeply troubling sentiment. Within a short time of his arrival in France in 1917, Patton came to feel that the conflict there was not real war.[45] Ever since he had first encountered warfare in history, real war had meant to him movement and decisiveness. West Point and his experience in Mexico had reinforced that view, so that he saw the static and indecisive trench warfare that he found in France in 1917 as an unhealthy aberration.[46] During the war and for the next dozen years afterward, Patton mulled the question of what had gone wrong, reaching the conclusion that the culprit was the mass army.

Patton's aristocratic upbringing, his classic and heroic value structure, and his ambition for preeminence left him little capacity to accept democratic values or institutions. By the time he had left West Point, Patton was a full-fledged Uptonian in his conviction that only professional military organizations were of any value.[47] Contact with reserve officers in subsequent years tended to reinforce these views.[48] In the late 1920s Patton became deeply interested in the writing of Ardant du Picq[49] and in that of current French and German military figures who extolled the values of the professional army. This reading helped Patton clarify his earlier views and led him to argue in 1930 and 1931 that while the huge conscript armies raised in 1914 and thereafter had been relatively easy to supply over Europe's magnificent transportation network, they were too massive and ill-trained to maneuver. As a result, the conflict in Europe had quickly stabilized along extended parallel lines so that war became a matter of attrition rather than movement.[50] For Patton, attrition degraded warfare from a form of human conflict into an industrial process in which "the inert human masses became fodder for their equally inert masses of machines."[51]

In Patton's mind, the obvious solution to this problem was to reject the wrong turn taken toward mass industrial warfare in 1914 and to return to the traditional warfare of maneuver, to be fought now by small, highly mobile, and fully professional armies. He spelled out this idea in great detail in his major student paper at the Army War College in 1932, giving it a broad historical introduction,[52] and it remained fundamental to his thinking during the rest of the decade. For a while he continued to claim that horse cavalry would play a number of major roles in such a force, arguing that mobility meant flexible speed, which could be gained only by a force made up of horse and machine units working in complementary fashion.[53] Later, however, he began to drop that argument, and the roles assigned to horse units in his imagined force began to diminish.

Thus, during the four years spent in the Office of the Chief of Cavalry and at the Army War College, Patton had come to accept a vision of warfare involving armored vehicles organized as self-contained units operating on a strategic as well as a tactical basis, a vision not too far removed from that of the mechanizationists.[54] Yet he got there principally by means of a reactionary line of thought, to the degree that he was still able to see himself as a defender of tradition. As such, he continued to criticize the "pure mechanizationists" vigorously and to point out repeatedly the limitations of armored vehicles. Thus, while there may have been a significant convergence between Patton and the mechanizationists in regard to the arms and doctrines both advocated, they were still as far apart as ever on the philosophic bases on which their ideas were founded. What the mechanizationists had proposed as a revolutionary means to overthrow an outworn traditional system of warfare, Patton had finally come to accept as an evolutionary means to restore it.[55]

Patton's subsequent assignments during the 1930s brought him into contact with other problems, and for a number of years his interest in mechanization faded.[56] Later, the Spanish Civil War and the growing feeling that a new European war was imminent rekindled that interest to some extent, leading to some refinement in his ideas. Patton was now willing to give significant reconnaissance and even tactical roles to aircraft and almost none to horse units.[57] At the same time he continued to attack mechanizationists for their lack of realism and for pandering to the public's craving for security from a draft.[58]

In July 1940 the Army committed itself to the creation of a mechanized force. Brigadier General Adna R. Chaffee, who had been one of the leaders of the mechanizationist movement since 1928 and who was now slated to head the new armored force, invited Patton to take command of a brigade in the new Second Armored Division. Patton accepted eagerly and threw himself immediately into training his unit. Gathering his unit for a lecture in early September, he explained, among other things, that the key to German success in this war was the fact that "they did not use weapons because they were new, but because through their use, age-old military tasks could be better accomplished."[59] Patton had joined the mechanizationists; yet he remained a traditionalist.

It would seem that at least two conclusions could be drawn from this brief survey of the development of Patton's vision of mechanized warfare. First, by the late 1930s Patton had developed a rather perceptive insight into the nature of the warfare that would emerge in the opening stages of the Second World War. Doing so required a major transformation in Patton's thinking on how tanks were to be used in combat. Giving them initially a role strictly subordinate to the traditional combat arms, he gradually came to accept a view of mechanized warfare similar to that of the mechanizationists. Yet this transformation in thinking was episodic in its development, with most changes taking place when Patton had responsibilities directly linked to tanks. At other times, interests created by other assignments and the inhibitions arising from his traditionalist vision of the nature of war and of legitimate change all but halted any development in his thinking in this area. These latter circumstances were common to many other officers in the Army, which may help explain the slowness of the Army in accepting the ideas of mechanization.

Second, while Patton came to adopt much of the mechanizationists' style of warfare and even to make himself a master of it, he did so by incorporating it into his own traditional outlook, so that the latter survived the transformation intact.[60] The fact that Patton and many of his fellow officers could modernize their style of fighting without disturbing their traditionalist outlook may partially explain their ability to maintain a sense of stability and self-assurance within the confusion of a new kind of warfare. It may also help explain why the Second World War so quickly assumed a traditional character.

NOTES

1. There are a number of works of varying quality on the history of mechanization in Europe and the United States. Among the most significant recent general works are Kenneth Macksey, *The Tank Pioneers* (London: Janes, 1980) and Charles Messenger, *The Blitzkrieg Story* (New York: Scribners, 1976). For individual countries, Basil H. Liddell Hart, *The Tanks* (London: Cassell, 1959), provides a two-volume chronicle of the development of British mechanization. Richard M. Carver, *The Apostles of Mobility: The Theory and Practice of Armoured Warfare* (New York: Holmes and Meier, 1979), provides an updated and far briefer survey. French, German, and Russian developments have not yet received coverage by individual books. The development of Italian armor is covered in John J. T. Sweet, *Iron Arm: The Mechanization of Mussolini's Army 1920-1940* (Westport: Greenwood Press, 1980). The standard, though now dated, work on the development of mechanization in the United States is Mildrid H. Gillie, *Forging the Thunderbolt: History of the Development of the Armored Force* (Harrisburg: Military Services, 1947).

2. By his own count, by 1934 Patton had written over 30 articles or papers on the subject. He had probably lectured on the topic even more often.

3. There are at least 16 biographies of Patton of one sort or another, most of which emphasize his career in the Second World War. By far the fullest is Martin Blumenson, *The Patton Papers* (Boston: Houghton Mifflin, 1972, 1975).

4. During his last year in high school, his final examination grade in history was 95, while his average grade in all other courses was 68. Stephen Cutter Clark, "Report of George S. Patton, Jr., for the term ending April 8, 1903." George S. Patton, Jr., Papers, Library of Congress, Box #5, "Chronological File: April-Dec. 1903." Hereinafter references from these papers will be cited as GSP followed by the box number and file title. Works by Patton himself will be cited without reference to the author.

5. Blumenson, pp. 150, 185.

6. "The Secret of Victory," 26 March 1926, GSP #50, Military Writings, 1926.

7. "Why Men Fight," 27 October 1927, GSP #50, Military Writings, 1927.

8. "Notes for Lectures," n.d. (1918-1920), GSP #12, Chronological File October-December, 1920.

9. "Final Examination in Roman History," 1903, GSP #48, Military Writings, 1903-1909.

10. This theme can be seen repeatedly in his work but was particularly evident in his poetry written during and after the First World War. See "End of War," 30 December 1917, and "Defeat," 16 January 1921, GSP #60, Poems.

11. "The Secret of Victory."

12. Patton was continually critical of his fellow officers for their lack of imagination, saying after

the First World War that the "lack of imagination is the besetting sin of our army with respect to tanks." "Notes for Lectures."

13. He took fifth place in the modern pentathlon, a contest involving use of the pistol and saber as well as running, swimming, and riding. Blumenson, pp. 248-55.

14. Patton took fencing lessons in France and later taught fencing to cavalry officers. He wrote an instructor's manual for the teaching of fencing, and published three articles in *Cavalry Journal* on the saber.

15. Blumenson, pp. 359-68.

16. One of his first assignments in France was to run the motor pool.

17. Letter to Beatrice Patton, 23 December 1917, Blumenson, p. 502.

18. Letter to Beatrice Patton, 5 July 1918, Blumenson, p. 597. Poem "Regret," 27 June 1918, and "Bill," 30 August 1919, GSP #60, Poems.

19. Letter to Beatrice Patton, 12 October 1918, Blumenson, p. 676.

20. Lecture, "Tank Tactics," 20 November 1920, GSP #48, Military Writings, 1918.

21. Ibid.

22. Letter to Beatrice Patton, 14 April 1918, Blumenson, p. 562.

23. Letter to Beatrice Patton, 22 November 1918, Blumenson, p. 700.

24. "Tanks in Future Wars," May 1919, GSP #58, Military Writings, 1918. Published as "Tanks in Future Wars," *Infantry Journal*, 16 (May 1920), 958-62.

25. This can be seen most clearly in his poems in this period, "Defeat," 16 January 1921, "The War Horses," n.d., and "The Curse of Kant," 20 January 1921, GSP #60, Poems.

26. Patton wrote and spoke relatively little on this subject during this period, and what he did say largely repeated ideas developed between 1918 and 1920.

27. This theme was elaborated for the first time in "The Cavalry Man," 1921, GSP #49, Military Writings, 1921.

28. "Drills for Fighting," 1926, Blumenson, p. 904.

29. "The Secret of Victory."

30. The appearance of prototypes of fast tanks in the United States was the result of several developments, none of which were linked directly to any distinct theory of mechanized warfare. These schemes were initially based on an ideal medium tank capable of long range and speeds of at least 20 m.p.h. overland. Interest in the development of such a vehicle in the United States, however, flagged soon after the National Defense Act of 1920 assigned responsibility for tank development to the infantry, whose interest in armored vehicles was limited to those that could accompany and support infantry (see George Hoffman, "The Demise of the U.S. Tank Corps and Medium Tank Development Program," *Military Affairs*, 36 [February 1973], 20-25). However, by the mid-1920s there was growing interest in the development of a cheap light tank which would use chassis and engines already in production for the civilian automotive market, thereby allowing easy and rapid mass production in the event of war. It was from these efforts, as well as those of independent inventor J. Walter Christie, that the prototypes for fast tanks appeared in 1929 (see Constance M. Green, Harry C. Thompson, Peter C. Roots, *The United States in World War II: The Ordnance Department: Planning Munitions for War* [Washington: Office of the Chief of Military History, 1955], pp. 189-98; C. C. Williams, "Mechanization and the New Era of the Armored Fighting Vehicle," *Army Ordnance*, 9 [May-June 1929], 301-07; and John Christmas, "Mechanization in Our Army Today," *Army Ordnance*, 13 [July-August 1932], 11-17). The appearance of these tanks, of course, made possible a mechanization of cavalry, attracting the interest of cavalry officers such as Adna Chaffee and Patton.

31. At this time Patton was a leading contributor to *Cavalry Journal* and a key member of an Army polo team.

32. "Armored Cars with Cavalry," *Cavalry Journal*, 33 (January 1924), 7.

33. "The 1929 Cavalry Division Maneuvers," *Cavalry Journal*, 39 (January 1930), 7-15.

34. Lecture, "Cavalry in the Next War," 4 February 1930, GSP #50, Military Writings, 1929.

35. Memorandum for the Chief of Cavalry, "Anti-Tank and Anti-Armored Car Weapons," 6 March 1930, GSP #58, World War I, Tanks 1918.

36. Ibid.

37. "Armored Cars with Cavalry," p. 186.

38. "Memorandum for the Chief of Cavalry," 20 June 1929, GSP #58, World War I, Tanks 1918. The career of J. Walter Christie and his effort to sell the Army a tank designed to run on

both wheels and tracks is described in George F. Hoffman, "A Yankee Inventor and the Military Establishment: The Christie Tank Controversy," *Military Affairs*, 39 (February 1975), 12-18, and in Macksey, pp. 90-94.

39. Lecture, "Modern Cavalry," 9 January 1931, GSP #56, Military Writings, 1931.

40. Lecture, "New Developments in Cavalry," 17 December 1930, GSP #51, Military Writings, 1931.

41. Memorandum to General Henry, 11 June 1931, GSP #52, Military Writings, 1931.

42. Lecture, "Is Cavalry Obsolete?" n.d., GSP #52, Military Writings, 1931.

43. Ibid.

44. Patton first began to clarify this idea in 1921 (lecture, "German and Allied Theory of War," n.d. [1921], GSP #49, Military Writings, 1921). It became a staple in his lectures and articles until well into the 1930s.

45. This can best be seen in his poem "Mud," July 1917, GSP #60, Poems.

46. This was one of his favorite topics of conversation with French officers, many of whom agreed with him. Letter to Beatrice Patton, 30 May 1918. Blumenson, p. 584.

47. Patton's first professional writing was a one-page typescript article entitled "National Defense" written in 1910 and which argued in favor of a professional army. GSP #48, Military Writings, 1910.

48. During the war Patton developed the theory that the sudden influx of poorly trained officers and soldiers led to specialization since they had learned to do only one thing well. From this specialization flowed not only the sterile character of the war but also the claims that single weapon systems, such as the tank, could produce victory unaided. Thus, Patton had early linked mechanizationists with the mass army and its essentially civilian character. "German and Allied Theory of War," "Tactical Tendencies," 26 November 1921, GSP #49, Military Writings, 1921.

49. Letter to Dwight D. Eisenhower, 9 July 1926, Blumenson, p. 873.

50. "Is Cavalry Obsolete?"

51. Lecture, "Modern Cavalry," 9 January 1931, GSP #59, Military Writings, 1931.

52. "The Probable Characteristics of the Next War and the Organization, Tactics and Equipment Necessary to Meet Them," 29 February 1932, GSP #52, Military Writings, 1932.

53. "Is Cavalry Obsolete?"

54. Patton had advocated the almost total motorization of the cavalry supply service during this time. Memorandum for the Quartermaster General, "Value of Animals to the Military Establishment," 28 August 1930, GSP #12, Chronological File, 1930-32.

55. Memorandum, "Mechanized Units," June 1931, GSP #52, Military Writings, 1931. It is also worth noting how little influence European theorists on mechanization such as J. F. C. Fuller and Basil Liddell Hart had on American development and even on the evolution of Patton's thought. For instance, Fuller's volume, *Lectures on F. S. R. iii (Operations between Mechanized Forces)* (London: Sifton Praed, 1932), considered by many to be the best exposition of his ideas on the subject, was virtually ignored by American military journals and schools. A speculative examination of possible reasons for this go beyond the scope of this paper, but one is worth noting. European theorists were transfixed by the First World War as experienced by their own nation and developed their ideas about mechanization as a means of avoiding a repetition of that experience. Both Fuller and Liddell Hart turned to the tank and to their visions of mechanized warfare as a means of overcoming the stalemated trench warfare that much of British opinion had seen as costly, indecisive, and meaningless. The central problem for both men, and many of their followers, was breaking through an entrenched line and exploiting that breakthrough in a decisive manner. (Both men have benefited from recent biographies centering on their ideas: Anthony J. Trythall, *"Boney" Fuller* [London: Cassell, 1977]; Brian Bond, *Liddell Hart: A Study of His Military Thought* [New Brunswick: Rutgers, 1977]. Jay Luvaas, *The Education of an Army* [Chicago: Univ. of Chicago, 1964], pp. 335-424, points out that this fixation also affected both men's visions of history.) In France, where the major lesson of the war was perceived to be the overwhelming power of the defense, mechanized warfare was largely ignored in deference to defensive systems based on the Maginot Line and artillery. Even Charles de Gaulle in his book *Vers l'armée de Metiér* (1934) emphasized the role of artillery. (See Andre Beaufre, "Liddell Hart and the French Army," in Michael Howard, ed, *The Theory and Practice of War* (Bloomington: Indiana Univ., 1965), pp. 129-42. In Germany the principal advocate of mechanization, Heinz Guderian, was an

acknowledged disciple of Liddell Hart, yet he turned to mechanization, in part, to provide the mobility necessary to overcome the disadvantage rising from Germany's central position, which many felt had left it surrounded and outnumbered in the First World War. (See Robert J. O'Neill, "Doctrine and Training in the German Army," in Howard, pp. 143-67, and Messenger, pp. 56-59.) Until the Ethiopian War, Italian armor was assigned the role of an infantry support weapon in defense of the Alpine passes threatened in the past war. (See Sweet, pp. 51-74.) American experience in the war was too brief to produce any such fixation, so that even those officers who, like Patton, generally kept up with the European military developments failed to share the concerns on which the various cases for mechanization were based. Many officers, including Patton, saw armored vehicles as necessary to military conditions peculiar only to northwest Europe, an area in which, for a long time, few Americans expected to be again involved militarily.

56. The lectures and writing on the subject during this period were limited and largely a hasty rework of earlier materials.

57. Lecture, "Defense Against Mechanization," 4 March 1936, GSP #51, Military Writings, 1936.

58. Memorandum, "Current Thought on Mechanization," 15 December 1936, GSP #51, Military Writings, 1937. For a decade and a half after the end of the war, Patton argued repeatedly that no society could stand the economic strain of mechanized war. While he dropped this argument in the mid 1940s, he still argued that within a few months of the opening of a general war, all sides would exhaust their supply of armored vehicles and it would require domestic industries a year to begin an adequate resupply. Lecture, "Mechanization," 11 April 1934, GSP #52, Military Writings, 1934.

59. Lecture, "Armored Operations in Poland," 3 September, 1940, GSP #12, Chronological File, 1940-41.

60. Anyone familiar with Patton's book, *War as I Knew It* (Boston: Houghton Mifflin, 1947) will realize that these traditional values also survived the Second World War intact.

This article appeared in the autumn 1985 issue of *Parameters*.

19

De Gaulle's Concept of a Mobile, Professional Army: Genesis of French Defeat?

by ROBERT A. DOUGHTY

The fall of France to the German blitzkrieg in June 1940 has generated a great deal of literature that attempts to pinpoint the causes of France's rapid collapse. Among the important immediate causes identified is the French failure to mass armored forces for use against the attacking German thrusts. It is clear that the French error ensued from an inability to recognize the potential of mechanized warfare, not from a shortage of armored vehicles. By May 1940, France and Germany were approximately equal in the number of tanks available for combat on the western front, France having 2431[1] and Germany 2439 (not counting command vehicles).[2] The Germans massed their ten armored divisions into an armored group, two separate corps, and one separate division, while France haphazardly scattered her three armored divisions, three mechanized divisions, and her remaining twenty-seven non-divisional tank battalions among the eight French armies.[3] While the Germans recognized the potential of massed armored forces in conducting rapid, mobile operations, French armored units were committed to battle in a piecemeal fashion, resulting in their "melting away one after the other like snow flakes in the sun, without having any appreciable effect on the course of the battle."[4]

One might validly conclude that the Germans had learned more than the French from the First World War, and that the German commanders were more innovative than the French. There are numerous statements by prominent French military leaders supporting these views. For example, Marshal Pétain admitted in 1947 his early lack of familiarity with combat involving tanks: "I had never worked with them. In the course of the War of 1914, I did not have armored divisions. This caused me to be somewhat disinterested in them."[5] But the problem of French employment of armor is more complex than this, since their consideration of armor was greatly influenced by the traditional French approach to national defense, which called for the entire nation to spring to arms during times of national emergency. This defense concept has been called "the nation in arms."[6] Many military and political leaders believed that an Armor Corps (i.e., a separate armor command having large homogeneous tank units) – because of its inherent offensive capabilities, its needs for a better-trained and longer-serving soldier, and its frequent association with elitism and professionalism – was not consistent with the basic tenets of the nation in arms. This negative view of armor became even more prevalent when General Charles De Gaulle offered his famous plan for the formation of a highly mobile army, insisting that it be formed with professional rather than citizen-soldiers. The question of armored units subsequently became subsumed by the controversy over professionalism, leading France to reject the creation of a highly professional mechanized force without adequately considering the potential of armored units. This crucial decision was brought about more by a belief that the Armored Corps violated the "republican" approach to national defense than by a consideration of the capability of a spearhead of tank forces.

The Nation in Arms versus the Professional Army

The concept of the nation in arms had originated in the French Revolution with the "cannonade of Valmy" in 1792 and the *levée en masse* in 1793. Its true spirit was reflected in the decree establishing the *levée en masse:*

Henceforth, until the enemies have been driven from the territory of the Republic, the French people are in permanent requisition for army service. . . . The young men shall go to battle; the married men shall forge arms and transport provisions; the women shall make tents and clothes, and shall serve in the hospitals; the children shall turn old linen into lint; the old men shall repair to the public places, to stimulate the courage of the warriors and preach the unity of the Republic and the hatred of kings.[7]

This reliance on the military potential of the citizenry became an important part of French republican tradition. Many Frenchmen came to believe that when the country was in danger, a mass of patriotic volunteers would rise and destroy the invading armies. The concentration of all national energies against an enemy would be morally and militarily sufficient to defend France. Even though she moved away from the armed nation to a professional army for a time after the Napoleonic Wars, the total commitment of the entire nation remained the theoretical basis of the French nation in arms.

The nation in arms was not reinstituted by the French until after the War of 1870-71, during which Germany dramatically reminded them that wars were no longer simply quarrels between governments of ruling families, fought by relatively small armies of professional soldiers.[8] Wars were now conducted between entire peoples, fought by armies of completely mobilized nations. From the time of that defeat, the foundation of the French national defenses rested on an unswerving faith in the massive mobilization of the citizenry in times of national peril. The resulting symbiotic bond between army and nation was well characterized in a 1904 report by a Chamber of Deputies

Commission: "The modern concept of the army is that . . . it is identical with the nation, draws from it all its resources, and has no separate and distinct existence outside the nation."[9] After the First World War, the principle of the citizenry in arms was expanded to include the notion of complete mobilization of every possible materiel resource. The concept came to be one of total war; France was convinced that her best defense lay in committing *all* her resources, both men and materiel, against an attacking enemy. The completely committed and mobilized nation, since it was peace loving, came to emphasize as well the defense as opposed to the offense, and the citizen soldier as opposed to professional. For many Frenchmen the three nation in arms, defense, and citizen soldier became synonymous.

There was little doubt that the nation in arms was based essentially on a defensive principle. An army composed of citizens performing their patriotic duty would be very reluctant to aggressively attack another state; however, they would willingly defend to the death their sacred French soil. The example of World War I also contributed to a continued belief in this defensive principle. French commanders – almost to a man – accepted the popular perception of the Great War as a heroic defensive effort by an armed nation. An aroused France had succeeded in 1914 in turning back the invading German forces; why shouldn't she again succeed in the future? They had learned too well the lessons of the First World War and could visualize only a war similar to the previous. Their vision rarely ranged above the trenches of that war, which had validated the principle of the armed nation. As a result of such outmoded thought, the offensive was de-emphasized, and France's strategy between wars became one of the armed nation gloriously defending its borders. France would wait for Germany to strike the first blow; then, after the initial attack had been repelled, she would undertake limited, methodical attacks of massed infantry, armor, and artillery. Armor would be used in these attacks, but its purpose would be to support the infantry, not to conduct rapid, independent maneuvers. The ultimate result of this thinking was the "Maginot Line Complex": the delusory belief that the fortifications on the northeast frontier would protect France or at least give her time to mobilize and commit the nation in arms. As Marshal Pétain envisioned, "The active metropolitan army will act as the covering force; under its protection, the principal mass of our forces will be mobilized"[10]

And with regard to the citizen-soldier, France had learned yet another important lesson from the First World War; in it the reservist demonstrated that he could perform admirably in battle. Since republican France traditionally feared the conservatism of the professional soldier, she possessed a natural bias in behalf of reliance upon citizen soldiers. Accordingly, France maintained short-term service for the conscript and held the size of the professional component to a comparatively low figure. The term of service for the conscript was reduced from three to two years in 1921, to 18 months in 1923, and to one year in 1928 (though later increased to two years in 1935).

During the same period the permanent component was gradually reduced to the point where it could be spared only for a few priority roles, e.g. in the frontier fortifications, the conscript training centers, and the planning staffs. The professional army thus became the cadre for training the citizen-soldier before returning him to civilian life; it also provided the umbrella of protection under which the armed nation would be mobilized. "France had no army in peacetime in the old sense of the word," according to Irving M. Gibson. "She had only a permanent frontier guard and 240,000 recruits under training."[11] The active army was described even in French law as a training rather than fighting force.[12] This system was to last through 1939 and the beginning of World War II.

In addition to the firm belief in the potential of a completely armed French nation, this predominant emphasis on the citizen-soldier was based on the beliefs that such an army would be totally loyal to the republican regime, that it could not be used in initiating an aggresive war. According to the republican view, there was little likelihood that the army could be persuaded to act against the republican regime if it consisted mostly of conscripts. Those who supported this view had only to look back to the professional army of Napoleon III to see the menace of such a military force. As for a professional army's being more prone to undertake international ventures, many Frenchmen agreed with their countrymen who asserted, "When one has such fine arms, there are always fools who are burning to try them out, [for] . . . soldiers, like iron, rust in times of peace."[13] In contrast, an armed nation would fight only in defense of its own territory or for essential national needs. Since the nation in arms was composed of citizen-soldiers, it would be impossible for France to fight an aggressive war undesired by the citizenry. Furthermore, the political left believed that a professional army was not necessarily a more effective fighting force. One leftist observer opined that "a professional army increases, in time of peace, the chances of war, and in times of war, . . . diminishes the chances of victory."[14] After all, a professional French army had lost the Franco-Prussian War of 1870-71, but a nation in arms had won the First World War.

The French, then, firmly believed in the principle of an aroused nation valiantly defending itself, this belief reaching its zenith during the 1930s when the political left acquired its greatest power. The principle accorded with their republican sentiments, furnished a means of controlling the potentially reactionary military, and provided what they considered to be the most effective national defense strategy. The army thus became a deterrent or defensive force, rather than an aggressive war-making institution. The close relationship between the nation in arms and the army, and its consequences, were noted in an army manual, *Provisional Instructions for the Tactical Employment of Large Units*, published by the French General Staff from 1921 to 1936 and often referred to as the "Gospel of the Army": "The very life of the citizenry is associated in an intimate fashion with that of the army, and thus the formula for the nation in arms is realized in every aspect. . . . [This] greatly influences the eventualities of war and consequently the formation of strategy."[15]

This common French perception of national defense strategy had a decisive influence upon the manner in which the French army organized its armor forces. Since armored units were more capable than foot soldiers of offensive action, many thought that lack of emphasis on large armored formations would reduce the possibility of France's starting a war. As one military observer noted, "The Germans, who are naturally aggressive and who prepare their army for the attack, must naturally have armored divisions. But France, being pacific and defensive, is bound to be anti-motorization."[16] Important political leaders also adopted this attitude toward large armored formations. For example, Léon Blum, leader of the Socialist Party and Prime Minister from 1936-37, was convinced that De Gaulle and the High Command were conspiring to create an aggressive army of "shock and speed." He felt that such a conception was a "menace to peace."[17] To meet the threat of German invasion, even by armored divisions, France would rely on a full-scale mobilization of French infantrymen to defend the northeast frontier, thereby avoiding the possibility of French armor-led aggression. The anti-tank gun, rather than the tank, was most accordant with France's approach to national defense, since it was less expensive, was primarily a defensive weapon, and could easily be handled by the citizen-soldier.

De Gaulle's Professional Army

There were some early attempts in France to create a modern armored corps. The most influential individual during the initial period was Colonel (later General) J. E. Estienne, now known as the "father of French armor."[18] An artillery officer, he conceived the idea of an armored fighting vehicle during the First World War and dubbed the French tank units as the *Artillerie d'Assaut*, or assault artillery. Yet, he clearly recognized the wider possibility of tanks and in 1922 called for a primitive type of armored division. His ideas fell on the deaf ears of the French High Command, and the separate headquarters of the armor command established during the war was soon abolished. In a decision that reflected France's future approach to the employment of tanks, questions regarding armor were placed under the purview of the infantry command. There were others who recognized the potential of mechanized warfare. In July 1927, General André Doumenc, who had served as General Estienne's chief of staff in the Great War and who was to serve in World War II as the chief of staff of the Armies of the Field under General Alphonse Georges, called for the formation of large armored units. Also, a continual trickle of articles and books emphasizing the need for French mechanization appeared in the interim between the wars.

One of the best known of these was *Vers l'armée de métier* by Lieutenant

Colonel (later General) Charles De Gaulle. This work, calling for the creation of a separate armored corps, first appeared in 1934. The thrust of the author's argument is suggested by his title. While the English translation of 1941 is entitled *The Army of the Future*, a better translation would be *Toward the Professional Army*. In this work, De Gaulle asserted essentially that quality is better than quantity. A professional army is superior to the nation in arms, and France should construct a strongly armored, professional army. The fundamental assumption of the French national defense, that is, the superiority of the nation in arms over other modes of defense, is fallacious.

De Gaulle observed several weaknesses in the theory of the nation in arms. First, he recognized that the geographical nature of France made it particularly vulnerable to attack. If converging attacks were made from Flanders, the Ardennes, Alsace, or Lorraine, and one attack broke through the defenses, it could "strike straight at the heart of France" – Paris. The armed nation was particularly vulnerable in this situation, since its slowness to mobilize made it more likely that a break could swiftly be made in the defenses along France's frontiers. De Gaulle also believed that the nation in arms could be mobilized only during periods of the greatest danger. Because commitment of the nation in arms to battle would necessarily entail heavy losses, he recognized that national security would have to be gravely imperiled before France would go to war. Yet, De Gaulle could envision instances when France would want to "seize the coveted prize as swiftly as possible, thus offering the adversary the alternative either of resigning himself to the *fait accompli*, or of assuming the risk and odium of a war of extermination."[19] He firmly believed there were instances when France would want to attack outside her own borders. Therefore, he rejected the defensive nature of the nation in arms and, in effect, called for the creation of an army that could launch a "preventive strike" or initiate an immediate offensive upon the declaration of hostilities.

De Gaulle also attacked the fighting capability of the citizen-soldier, and asserted that too much stress was being placed on numbers of personnel. With the increasing complexity of war machines, there existed a "latent opposition between mechanization and the exclusive system of numerical strength." Since war was becoming more and more technical, he could not believe a massively armed populace would have great military power simply because it was armed. He was particularly disturbed by the inadequate training the conscript received: "Soon, someone will set up as a principle that the less military training a nation has had, the better it fights, as Émile acquired learning through not having studied."[20] The increase in the technical level of warfare, in his view, demanded more highly trained troops, not simply more troops.

Thus, De Gaulle attacked the efficacy of the entire concept of the nation in arms. He asserted that "No form of battle is more bloody than that of nations in arms." The solution was to establish a professional army. "Without a professional army, there can be no French defense."[21] A professional army would have both an offensive and a defensive capability, could be used immediately without wasting precious time mobilizing, would compel economy in both personnel and in materiel, and could be highly trained in the use of modern weapons of war. France would still require a system of reserves, since this elite force could not possibly destroy all the forces of the enemy in an all-out war. But the "picked troops" of a professional army would be the foundation of France's defenses and would be the "vanguard of the mobilized nation."[22]

As for mechanized forces, De Gaulle's professional army would consist primarily of armored units. It would be composed of 100,000 volunteers, comprising six divisions. Each division would have three brigades (one each of armor, infantry, and artillery) with supporting engineer, signal, reconnaissance, and aerial units. The army would also have a light armored division for scouting purposes, a brigade of heavy tanks for attacking permanent fortifications, and assorted other support units. This professional army, then, would be a powerfully armed, swiftly moving body employing all the potential of armored forces. To use De Gaulle's descriptive terminology, "the aristocrats of war" would become "the chief element of maneuver."[23]

But De Gaulle had unfortunately linked the growth of French armored forces to the appearance of a professional army. This linkage required a rejection of the tradition of the nation in arms and was a direct affront to much French republican sentiment. Additionally, he had committed heresy by suggesting that France itself could initiate a war, and by intimating that expansion of her frontiers could be in her general interests. Thus, De Gaulle, by suggesting the possible use of armored forces in an aggressive role, corroborated many of the fears of those who opposed armored forces for France. In the debate over mechanization, his proposal shifted attention to the demand for a professional army, rather than to the merits of large armored formations.

The Political Reaction

There is little doubt that De Gaulle's argument aroused the suspicion and opposition of important political leaders. Léon Blum expressed the complaint that De Gaulle had "combined two ideas, which in my opinion should not be associated in any degree: one was the strategic employment of large armored units and the other was the return of the professional army. I was tempted by the first idea; I was a resolute adversary of the other."[24] Such sentiments on the part of the political left became increasingly apparent, for it considered itself the true heir and defender of French revolutionary and republican ideals. To the leftists, the shibboleth of the nation in arms was sacred. Many members of the political left would have preferred a militia rather than an active army, and nothing was more contradictory to their beliefs than a professional army. De Gaulle's book could not have been published at a more inopportune moment, for when it appeared France was attempting to amend the law of 1928 and convert from one-year to two-year service in the army. On March 15, 1935 (the eve of Hitler's denunciation of the clauses of the Versailles treaty providing for German disarmament), Blum cited the book as evidence in the Chamber of Deputies that while the High Command was apparently seeking two-year service it ultimately wanted to create a professional army.[25] Nothing could have been further from the military hierarchy's intentions.

Because of their controversial nature, De Gaulle's theories received little support from the War Ministers. Edouard Daladier, War Minister from December 1932 through January 1934 and from June 1936 through May 1940, asserted: "General de Gaulle systematized the [armored] doctrine with an incomparable brilliance, but, in my opinion, was mistaken to tie his concept to a professional army. For as much . . . as I understand the need for armored divisions, I say that I am hostile to the creation of a professional corps of 100,000 men that risks being engaged in an offensive adventure. . . ."[26] Jean Fabry, War Minister in three different cabinets between 1934 and 1936, felt that it was unnecessary to create a special mechanized corps that could not by itself protect the national territory. Such an elite unit would detract from overall defense needs; besides, such an organization had precisely the same objective as France's existent covering forces.[27] General Joseph-Léon-Marie Maurin, also War Minister in three different cabinets during the period 1934-36, also perceived as inappropriate De Gaulle's ideas: "How could anyone believe that we can still contemplate an offensive, when we have spent billions to establish a fortified barrier? Would we be foolish enough to go beyond this barrier, to I do not know what kind of adventure?"[28] With the addition of Marshal Pétain, War Minister from February through November 1934, to the opposition, every individual who had occupied or was to occupy the War Office from 1932 through May 1940 attacked De Gaulle's scheme, with their public objections concentrated on the professional and aggressive nature of his mechanized force.

Nonetheless, certain political leaders supported De Gaulle's ideas, chief among them being Paul Reynaud, who became the parliamentary champion of the armored corps. Reynaud was convinced France was again preparing for the war that had just been fought, while the Germans were preparing for the war of the future. He earnestly believed the key to a successful defense for France lay in mechanization, and he asserted that armored units "should be the gauntlet of steel with which you strike the adversary the decisive blow."[29] Reynaud saw a need for the French armored force to be an elite unit that would spearhead the national army, and described it as "the steel head of the lance while the national army would be the wood." He also accepted the idea that soldiers serving with armored units required additional training and expertise, and thus lengthier service in the army. As he described it, putting the complex, fragile, and expensive tank in the hands of short-term conscripts would be the same as "putting torpedo boats in the hands of neophytes."[30] Reynaud eventually offered legislation for the formation of an "elite corps" barely distinguishable from De Gaulle's professional army, but it proved impossible to disassociate armored units from the politically explosive issue of professionalism. De Gaulle's armored model could not be reshaped to fit the mold of the French nation in arms; it had been too closely linked to the bête noire of French politics, the professional army.

De Gaulle and the Military Hierarchy

All of the foregoing is in no way to claim civilian responsibility for French failure to recognize the potential of large armored units. Four generals – Henri Philippe Pétain, Marie-Eugène Debeney, Maxime Weygand, and Maurice-Gamelin – held the positions of Vice-President of the Superior War Council and Chief of the General Staff of the French Army from the early 1920s through 1940. Each of them openly opposed the ideas of De Gaulle. Though apparently recognizing that the political climate was not propitious for the formation of a professional armored force, they chose to reject that force on its own merits. Not surprisingly, their objections also revolved around the questions of professional army and the nation in arms instead of the value of mechanization.[31] In each case, they emphasized the special link between army and nation, frequently more vigorously than their civilian counterparts. They felt a national army was the most effective mode of defense, and that a professional army would actually detract from France's ability to defend herself. Marshal Pétain asserted, "Since modern struggles naturally involve putting to work the totality of the people's resources, our national defense should be established on the principle of the armed nation. This conception corresponds exactly to the political and social state of a nation lacking all territorial ambition and having no objection other than the safeguarding of its soil."[32] The national defense system existent in France in 1935 had been established by the organization law of 1927 and the recruitment law of 1928; these had firmly institutionalized – more than in any other period – France's tradition of the nation in arms. As General Debeney stated in 1930, "The metropolitan army, the army of the French territory, organized by the laws of 1927-1928 is entirely oriented toward a realization as complete as possible of the nation in arms."[33] In the period after 1930, there was little or no questioning of this situation by the military.

If there were any questions regarding France's approach to national defense, they revolved around whether Germany's army would remain small and whether a sufficient number of conscripts would be available to maintain the French army's strength at an appropriate level. With the rearming of Germany in March 1935 and the appearance of a number of lean recruiting years from 1935 to 1939 because of the low birth rate in World War I, these questions became critical. The predicament brought on a bitter period in French civil-military relations,[34] but there was still no concerted attack on the principle of the nation in arms. What the military sought was an increase in the term of service from one year to two years, not a change in the basic principle of the national defense. As Marshal Pétain asserted, "It is not necessary to change the principles upon which our military system rests."[35] When the term of service was increased in 1935, the mobilization system established in 1927-28 was retained. The armed nation remained the firm basis of the French military philosophy.

Once the military leaders had accepted this reality their other decisions and views on national defense followed from that acceptance. First, there was no doubt that the national army would have to be defensive. The active army was too small for initiating an offensive; further, it had been designed as a covering force for the mobilization of the entire nation. There was also some questioning of the ability of any national army to launch an offensive immediately upon mobilization, since in comparison to the defense the offensive required a greater degree of training and discipline on the part of the individual, as well as greater unit cohesiveness, training, and efficiency. In sum, the military hierarchy doubted that short-term conscripts could acquire sufficient skills in their brief period of service to be prepared for the offensive. For example, General Narcisse-Alfred-Gabriel-Louis Chauvineau, known as the "high priest of the defense," saw the nation in arms as eminently appropriate for the national defense. But when he entertained the possibility of an offensive immediately upon the beginning of hostilities, he suggested the creation of a "small, special army," specifically trained for the offensive. This "special army" would rely on servicemen with an obligation of no less than four years, rather than on conscripts of short-term service.[36] In the absence of the stiffening afforded by long-term service, French military leaders were reluctant to commit their army to an early offensive.

This is not to say that emphasis on the defensive was due solely to the armed nation principle, for the military view of the citizen-soldier and the defensive was obviously reinforced by other factors such as the great lethality of modern weapons, which enabled the defender to inflict heavy casualties on an attacker. It was normally assumed that the attacker required a massive superiority of "three times as much infantry, six times the artillery, and fifteen times the ammunition."[37] In view then of the prevailing army predilection for the defense, De Gaulle's attack on the nation in arms gained him little support among the military community, which firmly believed "The professional army is above all an offensive instrument."[38]

Military leaders also attacked De Gaulle's concept of a professional army for tending to split the national army into two armies, thereby causing the second-line army to suffer. This was not a theory solely constructed to counter De Gaulle. General Debeney had offered the objection as early as 1930, when he described the problems and limitations of a professional army for France. After De Gaulle offered his theory, Debeney's argument resurfaced[39] and was a continual theme in the works of the military hierarchy attacking De Gaulle. Essentially, these soldiers viewed the professional army as a siphon that would progressively act to drain resources from the legitimate needs of national defense. Even though the division into a professional and non-professional component might work initially, the second force would eventually suffer in peacetime when the question of finances became difficult. The needs of the professional force would probably be met at the expense of the remainder of the army, and the best personnel would also tend to gravitate toward the professional army. The defense of France would thus rest on an insufficiently prepared second-line force if the professional component did not prove equal to the task. General Debeney graphically predicted the armored corps' fate against a mass German army: "We will have a brilliant communique at the beginning, then silence, and after a few days, a useless S.O.S."[40]

With respect to the question of quality versus quantity, which De Gaulle had broached, General Weygand commented: "The question is not of opposing quality to quantity, this is a simple play on words, but of disposing at all times of quality in sufficient quantity, and very rapidly afterwards, of quantity provided with quality." France most of all had to "fear an abrupt attack, unleashed without a declaration of war." She had to have an army with enough strength in manpower and materiel to stop the initial attack, and enough potential to expand its size for the long war. A professional army, it was argued, detracted from both these capabilities. It could possibly be checked and shattered in its initial aggressive assault, leaving France ill-defended during national mobilization; furthermore, resources allocated to it would seriously detract from the potential for molding an effective national army. As General Weygand asserted, the second-line army would quickly "fall to the state of a resigned militia, without pride, without life."[41] Only a national army, supported by all the resources of the nation, could meet French defense requirements. Modern warfare was simply too vast an enterprise for an elite force alone to fight a nation's battles. As Marshal Pétain noted, "War . . . today is no longer only that of professional armies, but that of entire peoples, abundant with all their resources and with all their faith."[42]

General Émile Alléhaut, one of the most perceptive French officers of his day and one who labelled the argument for a purely defensive army as "abominable sophism," also opposed De Gaulle's conclusions. Alléhaut was a strong advocate of mechanization and recognized that there was some agreement between his ideas and those of De Gaulle, for example, recognition of the need for a strong covering force based on maneuver and armor. But he could not accept De Gaulle's insistence upon a professional army. The republicans, according to Alléhaut, "are distrustful, rightly or wrongly, a professional army will be considered a praetorian army, an army for a *coup d'état*. . . . Hence, of what use is a system based on an institution that domestic politics will not allow?" Alléhaut expressed his confidence in a national army as the "generator of the spirit of sacrifice and of abnegation which has permitted the writing of never-to-be-forgotten pages [of history]: the Marne, Verdun, the Somme, Champagne, and many others. . . ."[43] Thus, in the views of many soldiers, a professional army was a threat to a triumphant national martial spirit, for it would create an elite force apart from the populace. Only a national army responded to the French national spirit and to the egalitarian principle giving rise to this spirit.

The Eclipse of the Armored Corps

The French military hierarchy thus rejected De Gaulle's highly mobile, professional army without adequately studying the merits of large armored formations. At the same time they opted for the continued application of the methods learned from World War I. The introduction to the 1937 edition of *Instructions for the Tactical Employment of Large Units* stated: "The mass of doctrine that was objectively fixed, on the morrow of victory, by eminent leaders who had but recently exercised high command . . . remain[s] the authorized guide for the tactical employment of large units."[44] Implicit in the retention of the old precepts was the rejection of the newly proposed large armored units, even though the approach to armor was more realistic in the 1937 than in the 1921 manual. The French High Command still seriously questioned the potential of the tank, observing, "At the present time, the anti-tank weapon confronts the tank as, during the last war, the machine gun confronted the infantry."[45] Many officers considered the terrain on the Franco-German frontier to be unsuitable for armored formations, and the example of the Spanish Civil War was often cited to refute those praising the potential of mechanized warfare. Until the beginning of World War II, the High Command's answer to armor proponents was that armor "needed further study," and the operations bureau concluded that no change in French tactics was necessary despite Poland's frightening experience with the German armored blitzkrieg. The first French armored division was not created until October 1939, and when Germany attacked in May 1940 France had only three armored divisions in being with a fourth (commanded by De Gaulle) being formed.

France's consideration of armor had been far from zealous because of its perceived threat to the basic republican tenets of the nation in arms. De Gaulle's equation of a professional army with an armored corps, and his attack upon nation in arms, served only to solidify opposition to separate armored forces. While he may have been the French prophet of armor, his linking of a mobile army to professionalism was a major reason for the French failure to recognize the value of large armored forces. Others such as Blum, Daladier, Pétain, and Gamelin failed to understand the true potential of armor, but De Gaulle committed an equally grave error by associating armored units with professionalism and thus making it politically untenable for France to acquire large armored forces until the beginning of the war, when it was too late to gain sufficient experience in their use. Had he been more politic, seeking instead the creation of an armored force in a manner not directly challenging widely held French views on national defense, or more in agreement with the tradition of the nation in arms, the chances for the earlier creation of large armored units would have been materially enhanced. Political considerations and military traditions, not advances in military doctrine, had determined the shape of France's defenses, and ultimately her future.

NOTES

1. The number of French tanks is calculated by adding the 2,285 battle tanks given by Lieutenant Colonel Charles de Cossé-Brissac in ''Combien de chars Français contre combien de chars Allemands le 10 Mai 1940?'' *Revue de Défense Nationale* (July 1947), 81, to the 146 *automitrailleuses de combat* mentioned by General Maurice Gamelin in Servir (Paris, 1946), I, 157.

2. Heinz Guderian, *Erinnerungen eines Soldaten* (Heidelberg, 1951), p. 429.

3. *Commission d'enquête parlementaire: Les événements survenus en France de 1933 à 1945; Rapport*, Paris 1952), II, 306. (Hereafter abbreviated as *Commission d'enquête: Rapport*); and Gamelin, pp. 157-9.

4. A. Goutard, *1940: La guerre des occasions perdues* (Paris, 1956), p. 84.

5. France, Assemblée Nationale (1947), *Commission d'enquête parlementaire: Les événements survenus en France de 1933 à 1945: Témoignages* (Paris, 1951), I, 169-70 (hereafter abbreviated as *Commission d'enquête: Témoignages*).

6. On the entire question of the nation in arms, see Richard D. Challener, *The French Theory of the Nation in Arms, 1866-1939* (New York: Russell & Russell, 1965). His work is fundamental for an understanding of French military institutions.

7. David B. Ralston, ed., *Soldiers and States: Civil-Military Relations in Modern Europe* (Boston: Heath, 1966), p. 66.

8. See J. Monteilhet, *Les Institutions Militaires de la France, 1814-1932* (Paris, 1932), pp. 110-53.

9. *Journal Officiel de la République Francaise: Documents Parlementaires* (1904), p. 148.

10. Maréchal Philippe Pétain, ''La securité de la France aux cours des années creuses,'' *Revue des Deux Mondes*, 26 (1935), i.

11. Irving M. Gibson, ''Maginot and Liddell Hart: The Doctrine of Defense,'' *Makers of Modern Strategy*, ed. Edward Mead Earle (Princeton: Princeton Univ. Press, 1941), pp. 369-70.

12. Philip C. F. Bankwitz, *Maxime Weygand and Civil-Military Relations in Modern France* (Cambridge: Harvard Univ. Press, 1967), p. 41.

13. Jules Simon, *La politique radicale* (Paris, 1868), p. 181.

14. Monteilhet, p. xvi.

15. France, Ministere de la Guerre, *Instructions provisoire sur l'emploi tactique des grandes unités* (Paris, 1922), p. 11.

16. Général X (anonymous), ''L'armée de métier,'' *Mercure de France*, 267 (1936), 14-15.

17. Léon Blum, ''A bas l'armée de métier?'' *Le Populaire*, December 1, 1934, p. 1.

18. See Général P. A. Bourget, *Le général Estienne, penseur, ingénieur et soldat* (Paris, 1956); and Colonel Georges Ferré, *Le défaut de l'armure; Nos chars pouvaient-ils vaincre en 1940? - Enseignements et perspectives nouvelles* (Paris, 1948).

19. Charles de Gaulle, *The Army of the Future*, trans. Walter Millis (Philadelphia: Lippincott, 1941), p. 77.

20. *Ibid.*, pp. 58, 60.

21. *Ibid.*, pp. 43, 89.

22. Charles De Gaulle, ''Comment faire une armée de métier,'' in *Trois Études*, ed. L. Nachin (Paris, 1945), p. 122.

23. De Gaulle, *Army of the Future*, p. 69.

24. *Commission d'enquête: Témoignages*, I, 223.

25. *Journal Officiel de la République Francaise: Chambre Débats* (1935), p. 1025. (Hereafter abbreviated as *J. O. Ch. Déb.*)

26. *Commission d'enquête: Témoignages*, I, 22.

27. *J. O. Ch. Déb.* (1935), p. 2776.

28. *Ibid.*, p 1045.

29. *Commission d'enquête: Témoignages*, I, 97.

30. *J. O. Ch. Déb.* (1937), p. 297; (1935), p. 1041. See also *Commission d'enquête: Témoignages*, I, 103.

31. The High Command demonstrated its intolerance of any more ''new'' ideas in 1935, stating

that only the High Command was qualified to define military doctrine. Thenceforth, military writings did little more than mirror official doctrine. See Général André Beaufre, "Liddell Hart and the French Army, 1919-1939," in *The Theory and Practice of War*, ed. Michael Howard (New York: Praeger, 1966), p. 140.

32. Pétain, "*La securité de la France*," p. VII.

33. Général Debeney, *Sur la securité militaire de la France* (Paris, 1930), p. 28.

34. Some of the resistance of the military leaders to De Gaulle was undoubtedly due to their awareness of the reaction his ideas were producing in the political community. See Bankwitz, pp. 83-115, 151-67.

35. Pétain, "*La securité de la France*," p. VII.

36. Général Chauvineau, *Une invasion: Est-elle encore possible?* (Paris, 1939), pp. 149-50.

37. *Ibid.*, p. 122.

38. Pétain, "Preface" to Chauvineau, p. XIII.

39. Debeney, *Sur la securité militaire de la France;* "Encore l'armée de métier," *Revue des Deux Mondes*, 28 (1935), 279-95.

40. Debeney, "Encore," p. 283.

41. Général Weygand, "L'état militaire de la France," *Revue des Deux Mondes*, 35 (1936), 724; and "L'unité de l'armée," *Revue Militaire Général*, 1 (1937), 16, 18-19. Interestingly enough, Weygand opposed De Gaulle's ideas even though he had provided for the motorization of five infantry divisions and for the transformation of a cavalry division into a light mechanized division.

42. Maréchal Pétain, "Preface" to Colonel P. Vauthier, *La doctrine de guerre de Général Douhet* (Paris, 1935), p. XI.

43. Général Émile Alléhaut, *Être Prêts* (Paris , 1935), pp. 145, 179.

44. France, Ministry of War, *Instructions for the Tactical Employment of Large Units*, trans. Lieutenant Colonel Richard U. Nicholas (1937 ed.; Fort Leavenworth, 1938), p. 1.

45. *Ibid.*, p. 4.

This article appeared in the summer 1974 issue of *Parameters*.

20

Shaping the American Army of World War II: Mobility versus Power

by RUSSELL F. WEIGLEY

Their kettle-shaped helmets lent a medieval aspect to the horse soldiers clattering out of the twilight. The year was 1940, the occasion a preparedness parade, the helmets actually those of the 1917-18 style. Yet to a small boy catching his first glimpse of America's Army as it readied itself for the new war, the pennant-like guidons drooping in the chill, damp evening as well as the metallic headgear seemed to represent old wars rather than new, a military past yet more remote than the Mexican border skirmishes for which the troopers in fact were outfitted.

Early in the year of the German Blitzkrieg, the American Army was antique enough. There were only two Regular divisions in the continental United States amounting to more than the barest of skeletons, and one of these was traditional cavalry, the 1st Cavalry Division. Both this division and the other that was reasonably ready for combat, the 2d Infantry, were under VIII Corps headquarters at Fort Sam Houston, Texas to guard against trouble spilling across the Rio Grande from restless post-revolutionary Mexico. The 2d Infantry was mostly in garrison at the corps headquarters, while the 1st Cavalry was stretched out along the frontier.

There was a mystique of the horse in the American Army in those days. An artilleryman who distinguished himself later while commanding armor units remembered fondly: "There was nothing more delightful than to move out at the head of my battalion of 75s in the cool of a frosty morning, guns and caissons rolling, horses snorting, and trace-chains rattling as we trotted along the sandy roads."[1]

In August 1940, two months after the completion of the German Army's mechanized conquest of France, the final phase of the American Army's large-scale maneuvers in Louisiana between the IV and VIII Corps opened by pitting horse cavalry against horse cavalry – the latter's 1st Cavalry Division opposed to the 23d Cavalry Division. The 23d's National Guardsmen – from

Wisconsin, Illinois, Michigan, Louisiana, Georgia, and Tennessee – unfortunately had to rent horses for the occasion. The animals they could find turned out to be unsuited for military rigors and had to be removed by truck to rest areas at the end of the second day. But American war was still a war of cavalry horses, artillery horses, and infantry pack mules.

The horses were no mere embodiment of a conservatism suspicious of new military technology. Nor was the American Army's fondness for the horse at all as resonant with a social significance involving the class status of the officer corps as were equine passions in the British Army. Rather, in the American Army the importance of the cavalry was yet more fundamental, the quintessence of all that the Army was or ever had been. Historically, the American Army was not an army in the European fashion. It was a border constabulary for policing unruly Indians and Mexicans. The US Army of 1940 had not yet completed the transition that would have made it an appropriate instrument of its country's claims to world power.

Mobility and Power

The American Army's capacity to transform itself during the next few years was as impressive an achievement as any in military history. The achievement was possible in large part because the immense material resources of the United States were available to support it. It was possible also because the 12,000 to 13,000 officers of the old Army had succeeded in preparing themselves mentally for the transition more than the observer of mounted parades and maneuvers – and polo matches – might have suspected. The officers did so thanks largely to an excellent military school system modeled on European examples and long embedded somewhat incongruously within the frontier constabulary. But the limitations of the Indian-fighting past could not be entirely transcended so soon.

The American officer corps had been able to prepare itself mentally for the transition also because, along with the legacies of the Western frontier, the Army had inherited the traditions and institutional memory of one great European-style war of its own: The American Civil War. The Civil War had molded the American Army's conceptions of the nature of full-scale war in ways that would profoundly affect its conduct of World War II.

Yet the American Army's two principal inheritances from its past were mutually conflicting legacies, which would put the army at cross purposes with itself as it began in 1940 to prepare for European war. The memory of the Western border wars suggested that the primary military virtue is mobility: the history of the frontier was that of the horse soldier in blue or khaki forever challenged by the quicksilver elusiveness of Mexican irregulars or the Indian light cavalry of the Plains. At odds with this vestige from the past, the memory of the Civil War suggested that the primary military value is sheer power: General U. S. Grant's great blue army corps smothering the gray legions of

Robert E. Lee under the weight of their weapons and numbers. To reconcile mobility and power, to arrive at the appropriate military compound of the two, proved the central problem of the transformation of the old American Army of the frontier to the new Army of European war.

The Problem of Weapons

In 1917-18, during the American Army's single brief adventure in European war before World War II, American officers had betrayed hypersensitive awareness that they were embarked on their first contest in the military major leagues. Not the least of their sources of embarrassment was American dependence on foreign weapons for everything beyond shoulder arms and machine guns.

This awkward dependence provoked a postwar shakeup in the Ordnance Department, the Army's designer and in peacetime principal manufacturer of weapons; henceforth, the Department would attempt to ensure that American weapons would adequately serve the combat arms' requirements. One of the changes was a determination that the users of weapons must be able to decide what sorts of weapons Ordnance should provide; previously, the Ordnance Department blandly imposed its own decisions upon the users. This change proved less helpful, however, than might be assumed from the apparent common sense of letting the soldiers who had to face enemy fire decide what they needed to survive and overcome the fire. The Ordnance Department was more closely in touch than the combat arms with European weapon developments. It was consequently aware of and receptive to European tendencies in the late 1930s toward rapid enhancement of firepower through bringing increasingly heavier weapons closer and closer to the front. These European tendencies might have accorded with American strategic predilections about applying overwhelming power, but they conflicted with the attitudes and practices grown habitual in a frontier constabulary charged with patrolling vast distances and needing above all to be mobile.

The Tanks

In the post-World War I US Army, the tank was an infantry weapon. It was officially proclaimed an infantry weapon, and its use was restricted to the infantry by the basic organizational statute governing the Army – the National Defense Act of 1920. This law had terminated the wartime Tank Corps, which had begun to cultivate the notion that tanks were not mere appendages to the traditional combat arms but rather the foundation of a new mode of war. Rejecting such a heretical view, both the legislation and postwar Army doctrine (which each of the traditional combat arms – infantry, cavalry, coast artillery, and field artillery – prepared for itself) regarded tanks as mere aids to the foot soldier in his efforts to break enemy defenses and occupy ground.

Attaching tanks to the infantry might conceivably have encouraged the development of powerful, heavily armed tanks to increase the firepower of the infantry assault as much as possible. The actual effect ran in the opposite direction. If tanks were to assist the infantry, they must be able to move wherever a rifleman might go. Therefore, they must be light and agile. Establishing the principles to guide tank development in 1922, the Adjutant General's Office declared: "The primary mission of the tank is to facilitate the uninterrupted advance of the riflemen in the attack. Its size, armament, speed, and all the accessories for making it an independent force must be approached with the above mission as the final objective to be obtained in development." Specifically, the Adjutant General translated this dictum into a requirement for two basic tank types, both of them small and of necessity lightly armed: a five-ton tank that could be transported from rear areas to the front in trucks along with the infantry, and a "medium" tank that would not exceed the 15-ton weight limit of average highway bridges or of the Army's medium pontoon bridge. An outside limit of 25 tons was superimposed because any vehicle in excess of that weight would be too heavy for the emergency bridges of the Corps of Engineers.[3]

American tanks thus became machine-gun carriers designed to move with the infantry, and armored only against enemy machine guns. As late as 1935, this conception of the tank led to calls upon the Ordnance Department to develop a tank limited to three tons. The arbitrary weight limits of 25 tons at most, and preferably 15, governed the design of medium tanks until 1940 and influenced it thereafter. The Ordnance Department warned repeatedly in the late Thirties that American tanks were falling behind their European counterparts in both guns and armor, but the users persisted in demanding lightness and maneuverability.

In 1935, some ordnance officers urged the mounting of a 75mm pack howitzer in a tank turret, but not until 1938 were they permitted to do so in one experimental tank. By that time, the Germans were experimenting with an 88mm gun in a tank turret; however, the American Chief of Infantry still pronounced the 75mm a useless weapon for a tank. When the rival European armies fought the Battle of France in the spring of 1940 with 75mm guns in the main battle tanks of both sides – the German *Panzerkampfwagen IV* and the French *Char B* – the heaviest gun in an American tank was a 37mm. The War Department's approval to design a tank mounting a 75mm howitzer came not until July 1940. In the spring of 1944, when Anglo-American armies prepared for the invasion of northwest Europe in accordance with the American strategy of direct application of power, Germany's Panther tanks carried long-barrelled, high-muzzle-velocity 75s and her Tigers fired 88s. But the largest gun on an operational American tank was still a short-barrelled, low-muzzle-velocity 75, the standard armament of the then-standard M4 Sherman tank.

Tank Killers

Mobility rather than power similarly shaped the search for weapons with which the traditional American combat arms might protect themselves against enemy tanks. Just after the Armistice of 1918, as a result of concern about the deficiencies of American ordnance in the war, the Army Chief of Staff, General Peyton C. March, appointed a board of ordnance and artillery officers to convene in France, study existing American and foreign weapons, and draw up recommendations for the American artillery of the future. Headed by Brigadier General William I. Westervelt of the Ordnance Department, the Westervelt Board (or "Caliber Board") included among its recommendations development of an antitank gun of about 75mm, based on the board's projections of the strengthening of tank armor. If this recommendation had been heeded, it would have been just about right for World War II. But the War Department actually chose a 37mm antitank gun that served the infantry into the 1930s. When reports of thickening tank armor and new antitank guns in Europe led in 1936 to an effort to modernize the American weapon, the result was merely the adoption during the next year of a new model 37mm gun. By this time the Russians had achieved good results in the battle-testing of a 45mm antitank gun in Spain, and the Germans were adopting antitank guns of from 50mm to 80mm. Nevertheless, in response to questions about the small American gun raised by officers in touch with European progress, the infantry insisted on mobility and lightness and thus on retaining the 37mm gun. In 1938 the War Department explicitly instructed the Ordnance Department to expend no funds in fiscal 1939 or 1940 on antitank guns larger than 37mm.

The European war that began in 1939 swiftly demonstrated the shortsightedness of this decision and the emphasis on mobility alone that underlay it. The 37mm gun could not kill modern tanks, and mobility and lightness were irrelevant if the gun could not do the job it was intended to do. By 1939 and 1940, however, it was late for American gun designers to start catching up. In the spring of 1944, on the eve of the invasion of northwest Europe, the standard American antitank gun had grown to only 57mm, and it remained a weapon that could kill tanks only at short ranges and only by finding their lightly armored flanks, undersides, and treads. By that time, the standard German antitank gun was a mobile 75 mm piece, to say nothing of the Germans' famous dual-purpose 88mm antiaircraft gun that had become the terror of British (and American-made) tanks in the Western Desert.

With American tanks undergunned against enemy tanks, and the American Army lacking suitably powerful weapons with which the ground forces in general might take on enemy armor, an attempted solution consistent with the Army's habitual attitudes and practice developed in the form of the so-called tank destroyer. The tank destroyer was a special pet of the most influential single architect of the American ground forces in preparation for the European war, Major General (from June 1941 Lieutenant General) Lesley J. McNair. Chief of Staff of General Headquarters from its activation in 1940, and then Commander of the Army Ground Forces from March 1942, McNair was a bantam, efficient, decisive – some would say opinionated – artilleryman whose career as a staff officer and instructor and lack of field and combat experience did not temper his assurance that he knew what was good for the troops in combat. McNair's passion was to keep the American Army lean and mobile. Believing that existing tank design was satisfactory because tanks should not fight tanks anyway, he characteristically preferred in a tank killer a bigger gun mounted on a tank chassis, but with the vehicle stripped of heavy armor protection and its turret open to save weight and afford rapid mobility. By 1942, the M10 tank destroyer had become standard – a 3-inch, high-muzzle-velocity, flat-trajectory gun mounted on a Sherman chassis. By 1944, the need for still more gunpower to cope with German tanks brought into service the M18, with a 75mm gun in a shallow open turret on the new M24 light tank chassis, and the M36, an M10 redesigned to accommodate a 90mm gun. The troubles implicit in this effort to unite mobility and gunpower at the expense of a thick skin might have been apparent long before the final report of the First United States Army assessed them in retrospect:

The tank destroyer was created for the primary mission of destroying the hostile armor. Its initial superiority for this mission lay in its superior gun power. With the development of more adequate tank cannon and due to the offensive nature of operations the need for this special-mission type of unit has ceased. During operations tank destroyers were required to assume tank missions for which they were not equipped or trained adequately and to perform secondary missions as roving batteries, direct fire assault gun action, and augmentation of the fire of armored units. The tank destroyer mission as originally conceived has been superseded by the requirements for a killer tank. Tank destroyers should be replaced by a tank which can equal or outgun enemy tanks and which has sufficient armor to protect itself and its crew from normal anti-tank and tank weapons.[3]

In any event, the tank destroyer was no more able than the newer, more heavily armored tanks to go everywhere the infantry went, and so there remained the need for tank protection that the soldier on the ground could take with him – preferably an antitank weapon the infantryman could carry and fire from his shoulder. By the late 1930s, the Ordnance Department had developed an interest in an antitank grenade designed by a Swiss inventor, Henri Mohaupt. The Mohaupt grenade drew its special effectiveness from the shaped- or hollow-charge principle discovered by American physicist Charles E. Munroe as early as 1880: shaping a high explosive with a hollow cone at the forward end focuses the explosive to yield greater penetration per unit weight. Initially the Mohaupt grenade was fired from a spigot launcher resembling a mortar, which did not permit accurate aiming. Years before (in 1918, in fact), Robert H. Goddard of Clark University, the father of modern rocketry, had offered the Ordnance Department his "recoilless gun" or "rocket gun," a portable tube rocket launcher. After the Armistice the Army's interest in Goddard's work languished, but it never altogether died, and in 1941 the Ordnance Department returned to the recoilless gun as an instrument for launching the Mohaupt grenade. At the first test firing of the rocket grenade at Aberdeen Proving Ground in May 1942, the firing tube was dubbed the bazooka because it resembled a curious gas-pipe musical instrument of that name favored by a comedian named Bob Burns.

Unfortunately, the next month the Ordnance Department standardized a

2.36-inch model of the rocket and launcher. Introduced into battle in Tunisia, the bazooka was sufficiently troublesome to German tanks that the enemy soon began fitting *Pzkw IVs* with wire-mesh antirocket screens and eventually put solid metal covering skirts over the vulnerable bogey wheels. But the bazooka, like American antitank guns, was too small. It could not penetrate the heavy front armor of the German tanks. It demanded careful aim against soft spots, which was no easy chore for an exposed, nervous infantryman when a massive German tank came looming up so close upon him that he could hear the pulsating squeak of the bogies. The Germans promptly adopted the bazooka principles, and the resulting 88mm *Panzerfaust* was about twice as powerful. James M. Gavin was a colonel in the 505th Parachute Infantry of the 82d Airborne Division when his troops first used bazookas in Sicily in 1943. Expressing the men's disappointment, he wrote:

As for the 82d Airborne Division, it did not get adequate antitank weapons until it began to capture the first German *Panzerfausts*. By the fall of 1944 we had truckloads of them. We also captured German instructions for their use, made translations, and conducted our own training with them. They were the best hand-carried antitank weapon of the war.[4]

The United States did not initiate a project for a more powerful, 3.5-inch rocket until August 1944.

Some of the weapons with which the American Army entered World War II were excellent. The Western border constabulary had always cultivated expert marksmanship, using superb rifles from the time when rifles first entered general military service. The US Army's Garand .30-caliber M1 semi-automatic rifle was the best standard infantry shoulder arm of World War II. No other rifle of the war matched its combination of accuracy, high rate of fire, and reliability. The standard American medium artillery weapon, the 105mm howitzer, was at least the equal of its German counterpart of the same caliber. The effectiveness of this weapon and every other type of American artillery was multiplied by the best equipment and techniques of any army for fire direction, observation, and coordination. By 1944, the US Army Air Corps had more than caught up with the early lead of the the German *Luftwaffe* in quality of airplanes and tactics for direct support of the ground battle, though air-ground teamwork still left something to be desired.

Nevertheless, while American strategy relied not on maneuver or even on concentration, but on overwhelming the enemy with the exertion of superior power, American weapons had been designed first for mobility, and the weapons could not be counted on for power appropriate to the strategy.

The Infantry

When the Civil War and World War I had demanded that the mobile, frontier-constabulary American Army convert itself into a force of overwhelming power, the power came to reside primarily in Grant's and

Pershing's infantry divisions. In the years following World War I, American soldiers mainly believed that if the call came to apply a strategy of overwhelming power again, once more they would muster big, strong, resilient infantry divisions. In October 1938 the War Department General Staff restated that "the infantry division continues to be the basic combat element by which battles are won, the necessary enemy field forces destroyed, and captured territory held."[5]

The American infantry division of 1917-18 was big, strong, and resilient to the extent of employing about twice the manpower of other nations' divisions. This was the "square" division of four regiments organized into two brigades, the whole some 22,000 strong. From 1935 to 1941, the threat of a new war led the US Army to conduct the largest sequence of maneuvers in its history. Consistently, the American senior officer who boasted the most extensive command experience in World War I, Major General (from August 1939 Lieutenant General) Hugh A. Drum, commander of the First Army, affirmed that the maneuvers proved the necessity to retain the combat endurance and sustained power of the square division of 1917-18.[6]

Increasingly, Drum's colleagues thought otherwise. From the square division's origins in 1917, many officers had objected that it was too hard to maneuver and supply to be fit for anything except static trench warfare. General McNair faulted the square division because it obstructed his passion for mobility. In the late 1930s, McNair was commanding general of a division testing a "triangular," three-regiment structure that dispensed with brigade headquarters and was altogether tailored for lightness and mobility. General Pershing had recommended such a triangular division as early as 1920 as more suitable than the square division for the open, mobile warfare likely to return in the future, and the War Department had tentatively endorsed the design in 1935. As chief of staff of General Headquarters from 1940 to 1942 and later as commanding general of Army Ground Forces, McNair would be the main architect translating the concept of the triangular division into reality.

Under tables of organization drawn up in 1940, the Regular Army divisions shifted from square to triangular form by the time of Pearl Harbor. National Guard divisions were converted only after the United States went to war. In contrast to the square division, the triangular division had 15,514 officers and men under tables of organization of 1 June 1941. By 15 July 1943, General McNair had taken the lead in further paring the American infantry division to 14,253.

McNair's special contribution was to improve the mobility and flexibility of the new division through consistent application of "the sound fundamental," as he put it, "that the division or other unit should be provided organically with only those means which it needs practically always. Peak loads, and unusual and infrequent demands obviously should be met from a pool – ordinarily in the army or separate corps."[7] A combat infantry division should consist solely of combat infantry and the essential supporting arms and the barest necessities of supporting services. There should be no frills; anything beyond basic combat forces that might be required occasionally should be attached only for the occasion, coming when needed from an army or corps pool and then returning to the pool. Nothing unessential should hinder the division's movement. McNair liked his fighting units lean and tough.

The more fully the infantry division adhered to McNair's "sound fundamental" and carried as part of its table-of-organization strength only the men and equipment it would need under practically all conditions, the lighter and more mobile the division became. The more faithfully the whole Army observed the fundamental, putting nothing into a division unless the division "practically always" required it in combat, the more effectively the Army could use its limited manpower and resources. Men and equipment would be wasted if they were placed where they were not constantly used. The military principle of economy of force did not mean getting along with little, it was argued, but making maximum use of available resources, without waste.

Total principal armament of the infantry division designed by McNair was 6518 rifles, 243 automatic rifles, 157 .30-caliber machine guns, 236 .50-caliber machine guns, 90 60mm mortars, 54 81mm mortars, 557 bazookas, 57 57mm antitank guns, 54 105mm howitzers, and 12 155mm howitzers. This was an apparently formidable armament; yet, throughout, mobility rather than power had become the outstanding characteristic of the American infantry division. All elements of the division except the infantry were motorized. With the attachment of only six quartermaster truck companies, the infantry could be motorized as well. Or, as the infantrymen promptly demonstrated in combat, the appropriation of enemy transport and the mounting of infantry on the division's trucks, artillery vehicles, and attached tanks motorized the division still more easily. In pursuit, an American infantry division readily moved on wheels and tracked vehicles. No other army in the world was so mobile.

Whether the 1943 infantry division would prove to be a satisfactory reservoir of power was another matter. In combat power, the triangular division no longer heavily outweighed a German infantry division as the old square division had done, but instead mustered merely comparable strength. When the German Army was on the offensive in 1939-42, however, its infantry divisions played second fiddle to the *Panzer* divisions in exerting the power to achieve breakthroughs. But American armored divisions were not designed with the power to do what *Panzer* divisions had done. Whether the American infantry divisions, deprived of the decisive instruments of power, could suitably carry the burden of a strategy of head-on assault across the English Channel against German strength was the question raised by their remaining the principal locus of the American Army's power.

In 1943, the Americans had scarcely begun to reenact those painful lessons of World War I in the limitations of infantry's offensive power. These of course were the lessons that had driven the Europeans to search for substitutes, culminating in the *Panzer* division. As far back as 1921, Major George C.

Marshall, Jr., writing in the *Infantry Journal*, had warned American officers against generalizing about modern warfare from their 1918 experiences against a German Army already stumbling into exhaustion. American infantry had scored offensive accomplishments against a crippled and weary enemy that it could not expect to repeat against a fresh and first-rate foe.[8] The generalizing proceeded nevertheless, not least in unfaltering reliance on the infantry division as "the basic combat element by which battles are won."

The limitations of the battlefield power generated by the standard infantry division accounted for the custom of attaching a tank battalion to almost every infantry division. The attached tank battalions were to prove themselves essential to the forward advance of the infantry against recalcitrant opposition, and often on defense against enemy armor as well. Yet the attachment of a tank battalion to a division also underlined the defects of the design of the Army. If an attached tank battalion was essential to the effectiveness of the infantry division under most combat circumstances, as it proved to be, then by the logic of McNair's system the battalion should have been organic to the division. The number of separate battalions and the number of divisions did not quite match up. Occasionally in the campaign of France and Germany, an infantry division was to find itself without an available tank battalion, sometimes necessitating the detachment of substitute armor from an armored division, to the detriment of that force, to remedy the deficiency. More important, if the infantry division needed tanks consistently, infantry and tanks should have been able to train together and work together routinely to learn each other's ways. Deficiencies in infantry-tank teamwork were to prove a severe problem in Europe at the outset and a persisting problem even as the campaign wore on. Moreover, because the infantry division required consistent tank support, one tank battalion was scarcely enough. The infantry regiments might rotate and rest their battalions, but the infantry division's single attached tank battalion had to fight on, wearing out men and equipment, as long as the division was in action. Finally, the infantry-tank team especially suffered from the deficiences of the Sherman tank. Heavy firepower and armored protection comparable to the *Panzers'* were more valuable than mobility in a tank working with infantry.

Furthermore, mobile as the American infantry division was, its designers omitted an artillery weapon both mobile and powerful enough to work up close with the riflemen. The towed 105mm gun-howitzer was too cumbersome for this role, as any towed gun would have been. With this weapon, divisional artillery too often had to remain well behind the infantry, working with corps and army artillery rather than contributing uniquely and more directly to the division. The need was for a self-propelled gun able to keep pace with infantry movement, at least comparable to the 75mm self-propelled gun that the Germans used both to support the infantry platoon close at hand in the attack and to assist in repelling enemy tanks. By 1944, the German Army no longer had enough of these guns, to the great good fortune of the Allies; but losses of the guns had been high partly because they served so well and were therefore so much in demand on the Eastern Front. In general, relying principally on towed, roadbound guns meant that the artillery detracted from the mobility that was the primary characteristic of the American Army. This limitation of the artillery, its difficulties in displacing rapidly either forward or toward the rear, would become conspicuous, especially when the American Army had to go into retreat.

Nevertheless, an American officer observed that "We let the arty fight the war as much as possible."[9] For the sustained power that its other components lacked, the American Army had to look to its artillery. From the time American divisions first entered World War II against Germany in 1942, the same Germans who disparaged American infantry consistently praised American artillery. The artillery was the American Army's special strong suit.

For all the deadliness of American guns, there remained enough inconsistencies between the American strategy of overwhelming power, on one hand, and the American Army's actual design emphasizing mobility over power, on the other, that the strategy could have struck deep trouble against an alert, well-disciplined, well-equipped, and battlewise foe. Fortunately for the Americans, the German Army in 1944 as in 1918 would not be the German Army at the peak of its own power. Yet, this foe still had to be respected and feared, and the unresolved conflict within the American Army between the military values of mobility and power was to make his defeat a more difficult task than it need have been. In Normandy in the summer of 1944, and again along the West Wall all through the autumn and well into the winter of 1944-45, the Germans were able to grasp the allies in costly deadlocks, largely because the American Army lacked in force structure the combat power demanded by the Army's own power-drive strategy. After 25 July 1944, artillery, air power, and above all the German enemy's exhaustion were to rescue the American Army from its internal contradictions – but only after excessively high casualty tolls.

Whether the American Army's historic difficulties in balancing power and mobility have been resolved today is an issue that experience in World War II may well make worth pondering.

NOTES

1. Hanson W. Baldwin, *Tiger Jack* (Ft. Collins, Colo.: Old Army Press, 1979), p. 76. The officer quoted is the subject of Baldwin's biography, Major General John S. Wood.
2. Constance McLaughlin Green, Harry C. Thomson, and Peter C. Roots, *The Ordnance Department: Planning Munitions for War*, part of the official history series *US Army in World War II*, Vol. 6: *The Technical Services* (Washington: Office of the Chief of Military History, 1955), p. 190.
3. *First United States Army, Report of Operations, 23 February-8 May 1945*, 1 (Washington: GPO, 1946), 93.
4. James M. Gavin, *On to Berlin: Battles of an Airborne Commander, 1943-46* (New York:Viking, 1978), p. 52.
5. Wesley Frank Craven and James Lea Cate, eds., *The Army Air Forces in World War II*, Vol. 6: *Men and Planes* (Chicago: Univ. of Chicago Press, 1948-58), p. 197.

6. Jean R. Moenk, *A History of Large-Scale Army Maneuvers in the United States, 1935-1964* (Ft. Monroe, Va.: Headquarters US Continental Army Command, 1969), pp. 25, 39.

7. Kent Roberts Greenfield, Robert R. Palmer, and Bell I. Wiley, *The Organization of Ground Combat Troops*, part of the official history series *US Army in World War II*, Vol. 1: *The Army Ground Forces* (Washington: Historical Division, US Army, 1947), pp. 316-17.

8. George C. Marshall, "Profiting by War Experiences," *Infantry Journal*, 18 (January 1921), 34-37.

9. Chester B. Hansen Diaries, US Army Military History Institute, Carlisle Barracks, Pa., 25 June 1944, quoting an unnamed captain of the 12th Infantry Regiment.

This article appeared in the September 1981 issue of *Parameters*.

21

Lessons from the Past for NATO

by RICHARD F. TIMMONS

In some respects it does not appear that NATO, nor the US Army, has taken full advantage of the *Wehrmacht's* experience in confronting large Soviet forces during World War II. That, in a nutshell, is the inference that may be drawn from the recent reflections at the US Army War College of several high-ranking German officers who served in the *Wehrmacht* and had the occasion to observe NATO's military forces, in some cases as officers of the *Bundeswehr*.[1]

That the *Wehrmacht's* large-scale, post-Stalingrad operations offer potentially valuable insights for NATO's defense of Western Europe is virtually a truism. The Germans were defending against an overwhelmingly superior force. The dimension of the imbalance, and the effectiveness of the defense, can be grasped from consideration of the following: in January 1943 the *Wehrmacht* had, on the entire Eastern Front, approximately 500 operational tanks; the Soviets had five to eight times that number; yet the Germans were able to continue as an effective fighting force for more than another two years, even as they were fighting the war in the West and in Italy.

The key to the *Wehrmacht's* success was responsiveness – they were able to make good decisions and execute them rapidly. Several factors are responsible for the *Wehrmacht's* ability to do so, some of which are applicable to NATO today. But to understand the German war machine's superb defense of the Eastern Front, one must understand the context; it will be useful, then, to consider first some of the characteristics of the Red Army in the middle years of World War II.

The Germans considered the higher-level Russian field commanders to be soldiers of high quality and great ability. The caliber of leader and battle captain stopped at the corps level, however; those below often blundered badly at great cost to the Russian army. Marshal Zhukov personified the superb Russian professional; he is reported to have graduated from the *Kriegsakademie* in Berlin in 1935. On the whole, however, Russian leaders and soldiers alike lacked initiative and virtually always sought direction from their superior headquarters. Leadership in small units was especially inferior, as lower echelon leaders relied on "follow the book" solutions with a formality and rigidity of mind that made flexibility impossible and ruled out individuality. At

269

the root probably lay an overwhelming fear of making a mistake and suffering the consequences.

Posted within each unit was a political commissar with authority nearly equal to that of the unit commander; he had the power to exact life-and-death punishments for those found wanting in some aspect of their performance.[2] This threatening aura must have had much to do with why few exhibited initiative and why the units were only capable of conducting one mission at a time and were unable to reverse directions once started; it may also have had something to do with the general attitude of fatalism that seemed to pervade captured Russian soldiers.

The 1943 Russian soldier was thought by the Germans to be temperamental and unstable in battle. He was easy to panic and stampede, especially when confronted by the unexpected, and frequently fled from the battlefield. Mobile, fluid operations characterized by surprise often caused Russian units to break apart; the Russians would abandon both their equipment and their previous gains if panzer units found a flank and ruthlessly pressed the attack. The Russians generally seemed to overestimate the size of the German units when caught off guard, and they were herd-like in their efforts to disengage and break contact.[3]

When fully informed of the situation, and when no unexpected changes confronted him, the Russian could be a stubborn and fanatical fighter. In offensive operations the Russians were masters of infiltration, moving entire units and their equipment through German lines noiselessly to establish strongpoints 10 to 12 kilometers behind the lines. Such strokes were brilliantly executed. Defensive positions were prepared throughout the night, and by morning stocked and dug-in Russian troops would be able to thwart German efforts to eliminate them quickly, except at great sacrifice.[4] The Russians practiced the art of camouflage meticulously and generally were excellent at fieldcraft and the use of terrain.

The Red Army attempted to establish bridgeheads at every opportunity and of every size. This was often done during darkness, which the Russians routinely used to maximum effect. The Germans learned that delay in attacking these bridgeheads or penetration strongpoints could be fatal. The Soviets reinforced such positions steadily and expanded them with tremendous speed and determination, making the lodgements progressively more difficult and costly to clear the longer they were allowed to remain. As a consequence, it became almost automatic for the Germans to attack these sites immediately upon discovery with whatever forces were at hand, even if that meant piecemealing forces.[5]

Tactical sectors for German units on the Eastern Front were large (a 50-kilometer front for a panzer division was not unusual), so combat methods had to be improvised. To the German advantage, the Russians at first were unable to defend or delay effectively, and defeating their units was not difficult. As their experience increased they became more capable, although they were predictable in their use of artillery. German front-line units could anticipate barrages and avoid the consequences of heavy shelling. Even as the Russians improved, they did not practice the concept of coordinating artillery, aircraft, and mounted units to attack in unison. In one instance, the entire tank strength of the 5th Tank Army was destroyed bit by bit because of piecemeal commitment. Despite incredible casualties, however, the Russians were virtually always able to reconstitute decimated units; they regularly reappeared in the order of battle within several days' time. This ability constantly amazed the Germans.[6]

Given these strengths and weaknesses of the Red Army, the Germans learned that responsiveness was the key to conducting a successful defense. Such responsiveness comprises several factors – good intelligence, rapid decision-making, mobility, surprise, and independence.[7] The *Wehrmacht* discovered that exploiting these characteristics was critical.

German corps were able to capitalize on these traits by keeping the headquarters small, mobile, well forward, and capable of reacting rapidly.[8] The decision-making staffs normally numbered only three or four persons – the chief of staff or commander, G2, G3, and G4. They routinely had great trust and confidence in each other and talked frequently each day of the problems and contingencies facing them. The orders given were broad and without details, which were left to subordinate commanders to work out. Normally orders were given face-to-face or over the radio or telephone; they were rarely written in advance, though they always were completed after the fact for historical records and diaries.

This method of operation was possible because the corps commanders routinely spoke in person with their divisional commanders two or three times each day, and this degree of personal contact with subordinates was common for the army commanders as well. With this level of first-hand information, decisions could be made quickly by any commander as he and his staff were fully abreast of almost hourly developments.

Manstein, for example, made decisions very quickly. He told his staff what he intended to do and then asked if it was possible. He expected simple answers to be provided without great detail – then he decided. He left concern for details to others.[9]

Much of the time battlefield operations and techniques had to be improvised because of casualties, terrain, and unanticipated enemy formations or tactics and weapons. No set doctrine held for all situations. But to improvise successfully, the German leaders had to understand completely the current German doctrine and theory for war; then they could deviate from that with the expectation of success.[10]

One important lesson was that panzer divisions should never be used to attack fortified complexes; doing so failed to capitalize on their maneuver value and shock.[11] They were most effective in the counterstroke, where fixing forces held the enemy while maneuver units applied the full measure of their speed, shock, and mobility. This was especially effective if good intelligence was available. In these situations, radio intelligence was extremely valuable in revealing the strength of the enemy units in the opposing order of battle. In at least one major breakout operation, Manstein based his decision on where to punch through Red Army forces on intercepted enemy logistics transmissions that revealed Russian tank strengths unit by unit.[12]

The heart of German orders and operations was the concept of *Auftragstaktik* – mission orders. This was more than a method of giving orders, actually more akin to a habit of thought, and it depended heavily on the quality of the training received by the troops. Usually the commander would provide only a single statement about the operation, consisting of the who, what, when, where, and why. That's all. He was no more specific than that; the job of working out the details was left wholly to the subordinate commander, without supervision.[13]

This method of operation was possible because of the trust that existed throughout the ranks, all the way down to the private soldier. It was simply taken for granted that everyone would exercise initiative to get the mission accomplished.[14] As a result of this faith and trust in the unit's officers, troop morale was extremely high, even in the bitterest fighting. The troops felt superior to the Russians; they believed the Soviets could be beaten despite unfavorable conditions.

Sometimes the tactical situation dictated the degree of detail necessary in the orders. In the open terrain of France in 1940 only three sentences were necessary for the panzers, whereas on the Eastern Front, and later in the war, the conduct of complex withdrawal or defensive operations required more specific information. A typical panzer division order on the Eastern Front from corps would generally include the objective, route, speed, sequence, departure time, and the division commander's new location for the issuance of subsequent orders.[15]

Also of real importance in the German system was the fact that the battle intentions of division and regiment were virtually always made known to the battalions. Changes in operations or missions were simply handled by fragmentary orders issued by the quickest means – radio, telephone, or dispatch rider. But even without orders, commanders and men were expected to use initiative and not to delay necessary actions by waiting for direction from higher headquarters.

Tactical headquarters were kept as far forward as possible. This demonstrated resolve and stability to the soldiers and at the same time permitted the commander and his staff rapidly to size up a battle situation, make timely decisions, and act.[16] These tactical battle headquarters normally had a maximum span of control of about four subordinate units; divisions were not capable of controlling in battle six battalions at the same time. To help overcome span-of-control problems, it was mandatory that subordinate units assign liaison officers to the division headquarters. These were experienced officers who were permitted to see and hear what was going on and then report back to their units with messages, information, maps, orders, etc. Liaison officers were a vital link in the command and control of the division.

In the *Wehrmacht* experience the only way to defeat the Russian attack was to have defenses in depth with mobile reserves on hand to react immediately to enemy advances. As already pointed out, Russian strongpoints established in the rear of frontline defenses had to be eliminated quickly, before the Russians could reinforce them to the degree that they would become severe threats.[17]

The Germans continually sought to keep from piecemealing their tank units to cope with these advances. Panzers would often move at night with the infantry and attack to eliminate those enemy units that had infiltrated in the dark. It was more effective to wait and mass as much of the panzer division during the night as possible, even if the situation was bad. Although difficult to accomplish under the circumstances, unit commanders tried to allocate time for the units to prepare for these unanticipated missions, but this was not always possible.

The critical task for the commander and staff was to identify the *schwerpunkt* of the attack, that is, the main thrust or objective of the enemy effort. Without knowing this it would be impossible to know where and how to react to destroy and defeat him. This was the reason that German doctrine did not espouse killing zones or fire pockets; it was never certain where the enemy would attack, or whether it would be possible to destroy him in the pocket even if he arrived.[18]

When German front-line units were penetrated, they continued to fight independently and worked to reestablish a cohesive defensive line. If ordered to withdraw, the infantry was given a line and boundaries to establish, regardless of pressure. They fought at day and moved at night with little opportunity for rest, often exfiltrating through Soviet units to their rear. Even in these times of great stress, morale throughout the army was generally extremely high. During the great Eastern Front battles in 1943-44, divisions would not know until 1000 hours the next morning the approximate losses from the night before, and the commander would have to walk or drive his front line to discover where his units were positioned. Usually by the end of the day hundreds of the "casualties" reported in the morning would start to filter back in and find their units, having fought independently or having been cut off or wounded since the night before.[19]

This fluid situation demanded spirit and initiative from the troops. Fortunately, defending units were rarely surprised by the enemy attacks because Russian artillery and radio intercepts usually gave away the timing, location, and attack direction of the assaulting ground units. In most cases, the Germans knew everything but the strength of impending attacks. One objective in the defense was to degrade the tempo of enemy attacks by forcing units to deploy at critical points, then mauling the stalled formations in depth. To that end, an effective technique for rapid fire support was to station an air force liaison pilot in a tank close to the tank unit commander to coordinate immediate air strikes on enemy targets of opportunity. While the Germans used air to good advantage, Russian aircraft at this stage of the war had little influence on German operations. In the West, however, Allied Thunderbolts ranged inland throughout France up to 170 kilometers deep, making daytime movement difficult and hazardous.

The German army of this era was still mainly dismounted infantry with many horses in the supply and artillery columns. These units walked to Kursk and back without being destroyed or overrun by Russian mobile units. Despite Guderian's own mobile doctrine, the German infantry kept up. One effort to increase the mobility of the infantry was the formation of motorcycle battalions. These units were employed early in the war and were able to react rapidly, but they suffered too many casualties and were abandoned. Half-tracked vehicles provided much more protection. These Panzer Grenadier units were designed to accompany the tanks in battle as follow-on forces to mop up the bypassed enemy, or to lead on foot if the terrain dictated.

As the war progressed, experience taught that combat groups were the best configurations for battle units. These had artillery, infantry, tanks, and engineers and other specialists as required. Normally they were given the simple order to "Destroy the enemy." The German officers believed that destroying enemy forces was the correct aim and could be achieved by many means. A common mistake of inexperienced commanders was that of holding or focusing on terrain as an objective in itself.[20]

The German way of life had much to do with the education of the soldier and a German's approach to military service. Values such as self-sufficiency, independence, and taking the initiative lent themselves naturally to the development of good professional soldiers. But character came first. Of all things in war it has perhaps the greatest weight. Moreover, it cannot be broken between one's professional and private lives, but is a constant in both realms of a man's existence.[21]

In the *Wehrmacht* it was the subject of direct comment in officer reports, with those identified as lacking this essential quality (or recognized to be "climbers") removed from the service. An adage for the General Staff officer was "to be more than you seem, and do more than you appear to."[22]

At the core of the education of German officers were the ideals of duty, patriotism, and modesty. To these ideals were added such undergirding principles as the ability to take responsibility, intellectual flexibility, initiative, and decision-making strength and simplicity. Through all of an officer's education and training, the individual's decision was honored, and if wrong, corrected without condemnation. To do otherwise would have stifled initiative.

With this educational approach, officers who completed the military schools found it unnecessary to receive detailed specifics from higher headquarters in orders and directives. Their disciplined operational approach, analytical skills, and self-reliance had been instilled throughout the officer corps. Their thinking was not limited to specified doctrine or techniques but had more to do with a professional devotion to fulfilling the commander's intentions. Orders should make the commander's intentions clear; staffs and subordinates thereafter would take the actions needed to bring the intentions to fruition. The system hinged, however, on the selection of quality men for the officer corps; this was a singularly critical component for success.[23]

The officer education process began with a cadet officer being assigned to a unit and living with the troops as a private for six months. Thus all officer candidates learned the basic skills of war that enlisted men had to know. Following successful completion of this stage, the "private" cadet was promoted to corporal and, for the infantry officer, then sent to the infantry school for a year. Having done all this he finally arrived at the regiment, still a cadet, but now permitted to serve as a platoon leader. If he did well and received the recommendations of his superiors, he was given the opportunity to compete for attendance at the *Kriegsakademie* in Berlin by taking competitive examinations, which could be taken at the earliest after only six years' service.

The foundation of the General Staff was the *Kriegsakademie*, where the course of instruction took three years for those selected. Central to the instruction was an emphasis on the need for the officer to estimate a situation quickly, to draw from it the essence of the problem and the critical facts, and then to make quick, clear-cut decisions. Each day's study included different operational problems and compelled each student to analyze them and make decisions. The development and thought processes drove officers to work at least one rank above their present one to prepare them to assume greater responsibilities without hesitation or a lack of confidence.

One highly effective educational aid was the eight-day staff ride that all *Kriegsakademie* officers made under the watchful eye of a senior general. The focus was education of the officers at the division and corps levels, and the ride involved a combination of map and terrain work in the countryside. Each student's work was critiqued by the senior officer present. Of additional value in training officers was a two-sided free-play war game, whose goal really had nothing to do with winning; the game was designed, rather, to train officers to make decisions and to take responsibility and initiative.[24]

Coupled with this excellent military education system, most officers had lengthy service at the regimental level, which balanced the academic with the practical. Before the war, unit commanders would gather their officers in a group and review tactical lessons and procedures as reinforcement of what the schools and their experience had provided. An interesting footnote to this era is that Rommel's book *Infantry Attacks* was used extensively as a training document and was highly influential during the interwar years.[25]

During the war the various branch schools adapted their instruction to the lessons from the battlefield and the capabilities of new German equipment, but the *Kriegsakademie* closed except for a three-month refresher course. As the war progressed, the reduced emphasis on education created problems. Losses among the most skilled and well-trained officers made it necessary to issue longer and more detailed orders and directives; younger officers had not had the benefits of a thorough education, and to get the same results more specific information had to be given to subordinate commanders.[26]

General Heinz Guderian, chief of the armored forces, worked to overcome educational and training handicaps by publishing a bimonthly periodical with the latest information on tactics and equipment, and with useful information on the enemy. He often went straight to the units, bypassing all intermediate headquarters, with material he believed was critical to battlefield success. It was not uncommon for him to arrive unannounced at a battalion headquarters and quiz leaders and men on the latest information he had distributed.

One of the most significant contrasts that might be drawn against the German experience is that units today seem to evaluate procedural particulars that may have little use in combat. One of the keys to the German successes against the Russians was the ability to react quickly, reconstitute, and continue the mission despite the mauling their units endured day after day.[27] Division, corps, and army staffs were small and contained few decision-makers. The decision process was usually very fast and not characterized by exhaustive details and analyses by the staff and specialists. This was accompanied, however, by very competent and detailed ongoing staff work and superb staff planning and execution once decisions had been made. Moreover, the speed with which decisions could be reached was probably a result of the intangible but important intimacy, trust, and confidence the German officers developed among themselves over the many years of military sevice they had spent together. They were essentially familiar with their contemporaries' personalities and professional aptitudes.[28]

Some of the simple procedures used to avoid bureaucratic miring seem obvious enough, but in most armies they never seem to be used with the regularity needed to become ingrained and effective. The commanders generally visited their subordinate units three or four times each day, and the chief of staff went forward every three or four days to remain in touch with actual developments. In this way the key decision-makers were intimately abreast of developments and could quickly make sound decisions. Normally the chief of staff personally called the regiments each hour for situation reports, and every two hours personally called the corps chief of staff to update him. When a commander returned from his visits to the units, the chief briefed him and advised him of the decisions he had made, for the chief exercised the same force of authority as the commander, although it was clear that the commander always carried the weight of responsibility for the command and the final decision. While the commander was afield, he routinely informed the chief immediately if he made any important decisions so that both were constantly in the picture and could act interchangeably. Under such circumstances the chief and commander worked in synchronization in an atmosphere of mutual confidence.[29]

A rhythm was maintained in the headquarters operations whenever possible.

At the division level, orders were routinely received at about 2200 hours for the next day's operations, and by midnight the division had translated those orders into regimental objectives and dispatched them by the fastest means down to the regiments.[30] For a typical corps chief of staff, the most important part of the day was his 0600 staff meeting with the G2 and the G3 to review the latest situation, the plans for the day, and any adjustments that had to be made.[31]

The subject of sufficient planning time for new missions was viewed as an unknown. Units and staffs were not conditioned to expect "sufficient" time to think through each mission given, because in combat there was no way of knowing what the situation would allow. To come to rely on some imaginary increment of time as necessary to execute a mission properly would subtly inject a degree of doubt, if that time did not materialize, into the minds of the leaders before the operation ever commenced. That could create dangerous reservations among leaders and led before battle was joined. The men and unit must simply improvise and conduct the operation to the best of their capabilities under the prevailing conditions.

Intelligence played a continuing and important part of staff operations and was responsible for many successes. In fact, the Germans often had a thorough knowledge of Soviet troop dispositions; history has shown that their intelligence reports were amazingly accurate. The sources used were, in order of importance, radio intercepts, air reconnaissance, POW interrogation – especially of high-ranking POWs, captured documents, German agents behind the lines, and enemy agents.[32]

While NATO cannot duplicate the *Wehrmacht's* officer education and selection procedures and thereby recreate conditions wherein *Auftragstaktik* can be fully employed, it can take other actions to achieve the responsiveness that proved so important during World War II. First, NATO's corps and division headquarters, which are currently huge and unwieldy (both in decision-making and deployment), could be trimmed to the point of streamlined efficiency. They then could be deployed much closer to the front. Also, NATO exercises could be much more productive if made to incorporate free play. This would encourage initiative and boldness, which are essential to a successful defense against a Soviet invasion. Current exercises encourage an outlook reminiscent of the Maginot Line train of thought. In recent years NATO commanders have not participated in the war games except in a most perfunctory way, certainly a destructive trend in terms of developing sound tactics and clear staff officer thinking. We have given over to computers too many functions and so denied commanders and staff officers any real knowledge of the enemy, producing a wholly artificial perception of the realities of European combat.[33]

In addition to reducing headquarters staffs and improving field exercises, the United States Army could probably benefit from adopting some of the attitudes and personnel practices of the *Wehrmacht*. First, it is apparent that the importance of good staff work at the corps level and below was well appreciated in the *Wehrmacht*. This is often overlooked in the US Army; rather than understanding the importance of good staff officers, we too often tend to look upon staff work with some disdain, as something to be avoided if possible.

Second, neither do we appreciate the importance of individual intelligence in selecting officers for military schooling. The OER, which serves as the basis for virtually all selections in the US Army, is an imperfect tool designed to assess job performance. It has no capacity, other than through purely subjective comments, for evaluating potential intellectual abilities. Current procedures preclude the consistent selection of the best-qualified officers for higher military education. Surely we could profit from change in this regard. In the collegiate academic environment, standardized tests ensure that quality students receive the opportunities available from the finest institutions. Indeed, competitive examinations both for promotion and for advanced military education are common in most modern armies; they should be implemented in the American military system as well.

Third, the evidence is strong that German battlefield prowess resulted in large measure from their officer education process. The US Army should take this important cue and realize that German officers were *educated* in their profession, not simply trained. That is, they understood *why* a particular action should be taken, not just *how* to do it. Our schools often assume that a checklist of lessons is sufficient, although the man who created the list is frequently the only one fully able to apply the lessons properly.

Fourth, we should perhaps integrate officer candidates –from all sources of commissioning – with normal basic training. A shared experience forms the basis of a bond of trust and confidence, and graduates of the US Military Academy and the ROTC program routinely share no such common experience with their soldiers. Seeing future officers undergoing the basic soldier's experience should preclude any thought on the common soldier's part that soldiering is demeaning.

Fifth, soldiers of all ranks need to talk with each other candidly and often. Conversations between seniors and juniors should not be the one-way, pro forma sessions so often characterized on screen and page and too frequently emulated in the real Army. Moreover, formal staff briefings, which often inhibit real communication, might productively give way to less rigid discussions between commanders and their staffs. Genuine two-way communication is far more effective for information exchange; we need to pay more attention to what is said than to the form of presentation.

Sixth, the rapid exploitation of accurate intelligence confers a tremendous advantage. The Germans had the capacity to acquire and then use information about the Russians to great benefit. This is a weakness in the US military structure today, despite the staggering array of technical aids that surround the commander. Technology will not pay all the bills however. Doctrine, force structure, training, and education are the stones upon which the timely use of intelligence must be built.

Finally, it may be that the most important lesson is the most obvious, though the least recognized and the most challenging to absorb. The Germans had what can only be described as a "doctrinal anchor" around which the tactical and operational levels of war were built. It was consistent but flexible. Through concept and combat the Germans melded equipment, force structure, unit organization, tactics, techniques, and command and control measures into a battle doctrine which was clearly understood and which inspired great confidence. This was the blitzkrieg.

The American Army has no such doctrinal foundation today. Over the last decade or more, the Army seems to have navigated the doctrinal seas without a rudder, changing course so often as to confuse all the operators and executors from top to bottom. We have finally arrived at a port we expect to build upon in the years ahead, but it is certainly not ready for extensive use today – AirLand Battle. If this were not troublesome enough, blending the doctrinal philosophies and practical aspects of the several NATO partners into a cohesive, energy-charged battle force raises discomforting speculation on its effectiveness, especially when the most influential partner is himself confused. This handicap is not measurable and by its nature is certainly subjective, but it may be NATO's most significant weakness and the one with the greatest potential for exploitation by the Soviets.

In sum, the German experience on the Eastern Front in World War II continues to be a fertile field for ideas regarding our situation in Europe. We need not slavishly emulate the *Wehrmacht*, but we ignore their experiences at our peril. Since the Second World War the nature of soldiers has not changed radically, nor have the classic lessons of maneuver warfare been altered. For these reasons the *Wehrmacht* experience, properly considered, has substantial value and is worthy of serious reviews by all NATO partners.

NOTES

1. During the period 26-30 March 1984, the US Army War College hosted a symposium on operations on the Eastern Front 1942-43 as part of the Art of War Colloquium, an informal society of those dedicated to increasing the professionalism of the US Army officer corps. Entitled "Operations on the Eastern Front 1942-43 and Their Relevance to the Problem of Defending the Central Region of NATO," the symposium was a historic event. It attracted a highly respected group of former German officers and other participants, who freely exchanged experiences and thoughts on the Eastern Front campaigns and NATO. The objective of the symposium was to study large-unit operations against Soviet mechanized forces and to relate the lessons learned from these operations to the employment of mobile warfare in defense of NATO. The German contributors included: General Ferdinand M. von Senger, former NATO CINCENT; General a. D. Graf J. A. von Keilmansegg, Operations Section OKH (WW II) and NATO CENTAG Commander; General Hans von Blumroeder, G2, Army Group South (WW II); General a. D. Gerd Niepold, G3, 6th Panzer Division at Kursk (WW II) and NATO Corps Commander; Generalmajor a. D. Carl Wagener, Chief of Staff, 40th Panzer Corps (WW II), Chief of Staff, 5th Panzer Army (WW II); Generalmajor F. W. von Mellenthin, Chief of Staff, 48th Panzer Corps (WW II), Chief of Staff, Army Group "G" (WW II); Brigadiergeneral a. D. Edward Lingenthal, 11th Panzer Division (WW II) and *Bundeswehr*; Oberst a. D. Helmut Ritgen, 6th Panzer Division (WW II) and *Bundeswehr*; and Dr. Dieter Ose, Historian, Militaergeschichtliches Forschungsamt, FRG.

Other participants were: General Nigel Bagnall, British Army, CINC NORTHAG; Major General J. C. Reilly, British Army, Director of Battle Development; Brigadier Richard Simpkin, British Army, retired; Colonel Paul Adair, British Army; Brigadier General P. H. C. Carew, Canadian Armed Forces, Deputy Chief, Research and Analysis; Lieutenant Colonel Jack English, Canadian Armed Forces; Colonel Wallace Franz, US Army; Lieutenant Colonel David Glantz, US Army; and Professor Bela Kiraly, former head of the Hungarian War College (1951) who campaigned with the Soviets in WW II.

2. Remarks by Generalmajor von Mellenthin.
3. Idem.
4. Idem.
5. Idem.
6. Idem.
7. Remarks by Generalmajor Carl Wagener.
8. Idem.
9. Remarks by General von Blumroeder.
10. Remarks by General von Kielmansegg.
11. Remarks by Generalmajor von Mellenthin.
12. Remarks by General von Blumroeder.
13. Remarks by Generalmajor Carl Wagener.
14. Remarks by Generalmajor von Mellenthin.
15. Remarks by General Gerd Niepold.
16. Remarks by Generalmajor Carl Wagener.
17. Remarks by Generalmajor von Mellenthin.
18. Remarks by General Gerd Niepold.
19. Idem.
20. Remarks by Generalmajors von Mellenthin and Wagener.
21. Remarks by General von Kielmansegg, General von Blumroeder, Generalmajor Wagener, Generalmajor von Mellenthin, Brigadiergeneral Lingenthal.
22. Remarks by Generalmajor Carl Wagener.
23. Idem.
24. Remarks by General von Kielmansegg.
25. Remarks by Generalmajor von Mellenthin.
26. Remarks by General von Kielmansegg and Generalmajor Carl Wagener.
27. Remarks by General von Senger.
28. Remarks by General Gerd Niepold.
29. Remarks by Generalmajor von Mellenthin.
30. Remarks by General Gerd Niepold.
31. Remarks by Generalmajor von Mellenthin.
32. Remarks by General von Blumroeder.
33. Remarks by General von Senger.

This article appeared in the autumn 1984 issue of *Parameters*.

22

In the Laps of the Gods:
The Origins of NATO
Forward Defense

by JAMES A. BLACKWELL, JR.

In my opinion as a military man . . . the people of Western Europe, with our assistance, and given time, can build up a sufficient force so that they would not be driven out of Western Europe. Now just exactly where they could hold . . . is in the laps of the gods.

– General J. Lawton Collins
Chief of Staff, US Army
19 February 1951

The military strategy of the North Atlantic Treaty Organization is two-pronged, consisting of the principles known as flexible response and forward defense. While the flexible response doctrine has been subjected to intense scrutiny since its promulgation in 1967, the forward defense strategy more often has been neglected by analysts. This article addresses this less thoroughly examined side of NATO strategy, exploring the operational origins, rather than the strategic or political origins, of the forward defense strategy in the formative years of the alliance, 1945-55.

NATO's historians have traditionally agreed that in the early years the strategy of forward defense was mainly a political and psychological necessity to ensure eventual German rearmament and participation, as well as to allay French fears of a defeated *Reich* rearmed for the second time in half a century. The Allies did not believe that it was a strict military requirement to protect every square inch of West European soil with forces in being. Many modern-day commentators argue that since the Allies have constructed a layered scheme of national corps sectors across the inter-German border from north to south, NATO plans to fight a hopelessly linear forward defense. These conclusions are, at best, incomplete.

It is revealing to trace the military implementation of the strategy of forward defense through the early years of Allied defense planning. From the perspective of the operational level of war, it becomes apparent that the forward strategy was then, as it is now, subject to wide variation in interpretation in spite of the political unity that prevailed in the articulation of the strategy itself.[1]

This variation derived from many sources, but principally from differing operational concepts, contrasting national styles of war, and the clash of military personalities.

Initial Planning: 1945-49

On Victory in Europe Day, 8 May 1945, the armies of the Western Allies had three enormous tasks ahead of them: occupation, redeployment to the Pacific Theater, and demobilization. By the winter of 1945-46, the absence of a fighting enemy, combined with the problems inherent in demobilization and redeployment, caused a serious deterioration in the battle-seasoned units of one of history's largest land armies. The discipline, morale, and supply problems in Europe were of such proportions that General Eisenhower's first replacement as commander of US forces in the European Theater, General Joseph T. McNarney, remarked that his troops "could operate in an emergency for a limited period at something less than 50 percent normal wartime efficiency."[2]

Yet as Allied soldiers indulged themselves in the spoils of victory and awaited their turn to go home, Western leaders grew more concerned with the postwar intentions of the Soviet Union. On 12 May 1945, British Prime Minister Churchill sent his "Iron Curtain" telegram to President Truman. That same month, Field Marshal Montgomery, in command of occupation forces in the British sector, was ordered not to destroy any more captured German arms, "in case they might be needed by the Western Allies for any reason."[3]

By the time of Churchill's "Iron Curtain" speech in the United States in January 1946, military planners in the West began to redirect their thinking from occupation duties to contingency planning for the possibility of an attack from the Red Army, which had neither demobilized nor redeployed to the extent that British and American forces had. American occupation forces by July 1947 were stabilized at a low point in strength of 135,000 troops, a level at which they remained until the early 1950s.[4] The US forces had been reorganized in 1946 into three components: a constabulary – roughly a division in size – dispersed in small units throughout the American sector; the 1st Infantry Division; and various theater and military government supporting units. Secretary of State James F. Byrnes signalled a formal change in the attitude of the American government as to the purpose of these troops in a speech at Stuttgart on 6 September 1946, when he indicated that the Americans were now in Germany not only for occupation, but also for defense.

Accordingly, the constabulary was given primary responsibility for maintaining law and order, and the 1st Infantry Division was assigned a reserve mission to be ready to block any Russian advance. As the events of 1947 in Berlin, East Europe, and Greece were marked by the creation of Bizonia, the Marshall Plan, and the Truman Doctrine, US military leaders more fully comprehended the implications of the Cold War. On 4 August 1947, after the June failure of the Allied talks on troop withdrawals, the US military governor,

General Lucius D. Clay, sent a wire to his superiors concerning a British proposal to the Americans for unilateral withdrawals; in his opinion the idea of leaving Western Europe in large numbers was tantamount to abandoning Germany to the communists.[5]

While American military planners were reorienting their thinking, Montgomery, now preparing himself for his future duties as Chief of the Imperial General Staff, directed his own Occupation Zone Staff in May 1946 to prepare a paper discussing defense against an external threat. In that paper he argued for a British presence on the Continent alongside potential allies.[6] Montgomery submitted his staff paper to the Ministry of Defense amid frequent trips back to the Continent in 1947 to inspect the British Army of the Rhine. By December 1947, the joint planners in the Ministry of Defense had considered his paper and proposed three possible strategies in the event of a Russian attack: an air offensive; a Continental defense; or a Pyrenees defense, followed by a liberation operation based from Spain and Portugal. The preference of the Ministry of Defense staff was the air strategy, with the land defense of the Continental strategy being summarily dismissed. Montgomery's reaction was not subtle: "I blew right up, saying that I disagreed completely . . . . We must defend Western Europe, not liberate it."[7]

While British Foreign Secretary Ernest Bevin was preparing to make his public call for a Western European Union in January 1948, Montgomery was personally preparing a response to the Defense Ministry's European strategy paper. In his reply, dated 30 January 1948, he not only reiterated his argument for a conventional land defense, he also proposed his formula for effecting his strategy: "We must agree that, if attacked, the nations of the Western Union will hold the attack as far to the east as possible."[8] This is the earliest public record of an official postwar reference to a forward defense of Europe. Thus, at the operational level of war, Montgomery should be credited with being a fundamental proponent of forward defense.

Bevin's Western European Union proposal was welcomed, of course. The Brussels Treaty, signed on 17 March 1948, marked the beginning of joint military planning by Western armed forces. The first steps were the appointment of a military committee and the selection, in late September 1948, of Field Marshal Montgomery as Chairman of the Commanders-in-Chief Committee, with headquarters in Fontainebleau, France. His committee began its planning in secrecy, but immediately came under public scrutiny and criticism as a debate ensued over where the defensive line should be drawn in Europe.

The public discussion was wide-ranging. Arguments were heard from a number of sources, contending that the line ought to be drawn variously at the Vistula, Oder-Neisse, Elbe, Rhine, Brittany Peninsula, or Pyrenees Mountains. In particular, the French generally were suspicious of British intentions to defend the Continent, based on their initial experience in the two previous world wars. Although Montgomery publicly declared, "Together we will fight to prevent this and we will win,"[9] many Frenchmen remained unconvinced. In the words of one French official, "If we must one day evacuate France it must not be a British officer who orders it."[10] General De Gaulle joined in this sentiment with his own brand of French nationalism, decrying alleged British intentions of planning an early withdrawal from the Continent in the event of a Soviet attack.[11]

As the Berlin crisis carried over into 1949, the public debate intensified and concern over American intentions rose. On 28 February 1949, French Premier Henri Queille pleaded for the United States to prevent a Soviet advance beyond the Elbe.[12] He expressed his concern graphically in a later interview when he said, "We know that once Western Europe was occupied, America would again come to our aid and eventually we again would be liberated. But the process would be terrible. The next time you probably would be liberating a corpse."[13] French Prime Minister Paul Ramadier gave official endorsement of the strategy of forward defense. In response to questions from the French communist opposition he mentioned the Rhine River as a defensive line, but then concluded, "We shall endeavor to halt the aggressor as far as possible from our frontier."[14]

Finally, once the North Atlantic Treaty was signed on 4 April 1949, the United States committed itself publicly to the concept of forward defense. The day after the signing of the treaty, General Omar N. Bradley, then Chairman of the US Joint Chiefs of Staff, said in a speech to Jewish war veterans in New York that America's commitments "have carried its international obligations east of the river Rhine."[15] Thus, at least in public, the Allies were agreed in principle that Western Europe must be defended forward. However, while the North Atlantic nations were publicly subscribing to the forward strategy, military planners were facing up to the realities of the military balance in 1948-49.

The Soviet Union could count on perhaps a hundred fully combat-ready divisions within a short time, including 22 in place at full strength in Eastern Europe which needed only orders to attack – contrary to the then-popular notion that they needed only shoes, which of course they already had. The Western powers had only ten divisions, all of which were at less than full strength and readiness, and no quickly available reserves.[16] On 16 June 1948, the Allied Commanders-in-Chief – US General Clay, British General Robertson, and French General Koenig – agreed that the Rhine would be the defensive line in the event of an attack, and requested the immediate appointment of a supreme commander and the formation of an Allied staff to plan the "coordinated defense of the Rhine."[17] In August came the authority to conduct the planning effort, and General Clay could inform his superior, General Bradley, that a tripartite staff had begun its work in Wiesbaden. This staff operated in accordance with a directive that discussed plans to defend along the Rhine River, specifically incorporating the work of previous consultations which already had provided for initial positioning of forces.[18]

Thus, despite the somewhat ambiguous public statements on the nature of the notion of forward defense, and despite the lack of a formally integrated military structure or a supreme commander, there were by mid-1948 three separate but coordinated plans for a defense on the Rhine River, and there was a committee tasked to prepare a more fully developed combined forces plan. The military commanders of the occupation zones, recognizing that the defense of the separate zones had to be coordinated, anticipated that a more formal Allied command structure would be established in the event of war. They were reluctant to delay planning on the formation of Western European Union organizations, so they prepared the contingency plan for forward defense at the operational level in an informal, somewhat ad hoc fashion, knowing that if war came they would be held accountable for stopping the Red Army.

In September 1948 Montgomery became Chairman of the WEU Defense Organization. His first task was to select the high-level staff officers who would work with him in conducting the overall planning effort and who would hold, presumably, although not by explicit agreement, supreme command over the Brussels Treaty forces in the event of war. He selected British officers for the air and sea staff positions, but looked to the French for a land force representative. Montgomery reasoned that the French would make the greatest contribution to the land forces, and he was aware of French sensitivities to British command over Continental defense.

The first choice for the land forces position was General Alphonse-Pierre Juin, who declined the position. It was suggested in the press that General Juin shared General De Gaulle's misgivings about British domination of Western European Union forces, and for that reason did not take up the post.[19] The job then fell to General de Lattre de Tassigny, who had commanded the French First Army under US General Devers in the Southern Army Group during the Allied forces European offensive. General de Lattre brought with him an officer named André Beaufre, who would later become a significant contributor in his own right to forward defense concepts. By mid-November 1948, Montgomery's staff had pieced together the first joint defense plan for the WEU.

This plan was much more than the earlier effort of the local commanders to coordinate their separate defense plans. It called for three potential operations, depending on the level of forces available to the WEU on the Continent at the time of attack. The initial plan, based on existing force levels, was called the Short-Term Plan; it called for an emergency evacuation of the Continent behind a forward delaying action and a stout defense at the Pyrenees.[20] At a second level was the Medium-Term Plan, so named in anticipation of the time it would take to generate the forces necessary to implement it and to shift the logistical infrastructure away from the relatively exposed north-south axis of the occupation forces to a more secure east-west system. This plan called for a mobile defense in which the US constabulary, organized into armored cavalry units, would conduct the screening operation east of the Rhine along the border, in front of 18 divisions between the border and the Rhine. The bulk of the WEU forces, 36 divisions, would be employed in defensive positions along the Rhine River. This force was to hold the Rhine until European and American reserves could be mobilized and deployed in a counteroffensive to force the aggressor's withdrawal back to the east.[21] The third plan, the Long-Term Plan, anticipated the day when up to 100 divisions would be available in Europe to conduct a linear defense along the border between East and West Germany. There apparently was no plan to construct heavy fortifications; rather, the divisions would be deployed to take advantage of terrain favorable for defense, weighting forces along the more vulnerable avenues of approach.[22]

Despite later public statements, there developed at about this time some important differences in approach between the French and British staffs at Fontainebleau.[23] To be sure, it was agreed by all that existing forces were incapable of holding even at the Rhine.[24] The disagreement arose over where the line of the main defensive effort was to be drawn once the Brussels Treaty states began to meet their commitments for additional forces. For the British, especially Montgomery, forward defense would be achieved by screening and delaying forces between the Elbe and the Rhine, with the Rhine River being the line along which the final stand would be taken.[25] To the French, particularly to General de Lattre de Tassigny, forward defense meant a stand closer to the Iron Curtain.[26] Thus there might have been a difference of opinion amounting to as much as 150 kilometers, considering the depth of the Fulda-Mainz corridor.

This first period of Western European military planning was marked by significant differences between the British and the French in the operational dimension of war. Although much of the planning at first consisted of ad hoc efforts, the military commanders recognized a need to be prepared to fight the Russians. The differences were both conceptual and personal, and they were present not only between Allies but sometimes, as in the British case, within the defense establishment of a single country. The formation of the WEU Defense Organization resulted in a coordinated plan, but the Union did not reduce the effect of the differences because it lacked sufficient troops to do much more than protect an evacuation of the Continent, and because it lacked a supreme commander with the authority to resolve the differences. But the danger of the Cold War suddenly going hot in 1950 soon imparted a sense of urgency at the operational level that was to produce temporary resolutions.

A Sense of Urgency: 1949-52

Although the Berlin Airlift had been an overwhelming success by May 1949, and the April signing of the North Atlantic Treaty had seemed to signal for the Allies that the Russians might be contained in Europe with no further encroachments on the Free World, a number of subsequent events rapidly brought to the West a fear of imminent war with the Russians in Europe. The announcement on 22 September 1949 that the Soviet Union had detonated an atomic device caused consternation in Western military circles, more because of the unexpected quickness with which the Soviets had developed the bomb than from fear of their ability to deliver it in 1949 or 1950. The second event was the outbreak of the Korean War, half a globe away, in late June 1950. The Korean attack seemed to signal a Soviet willingness to use armed force in the Cold War, and Western Europe looked like an easy target for the massive Red Army in Eastern Europe. What had become obvious by late 1949 was that any defense of Western Europe, forward or otherwise, would require a contribution of troops in some form from West Germany. The unanimity of this view among the Western Allies did not, however, lessen the differences in approach to Continental defense, especially between the French and British military planners.

In the fall of 1949, Montgomery had told Bevin that a German contribution to WEU forces would be necessary. In November, Monty carried the same message to President Truman and to General Eisenhower – then President of Columbia University – in the United States.[27] Equally obvious was the implication that if the conquerors were going to expect the conquered people to provide soldiers to oppose the new enemy, the territory of the occupied country would also have to be included in the defense plans. Accordingly, the protection of the North Atlantic Treaty was extended to Germany, and the doctrine of forward defense was adopted by the North Atlantic Council in its September 1950 meeting.[28]

The Brussels Treaty powers merged the military planning organizations of the Western European Union with analogous NATO structures in December 1950, and General Eisenhower was appointed the first Supreme Allied Commander Europe (SACEUR) on 19 December. Supreme Headquarters Allied Powers Europe (SHAPE) was activated on 2 April 1951, and by February 1952 the council at Lisbon approved force goals for the implementation of the forward strategy. It is significant that in the September 1950 communique, ''forward defense'' was not established on any specific line, nor even was it specified that the defense would be mounted ''as far east as possible.'' Indeed, the term ''forward defense'' is used nowhere in the text. Thus, the military planners were allowed some room for interpretation as to the operational implementation of forward defense.

Using this latitude on interpretation, the military planners prepared an operational concept that was in accordance with the spirit of the forward strategy, yet which sought to minimize the risk of a military defeat in the face of overwhelmingly unfavorable force balances. The solution was a mobile defense, calling for a delaying operation from the intra-German border westward to a final defensive stand along the Rhine. The defensive force would be required to hold until reinforcements from mobilized Continental reserves and from the United States, Canada, and Great Britain could be formed and launched into a counteroffensive.

The newly formed SHAPE staff began its work by drawing upon the staff work done by the Western European Union Defense Organization, the Short-, Medium-, and Long-Term Plans. In the summer of 1950 the WEU had conducted an exercise under General de Lattre de Tassigny called "Triade." This exercise tested the ability of the deployed forces to conduct defensive operations to stop an attack. According to General Beaufre, both British and French Ministers of Defense concluded that the exercise was a success[29]. The plans called for stiff fighting east of the Rhine, using delaying tactics in order to stop the Red Army as far east as possible. In March 1951, the operational plans were being implemented; roads and bridges east of the Rhine were prepared for demolition, an important indicator of the plan to fight a delay east of the river.[30]

The fact that SHAPE was planning a mobile defense became clear in the public testimony of US officials in February 1951 Senate hearings on stationing US troops in Europe. At those hearings, General of the Army Omar Bradley, Chairman of the Joint Chiefs of Staff, spoke of the "greater depth" that NATO forces could fight in with the four divisions that the United States planned to deploy in Europe.[31]

General J. Lawton Collins, Chief of Staff of the Army, stated clearly that a mobile defense was planned, using demolitions, antitank weapons, and mobile reserves,[32] all characteristics of a mobile defense rather than a linear or area defense. The Chief of Naval Operations, Admiral Forrest P. Sherman, confirmed that delaying tactics would initially be employed.[33] Even the Air Force Chief of Staff, General Hoyt S. Vandenberg, supported the delaying operation,[34] although other unofficial air power advocates at the hearings argued that ground forces might not be necessary at all in the light of the capabilities of the Strategic Air Command.[35] In retrospect, Drew Middleton's report in September 1951 on SHAPE's plans was probably accurate: "deliberate withdrawal in front of the Soviet attack across the North German plains and through the Fulda gap, followed by concerted attacks on the flanks of the Soviet advance by strong forces stationed around the base of the Jutland Peninsula and in the area of the Main River."[36]

The official pronouncements by the North Atlantic Council in September and December 1950 thus gave SHAPE planners some leeway in planning for a forward defense which would conform to the realities of the military balance of the early 1950s. The mobile defense concept would ensure that the Russians would meet some organized resistance from the moment they crossed the border, but Allied delaying tactics, with large forces refusing to become decisively engaged, would prevent an early defeat at the hands of a foe with superior numbers. The Lisbon Conference of February 1952 called on Alliance members to provide sufficient forces by 1955 to mount a credible defense east of the Rhine without giving up territory. Nevertheless, critics of SHAPE's operational concept were quick to point out that the planned delay looked very much like an American and British plan to abandon the Continent in the event of an attack, much like the WEU Short-Term Plan.

In spite of repeated denials by General Eisenhower himself, this criticism persisted.[37] The principal sources of criticism were the French Gaullists and the West German Social Democrats. It is not insignificant that both groups were in the opposition to their governments in their national legislative bodies. For the West German Social Democrats (SPD), the issue was not so much forward defense as it was the implication of the strategy for the issues that the SPD considered most important: rearmament and reunification. The SPD leader, Kurt Schumacher, spoke in 1950 of establishing Western protection for Germany, "such as to enable a military decision on the Vistula and Niemen."[38] After initially voicing the SPD's opposition to *Vorfeld-Verwendung* (forefield employment) because of inadequate plans to rearm Germany, Schumacher late in September 1950 said, "We are ready to bear arms once again if, with us, the Western Allies take over the same risk and the same chance of warding off a Soviet attack, establishing themselves in the greatest possible strength on the Elbe."[39] For the SPD, apparently, a mobile defense was not an adequate return on the investment of Germans to rearm themselves. Chancellor Adenauer nevertheless contended that the September 1950 decision marked the end of a Rhine defense and the beginning of Allied abilities to mount a forward defense beginning at the border.[40]

In France, De Gaulle continued to allege that the true intention of the United States and Britain was to abandon the Continent in case of war. He pointed to the concept of a delay as merely a cover for another Dunkirk-style evacuation. Although Eisenhower appointed Marshal Juin to replace de Lattre de Tassigny as land force commander, De Gaulle was not appeased. He argued that the Allies were not committed to defense of the Continent, but were "disposed to limit their effort to defense of a few points: England, Spain, a Breton redoubt."[41]

De Gaulle's reference to "a Breton redoubt" was apparently taken from an account of General Eisenhower's congressional testimony in 1951. Although General De Gaulle's accusation may have been politically motivated with a view toward getting votes in the upcoming French national election, Eisenhower felt it was serious enough to warrant a public denial.[42] Furthermore, De Gaulle's charges were not without a basis in fact. As President of Columbia University, Eisenhower had said in October 1950, before the North Atlantic Council asked Truman to make him available for the SACEUR position, that American soldiers should not be stationed outside our continental limits; rather, they should serve as a global central reserve.[43] Other American conservative leaders had taken a similar public stance. For example, Senator Taft urged that the United States could not hold the Elbe line, and that therefore we ought to concentrate instead on the Navy and Air Force for defense.[44] In his congressional testimony in February 1951, General Eisenhower reworded his position but did not categorically support stationing US troops in Europe.[45] No amount of reassurance from the Americans could subsequently assuage the fears of the German and French opposition parties.

In spite of the misgivings of the aspirants to political power, the February 1952 Lisbon Conference marked a unity in the Alliance at the operational level that certainly has not been achieved since. The widely accepted perception of the willingness of the Soviet Union to use force to achieve its hegemonic goals served to rejuvenate the wartime alliance relationships among the Western powers, particularly under the leadership of the former Supreme Commander of the coalition armies. As economic realities set in to cast doubt on the attainability of the Lisbon force goals, and as concern over Soviet use of force declined, the unity began to erode.

Stretch-Out: 1952-55

The Lisbon force goals were overly optimistic in terms of the Allies' abilities to provide fully combat-ready divisions for the Central European region. Indeed, there are, among those who participated in the Lisbon talks, some who believe that many Alliance members knew they could not meet their commitments even as they were making them.[46] This period was a time when the military planners occupied themselves with somehow reconciling the need for a forward strategy with the lack of sufficient conventional forces to conduct a defense at the border.

One potential solution that began to receive serious attention early in 1952 was the use of nuclear weapons to stop a Russian breakthrough east of the Rhine. General Beaufre was given the task of studying this potential, even as SHAPE's staff had completed its plans for the conventional mobile defense.[47] While General Beaufre began work on what was to become the important nuclear doctrine, two events dominated SHAPE in April 1952. The first of these was an early command cell exercise, which was held 2-13 April. The second event was Eisenhower's replacement on 28 April by General Matthew B. Ridgway.

The SHAPE exercise of April 1952 was the first of its kind. It was important not only for its role as a vehicle for practicing agreed NATO strategy and operations, but also for the method involved in the conduct of the exercise. In the event, known as "Venus de Milo" (no arms and all SHAPE[48]), the mobile defense was exercised on maps by SHAPE commanders and staffs under the overall supervision of the Deputy SACEUR, Field Marshal Montgomery. Montgomery handled it as a classroom exercise, challenging participants to react instantly to his prepared scenario.[49] By controlling the scenario and the procedures for this and subsequent exercises at SHAPE, Montgomery was able to influence the particular interpretation of forward defense practiced by SHAPE in the early years. Thus the idea that the Russians would concentrate their drive along the North German Plain approach came out of these "teaching exercises in which the great tactician lectured to his subordinate NATO commanders and their staffs in an entertaining but very positive way."[50] Montgomery would then have the main Soviet attack come out of the

Magdeburg area, cross the Weser River, and dash to the Channel ports. He considered the larger Central Army Group region to be the more easily defensible, thus rendering a Soviet main effort there unlikely.[51]

The second critical event of April 1952 was Eisenhower's replacement as Supreme Allied Commander Europe by General Matthew B. Ridgway. In leaving the post to seek the Republican nomination for the US Presidency that year, General Eisenhower reported on the year's activities at SHAPE to the Standing Group. In this report, he stated his desire to have the forces required to fight a defense in depth in Europe.[52] In his assessment, NATO was not yet capable of forward defense at the Rhine River: "As of today, our forces could not offer prolonged resistance East of the Rhine barrier."[53] With General Eisenhower went a certain ability to produce consensus and urgency in operational matters among the Allies.[54]

General Ridgway ran head-on into the problems of differing national perspectives and personality conflicts as SACEUR. General Ridgway faced great problems of suspicious partners who doubted that French, British, or American troops would defend the smaller countries forward.[55] In responding to these suspicions, Ridgway went so far as to speak personally to the Dutch cabinet at length to reassure them of the intentions of SHAPE to defend the territory of all members of NATO, but made clear that he would fight a delaying action rather than risk losing his entire force by taking a final stand too far forward.[56]

General Ridgway had a particularly difficult time resolving the personality conflicts within SHAPE. This was especially true in his own relationship to his Deputy Supreme Commander, Field Marshal Montgomery. By this time Montgomery had seen several Western European staffs come and go: two of his own in the Western European Union Defense Organization, and before that his staff in the British Occupation Zone, as well as Eisenhower's first SHAPE staff. Now he was to be subordinated to an American who had been a two-star general and division commander during the D-Day invasion, at a time when Montgomery had already been appointed a Field Marshal, the equivalent of a four-star general. Ironically, during the Normandy operation, Ridgway had worked under Montgomery in the Army Group responsible for the northern portion of the Allied invasion. At the outset of his new command, General Ridgway attempted to defuse any potential misunderstandings with Montgomery as to who was in charge; but apparently Montgomery would take matters into his own hands. Occasionally the Deputy SACEUR would give unofficial, personal recommendations to field commanders that were contrary to official SHAPE policy. When Ridgway would confront him with such veiled disloyalty, the result was less than satisfactory: " 'You're right Matt,' he'd say. 'You're quite right.' Then he'd go out and do it again."[57] Meanwhile, the public debate over forward defense was renewed as the failure to meet the ambitious Lisbon force goals became publicly apparent.

In the summer of 1952 there were a number of reports that the French had arrived at a concept of a withdrawal into a "French Fortress" if the Russians were to attack in central Europe.[58] These reports drew repeated denials from SHAPE in the fall of 1952 upon the conclusion of a large-scale maneuver involving NATO forces, including the newly deployed US, French, Belgian, and Dutch units, practicing delaying operations east of the Rhine River in Exercise Rosebush.[59] However, these denials failed to clear up the confusion regarding SHAPE's intentions, because SHAPE spokesmen seemingly contradicted each other. Specifically, Marshal Juin issued a statement in September 1952 asserting that his NATO land forces could delay east of the Rhine and hold firm at the river.[60] Juin's statement elicited an immediate critical response from the German Social Democrats who demanded a defense farther east.[61] In response to this demand from the SPD, the US forces commander in Europe issued a statement the following day, pointing out that in delaying operations terrain sometimes is traded for time, but denying that Exercise Rosebush revealed any operational plans for wartime contingencies.[62]

The apparently contradictory statements coming out of SHAPE caused consternation at the diplomatic level. At the Council of Europe's Consultative Assembly, J. J. Fens, from the Netherlands, condemned any prepared plan to relinquish territory.[63] This brought a response from General Ridgway himself, who reiterated the mobile defense concept and again called for large numbers of reserves.[64] Marshal Juin rephrased his declaration into terms more acceptable to critics in the West German SPD.[65] Finally, the Standing Group itself stepped in to reassure the Allies of SHAPE's intentions, and it "reiterated the accepted strategy, namely the defense of all peoples and territories for which the North Atlantic Treaty Organization is responsible."[66]

Despite the best of intentions, the SHAPE staff was unable to convince its critics in this period that its concept of a mobile defense between the Rhine and the intra-German border was the most forward defense possible within the constraints of the conventional forces that were available or planned for in 1952. By the autumn of 1952, the operational planners began to look seriously to battlefield nuclear weapons as the primary guarantor of forward defense at the border.

In September 1952, General J. Lawton Collins, US Army Chief of Staff, told a NATO press conference that atomic weapons "will result ultimately in the ability to do the job with a smaller number of divisions."[67] The first attempt to integrate nuclear weapons into SHAPE plans involved a plan to use atomic devices to destroy the Soviet army while keeping NATO forces deployed as they would be in a nonnuclear defense; it was known as the Ridgway Plan of 1952-53.[68] The results of war-gaming this plan were that conventional forces were destroyed faster and more completely in the firepower of atomic weapons, generating requirements for even more replacements of conventional forces to maintain the forward defense.[69]

The planners therefore started over by reexamining their assumptions and strategic concepts. The result was a plan called the New Approach doctrine of

1954-56, which "called for a tactical nuclear response to Soviet aggression in Europe from the outset."[70] This strategy was a trip-wire operational concept in which conventional forces were not needed for maneuver; instead, "manpower requirements are limited to those needed to force concentrations on the attacker, identify these . . . and deliver the nuclear firepower."[71]

General Beaufre confirms that the conventional forces took on the role of a trip-wire under the New Approach strategy.[72] US Secretary of State Dulles announced the strategy in his January 1954 "Massive Retaliation" speech. This strategy was not particularly secret[73] but the issue of the tactical use of nuclear weapons in forward defense, so controversial in later years, was lost in the background of the major issue of 1954: German rearmament.

It had become apparent in the early 1950s that the Germans would have to contribute to the conventional defense of the central region of Western Europe. Indeed, we have seen that this consideration was part of the rationale for the forward defense strategy. The Pleven Plan for a sort of European, non-national army became the vehicle expected to carry German rearmament through all the sensitivities of the Europeans' fears of a resurgent Germany. When the French National Assembly failed to ratify the European Defense Community Plan in August 1954, the Western powers, two months later, officially ended the occupation. They also offered sovereignty and accession to the Brussels Treaty to the West German state.

In anticipation of eventual rearmament, Chancellor Adenauer had appointed Theodore Blank as a special adviser on the question. Blank had a notable staff, including former *Wehrmacht* strategists of considerable success during the war who had been cleared of National Socialist ties. The West Germans for the most part concurred with both the forward defense strategy and the mobile defense concept.[74] There was at least one member of Blank's staff, however, who did not go along with the mobile defense idea, Colonel Bogislaw von Bonin.

Von Bonin proposed a linear defense at the border that would not yield an inch of German territory. What is significant about Von Bonin's proposal is not so much that it called for a truly forward defense with conventional forces, but the fact that his concept was rejected by the West Germans. Upon the rejection of his plan, Von Bonin went public with his dispute and was promptly dismissed. He was later connected to communist front organizations in West Germany.[75] It was ironic that his was a truly forward concept; supposedly that was what the Germans, French, and the smaller Continental states wanted, yet the proposal was nevertheless unacceptable to the most threatened ally, West Germany.

Conclusion

By 1955, Western Allied military strategy had come full circle. Starting in the occupation years of the 1940s, there was at the operational level an initial emergency defense plan, coordinated by the French, British, and American zone commanders. The Western European Union Defense Organization plan under the chairmanship of Field Marshal Montgomery produced the first integrated defense plan for the Brussels Treaty Powers. When NATO formed SHAPE, General Eisenhower's staff took over the work and developed a plan for a mobile defense between the border and the Rhine. As the sense of urgency of 1945-52 abated, NATO members fell short of their goal of providing the nearly 100 divisions that would be required to fight a linear forward defense in accordance with the September 1950 council declaration on the forward strategy. The allied effort had begun, because of lack of forces in 1948, as an impossible forward conventional defense; it had evolved into a more practical mobile defense by 1952; but then it had regressed into an impossible forward conventional defense again and a reliance on nuclear weapons.

The early history of NATO thus demonstrates the complex operational origins of the forward strategy. All the factors affecting the operational level of war were present in vivid illustration in this time. Differing operational concepts were proposed by the various factions interested in forward defense, ranging from the British Ministry of Defense option of the Pyrenees defense to Von Bonin's linear defense proposal. The cultural, historical, and geographical makeup of the factor of a national style of war is amply portrayed in the tension among the French, British, American, and Benelux reactions to the various plans for forward defense throughout these years. And certainly the force of personality was a major contributor in determining the operational concept for the implementation of forward defense; plans changed with changes in command and as strong personalities came into conflict with each other. Still today, these several complexities continue to nag the operational dimension of NATO forward defense.

NOTES

1. See James A. Blackwell, Jr., "Conventional Doctrine: Integrating Alliance Forces," in James R. Golden, Asa A. Clark, and Bruce E. Arlinghaus, eds., *Conventional Deterrence: Alternatives for European Defense* (Lexington, Mass.: Lexington Books, D. C. Heath and Company, 1984).
2. Quoted in Franklin M. Davis, Jr., *Come As A Conqueror: The United States Army's Occupation of Germany 1945-1949* (New York: Macmillan, 1967), p. 133.
3. Bernard Law Montgomery, *The Memoirs of Field Marshal The Viscount Montgomery of Alamein, K.G.* (Cleveland: The World Publishing Company, 1958), p. 321.
4. Davis, p. 135.
5. Jean Edward Smith, ed., *The Papers of Lucius D. Clay: Germany 1945-1949*, Vol. I (Bloomington: Indiana Univ. Press, 1974), p. 393.
6. Montgomery, p. 390.
7. Ibid., pp. 448-49.
8. Ibid., p. 449.
9. "Montgomery Says War Can Be Balked," *The New York Times*, 10 July 1948, p. 4.
10. "Frenchman Refuses to Head Armies of Europe," *The New York Times*, 3 October 1948, p. 10.
11. *The New York Times*, 10 November 1948, p. 1.
12. "Pact's Value Doubted," *The New York Times*, 1 March 1949, p. 20.
13. "Arms Tie to Atlantic Pact Being Debated in Capital," *The New York Times*, 4 March 1949, p. 4.

14. "Ramadier Regrets Atlantic Pact Delay," *The New York Times*, 4 March 1949, p. 4.
15. "Text of Bradley Address Hailing Atlantic Pact," *The New York Times*, 6 April 1949, p. 3.
16. Soviet and Western strength figures are given by General André Beaufre, *NATO and Europe*, trans. Joseph Green (New York: Vintage Books, 1966), p. 24.
17. Smith, p. 679.
18. Ibid., pp. 772-73.
19. "Frenchman Refuses," *The New York Times*, p. 1.
20. Roger Hilsman, "NATO: The Developing Strategic Context," in *NATO and American Security*, ed. Klaus Knorr (Princeton: Princeton Univ. Press, 1959), pp. 18-20; and Beaufre, p. 24.
21. Hilsman, pp. 14-15; Beaufre, p. 25.
22. Hilsman, pp. 15-16.
23. "Montgomery Confirms Unity," *The New York Times*, 10 August 1949, p. 7.
24. Montgomery, p. 457; Hilsman, p. 14; Beaufre, p. 24.
25. Beaufre, p. 26.
26. Ibid.
27. Montgomery, p. 458.
28. Federal Republic of Germany, The Press and Information Office of the Federal Republic, *Germany Reports*, 3d ed., 1961, pp. 283-84; Gordon A. Craig, *NATO and the New German Army* (Princeton: Center of International Studies, Princeton Univ., 1955), pp. 1-2; "Text of West's Three-Power Agreement on Rearming Bonn Regime,"*The New York Times*, 20 September 1950, p. 12; Robert Endicott Osgood, *NATO: The Entangling Alliance* (Chicago: Chicago Press, 1962), pp. 37-38; and Hilsman, pp. 17-18.
29. Beaufre, pp. 26-27.
30. "First of Rangers Now in Germany," *The New York Times*, 14 March 1951, p. 17; Robert J. Wood, "The First Year of SHAPE," *International Organization*, 6 (No. 2, 1952), 180.
31. US Congress, Senate, *Assignment of Ground Forces of the United States to Duty in the European Area*, hearings before the Committee on Foreign Relations and the Committee on Armed Services, 82d Cong., 1st Sess. (Washington: GPO, 1951), pp. 131-32.
32. Ibid., pp. 154-55, 168, 194.
33. Ibid., p. 214.
34. Ibid.
35. Ibid., testimonies of General LeMay and Major Seversky.
36. "Allies Map Strategy East of the Rhine as Strength Rises," *The New York Times*, 9 September 1951, pp. 1, 14.
37. *The New York Times*, 2 February 1951, p. 4; 17 March 1951, p. 3; 27 November 1951, p. 12.
38. *Germany Reports*, p. 292.
39. Ibid.
40. "Adenauer Expects Defense By West," *The New York Times*, 12 October 1950, p. 24.
41. "De Gaulle Charges Allies Plan 'Redoubt'," *The New York Times*, 13 April 1951, p. 8.
42. Ibid.
43. "Eisenhower Urges Armed Alertness," *The New York Times*, 20 October 1950, p. 17.
44. "Taft Opposes Troops For Europe," *The New York Times*, 6 January 1951, pp. 1, 4.
45. *Assignment of Ground Forces of the United States*, p. 5.
46. F. W. Mulley, *The Politics of Western Defense* (New York: Praeger, 1962), p. 122.
47. Beaufre, pp. 50-51.
48. "Eisenhower Opens 'Paper War' Today," *The New York Times*, 7 April 1952, p. 5.
49. Ibid.
50. James H. Polk, "The North German Plain Attack Scenario: Threat or Illusion?" *Strategic Review*, 8 (Summer 1980), 60-61. This point was also made in an interview with Colonel Lewis Treleaven, USMC Ret., in June 1983. Colonel Treleaven was on Montgomery's personal staff at SHAPE and attended these exercises. He is now Special Assistant to the President, Kenyon College, Ohio.
51. Ibid., p. 61.
52. Dwight D. Eisenhower, *Annual Report to the Standing Group North Atlantic Treaty Organization* (Paris: SHAPE, 2 April 1952), p. 22.
53. Ibid., pp. 21-22.
54. Matthew B. Ridgway, *Soldier: The Memoirs of Matthew B. Ridgway*, as told to Harold H. Martin (New York: Harper & Brothers, 1956), pp. 239-40.

55. Ibid., pp. 247.
56. Ibid., pp. 247-48.
57. Ibid., pp. 252-53.
58. *The New York Times*, 10 May 1952, p. 3.
59. "Rhine Defense Key, NATO Games Show," *The New York Times*, 19 September 1952, p. 4.
60. "Juin Says Allies Could Hold Rhine," *The New York Times*, 9 September 1952, p. 5.
61. "Eddy Denies Test of Rhine Defense," *The New York Times*, 10 September 1952, p. 5.
62. Ibid.
63. "Equal Security Asked For West," *The New York Times*, 28 September 1952, p. 6.
64. "Ridgway Deplores False Confidence," *The New York Times*, 15 October 1952, p. 12.
65. *The New York Times*, 18 October 1952; 4 January 1953.
66. "NATO Chiefs Press Build-up of Armies," *The New York Times*, 29 October 1952, p. 8.
67. "Atom Arms to Ease Europe Troop Need, Collins Declares," *The New York Times*, 7 September 1952, p. 1.
68. Robert C. Richardson III, "NATO Nuclear Strategy: A Look Back," *Strategic Review*, 9 (Spring 1981), 38.
69. Ibid.
70. Ibid., p. 41.
71. Ibid.
72. Beaufre, p. 57.
73. "Eisenhower Asserts Allies Must Plan Arming For Years," *The New York Times*, 24 April 1953, p. 1.
74. Craig, pp. 1-2, 20-21.
75. On the details of the Von Bonin affair, see Craig, pp. 22-25; "The Bonin Case: A German Controversy Over Rearmament, By a Former German General," US Air Force Project RAND Research Memorandum No. RM-1538, 1 July 1955; and Hans Speier, "German Rearmament and Atomic War," US Air Force Project RAND Research Memorandum No. R-298, 15 February 1957.

This article appeared in the winter 1985 issue of *Parameters*.

About the Editors and Contributors

DR. EDWARD N. LUTTWAK is a Senior Fellow, Center for Strategic and International Studies, Washington, D.C. He has served as a consultant to the Department of Defense, the U.S. Army, the National Security Council, and the Department of State, and has taught at the Johns Hopkins University and at Georgetown University. In addition to scores of articles on military affairs, Dr. Luttwak has written six books, including *The Grand Strategy of the Roman Empire: From the First Century A.D. to the Third* (1976) and *The Pentagon and the Art of War: The Question of Military Reform* (1985). His latest book, *Strategy: The Logic of War and Peace*, was published in 1987.

COLONEL LLOYD J. MATTHEWS, USA RETIRED, is editor of *Parameters: Journal of the U.S. Army War College*. He holds a Ph.D. from the University of Virginia, an M.A. from Harvard, and a B.S. from the U.S. Military Academy. Colonel Matthews served as an infantry officer in Vietnam during the period 1964–65 and was subsequently a professor and associate dean at the Military Academy.

CAPTAIN DALE E. BROWN, USA, is assistant editor of *Parameters: Journal of the U.S. Army War College*. He earned an M.A. in history from The Ohio State University. Captain Brown is an air defense artillery officer and has served in a variety of air defense assignments in the United States and Europe.

MAJOR JAMES A. BLACKWELL, JR., USA, is serving with the 9th Infantry Division, Ft. Lewis, Washington. He holds a Ph.D. in International Law and Diplomacy from the Fletcher School, Tufts University. He is a former assistant professor of politics and government at the U.S. Military Academy.

CHAPLAIN (MAJOR) JOHN W. BRINSFIELD, USA, is assigned to the Staff and Faculty, U.S. Army Chaplain School, Fort Monmouth, N.J. He received the Master of Divinity from Yale, Ph.D. from Emory University, and D.Min. from Drew University. He is a graduate of the Armed Forces Staff College and served from 1980 to 1984 as an assistant professor in the Department of History at the U.S. Military Academy.

COLONEL WILLIAM E. BUSH, JR., USA, is Director of Personnel and

Community Activities, Fort Gordon, Georgia. He is a graduate of Middle Tennessee State University, holds an M.A. from Wayne State University, and is a 1985 graduate of the U.S. Army War College.

DR. HUGH M. COLE was the 1976-77 Visiting Professor of Military History at the U.S. Army Military History Institute. He received his undergraduate degree from Wheaton College and his master's and doctoral degrees in history from the University of Minnesota. He is a retired colonel in the U.S. Army Reserve and served during World War II in the G3 Section, Third U.S. Army, and as Deputy Theater Historian, European Theater of Operations, where he worked with S.L.A. Marshall. He has been military writer for the *Chicago Sunday Tribune* and the *Chicago Sunday Times* and is author of two volumes of the official historical series, *US Army in World War II*.

DR. BENJAMIN FRANKLIN COOLING is Chief, Special Histories Branch and Senior Historian for Contract Programs, Office of Air Force History, Washington, D.C. He has previously been associated with the U.S. Army Center of Military History as a historian, and more recently as Assistant Director for Historical Services, U.S. Army Military History Institute, Carlisle Barracks, Pennsylvania. A graduate of Rutgers University, he holds the M.A. and Ph.D. degrees in history from the University of Pennsylvania. He has written and edited numerous articles, volumes, and series in the field of military and naval history.

DR. HAROLD C. DEUTSCH is a retired professor of military history at the U.S. Army War College. He is a graduate of the University of Wisconsin (B.A., M.A.) and Harvard University (M.A., Ph.D). During World War II, he was chief of the Political Subdivision for Europe, Africa, and the Middle East of the Office of Strategic Services, and then headed the Research and Analysis Branch of the OSS Mission in Germany. Dr. Deutsch, a leading authority on ULTRA, is the author of five books, including *Hitler and His Generals: The Hidden Crisis of January-June 1938* (1974).

COLONEL ROBERT A. DOUGHTY, USA, is the Head of the Department of History at the U.S. Military Academy. He has taught history at the Command and General Staff College and Yale University. A graduate of the Command and General Staff College, he received his Ph.D. in history in 1979 from the University of Kansas. Colonel Doughty is the author of *The Seeds of Disaster: The Development of French Army Doctrine, 1919-1939* (1986).

DR. JOHN M. GATES is a professor of history at the College of Wooster, where he teaches military, American, and Latin American history. He received his B.A. and M.A. from Stanford and his Ph.D. from Duke. Dr. Gates is the author of *Schoolbooks and Krags: The United States Army in the Philippines, 1898-1902* (1973). His article, "The Alleged Isolation of U.S. Army Officers in the Late 19th Century," received the Harold L. Peterson Award for exemplary work in American military history.

COLONEL J. FRANK HENNESSEE, USA, is commander of the 3rd U.S. Infantry (The Old Guard). He is a graduate of the U.S. Military Academy, holds an M.S. from Georgia Tech, and is a 1985 graduate of the U.S. Army War College. Prior to assuming his current duties, he served in the Organization of the Joint Chiefs of Staff as Chief of Warfare Policy.

DR. D. CLAYTON JAMES (Ph.D., University of Texas) held the Harold K. Johnson Chair of Military History at the U.S. Army Military History Institute, Carlisle Barracks in 1979-80. Subsequently he held the John F. Morrison Chair at the U.S. Army Command and General Staff College, Fort Leavenworth and the Harmon Memorial Lectureship at the U.S. Air Force Academy. Currently, he is Distinguished Professor of History at Mississippi State University. He has published five books, notably *The Years of MacArthur* (3 vols., 1970-85). At present he is completing a book on the American high command in World War II and is beginning a book on the Korean War.

DR. DOUGLAS KINNARD (Brigadier General, USA Retired), a 1944 graduate of the U.S. Military Academy, saw combat in World War II in Europe, in the Korean War, and twice in the Vietnam War. Following retirement from the Army in 1970, he earned the Ph.D. from Princeton University, and subsequently taught for twelve years at the University of Vermont at which he is now Professor Emeritus of Political Science. Dr. Kinnard is the author of *President Eisenhower and Strategy Management* (1977), *The War Managers* (1977), and *The Secretary of Defense* (1980). He is presently completing a book on Maxwell Taylor.

COLONEL WALTER P. LANG, JR., USA, is the Defense Intelligence Officer for the Middle East and South Asia in the Defense Intelligence Agency. He is a graduate of the Virginia Military Institute, holds an M.A. from the University of Utah, and is a 1985 graduate of the U.S. Army War College.

DR. JAY LUVAAS is Professor of Military History at the U.S. Army War College, where he holds the Maxwell Taylor Chair of the Profession of Arms. He is a graduate of Allegheny College and earned the M.A. and Ph.D. degrees at Duke University. Dr. Luvaas taught at Allegheny from 1957 to 1982, and he has been visiting professor of military history at the U.S. Military Academy and at the U.S. Army Military History Institute. His latest book is *The Battle of Gettysburg: The U.S. Army War College Guide* (co-authored; 1986), and he is working on future volumes in the series.

DR. KEITH D. MCFARLAND is Dean for Graduate Studies and Research and Professor of History at East Texas State University in Commerce, Texas. A former Army officer, he is a graduate of Kent State University and holds M.A. and Ph.D. degrees from The Ohio State University. Dr. McFarland is the author of *Harry H. Woodring: A Political Biography of FDR's Controversial Secretary of War* (1975) and *The Korean War: An Annotated Bibliography* (1986).

DR. JAMES KIRBY MARTIN is Professor of History at the University of Houston, where he has also served as department chairman. A graduate of Hiram College, he earned the M.A. and Ph.D. degrees at the University of Wisconsin. Among Dr. Martin's works are *Men in Rebellion: Higher Governmental Leaders and the Coming of the American Revolution* (1973); *In the Course of Human Events: An Interpretive Exploration of the American Revolution* (1979); *'A Respectable Army': The Military Origins of the Republic 1763-1789* (co-authored; 1982) and *Citizen-Soldier: The Revolutionary War Journal of Joseph Bloomfield* (1982). Dr. Martin is currently finishing a biography of Benedict Arnold.

DR. JANOS RADVANYI is a professor of history at Mississippi State University. From 1948 to 1967 he was a member of the Hungarian Diplomatic Service. He rose to the position of Chief of Mission in the United States, and in that capacity was personally involved in the wartime negotiations between the United States and North Vietnam, particularly in 1965–66. Professor Radvanyi obtained political asylum in the United States in 1967. He is the author of *Hungary and the Super Powers* (1972) and *Delusion and Reality: Gambits, Hoaxes and Diplomatic One-Upsmanship in Vietnam* (1978).

LIEUTENANT COLONEL JAMES W. RAINEY, USA, is the executive director of the Office of the Deputy Chief of Staff, Intelligence, United States Army, Europe. He was an assistant professor of history at the U.S. Military Academy and holds a Ph.D. in history from Temple University.

MAJOR JOHN F. SHORTAL, USA, is an assistant professor in the Department of History, U.S. Military Academy. He is a 1974 graduate of the Academy and holds an M.S. from the University of Southern California and M.A. and Ph.D. degrees from Temple University. Major Shortal has served in command and staff assignments in the United States and in Korea. He is the author of a forthcoming biography of Robert L. Eichelberger.

FATHER DONALD SMYTHE, S.J., is Professor of History at John Carroll University. He holds an M.A. in history from Loyola University (Chicago) and a Ph.D. from Georgetown University. Father Smythe is the author of *Pershing: General of the Armies* (1986).

COLONEL RICHARD F. TIMMONS, USA, is an infantry brigade commander at Ford Ord, California. He is a graduate of the Virginia Military Institute and the U.S. Army War College, and holds M.A. degrees from the University of Alabama and Central Michigan University.

DR. RUSSELL WEIGLEY is Distinguished University Professor of History at Temple University, having taught there since 1964. He holds M.A. and Ph.D. degrees from the University of Pennsylvania and was a visiting professor of history at the Army War College. Professor Weigley is the author of such books as *The American Way of War: A History of U.S. Military Strategy and Policy* (1975) and *Eisenhower's Lieutenants: The Campaigns of France and Germany, 1944–1945* (1981).

DR. WILLIAM J. WOOLLEY is Professor of History and chairman of the History Department at Ripon College, Wisconsin. He is a graduate of Dartmouth College and earned his M.A. and Ph.D. at Indiana University. A U.S. Navy veteran, he is an authority on the use of military history in professional military education.

THE
DINOSAUR PRINCESS
and Other
Prehistoric Riddles

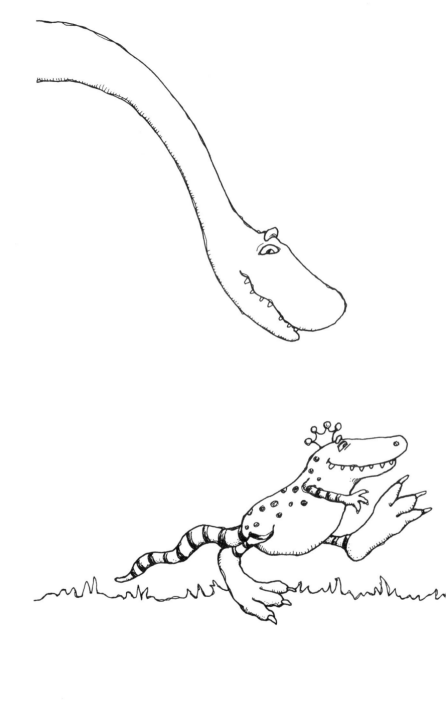

THE
DINOSAUR PRINCESS
and Other
Prehistoric Riddles

David A. Adler

illustrated by
Loreen Leedy

A BANTAM SKYLARK BOOK®
NEW YORK • TORONTO • LONDON • SYDNEY • AUCKLAND

To Eddie, who loves dinosaurs

This edition contains the complete text
of the original hardcover edition.
NOT ONE WORD HAS BEEN OMITTED.

RL 2 005–008

THE DINOSAUR PRINCESS AND OTHER PREHISTORIC RIDDLES
A Bantam Skylark Book / published by arrangement with
Holiday House Inc.

PRINTING HISTORY
Holiday House edition published April 1988
Bantam edition / January 1990
Bantam reissue / April 1992

Skylark Books is a registered trademark of Bantam Books,
a division of Bantam Doubleday Dell Publishing Group, Inc.
Registered in U.S. Patent and Trademark Office and elsewhere.

ISBN 0-553-15793-0

Published simultaneously in the United States and Canada

Bantam Books are published by Bantam Books, a division of Bantam
Doubleday Dell Publishing Group, Inc. Its trademark, consisting of the
words "Bantam Books" and the portrayal of a rooster, is Registered in U.S.
Patent and Trademark Office and in other countries. Marca Registrada.
Bantam Books, 666 Fifth Avenue, New York, New York 10103.

PRINTED IN THE UNITED STATES OF AMERICA

CWO   0 9 8 7 6 5 4 3 2

What's a caveman who has never been
to the big city?

A pre-hick-storic.

Why did Apatosaurus miss the train?

He got stuck in a turnstile.

What's the difference between cavemen and sewn socks?

Cavemen are dead men. Sewn socks are men-dead.

What's the name of the leaky dinosaur?

Bronto-porous.

How did scientists find the dinosaur princess?

They followed the dinosaur prints (prince).

What happened when Brachiosaurus walked
through the spinach fields?

He made creamed spinach.

Did woolly mammoths get ticks and fleas?

No, just moths.

What's a dinosaur curse?

A Tyrannosaurus hex.

How did cavemen and women make wooden tools?

A whittle at a time.

Did Tyrannosaurus Rex entertain a lot?

Sure. He always had friends for lunch.

The woolly mammoth is the ancestor of what animal?

The polyester mammoth.

How would you get milk and eggs from a dinosaur?

By stealing its shopping cart.

What kept cavemen and women up at night?

Dino-snores.

What would you get if you crossed a dinosaur with a game-show host?

A dead giveaway.

What did the cranky dinosaur tell the
paleontologist?

"Don't jostle my fossil."

Why did dinosaurs turn into fossils?

When the band started to play, the music
made the dinosaurs rock.

What would you get if you crossed a cat
with Tyrannosaurus Rex?

A big ugly puss.

Where do dinosaurs still follow cavemen?

In the dictionary.

What do you get when you cross a dinosaur with a magician?

A dino-sorcerer.

What steps did cavemen and women take to
protect themselves from dinosaurs?

Big steps.

Was it surprising when scientists first
found dinosaur bones?

No. It was surprising they could lose
anything that big.

What happened when Pteranodon flew into
a soda can?

Nothing. It was a soft drink.

How would you make stegosaurus soup?

In a big pot.

What did dinosaurs have that no other animals had?

Baby dinosaurs.

What happens when Apatosaurus beats the drums
and Allosaurus strums a guitar?

Tyrannosaurus rocks.

What does Triceratops sit on?

His tricera-bottom.

What's really old, has two tongues and lots of eyes?

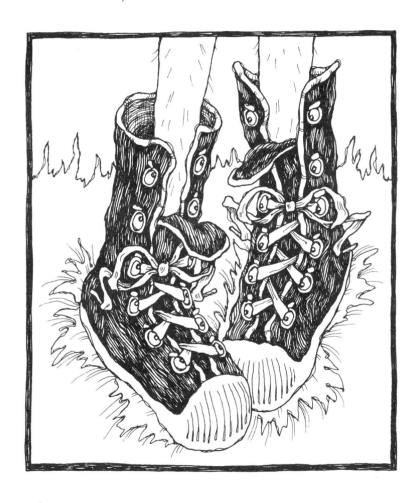

A cave woman's sneakers.

What would you get if you crossed Triceratops with a kangaroo?

Tricera-hops.

What would you say if you saw a three-headed dinosaur?

"Hello, hello, hello."

Name five members of the dinosaur family.

Mommy dinosaur, Daddy dinosaur and the
three baby dinosaurs.

What do you get when you cross a dinosaur with
the back half of a horse?

A dead end.

What's inside every dinosaur?

A dino-core.

When did cavemen and women keep saying "please" and "thank you"?

In the Nice Age.

Why didn't anyone play with Brontous?

He was a saur loser.

Where did Bagaceratops sleep?

In the riverbed.

How did Allosaurus get so rich?

He charged everyone he saw.

How would you make a dinosaur lighter?

Put some kerosene in his mouth and then
stick in a wick.

What followed the Mesozoic Age?

The Clean-up-zoic Age.

Why don't dinosaur skeletons get up and leave the museum?

They don't have the guts.

How would you spell ankylosaurus?

Slowly.

What would you give a seasick hadrosaurus?

Plenty of room.

Which prehistoric animal lived in a change purse?

The dimetrodon.

Was anyone safe from man-eating dinosaurs?

Sure, women and children.

What does Grandma Protoceratops carry in her wallet?

Photoceratops.

How do you get into a dinosaur cave?

By using a skeleton key.

What would you find in a dinosaur's ear?

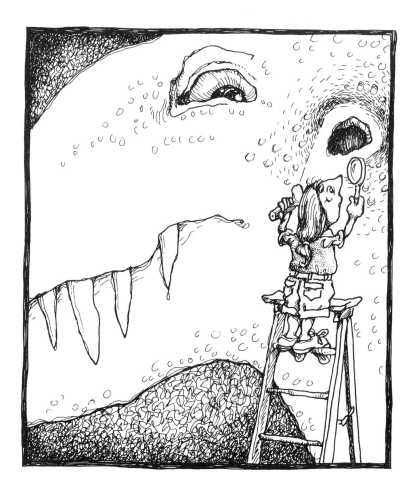

Tyrannosaurus wax.

What should you do if you dream you are in
a cave filled with iguanodons?

Wake up.

Why didn't Stegosaurus stand up straight?

He didn't want to drop the plates off his back.

What happened to the caveman who
swallowed a wheel?

It turned his stomach.

What did cave children have to eat before
they got dessert?

Their broccoli-saurus.

Why didn't Ankylosaurus dance ballet?

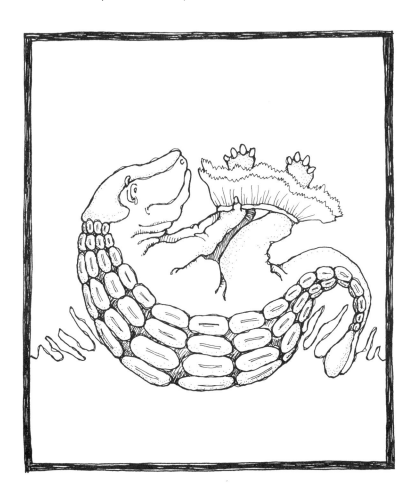

She couldn't fit into her tutu.

What did the cavemen and women say when
they discovered fire?

"Now we're cooking."

How much did it cost Brachiosaurus to get
a haircut?

Ten dollars for the haircut. One dollar for the
tip. And five hundred dollars for the chair.

How did iguanodons catch flies?

With baseball gloves.

Why did so few dinosaurs fly?

Most couldn't fit in the cockpit.

Which was the fastest dinosaur?

The pronto-saurus.

Why did Brachiosaurus have such a long neck?

Because his head was so far from the rest of him.

What do dinosaurs eat for lunch?

Cream of caveman soup.

How did cavemen and women discover the sun?

It just dawned on them.

Why was the dinosaur trolly late?

It fell off its trachodon.